DESIGNING FINANCIAL SYSTEMS IN TRANSITION ECONOMIES

DESIGNING FINANCIAL SYSTEMS IN TRANSITION ECONOMIES
Strategies for Reform in Central and Eastern Europe

edited by Anna Meyendorff and Anjan Thakor

The William Davidson Institute

The MIT Press
Cambridge, Massachusetts
London, England

This book was set in Times New Roman on 3B2 by Asco Typesetters, Hong Kong.
Printed and bound in the United States of America.

Library of Congress Cataloging-in-Publication Data

Designing financial systems in transition economies : strategies for reform in Central and
  Eastern Europe / edited by Anna Meyendorff and Anjan Thakor.
    p. cm.
  Includes bibliographical references and index.
  ISBN 0-262-13391-1 (hc. : alk. paper)
  1. Finance—Europe, Eastern. 2. Europe, Eastern—Economic policy—1989– 3. Finance—Europe,
Central. 4. Europe, Central—Economic policy. I. Meyendorff, Anna. II. Thakor, Anjan V.
HG186.E82 D47   2001
332′.0947—dc21   2001032618

Contents

Contributors

Philippe Aghion
Harvard University

Patrick Bolton
Princeton University

John Bonin
Wesleyan University

Arnoud Boot
University of Amsterdam

Steven Fries
Oxford University

Stanislav Gelfer
EBRD

Gary Gorton
The Wharton School, University of Pennsylvania

Thomas Hellmann
Stanford University

Lubomír Lízal
CERGE EI

Anna Meyendorff
The William Davidson Institute

Janet Mitchell
University of Saint-Louis

Kevin Murdock
McKinsey & Company

Georgiy Nikitin
Boston University

Enrico C. Perotti
University of Amsterdam

Raghuram G. Rajan
University of Chicago

Mark E. Schaffer
Heriot-Watt University

Anjolein Schmeits
Washington University

Joseph Stiglitz
Stanford University

Jan Svejnar
The William Davidson Institute and the University of Michigan Business School

Anjan Thakor
The University of Michigan Business School and the William Davidson Institute
Andrew Weiss
The Kellogg School, Northwestern University
Andrew Winton
Boston University

DESIGNING FINANCIAL SYSTEMS IN TRANSITION ECONOMIES

1 Introduction: Financial Systems in Transition

Anna Meyendorff and Anjan Thakor

The dramatic political and economic transformation of Central Europe that began 10 years ago with the fall of the Berlin Wall has provided new opportunities and raised new challenges in finance and economic research. On the one hand, rapid liberalization of both financial and real markets in the formerly state-controlled economies of Central Europe provides a new testing ground for existing theory. On the other hand, the noisy environment and poor data quality has made empirical research difficult. The unprecedented experiment being conducted in reforming centrally planned economies has also drawn academics into the inner circles of policymakers, as newly elected governments are struggling to create markets and institutions virtually overnight.

The William Davidson Institute organized a conference on the design of financial systems in Central Europe in May 1998. The conference brought together leading academics from Europe and North America, including both experts in the area of finance and banking and scholars specializing in the transition of Central European economies. The conference was intended to generate discussion about financial system design for transition economies, drawing on recent advances in research on financial restructuring, bankruptcy law, prudential regulation, and the role of banks. This volume is one result of that conference.

Collectively, the chapters address four important questions about economic reform in transition economies. The first two questions relate to the reform of financial institutions and markets, whereas the last two questions relate to the efficient structure of firms in transition economies. The four questions are:

1. How should we deal with the fact that banks in transition economies often have balance sheets that are burdened with excessive nonperforming assets?

2. What are the optimal policies for financial sector reform in transition economies?

3. What is the effect of ownership structure on economic performance?

4. Is conglomeration of nonfinancial firms optimal in transition economies?

The chapters that address the first question focus on financial restructuring in transition economies. Prior to the transition period, the primary function of Central European banks was to maintain the accounts of and channel subsidies to state-owned enterprises. Not surprisingly, the majority of loans on the books of these banks were not viable, and cleaning banks' balance sheets is a first and important step in imposing hard budget constraints on both firms and banks. In chapter 2 Janet Mitchell develops a general framework for analyzing trade-offs among various policies for cleaning banks' balance sheets of bad debt. Mitchell applies her frame-work—a two-tier hierarchy consisting of regulators, banks, and firms—to analyze three types of policies that have been advocated or employed in transition economies. Her analysis identifies two effects of policy choice: a direct effect of the policy on bank behavior and an indirect effect on firm behavior. A central insight of the chapter is that a tough recapitalization policy results in banks' rolling over loans in default in order to conceal the full extent of their loan losses, with the resulting indirect effect of extending soft budget constraints to firms.

Philippe Aghion, Patrick Bolton, and Steven Fries, extend this approach, in chapter 3, emphasizing the information asymmetry inherent in transition economies, where institutions for evaluating and disclosing the banks' credit-worthiness are weak. In addition to reproducing Mitchell's result that tough recapitalization policies lead to a softening of firms' budget constraints, they find that a soft approach to recapitalization leads banks to be excessively tough on firms and to exaggerate their own recapitalization requirements. The chapter finds a socially optimal outcome when recapitalization occurs through the buying out of nonperforming loans rather than a simple injection of funds, using a nonlinear transfer pricing mechanism to combat healthy banks' overreporting of bad loans.

The second set of chapters addresses the question regarding optimal policies for financial sector reform in transition economies. In chapter 4 John Bonin and Mark E. Schaffer provide an important cautionary lesson about the design of financial sector reforms, which can have significant detrimental effects if the particular institutional framework is not taken into account. They describe Hungary's experimentation with an "automatic trigger" requiring liquidation or reorganization proceedings by firms with overdue debt to any creditor. Whereas the legislation intended to impose financial discipline on firms and speed restructuring, the absence of mechanisms to promote efficient resource allocation created a situation in which many viable firms were faced with temporary liquidity constraints. By not distinguishing among the various causes of overdue debt, the automatic trigger took down "good" firms along with the "bad." This also forced the government into very rapid recapitalization of banks.

Anna Meyendorff, in chapter 5, similarly describes unintended effects of financial-sector policy measures. Using a simple theoretical model, she shows the negative effect Russia's policy of enforcing corporate tax payment through the banking system has had on credit allocation in Russia. This type of enforcement, inefficient in any economy, is particularly costly when fiscal authorities are weak. As the chapter indicates, it significantly retards financial sector development by discouraging the most profitable firms from interacting with the banking sector.

In chapter 6 Thomas Hellmann, Kevin Murdock, and Joseph Stiglitz point out pitfalls in the process of financial liberalization, discussing the impact of various forms of prudential regulation on bank behavior at a time when banks have not yet attained the desired level of capital. They argue that deposit rate restrictions will be more effective than increases in capital requirements in imposing discipline on banks' lending practices and that a policy of "regulatory overshooting" ensures both a faster and safer transition to a liberalized banking sector. Gary Gorton and Andrew Winton similarly argue in chapter 7 that high capital requirements imposed on banks may be detrimental to the development of a banking sector in the transition setting. As an alternative, they recommend that regulators seek foreign bank capital, grant domestic banks implicit capital through monopoly rents, or simply allow banks to operate with lower capital requirements.

The issue of financial reform is also examined by Anna Meyendorff and Anjan Thakor in chapter 8. They analyze the current state of the Romanian banking sector and prospects for reform and outline a set of policy recommendations applicable to many other emerging markets. In addition to discussing the problem of bad debts in the existing banks, they take a broader view of financial-sector development, stressing the interaction between real-sector reforms and the development of both bank lending and equity markets.

Picking up on Bonin and Schaffer's ideas in chapter 4—that optimal policies depend on initial conditions—Raghuram Rajan discusses the permissible scope of banking in chapter 9. Rajan argues that universal banking and unrestricted competition in the provision of financial services may not result in the creation of efficient institutions. In particular, if the markets in which the institutions compete are not naturally competitive, choosing inefficient structures may be a dominant strategy for institutions. This is of particular importance to transition economies because of the legacy of nontransparency and poor accounting they have inherited from the days of central economic control.

The third group of chapters addresses the question of ownership structure and its effect on firm performance. These chapters focus more directly on the interaction between real- and financial-sector reform in the context of the Czech Republic. Andrew Weiss and Georgiy Nikitin, in chapter 10, use survey data to assess the effect of ownership structure of Czech firms on their economic performance by measuring the relationship between changes in performance and changes in the composition of ownership structure at the firm level. They find that ownership concentration in the Czech Republic is associated with improvements in the performance of operating companies, but only if ownership is concentrated in hands other than investment funds. Whereas Czech investment funds were designed to counteract the diffuse firm

ownership created by the Czech voucher privatization program, the incentive structure of the investment fund managers undermined this original intent.

In chapter 11 Lubomír Lízal and Jan Svejnar, using data from most of the industrial firms located in the Czech Republic between 1992 and 1995, find that domestic
firms cannot easily borrow investment funds externally and that investment varies
with and is financed from retained earnings. Although the finding that investment is
constrained by internal cash flow has also been documented in the United States,
this chapter lends support to the argument that the financial sector in the Czech Republic is not yet playing the necessary role of intermediary.

The final set of chapters examines the fourth question regarding the role of conglomerates and financial-industrial groups in the transition setting. In chapter 12
Arnoud Boot and Anjolein Schmeits make the analytical argument that conglomeration in banking seems to be optimal when rents are low and market discipline weak.
Internal cost-of-capital allocation schemes may create an internal discipline that complements the weak external market discipline. Enrico Perotti and Stanislav Gelfer
close the volume in chapter 13 with a focus on Russian financial-industrial groups,
in which large firms are affiliated with one or more large banks in a complicated
pattern of cross-ownership. Their empirical analysis shows that firms that belong to
one of these financial-industrial groups allocate capital better than firms that do not.

Several important themes emerge from the chapters in this volume. The first is the
critical interaction between financial- and real-sector reform. On the one hand, the
way that policymakers and banks address the issue of bad loans has a significant
impact on firms, either subsidizing the continued existence of firms that should be
liquidated or prematurely liquidating firms that could be profitable. On the other
hand, the quality of firms in the real sector circumscribes financial-sector development. When banks cannot find good credit risks, they cannot improve the quality
of their portfolios. Until there is a critical mass of viable firms in an economy, its
equity markets will be thin and ineffective.

The second important theme is that policies that are successful in developed market
economies may have substantially different and even undesirable outcomes in less
developed or transition economies. In Central and Eastern Europe, both markets
and the institutions that support them have developed at a slow and often uneven
pace. Missing markets and institutions have distorted policy outcomes. Thus, both
researchers and policymakers must think creatively about how to avoid these distortions. As argued in several of the chapters, policy solutions and institutional
arrangements which have been rejected outright in developed market economies
could be particularly appropriate, if only on an interim basis, in economies in transition from socialist to market-based systems.

2   Banks' Bad Debts: Policies, Creditor Passivity, and Soft Budget Constraints

Janet Mitchell

2.1   Introduction

Economies in transition, like those of many other countries around the world, have suffered banking crises in recent years. Like those in other countries, troubled banks in transition economies (TEs) have not always openly revealed the extent of bad debt on their balance sheets. Despite their inaccurate knowledge of the amounts of bad debt on banks' balance sheets, governments in TEs have acknowledged the problem of bad debt relatively rapidly, and they have employed a variety of policies to clean banks' balance sheets. As a consequence, considerable discussion has taken place in these economies regarding which policies to apply to banks in distress.[1]

A unique set of historical conditions faced by the TEs explains both a greater vulnerability to banking crises in TEs than in other emerging market economies and authorities' recognition of banks' problems. In particular, each country's commercial banks received a sizeable (though unknown) quantity of bad loans on their books at the point of their inception, and each of these economies had a history of soft budget constraints.[2] Because of this history, one of the objectives of the transition has been to harden firms' budget constraints. However, whereas in these previously socialist economies the government was formerly the source of soft budget constraints (SBCs) through its bailout of loss-making state-owned firms, their transition to market economies has given rise to a new source of SBCs via banks' rollover of loans (and potential refinancing).

This chapter reports on a line of research that views banks as sources of SBCs and models banks' decisions to roll over or refinance loans in default. The assumptions on bank behavior in the model presented here derive from the analysis of creditor passivity in Mitchell 1993, which defined the concept (banks' passively rolling over their loans in default rather than actively pursuing their claims) and identified a number of potential explanations for the behavior.

The observation that banks may be responsible for SBCs is not new. In the first paper to formalize Kornai's notion of SBCs, Dewatripont and Maskin (1993) show that banks that are "too large" may create SBCs (since the amount of available funds prevents them from committing to not refinancing "bad" projects for which it is actually efficient to refinance after default). Dewatripont and Maskin (D-M) demonstrate that commitment problems are at the heart of SBCs and focus on sunk costs as the source of these commitment problems. This focus somewhat limits their model's usefulness for analyzing banking crises and potential policy responses. In contrast, I show that the motivations for bank passivity generate SBCs in situations in which they would not arise in the D-M model and that a model allowing for bank passivity is well suited to analysis of banking crises.

The model of bank behavior that I present in this chapter illustrates an important motivation for bank passivity: troubled banks may have an incentive to roll over loans in default in order to avoid revealing the default. It also illustrates how this passivity can actually worsen banks' financial conditions, thereby exacerbating any resulting banking crisis. I incorporate this model of bank behavior into a general framework for analyzing real trade-offs among policy choices for dealing with troubled banks. Because the explanations for (and the observation of) banks' rolling over of loans are actually quite general and are not limited to TEs, the model elaborated here may be easily applied to analyzing banking crises in other settings.

Despite the frequent occurrence of banking crises in TEs and around the world, no research has formalized trade-offs between policies for dealing with troubled banks' bad loans. This chapter and the model it presents constitute the first to attempt to fill this vacuum. (A more detailed analysis of the model appears in Mitchell 1998.) The model's framework consists of a two-tier hierarchy comprising a regulator, banks, and firms. Hidden information and moral hazard are present at each tier of the hierarchy.

Analysis of the results obtained using the model demonstrates that the policy chosen by the regulator (who is unable to observe banks' precise levels of default) to clean troubled banks' balance sheets will influence banks' decisions to be active or passive in pursuing claims in default. A particular bank's response to the regulator's policy is labeled the *direct effect* of the policy. The bank's choice to be active or passive—referred to in the model as a choice of *workout* versus *rollover*—affects the amount of a loan that the bank will ultimately recover; therefore, it affects the bank's value. A policy to which banks respond by rolling over their loans in default will cause the level of default on banks' balance sheets to appear lower than it actually is and will result in lower bank values than a policy that induces banks to work out their claims. In contrast, workout (a term that refers to actions such as bankruptcy procedures or out-of-court workouts) is costlessly observable; hence, the level of default becomes known when a bank chooses this action. Revelation of a high amount of bad debt in a particular bank may be detrimental to the bank's manager if she suffers penalties or a loss in private or reputational benefits as a result.

In addition to the direct effect policies have on bank behavior, they also affect firm behavior. A bank's choice of workout or rollover of loans will influence the decision by the manager of the borrower firm on whether to divert the firm's assets (or its earnings) for the manager's private benefit. Asset dissipation by the firm manager decreases the firm's future value and the amount of the bank loan the firm ultimately repays. A choice of rollover by the bank motivates firm managers to choose higher levels of asset dissipation than does a choice of workout. A firm manager's choice of asset dissipation as a function of the occurrence of default and of the bank's choice of workout or rollover is referred to as the *indirect effect* of the policy. Whereas existing models of bank closure policies such as those in Boot and Thakor 1993 and Mailath and Mester 1994 focus entirely on the direct effects of policies, the analysis in this chapter of policies' indirect effects is new to the literature and shows that indirect effects can be important.

The framework presented for evaluating policy trade-offs is applied in the chapter to analyze three policies that have been either advocted or employed to clean banks' balance sheets in TEs. The policies considered are *debt transfer*, whereby the debt is left on firms' balance sheets but transferred from commercial banks' balance sheets to a specialized "bad-debt bank"; *self-reliance*, whereby the debt is left on firms' and commerical banks' balance sheets and the banks are required to work out their own problems; and *debt cancellation*, whereby the debt is cancelled from firms' and banks' balance sheets. It is straightforward to extend the framework to analyze additional policies (for example, see Aghion, Bolton, and Fries, this volume).

One finding of the analysis of policy trade-offs is that policies that leave debt from a past regime on firms' books may be beneficial. Default on this debt triggers a process of information gathering by the bank and valuation of the firm (see Harris and Raviv 1990). If this information allows the bank to better monitor the firm manager and to slow asset dissipation, then the sum of the net worths of the firm and the bank will be higher than it would have been if the debt were canceled and no default had occurred.

This observation implies that debt cancellation in TEs may actually lower bank and firm values. This is a significant result, in part because it runs counter to the intuition invoked by a number of prominent economists advocating debt cancellation in TEs,[3] who have argued that cancellation of the inherited debt from state-owned firms' and banks' balance sheets early in the transition would have no net effect on the value of state-owned assets.

A second finding of the analysis of policy trade-offs is that different policies that leave bad debt on firms' books may differ in their effects on asset values. Policies of self-reliance require that banks restructure or work out their bad debt on their own. Although workout involves resource costs, a policy of self-reliance allows commercial banks that choose workout to make use of "inside" information about the debtor that the commercial bank has acquired through its relationship with the debtor but that a bad-debt bank may not possess. This inside information is useful both for valuing the debtor and for limiting the degree of asset dissipation. Commercial banks may thus have a higher rate of loan recovery in the course of a workout than would the bad-debt bank. Indeed, the assumption that banks acquire private, inside information about their debtors is common in the financial economics literature (see, for example, Rajan and Petersen 1994 and Gorton and Winton, this volume). Slovin, Sushka, and Polonchek 1993 and James 1991 provide empirical evidence supporting the claim that information is lost when loans are transferred from the original commercial bank to other institutions.

Whereas commercial banks may be better able to recover loans through workouts than a bad-debt bank, a commercial bank in financial distress may have the incentive to roll over rather than work out its loans. In this case the benefits of workout (and the policy of self-reliance) are lost. Loan recovery (and bank value) is lower in such a case than it would have been with a policy of debt transfer, provided that the bad-debt bank to which the loan is transferred is reasonably skilled at undertaking workout. On the other hand, if the bad-debt bank is poorly skilled at workout and if the problem of asset dissipation among firms is not too serious, then debt cancellation may yield higher bank value than debt transfer, since it avoids costly workouts by the bad-debt bank.

In any particular case, the regulator chooses the policy that maximizes the expected value of bank and firm values, where the expectation is taken over the regulator's prior regarding the level of default on banks' balance sheets. The policy trade-offs described above imply that no policy will be optimal in all situations. Which policy is optimal in a given economy will depend on the expected levels of default on banks' balance sheets, the seriousness of the problem of asset dissipation among firms, and the potential skill of a bad-debt bank relative to commercial banks at recovering loans. It should be a straightforward task in practice to evaluate the importance of each of these factors. The trade-offs analyzed here can thus be useful for policymakers in the actual selection of policies.

This chapter is one of only a few studies to examine banks' actions in response to debt in default as opposed to banks' ex ante choices of riskiness of investment. Mitchell 1997 analyzes a model in which creditors may choose to be passive in response to default and the appearance of too many troubled banks may force regulators to undertake multiple bank rescues. This model of "too many to fail" complements that in the current chapter by taking account of the potential effects of systemic risks created by a banking crisis on regulatory response to the crisis and on the design of banking regulation. Perotti 1993 studies the incentives of banks to "throw good money after bad" as a result of the debt overhang created by inherited debt at the beginning of transition.

Other research treats bank response to default in developed market economies. O'Hara 1993 points out the possibility of banks' rolling over their bad loans in response to market value (as opposed to book value) accounting rules. Rajan 1994 analyzes a model of bank behavior in which banks may choose to be passive (lenient, in his terminology) to avoid a negative reputational effect associated with the revelation of loan defaults.

The chapter proceeds as follows. Section 2.2 discusses the links between bank behavior and SBCs. It provides a taxonomy of cases in which SBCs may occur and identifies the cases corresponding to the D-M model and those that arise with the model of creditor passivity. Section 2.3 outlines the merits of the policy of debt cancellation and describes actual policies applied in the banking crises in Hungary, Poland, and the Czech Republic. Section 2.4 presents the model and analyzes trade-offs among the policies of debt cancellation, self-reliance, and debt transfer. Section 2.5 discusses policy implications and concludes the chapter.

2.2   Soft Budget Constraints and Creditor Passivity

Although Kornai proposed the concept of SBCs, there is no consensus on the exact definition of the concept. For example, D-M's interpretation of SBCs differs from Kornai's original discussion of government bailout of loss-making firms. Even Kornai's own interpretation of SBCs has evolved over time.[4] For the purposes of this chapter, I formulate a definintion of SBCs that is general enough to encompass both the D-M interpretation and Kornai's original description.

DEFINITION 2.1   A firm has a soft budget constraint if (1) it has negative expected net present value but receives financing, or (2) a financial decision of a creditor or the government following default allows the firm to continue in operation although its assets would yield a greater return in an alternative use.

This definition allows for a number of differing cases of SBCs. It is possible to classify these cases according to two criteria: whether the decision to finance a firm is ex ante efficient, and whether a continuation decision is ex post efficient. Ex ante decisions are those made prior to default; ex ante efficiency corresponds to the financing of only firms (or projects) with positive expected net present value. Ex post decisions are those made following default; ex post efficiency refers to the continuation of only those firms whose returns to creditors are higher in continuation than in liquidation.

The table below presents the possible combinations of ex ante and ex post characteristics of firms and identifies the cases that would qualify as SBCs if firms in these cases were to receive financing or were to be continued in operation following default. For example, the right column in the first row represents the case of a firm with positive expected (NPV) at the ex ante financing stage; upon default, however, the return to creditors in this case is higher in liquidation than in continuation. If a firm in this case is continued in operation following default, it has an SBC. The entries in the second row both represent firms with negative expected net present value (NPV). If firms in these cases receive finance, they have SBCs, independent of the continuation and liquidation values of their assets upon default. Note that the only case in which the provision of finance combined with a continuation decision following default is consistent with hard budget constraints is the case appearing in the left column of the first row. Initial financing or continuation decisions lead to SBCs in all other cases.

	Ex post efficiency	Ex post inefficiency
Ex ante efficiency		SBC
Ex ante inefficiency	SBC	SBC

We may now identify the cases that correspond to various interpretations of SBCs. The D-M model represents the case in the left column of the table's second row and applies to a situation in which it is ex post efficient to refinance; ex ante, however, it is inefficient to provide finance. Firms with negative expected NPV receive finance at the ex ante stage because banks are unable at this stage to distinguish between firms with positive and negative expected NPVs. Firms with negative expected NPVs that default for which it is ex post efficient to refinance are refinanced because at the ex post stage the original loan is sunk. Firms for which it is ex post inefficient to refinance (the right column of the second row) would not be continued in operation in the D-M model.

Cases represented by the right column correspond either to Kornai's original description of SBCs (when the government provides refinance or makes the continuation decision) or to the case of creditor passivity (if banks or other nongovernmental creditors make the decision). There are, in fact, a number of potential explanations for the appearance of these cases, that is, those in which firms are continued in operation following default, despite the ex post inefficiency. These explanations include the following:

1. Creditors do not want to signal default because of their own weak financial positions.

2. Creditors believe that they or the debtor will ultimately be rescued.

3. The amount that the creditor may recover from liquidation may be less than the amount recovered in continuation because of bankruptcy costs, for example, or the creditor's placement in the absolute priority ordering, which determines which creditors are paid first.

4. The government has an objective, such as minimizing unemployment, that is inconsistent with maximizing the value of the firm.

Explanations 1–3 are among the motivations for creditor passivity discussed in Mitchell 1993; each belongs to a separate category that relates to, respectively, the value of the creditor, the creditor's relationship with the government, and the value of the debtor. The model presented in section 2.4 illustrates how explanation 1, which is in the category relating to the value of the creditor, can lead troubled banks to be passive. Explanation 4 is consistent with Kornai's original view of a paternalistic government.

As an aside, note that explanations 2 and 4 imply the existence of a commitment problem: the government cannot commit itself not to bail out (at least some) creditors or debtors that are insolvent. As discussed in Mitchell 1993, one potential reason for such a commitment problem on the part of the government is the existence of externalities arising from the default of a large number of banks or firms.[5] In such cases, the government's commitment problem, but it is unrelated to sunk costs. Even if it has made no prior investment in banks or firms before their financial difficulties appear, it may still face a commitment problem, because of the existence of externalities, when these banks or firms become insolvent.

The analysis in this chapter focuses on cases involving ex post decisions, that is, those in which banks must decide how to react to loan defaults and in which a regulator must choose which policy to apply to troubled banks. The next section reviews the policies that have been proposed or employed to clean banks' balance sheets in TEs.

2.3   Policies to Clean Banks' Balance Sheets

Commercial banks in all of the economies currently in transition were created by breaking off divisions of the central (monopoly) bank in the previous regimes. These banks inherited nondiversified portfolios with large portions of bad assets. Yet, the quantities of bad debt in these banks also increased in the first few years following their creation. Policymakers therefore realized that it would be necessary to "clean" banks' balance sheets before they could be successfully privatized.

A number of factors undoubtedly enter into governments' objective functions in determining the choice of policy to be implemented in cleaning banks' balance sheets in TEs. Yet although the objective function determining a government's policy choice may contain several variables, I argue that the value of (state-owned) banks' and firms' assets is likely to be one of that function's important arguments. In this chapter I employ the effect of a particular policy on the value of firms' and banks' assets to evaluate trade-offs among policies to clean banks' balance sheets. State-owned banks in TEs will eventually be privatized, hence their net worth is important in policy decisions concerning them. The net worth of state-owned firms that are being privatized is also important, whether firms are privatized by sale or through voucher methods. Privatization by sale yields government revenue. Alternatively, the net worth of a firm that is privatized through voucher methods determines the probability that the firm stays out of bankruptcy and the size of dividends that the firm may distribute. Both of these factors are important for maintaining political support for privatization and possibly for the entire transition process.

Policies applied to troubled banks have effects on both bank and firm behavior; therefore, the behavior of borrower firms' managers must be taken into account when choosing a policy for cleaning its balance sheets. The economics and finance literature commonly employs the assumption that firm managers may appropriate returns or the firm's assets for their personal benefit.[6] This assumption is especially relevant in the TEs, in which property rights are much less clearly defined than in developed market economies. The devolution of control from central authorities to state-owned firms' managers at the beginning of transition has resulted in a lack of effective corporate governance and has created a potential, uncontrolled leakage of assets to the private sector through managerial diversion of resources for perquisites and through direct transfer of assets to managers. Because of managers' ability to divert resources from state-owned firms, the timing of privatization of firms is also an important determinant of these firms' value. The longer the time required for privatization, the greater the potential for leakage and subsequent reduction in firms' values.[7] Even fast, mass privatization programs have not necessarily led to the rapid establishment of effective corporate governance. (See, for example, Brada 1996.)

Debt cancellation entails writing off the inherited debt of a bank at the beginning of transition.[8] Because debt cancellation lowers the (book) value of banks' assets, it will likely need to be accompanied by some measure, such as recapitalization, that restores bank solvency. Similarly, since the policy of debt transfer involves removing inherited assets from the banks' balance sheets, such a policy may also require recapitalization of banks. In addition, if the policy of self-reliance results in banks' writing off of a large quantity of debt, recapitalization will be necessary under that policy as well. Recapitalization has accompanied both debt transfer and self-reliance policies in practice.

The obvious motivation for recommending debt cancellation in a particular case is that if the inherited debt no longer exists, then it cannot pose any of the problems associated with large quantities of bad debts on banks' balance sheets. In addition, removal of the debt overhang eliminates from firms' balance sheets a burden from the past. In the absence of capital market imperfections, the argument that debt cancellation will eliminate problems associated with bad debt without changing the net worth of government assets is compelling. Yet debt cancellation has almost never been implemented in practice.[9] The fact that it creates a credibility problem is the most frequently cited explanation of why governments have not chosen such a policy: if the government is willing to cancel debt once, then agents may believe that the government will be willing to cancel debt in the future.

The feature of debt cancellation that gives rise to the credibility problem, however, is recapitalization rather than cancellation of the debt per se. If banks were not recapitalized in conjunction with debt cancellation, then they would oppose this policy, since it would require them to write down their assets. Since recapitalization has accompanied both the debt transfer and the self-reliance policies that governments have actually implemented, however, these policies also give rise to an analogous credibility problem.[10] The credibility argument, then, cannot completely explain why policies other than debt cancellation have been chosen. This chapter offers an alternative explanation relating to the effects of policy choices on banks' and firms' asset values. I show that whereas the removal of a bank's or firm's debt overhang from the past may have some benefit, the negative effect of unmonitored asset dissipation may outweigh any benefit if the problem of asset dissipation among firms is important. Self-reliance or debt transfer will, in such a case, yield higher bank and firm values. Appendix 2.1 describes the actual policies of debt transfer and self-reliance implemented in the Czech Republic, Hungary, and Poland.

2.4 The Model

The timing of events in the model described in this chapter is as follows. In period 0 each commercial bank in the economy has a continuum of debtors of measure 1 with loans equal to d for each debtor. Each bank has an amount H in deposits. Total debt repayments for a firm equal $d(1 + s)$, where s represents the interest rate. Interest sd is assumed to come due in period 1, whereas principal d comes due in period 2. Prior to the beginning of period 1 and before the precise level of default on banks' balance sheets is known, the government (G) chooses a policy: debt cancellation, debt transfer, or self-reliance.

At the beginning of period 1 firms realize their period 1 income and learn their continuation and liquidation values. The combination of income and continuation and liquidation values determines each firm's debtor type (good or bad). All of this information is private to firms.

After firms have realized their income and learned their types, banks receive income from good debtors, and they observe default by bad debtors if a debt cancellation policy has not been chosen. (When debt cancellation has been chosen, loans are written off the banks' and the firms' books prior to period 1, and default does not occur in period 1.) Information regarding default is private to the bank. If default has occurred, banks decide whether to roll over or work out the loans in default. The term "workout" will be used here to denote any action, such as a bankruptcy proceeding or an out-of-court workout, in which the bank attempts to recover some of its loan and possibly to reorganize the firm. Workout of a loan enables a bank to value the firm and to slow or halt the dissipation of its assets. The process of valuation is assumed to be costly. Once banks have decided whether to work out or roll over their defaulting loans, firms then choose their levels of asset dissipation.

During period 1 firms operate under government ownership. Asset dissipation and managerial appropriation of profit will occur during this period (if managers have chosen positive levels of asset dissipation) unless managers' activities have been constrained as a result of a loan workout. At the beginning of period 2 all firms are privatized (or some possibly liquidated).[11] If asset dissipation has occurred during period 1, the value of a firm's assets that is realized upon privatization will be lower than the value that would have been realized had no asset dissipation occurred. Loans that are still outstanding are repaid in period 2.

The timing of events in the model can be summarized as follows:

Period 0

G chooses a policy.

Period 1

Firms realize income, learn their continuation/liquidation values (hence, learn their types).

Default on loans occurs.

Banks observe default.

Banks choose action.

Firms choose their level of asset dissipation.

Period 2

Privatization of firms.

Outstanding loans repaid.

A bank that observes default in period 1 and decides whether to work out or roll over debt will be a bad-debt bank if debt transfer is the policy choice and a commercial bank if self-reliance has been selected.

Privatization of firms at the beginning of period 2 is assumed to occur through individual sale. A sufficient number of buyers is assumed so that if a firm's continuation value minus its outstanding debt obligations exceeds its liquidation value, the firm will be privatized.

2.4.1 Firm Behavior

The amount of asset dissipation that occurs during period 1 affects the firm's value in period 2. Let the proportion of the firm's assets that are dissipated be given by Δ.

ASSUMPTION 2.1 The maximum feasible value of Δ is given by $\bar{\Delta} \leq 1$.

$\bar{\Delta}$ is determined by existing institutions and regulations and will differ from economy to economy. For instance, if regulation of managerial behavior is nonexistent, then managers are free to steal the firm's assets and $\bar{\Delta} = 1$. (This is indeed what occurred in a number of countries at the beginning of transition.) If there is some degree of regulation of managerial behavior, then $\bar{\Delta} < 1$.

Let $x_i(\Delta)$ denote the continuation value (gross of debt repayments) in period 2 for firm i, for a given period 1 level of asset dissipation Δ. $x_i(\Delta)$ is assumed to be decreasing, with $x_i(0) = \bar{x}_i$ and $x_i(1) = 0$, where $\bar{x}_i$ represents the period 2 continuation value of the firm if no asset dissipation occurs in period 1. This is the firm's maximum possible continuation value; asset dissipation during period 1 lowers the firm's period 2 continuation value. When $\Delta = 1$, there are no assets left in the firm to enable it to operate in period 2.

Define the liquidation value $l_i(\Delta)$ of firm i in period 2 in a similar manner: $l_i(\Delta)$ is nonnegative and decreasing, with $l_i(0) = \bar{l}_i$, and $l_i(1) = 0$. The firm's period 2 value, gross of debt obligations, is then given by the maximum of the firm's continuation and liquidation values: $V_i(\Delta) = \max\{x_i(\Delta), l_i(\Delta)\}$. Suppose that the firm is continued in operation in period 2 and that the debt obligation remains on the firm's books; then its period 2 continuation value is given by $x_i(\Delta) - d$, with Δ amount of asset dissipation in period 1.

DEFINITION 2.2 A firm i is *viable* if $\bar{x}_i > \bar{l}_i$.

A firm will be called "viable," according to definition 2.2, if its maximum possible continuation value is greater than its maximum possible liquidation value. That is, in the absence of any asset dissipation and in the absence of a debt overhang, a viable firm would have higher value in continuation than if it were liquidated.

Asset dissipation by firm managers in period 1 determines two sources of private managerial benefits. On one hand, asset dissipation confers current (period 1) private benefits on managers. On the other hand, asset dissipation reduces the firm's future value and thus potentially reduces the manager's future private benefits (if the firm is not liquidated). Denote the value of current private benefits from a level Δ of asset dissipation by $b(\Delta)$, where $b(0) = 0$ and $b(\cdot)$ is increasing.

Denote the manager's future private benefits by a function $P_i(\Delta)$, which is assumed to equal a fraction ξ of the firm's continuation value. For example, if the debt is left on the firm's balance sheet and if the firm is not liquidated in period 1, then $P_i(\Delta) = \xi \cdot [x_i(\Delta) - d]$. The quantity ξ takes on a value between 0 and 1 and represents the degree to which the manager's future private benefits from continued operation of the firm are tied to the firm's value. For example, if the manager is the sole owner of the privatized firm, $\xi = 1$. On the other hand, if the manager is sure to have no relationship with the privatized firm, $\xi = 0$. The value of ξ is determined at least partly by the method of privatization. Note that since $x_i(\cdot)$ is decreasing in Δ, $P_i(\cdot)$ is also decreasing in this variable. Clearly, if the firm is liquidated before period 2, $P_i(\Delta) = 0$.

ASSUMPTION 2.2   The manager's utility is $U_i(\Delta) = b(\Delta) + P_i(\Delta)$.[12]

The manager's salary from working in the firm is normalized to zero in the utility function specified by assumption 2.2. This function reflects the trade-off between current and future benefits that the manager faces in dissipating the firm's assets.

Assumption 2.3 states that asset dissipation is inefficient:

ASSUMPTION 2.3   One dollar's reduction in period 2 firm value yields less than a dollar's increase in current private managerial benefits.

There are two types of firms in the model: good debtors and bad debtors. Definitions of the types reflect combinations of assumptions about period 1 incomes and about the viability of firms:

DEFINITION 2.3   A *good debtor* has the following characteristics: (1) period 1 income exceeds interest payments sd; (2) $x_i(0) - d \geq 0$.

DEFINITION 2.4   A *bad debtor* has the following characteristics: (1) period 1 income is less than interest payments sd; (2) $V_i(0) - d < 0$.

That firms are assumed to be either good debtors or bad debtors reflects some implicit restrictions on income flows. These restrictions are imposed for expositional convenience only and do not affect the model's qualitative results.[13] Definition 2.3 implies that all firms that earn enough income in period 1 to meet interest repayments are solvent (in the absence of asset dissipation); profit from continuation in period 2 exceeds debt repayments. Definition 2.4 implies that all firms that default on interest payments in period 1 are insolvent and, simultaneously, that all firms that are insolvent cannot avoid default on interest repayments in period 1. An assumption on income flows that is consistent with the above definitions is that solvent firms earn period 1 income equal to sd and insolvent firms earn period 1 income equal to 0.[14]

Bad debtors have so much debt on their books relative to potential earnings that default is inevitable. That these firms have a large debt overhang, however, does not necessarily imply that they are not viable. Some of these firms may become viable if the debt overhang is removed via debt cancellation or via a bank workout in which some debt is written off.

The level of asset dissipation a firm manager chooses is endogenous and is a function of the firm's type (good or bad debtor), G's choice of policy, and bank response to default (when debt cancellation is not the policy). In subsequent sections I analyze bank behavior and firms' resulting asset dissipation decisions for each policy.

2.4.2 Self-Reliance

ASSUMPTION 2.4   A banker's utility function is $W(\prod, \rho) \max[\prod, 0] + \rho$, where $\prod$ represents two-period bank profit and ρ represents a private benefit to the banker of maintaining the bank in operation.[15]

The private benefit ρ in assumption 2.4 can actually be interpreted in a number of ways. One interpretation is that given in the assumption: ρ is the private benefit of keeping the bank in operation (under the implicit assumption that the bank will be closed or the manager replaced if the bank becomes insolvent), where in this model two-period bank profit is equivalent to bank net worth. Note that if the bank is insolvent but liquid and if the insolvency is not discovered until profit is realized in period 2, the bank manager still enjoys the private benefit of keeping the bank in operation during period 1. In contrast, if the insolvency is observed in period 1, the manager will lose the private benefit and will have a level of utility of zero. The presence of ρ in the bank manager's objective function thus creates an incentive to hide the bank's insolvency by rolling over loans in default.

A more general interpretation of ρ is that it represents a private benefit from managing a solvent bank. The implicit assumption here is that $\rho = 0$ if the bank is known to be insolvent, even if the government rescues the bank. That is, the bank manager's reputation or future career advancement—for example, the likelihood of her staying on as the manager once the bank is privatized—is greatly diminshed if the manager is known to be in charge of an insolvent bank, even if the government recapitalizes the insolvent bank.[16]

A bank with some proportion α of its loan portfolio in default chooses between two actions: workout or rollover.[17] Workout and rollover policies are defined as follows.

Workout

Bank pays a cost $c(\alpha)$, which allows it to learn $V_i(\Delta)$ for each firm in default and to halt asset dissipation. $c'(\cdot) > 0$; $c''(\cdot) \geq 0$.

Bank may write off some debt.

Rollover

Loans are rolled over; therefore, on the bank's balance sheet the loans appear to be performing.

The function $c(\alpha)$ reflects costs associated with the process of information gathering and valuation of the firm that must accompany workout, whether it is through a bankruptcy reorganization procedure or an out-of-court workout. Even if the bank can access inside information concerning its debtors, the process of valuation and of determining the best course of action for the firm is costly. In addition, the function $c(\cdot)$ may also reflect the costs of raising capital when the bank suffers loan defaults.

ASSUMPTION 2.5   The bank's choice of workout is observable.

Assumption 2.5 states that when the bank chooses workout, this action is observable to the regulator. An obvious example is when the bank initiates a bankruptcy procedure against a defaulter. Yet even out-of-court workouts require banks to undertake easily observable actions. In addition, writing off debt requires visible changes to a bank's balance sheet. The choice of workout, therefore, reveals the level of default on the bank's balance sheet.

Assumption 2.5 implies that the bank cannot simultaneously roll over its loans so as to disguise its default and surreptitiously undertake a workout to value its debtors. Whereas the benefit to the bank of rolling over loans is that the value of α remains unobserved, its cost is that the bank does not learn the continuation and liquidation values of its defaulters; therefore, it cannot force them to liquidate or restructure, and it cannot halt their asset dissipation. The bank does know, however, the probability distribution of continuation and liquidation values of bad debtors and can thus calculate a firm's expected value given that it is a bad debtor. These calculated expected values will influence the bank's decision regarding whether to work out or roll over loans in default.

Obviously, a particular firm's expected value will be a function both of its type (good or bad debtor) and of the level of asset dissipation the firm manager has chosen. Define the expected continuation and liquidation values in period 2 of a bad debtor (gross of debt repayments), given some period 1 level of asset dissipation Δ, by $x(\Delta \mid B)$ and $l(\Delta \mid B)$, respectively. The firm's expected value in period 2 is then given by $V(\Delta \mid B) = E\{\max[x(\Delta \mid B), l(\Delta \mid B)]\}$. The expected value in period 2 for a good debtor is defined analogously: $V(\Delta \mid G) = E\{\max[x(\Delta \mid G), l(\Delta \mid G)]\}$. ($B$ corresponds to bad, and G to good.)

Recall that bad debtors have asset values that are lower than the face value of their debt: for each bad debtor i, $V_i(0) - d < 0$. This implies that if none of a bad debtor's debt is written off (i.e., if the bank chooses rollover), the firm will not be sold in period 2 when it is put up for privatization, since no buyer would be willing to pay a positive price for it. This observation raises the question of the treatment of firms that the government does not succeed in selling in period 2. This question is important, since the answer to the question affects policy trade-offs.

The government has two potential responses with regard to unsold firms in period 2: liquidation (piecemeal sale) or a giveaway of the firms, for example, to their employees. In the case of the first response, the liquidation of unsold firms would effectively eliminate the SBCs created by banks' rolling over loans in default. As it turns out that, this policy response may lead to excessive liquidation of firms, since it will result in viable firms' being liquidated because of the debt overhang.[18] In contrast, the second policy response, the giveaway of unsold firms, may lead to excessive continuation of firms, since it results in the continuation of nonviable firms in period 2. Privatization policies thus affect trade-offs among policies for cleaning banks' balance sheets.

To keep the exposition of the model as simple as possible, I assume that firms not sold in period 2 are given away. Another motivation for this assumption aside from model simplicity is that it renders the environment analyzed in this chapter more comparable to that of a nontransition economy, in which firms are already privately owned and thus bad debtors whose loans have been rolled over would automatically remain in operation in period 2.

ASSUMPTION 2.6   The government gives away firms that it is unable to sell through the privatization process in period 2.

Defaulting firms whose loans are rolled over will thus be continued in period 2. Given that $x_i(0) < d$ for bad debtors, the total repayment to the bank will be given by $x_i(\Delta)$, even if the firm's period 2 liquidation value exceeded its continuation value. Assumption 2.6, then, implies that self-reliance with rollover generates two potential sources of inefficiency: it does not halt asset dissipation, resulting in lower values of firms than if there were no asset dissipation; and firms may be inefficiently continued in operation.

Note that self-reliance with workout does not lead to inefficient continuation of firms. During the course of a workout in period 1 the bank learns $x_i(\cdot)$ and $l_i(\cdot)$. If $x_i(0) < l_i(0)$, the bank will liquidate the firm.

For the bank to evaluate its expected profit with workout and with rollover and to choose between these actions for its bad debtors, it must know the level of asset dissipation that these debtor firms would choosen given the bank's choice of action. The following sections identify firms' asset dissipation choices. These decisions by the firms about asset dissipation are then taken into account in the expression for the bank's expected profit given a choice of workout and its profit with rollover.

2.4.2.1   Asset Dissipation by Good Debtors

Call the manager of a good debtor a "good" manager. It is tempting to conjecture that since asset dissipation is inefficient (by assumption 2.3) and since the good debtor is solvent, a good manager will always choose a lower level of asset dissipation than will managers of bad debtors. This intuition, however, proves not to be entirely correct. The fact that the manager's private benefits from continuation of the firm constitute only a fraction of the firm's period 2 value may give the manager the incentive to dissipate the maximum possible amount of assets in period 1, leading to default of the firm on its debt repayments in period 2.

Only if the fraction ξ in the manager's private-benefit function $P_i(\Delta) = \xi \cdot (x_i(\Delta) - d)$ is high enough or if the firm's period 2 continuation value $x_i(0) - d$ is high enough will a good manager be encouraged to choose less than the maximum level of asset dissipation. The following technical assumption is therefore necessary to guarantee that good managers will not dissipate assets to the point of default on debt repayments in period 2:

ASSUMPTION 2.7 $P_i(0) > b(\bar{\Delta})$ for all good debtors i.[19]

The following claim follows directly from assumption 2.7 and characterizes the asset dissipation decision of the good manager:

CLAIM 2.1   The good debtor i will choose a level of asset dissipation Δ_i^G, such that $0 \le \Delta_i^G \le \bar{\Delta}$, with $\Delta_i^G < \bar{\Delta}$ if $[x_i(\bar{\Delta}) - d] \le 0$.

Proof Suppose that $\Delta_i^G = \bar{\Delta}$ and $[x_i(\bar{\Delta}) - d] \leq 0$. The manager's utility is given by $b(\bar{\Delta}) + P_i(\bar{\Delta})$, which equals $b(\bar{\Delta}) + 0$, or $b(\bar{\Delta})$. Assumption 2.7 implies that the manager's utility would be higher with a choice of $\Delta_i^G = 0$; therefore, a choice of $\Delta_i^G = \bar{\Delta}$ cannot be utility-maximizing.

Claim 2.1 states that a good manager will never choose asset dissipation equal to $\bar{\Delta}$ if so doing would cause the firm to become insolvent in period 2. Note that Δ_i^G is independent of the bank's choice of action in response to default of bad debtors.

2.4.2.2 Asset Dissipation by Bad Debtors

Recall that bad debtors are insolvent: $V_i(0) < d$ for every bad debtor i. This implies that for all Δ and for every bad debtor i, $P_i(\Delta) = 0$, whether the bank chooses rollover or workout in response to default. When the bank chooses rollover, the debt overhang is not removed, and the firm remains insolvent in period 2. Yet even if the bank chooses workout and writes off the debt of some firms to allow viable firms to be sold, $P_i(\Delta)$ will still equal zero. The bank will write down an amount of debt that leaves the new level of debt repayment exactly equal to $x_i(0)$. (The writing off of debt in workout to guarantee that the firm will be sold in period 2 is obviously more important in the situation where the government liquidates unsold firms.) That $P_i(\Delta) = 0$ for all α implies that there no longer exists a trade-off between current and future private benefits: increasing the bad debtor's current dissipation of assets does not result in a reduction of the manager's future benefits.

Workout If the bank undertakes workout of its defaulters, it will be able to halt asset dissipation. Thus, the firm manager's utility will be equivalent the payoff that she would have received in the absence of any asset dissipation: that is, for all Δ, $U_i(\Delta) = b(0) = 0$. Since $U_i(\Delta) = 0$ for all Δ, the manager has no incentive to choose a positive level of Δ.

Rollover If the bank rolls over the loan of a firm in default, then asset dissipation will not be halted. The manager's utility is thus $U_i(\Delta) = b(\Delta)$. The manager maximizes utility by choosing $\Delta = \bar{\Delta}$. Claim 2.2 follows immediately:

CLAIM 2.2 A bad debtor will choose $\Delta = 0$ if the commercial bank chooses workout and $\Delta = \bar{\Delta}$ if the bank chooses rollover.

Claim 2.2 illustrates that asset dissipation is higher with rollover than with workout.

2.4.2.3 Banks' Actions

The two-period expected profit for a bank given a proportion α of the portfolio in default and given workout[20] is

$$\Pi^w(\alpha) = (1 - \alpha)(1 + s)d + \alpha \cdot V(0 \mid B) - c(a) - H. \tag{2.1}$$

The two-period expected profit for a bank given α and rollover, taking into account bad debtors' choices of asset dissipation, is

$$\Pi^r(\alpha) = (1 - \alpha)(1 + s)d + \alpha \cdot x(\bar{\Delta} \mid B) - H. \tag{2.2}$$

Note that workout allows the bank to recover repayments equal to the expected value $V(0 \mid B)$ of firms; this expected value reflects the expected continuation value for viable firms and the expected liquidation value for nonviable firms. In contrast, rollover results in the bank's recovering repayments equal only to the expected continuation values of all firms. Assumption 2.8 implies that workout by a commercial bank is always socially desirable: $\Pi^w(\alpha) > \Pi^r(\alpha)$ for all α.

ASSUMPTION 2.8 $\alpha \cdot [V(0 \mid B) - x(\bar{\Delta} \mid B)] > c(a)$ for all α.

Although workout is more profitable than rollover, the presence of ρ in the banker's objective function motivates the banker to choose to roll over loans whenever $\Pi^w(\alpha) \leq 0$. Define α^* as the value of α such that $\Pi^w(\alpha^*) = 0$. The bank manager will then choose rollover for all $\alpha \geq \alpha^*$.[21]

2.4.3 Debt Cancellation

With debt cancellation commercial banks' inherited debt is canceled and firms' balance sheets in period 0, and the banks are recapitalized. Because no default occurs in period 1, the bank has no choice to make between workout and rollover. Yet because there is no default in period 1, there is no mechanism to halt asset dissipation. It is straightforward to show that the level of asset dissipation chosen by a "good debtor" i (i.e., a firm that would have been a good debtor if its debt had not been canceled) remains Δ_i^G, the level chosen under a policy of self-reliance. Although the future private benefits for a good debtor are now given by $P(\Delta) = \xi \cdot x_i(\Delta)$ rather than $\xi \cdot [x_i(\Delta) - d]$, the value of Δ that maximizes the manager's objective function does not change.

Now consider "bad debtors" (analogously, those that would have been bad debtors had their debt not been canceled). Assuming, as before, that the government gives away unsold firms, the future private benefits for the managers of bad-debtor firms increase from $P_i(\Delta) = 0$ to $P_i(\Delta) = \xi \cdot x_i(\Delta)$. Managers of these firms may well respond to the increase in future benefits by choosing an amount of asset dissipation less than $\bar{\Delta}$. Define $\Delta_{i,dc}^B$ to be the value of Δ that maximizes the utility of a bad manager (i.e., the manager of a bad debtor) i when there is no debt overhang. Then $\Delta_{i,dc}^B \leq \bar{\Delta}$.

The policy of debt cancellation thus generates two trade-offs relative to the policy of self-reliance. On the one hand, the asset dissipation of bad debtors is not halted, whereas with workout it is. Firms' values are thus lower with debt cancellation than they would have been if the debt had remained on their balance sheets and workout had been undertaken. On the other hand, removal of the debt overhang can increase the continuation values of bad debtors and thus lower levels of asset dissipation relative to levels occurring with self-reliance and rollover.

2.4.4 Debt Transfer

With debt transfer all of commercial banks' inherited debt is transferred to a bad-debt bank in period 0 and the commercial bank is recapitalized. I initially assume that the bad-debt bank is created for the purpose of working out the debt that is transferred to it and will be closed on termination of its duties. Because the bad-debt bank is not a commercial bank and does not accept deposits, its "solvency" is not an issue. I assume that G is thus able to structure the compensation scheme of the bad-debt bank's managers so that they have an incentive to maximize debt collection and to choose workout (when the gains from workout exceed the costs).

Obviously, these assumptions do not represent the only possible scenario regarding the operation of a bad-debt bank. For example, if there is a possibility that the bad-debt bank will not be closed after it has finished handling the debt that has been transferred to it or if G is not able to appropriately align the bad-debt bank managers' incentives with social interests, then these managers may sometimes choose rollover, which would create some additional policy trade-offs. Indeed, one could make a number of reasonable but competing assumptions regarding the functioning of a bad-debt bank. The existence of these competing assumptions implies that it is impossible to establish a definitive model of a bad-debt bank. Rather than attempting to argue that a particular set of assumptions is more realistic than another, therefore, I analyze trade-offs among policies under differing sets of assumptions. That is, in addition to describing policy trade-offs under the assumption that the bad-debt bank always chooses workout, I indicate how the trade-offs would change if the bad-debt bank were to choose rollover for some levels of bad debt.

I show below that under the assumption that the bad-debt bank always chooses workout, if the costs of workout for the bad-debt bank are the same as those for commercial banks and if the bad-debt bank is as skilled as the commercial banks at recovering loans, then debt transfer will always be preferred to self-reliance. There is, however, reason to believe that the bad-debt bank may not be as effective as the commercial banks in undertaking workout. In particular, if the commercial banks have access to inside information about borrowers' values, then workout by the bad-debt bank will not be as effective as workout by the commercial bank.

ASSUMPTION 2.9   Because of informational asymmetries between commercial banks and bad-debt banks, commercial banks are better able to determine their borrowers' values and to recover loan repayments with workout.

Assumption 2.9 can be translated into an assumption that a bad-debt bank is able to slow, but not to halt, asset dissipation when it undertakes workout. Let $\hat{\Delta}_{DT}$, where $0 < \hat{\Delta}_{DT} \leq \bar{\Delta}$, be the expected level of asset dissipation that remains unrecovered when the bad-debt bank undertakes workout. When bad debtors choose a level of asset dissipation equal to at least $\hat{\Delta}_{DT}$, the expected value of a bad debtor will be $V(\hat{\Delta}_{DT} \mid B)$, where $V(\bar{\Delta} \mid B) \leq V(\hat{\Delta}_{DT} \mid B) < V(0 \mid B)$. In addition, because $\hat{\Delta}_{DT}$ of asset dissipation remains unrecovered, the manager of a bad debtor receives utility of $b(\hat{\Delta}_{DT})$ when the bad-debt bank undertakes workout, as opposed to a utility of zero when the commercial bank undertakes workout.

CLAIM 2.3   A bad debtor will choose $\Delta = \hat{\Delta}_{DT}$ when debt transfer is the policy.

The level of asset dissipation chosen by bad debtors with debt transfer is greater than that chosen with self-reliance and workout but less than the level chosen with self-reliance and rollover.

2.5   G's Policy Choice

G must choose a policy before α is known.[22] G's objective is to select the policy that yields the highest expected net worth of banks and firms, where the expectation is taken over α and where G takes into account banks' and firms' optimal behavior at each value of α. The optimal policy for G to choose will thus depend on G's prior distribution over α and on values of other parameters. Pairwise comparison of policy choices provides the intuition for characterization of the optimal policy. G's balance sheets with workout, rollover, debt cancellation, and debt transfer are given in appendix 2.1.

2.5.1   The Choice between Debt Cancellation and Self-Reliance

Consider a value of $\alpha < \alpha^*$, that is, a value of α for which the bank would choose workout with self-reliance. Define $x(\Delta_{dc}^{B} \mid B)$ to be the expected continuation value of a bad debtor given a policy of debt cancellation and given assumption 2.6. Comparison of G's balance sheets with workout and debt cancellation indicates that G will prefer workout to debt cancellation for this value of α if $\alpha[V(0 \mid B) - x(\Delta_{dc}^B \mid B)] > c(\alpha)$.

Assumption 2.8 guarantees that $\alpha \cdot [V(0 \mid B) - x(\bar{\Delta} \mid B))] > c(\alpha)$; if Δ_{dc}^B is low enough, however, debt cancellation may be preferred to workout for some values of α. This can only be the case when removal of the debt overhang enables bad managers to gain enough extra private benefits from firm privatization that they no longer have a strong incentive to dissipate their firms' assets.

Now consider a value of α such that the commercial bank chooses rollover. Debt cancellation will be preferred to rollover if $x(\Delta_{dc}^B \mid B) \geq x(\bar{\Delta} \mid B)$, which always holds. Debt cancellation is thus preferred (possibly only weakly) to self-reliance for all $\alpha \geq \alpha^*$.

2.5.2 The Choice between Debt Transfer and Self-Reliance

Consider a value of α such that a commercial bank chooses workout. Debt transfer will be preferred to workout if and only if $V(\hat{\Delta}_{DT} \mid B) \geq V(0 \mid B)$, which never holds (assumption 2.9); therefore, workout is preferred to debt transfer. For a value of α such that a commercial bank chooses rollover, debt transfer will be preferred to rollover if and only if $\alpha[V(\hat{\Delta}_{DT} \mid B) - x(\bar{\Delta} \mid B)] - c(\alpha) > 0$. Debt transfer will be preferred if the gain to workout by a bad-debt bank relative to rollover justifies the cost of workout.

2.5.3 The Choice between Debt Transfer and Debt Cancellation

Debt transfer will be preferred to debt cancellation for all values of α such that $\alpha\{V(\hat{\Delta}_{DT} \mid B) - x(\Delta_{dc}^B \mid B)\} - c(\alpha) > 0$. Whether or not this inequality holds depends on the skill of a bad-debt bank in undertaking workout and upon the degree to which debt cancellation mitigates the problem of asset dissipation of bad debtors. Note that although debt transfer may be preferred to self-reliance with rollover, debt cancellation may nevertheless be preferred to debt transfer.

2.5.4 The Optimal Policy

Although the above discussion makes it obvious that the optimal policy in a given situation will depend on parameter values and on the probability distribution of α, some general observations can nonetheless be made with respect to optimal policy. First, note that the asset dissipation of good managers is invariant to G's policy choice; G's policy choice thus influences only the behavior of bad managers.

That a number of analysts have proposed the policy of debt cancellation raises the question of the conditions in which this policy would be optimal. Obviously, one necessary condition for debt cancellation to be the optimal policy is that it is preferred to debt transfer. The following definition aids the discussion of this question:

DEFINITION 2.5   A bad-debt bank is *effective* if

$$\int_0^1 \{\alpha[V(\hat{\Delta}_{DT} \mid B) - x(\Delta_{dc}^B \mid B)] - c(\alpha)\} f(\alpha) \, d\alpha > 0, \tag{2.3}$$

where $f(\alpha)$ represents G's prior over α.

Definition 2.5 states that a bad-debt bank will be called "effective" if expected firm value resulting from workout by the bad-debt bank, net of the costs of workout, exceeds expected firm value with debt cancellation. If a bad-debt bank is not effective, then debt cancellation will be preferred to debt transfer. Definition 2.5 makes it clear that the more skilled a bad-debt bank is at workout and the more serious is the problem of asset dissipation with debt cancellation, the more likely it is that the bad debt bank will be effective.

The following proposition provides necessary and sufficient conditions for debt cancellation to be the optimal policy choice:

PROPOSITION 2.1   Debt cancellation is optimal if and only if

(i) The bad-debt bank is not effective.

(ii) $\int_0^{\alpha^*} \{\alpha[V(0 \mid B) - x(\Delta_{dc}^B \mid B)] - c(\alpha)\} \cdot f(\alpha) < \int_{\alpha^*}^1 \alpha\{x(\Delta_{dc}^B \mid B) - x(\bar{\Delta} \mid B)\} \cdot f(\alpha).$

Condition (i) of proposition 2.1 states that debt cancellation will be the optimal policy only if it is preferred to debt transfer. Condition (ii) follows from comparison of G's balance sheets with self-reliance and with debt cancellation and states that for debt cancellation to be the optimal policy choice, the expected gains to self-reliance and workout relative to debt cancellation cannot exceed the expected losses of self-reliance and rollover relative to debt cancellation. The lower are α^* and Δ_{dc}^B, the more likely debt cancellation is to be preferred to self-reliance.

Corollary 2.1 identifies the necessary conditions for optimality of debt cancellation:

COROLLARY 2.1   Necessary conditions for debt cancellation to be optimal are

(i) The bad-debt bank is not effective.

(ii) For some bad debtors i, $\Delta_{i,dc}^B < \bar{\Delta}$.

Condition (ii) of the corollary formalizes the point made in section 2.3 that if asset dissipation is a serious problem, debt cancellation may lead to lower firm and bank values than other policies. Specifically, if the expected level of asset dissipation with debt cancellation is not strictly lower than that expected with self-reliance and rollover, then self-reliance will always be preferred (at least weakly) to debt cancellation, and self-reliance will be strictly preferred if at least one realization of α occurs with positive probability for which a commercial bank would undertake workout.

Factors affecting the level of $\Delta_{i,dc}^{B}$ relative to $\bar{\Delta}$ include the extent of the debt overhang, the viability of its bad debtors, the nature of the privatization process, and the degree to which debtor firms' managers will derive private benefits from firms once they are privatized. The greater the debt overhang, the more firms' continuation values will rise when the debt overhang is eliminated via debt cancellation and the greater the potential incentive for managers to reduce asset dissipation to benefit from the higher continuation value. On the other hand, if bad debtors are not viable, their maximum continuation values ($\bar{x}_i$) will be lower than their liquidation value ($\bar{l}_i$), implying weaker incentives for their managers to reduce asset dissipation.

The nature of the privatization process will also affect firm managers' willingness to abstain from dissipating assets when debt cancellation is the policy chosen. The higher the probability that a manager will be replaced upon privatization, the greater his incentive to dissipate assets in period 1. On the other hand, if the probability that the manager will be replaced is linked to the firm's continuation value at the point of privatization, then the manager will have less incentive to dissipate the firm's assets. Thus, the nature of the privatization process can affect the seriousness of the problem of asset dissipation associated with the policy of debt cancellation.

The above discussion indicates that when problems of asset dissipation are serious, debt cancellation cannot be the optimal policy; either self-reliance or debt transfer will be optimal in such cases. Whether or not debt transfer is the optimal policy in these cases depends on a bad-debt bank's ability to value firms and to recover repayments with workout, which the model captures in the bad-debt bank's ability to halt asset dissipation. Policy trade-offs involving debt transfer are first presented under the assumption that the bad-debt bank always undertakes workout. These policy trade-offs are then reinterpreted under the assumption that the bad-debt bank chooses rollover for some values of α.

The following proposition provides conditions for the optimality of debt transfer:

PROPOSITION 2.2   Necessary and sufficient conditions for debt transfer to be optimal are

(i) The bad-debt bank is effective.

(ii) $\int_0^{\alpha^*} \{\alpha[V(0\,|\,B) - V(\hat{\Delta}_{DT}\,|\,B)]\} \cdot f(\alpha) < \int_{\alpha^*}^1 \alpha\{V(\hat{\Delta}_{DT}\,|\,B) - x(\bar{\Delta}\,|\,B) - c(\alpha)\}f(\alpha)$.

Proposition 2.2 follows from comparison of G's balance sheets under the differing policies (see appendix 2.1).

COROLLARY 2.2   A sufficient condition for debt transfer to be optimal is that the bad-debt bank is effective and $\hat{\Delta}_{DT} = 0$.

Corollary 2.2 restates an obvious result discussed earlier. If a bad-debt bank is able to completely halt a firm's asset dissipation (i.e., is as skilled as a commercial bank at workout), then debt transfer will be preferred to self-reliance, since debt transfer never results in rollover.

Identification of the necessary conditions for debt transfer to be optimal is useful for distinguishing policy trade-offs under the assumption that a bad-debt bank always undertakes workout from those that would exist if the same bank chose rollover for some values of α. Given that self-reliance dominates debt transfer for all values of $\alpha < \alpha^*$, a necessary condition for debt transfer to be the optimal policy is that debt transfer dominates self-reliance for at least some values $\alpha \geq \alpha^*$.

Define $\hat{\alpha}$ as the minimum value of α such that $\hat{\alpha} \cdot [V(\hat{\Delta}_{DT} \mid B) - x(\bar{\Delta} \mid B)] - c(\hat{\alpha}) \leq 0$. For all $\alpha > \hat{\alpha}$, self-reliance and rollover is preferred to debt transfer. Then a necessary condition for debt transfer to be the optimal policy choice is that $\hat{\alpha} > \alpha^*$. There must then exist some range of α for which debt transfer is preferred to self-reliance. Proposition 2.3 summarizes the discussion:

PROPOSITION 2.3   Necessary conditions for debt transfer to be the optimal policy are

(i) The bad debt bank is effective.

(ii) $\hat{\alpha} > \alpha^*$.

If $\hat{\alpha} < 1$, then there exists some value of α for which the gains to workout by a bad-debt bank relative to rollover of loans do not justify the costs of workout. Obviously if this point is reached for a level of α for which a commercial bank would undertake workout, debt transfer cannot dominate self-reliance.

On the basis of the above discussion, it is now possible to identify sets of sufficient conditions and of necessary conditions for self-reliance to be the optimal policy choice.

COROLLARY 2.3   Sufficient conditions for self-reliance to be the optimal policy are that $\hat{\alpha} < \alpha^*$ and $\Delta_{dc}^{B} = \bar{\Delta}$.

The first condition of the corollary is sufficient for self-reliance to dominate debt transfer. The second condition implies that debt cancellation cannot dominate self-reliance.

COROLLARY 2.4   Necessary conditions for self-reliance to be optimal are

(i) $\hat{\Delta}_{DT} > 0$.

(ii) $\Delta_{dc}^{B} > 0$.

If $\hat{\Delta}_{DT} = 0$, then debt transfer dominates self-reliance. If $\Delta_{dc}^B = 0$, the problem of asset dissipation (among bad debtors) is nonexistent; therefore, debt cancellation dominates self-reliance.

It is also now possible to identify how policy trade-offs would change if a government does not succeed in aligning the incentives of a bad-debt bank's managers with government objectives and if that bad-debt bank rolls over loans for some values of α. Define $\tilde{\alpha}$ to be the lowest value of α for which a bad-debt bank begins rolling over debt. Clearly, for values of $\alpha \geq \tilde{\alpha}$ managers of bad debtors will choose levels of asset dissipation equal to $\bar{\Delta}$, and self-reliance and rollover will be weakly preferred to debt transfer, since $\tilde{\alpha} \cdot [x(\bar{\Delta} \,|\, B) - x(\bar{\Delta} \,|\, B)] = 0$. The definition of an effective bad-debt bank must therefore now be modified:

DEFINITION 2.5   A bad debt bank is *effective* if

$$\int_0^{\tilde{\alpha}} \{\alpha[V(\hat{\Delta}_{DT} \,|\, B) - x(\Delta_{dc}^B \,|\, B)] - c(\alpha)\} f(\alpha) + \int_{\tilde{\alpha}}^1 \alpha \{x(\bar{\Delta} \,|\, B) - x(\Delta_{dc}^B \,|\, B)\} f(\alpha) \, d\alpha > 0,$$

(2.4)

where $f(\alpha)$ represents G's prior over α.

Clearly a bad-debt bank is less likely to qualify as effective when it rolls over debt for some values of α. Changes to policy trade-offs are straightforward. As an example, we may restate proposition 2.3 as follows:

PROPOSITION 2.3′   Necessary conditions for debt transfer to be the optimal policy are

(i) The bad debt bank is effective.

(ii) $\tilde{\alpha} > \alpha^*$.

2.6   Conclusion

This chapter illustrates how troubled banks may react to loan default by passively rolling over loans and how this behavior and the resulting SBCs of firms affect trade-offs among policies designed to clean banks' balance sheets. The chapter proposes a new framework for analyzing policy trade-offs that consists of a two-tier hierarchy comprised of a regulator, banks, and firms. This framework is used to analyze the trade-offs among three policies—debt cancellation, debt transfer, and self-reliance—that have either been advocated or applied to clean banks' balance sheets in economies in transition. It is straightforward to extend the framework to analyze a wider range of policies, to treat firms and banks in developed economies, and to include restructuring or firms' asset dissipation decisions that affect their probability of default.[23]

The analysis presented in the chapter indicates how policies to clean banks' balance sheets have differing real effects on banks' and firms' asset values. Policies have direct effects on banks' treatment of defaulters and indirect effects on firm managers' activities relating to dissipation of their firms' assets. A policy's indirect effects can be an important determinant (in addition to its direct effects) of its outcome on banks' asset values.

Inclusion in the model of the indirect effects of policies for cleaning banks' balance sheets helps illuminate discussion of the policy of debt cancellation as a means of eliminating the problem of inherited bad debt in TEs. For example, one argument that has been made in favor of removing inherited debt from firms' balance sheets in TEs is that these firms should not be shackled during the transition with the burden of debts from the past. (See Blanchard et al. 1991, 49.) The model described in this chapter confirms that a potential benefit exists along these lines associated with debt cancellation. That is, removal of a firm's debt overhang may induce its managers to reduce their levels of asset dissipation below the levels that they would choose if the debt were to remain on the firm's balance sheets and banks rolled over debt in default. This potential benefit of debt cancellation may be overshadowed, however, by a disadvantage arising from the fact that managers of firms whose debt has been canceled may nevertheless choose to dissipate some of their firms' assets. Yet if debts have been canceled, the asset dissipation will remain unchecked, because of the absence of default and the ensuing process of valuation and monitoring of firm management by creditors who work out loans in default. If asset dissipation is a serious problem, debt cancellation may actually lead to more asset dissipation and lower firm values than policies that leave the debt on firms' balance sheets.

Analysis of the merits of the policy of debt transfer reveals the sensitivity of policy trade-offs to the ability of a bad-debt bank to recover repayments on debt transferred to it and to the incentives of the bad-debt bank's manager to work out the bad debt. The conditions under which a bad-debt bank is established, its likely life span, and the remuneration of its managers will all determine the incentives these managers have to be active or passive with respect to the bad debt and, consequently, the desirability of this policy relative to other policy choices.

Finally, the model illustrates how privatization methods in TEs can influence trade-offs among policies applied to clean banks' balance sheets. Privatization of firms by sale, followed by the piecemeal sale of firms that cannot be sold as a whole, may cause a policy of self-reliance to lead to inefficient liquidation of firms when banks have rolled over their bad loans. (The debt overhang in this case causes viable firms to be inefficiently liquidated.) The effects of SBCs created by loan rollovers are thus reversed via the privatization process. In contrast, if privatization of firms by sale is followed by giveaways of unsold firms or if firms are privatized via mass privatization methods rather than by sale, then self-reliance and rollover may lead to inefficient survival of firms. In this case the effects of SBCs created by rollover will persist.

Appendix 2.1

Policies Adopted to Clean Banks' Balance Sheets in Three Eastern European Economies

Czech Republic

• Debt transfer and self-reliance.
• Three commercial banks created on January 1, 1990.
• 40 percent of loans to the country's two largest banks were revolving inventory credits extended at negative interest rates.
• Two thirds of revolving inventory credits transferred in 1991 to consolidation bank.
• Commercial banks recapitalized with government securities.

Hungary

• Self-reliance; switch to debt transfer.
• Five commercial banks created on January 1, 1987.
• Bank provisioning and bankruptcy used until 1993.
• Loan consolidation program begun in 1993.
• Banks recapitalized in 1991, 1992, 1993, and 1994 (total recapitalization estimated at $3.5 billion).

Poland

• Self-reliance.
• Nine commercial banks created in February 1989.
• Banks instructed to create bad-loan divisions in 1992.
• Law on financial restructuring in 1993 required banks to undertake U.S. Chapter 11–type restructuring agreements.

G's Balance Sheets for Differing Policy Choices

Assume that y_G is the expected period 1 income earned by a good debtor and that the expected period 1 income of a bad debtor is zero. Denote by R the value of government securities used to recapitalize banks when debt cancellation or debt transfer is chosen.

G's balance sheet with self-reliance and workout

Assets

Expected income from good debtors $(1 - \alpha) \cdot [y_G + V(\Delta^G \,|\, G)] - (1 - \alpha) \cdot (1 + s)d$

Expected bank net worth $(1 - \alpha) \cdot (1 + s)d + \alpha \cdot V(0 \,|\, B) - c(\alpha) - H$

Liabilities

None

G's balance sheet with self-reliance and rollover

Assets

Expected income from good debtors $(1 - \alpha) \cdot [y_G + V(\Delta^G \,|\, G)] - (1 - \alpha) \cdot (1 + s)d$

Expected bank net worth $(1 - \alpha) \cdot (1 + s)d + \alpha \cdot x(\bar{\Delta} \,|\, B) - H$

Liabilities

None

G's balance sheet with debt cancellation

Assets

Expected income from good debtors $(1 - \alpha) \cdot [y_G + V(\Delta^G \,|\, G)]$

Expected income from bad debtors $\alpha \cdot V(\Delta_{dc}^B \,|\, B)$

Expected bank net worth $R - H$

Liabilities

Securities R

G's balance sheet with debt transfer

Assets

Expected income from good debtors $(1 - \alpha) \cdot [y_G + V(\Delta^G \,|\, G)] - (1 - \alpha) \cdot (1 + s)d$

Expected commercial bank net worth $R - H$

Expected bad-debt bank net worth $(1 - \alpha) \cdot (1 + s)d + \alpha \cdot V(\hat{\Delta}_{DT}) - c(\alpha)$

Liabilities

Securities R

Notes

I would like to thank Mathias Dewatripont, Patrick Legros, Maureen O'Hara, Gerard Roland, Anthony Saunders, Mark Schaffer, and the participants at the William Davidson Institute conference "The Design of Financial Systems in Central Europe" for helpful comments. I owe special thanks to John Bonin for helpful advice and collaboration. The research for the chapter was financed by the National Science Foundation and the International Research and Exchanges Board.

1. See, for example, Abel and Bonin 1993; Begg and Portes 1993; Bonin 1993; Bonin and Schaffer 1995; Brainard 1991a, 1991b; Calvo and Frenkel 1991; Caprio and Levine 1992; Coricelli and Thorne 1993;

Dornbusch 1991; Estrin, Hare, and Suranyi 1992; Levine and Scott 1992; Marrese 1994; Saunders and Sommariva 1993; and Thorne 1993.

2. The term "soft budget constraints" originated in Kornai 1980.

3. See Begg and Portes 1993; Blanchard et al. 1991, 49; Calvo and Frenkel 1991; and Dornbusch 1991.

4. See Schaffer 1998 for a discussion of the evolution of the interpretation of SBCs and for a slightly different current definition than that proposed here.

5. Mitchell 1997, discussed above, formalizes the discussion in Mitchell 1993 by focusing on externalities linked to multiple bank insolvencies. Independently, Perotti 1993 has modeled externalities arising from the insolvencies of many firms.

6. Examples include Bolton and Scharfstein 1990, 1994; Grossman and Hart 1982; Hart and Moore 1990, 1996; Jensen 1986; and Shleifer and Vishny 1992.

7. Most discussions of privatization in the TEs acknowledge the problem of managerial malfeasance and dissipation of asset values. See, for example, Lipton and Sachs 1990; Blanchard et al. 1991, 36; and Boycko, Shleifer, and Vishny 1993. None of the discussions of the problem of bad debt on banks' balance sheets, however, has recognized the relevance of this phenomenon.

8. It may appear to be an extreme assumption that all of the inherited debt of the bank is written off; the actual problem of identifying the portion of the inherited debt that was bad in the economies in transition, however, has been extremely difficult. More generally, in most countries where some bad debt has been discovered on banks' balance sheets, it has proven difficult to determine the true amount of bad debt.

9. Bulgaria undertook a cancellation of bank debt in 1993.

10. Several authors have noted this point, e.g., Bonin 1993; Brainard 1991a; and Marrese 1994.

11. Although the assumption of state ownership of firms in period 1, followed by privatization in period 2, allows for analysis of the effects of differing methods of privatization on policy trade-offs, it is not essential to the analysis of policy trade-offs in general. It is straightforward to apply the framework developed here to economies with privately owned firms.

12. For expositional simplicity I assume no discounting in the managerial utility function or in bank profit.

13. More precisely, these assumptions rule out the need to take into account the case in which defaulters are illiquid but not insolvent and that in which nondefaulters are insolvent but liquid.

14. The assumption that firms' types are realized (exogenously) at the beginning of period 1 is made to simplify the exposition. It can be justified in the current context by the fact that at the beginning of transition, changes in relative prices in the economy due to price and trade liberalization will cause some firms to become profitable and others not. The assumption of exogenous determination of types, however, is not essential to the model. Mitchell 1998 discusses results that would obtain with a more general model in which firms' choices of levels of asset dissipation determine their type in period 1.

15. This objective function is also employed in Aghion, Bolton, and Fries 1996. Rajan 1994 uses a similar type of objective function in which ρ is endogenous.

16. The Japanese banking crisis illustrates this point. Although the Japanese government decided to rescue banks via an offer of recapitalization, it was feared that Japanese bank managers would be reluctant to take advantage of the offer because of the negative consequences for them ("Obuchi's Big Bail-Out," *Financial Times*, Oct. 14, 1998).

17. I assume that the bank either works out or rolls over all of its debt. Its optimal strategy in some cases may be to work out some portion of its defaulting debt and to roll over the rest. Allowing for partial workout and partial rollover would complicate the model unnecessarily as it does not change the model's qualitative results.

18. Mitchell 1998 analyzes the effects on policy trade-offs of different privatization methods, including a decision to liquidate unsold firms.

19. This assumption implicitly imposes some restrictions on parameter values, such as a minimum value on ξ. For example, if $\xi = 0$, then $P_i(0) = 0 < b(\bar{\Delta})$. This assumption is made only to simplify the exposition of the model. If good debtors had the incentive to dissipate assets to the point of default in period 2, the bank would have to make a decision in period 1 about the level of monitoring of good debtors during this period. Including a monitoring decision would complicate the model without adding insights.

20. I assume that deposits are not withdrawn until period 2.

21. In this simple version of the model only managers of insolvent banks ever choose rollover. In a more general model solvent but financially distressed banks would also choose to roll over loans. For example, Mitchell 1997 shows that if rollover is a riskier action than workout, then solvent but financially troubled banks may choose rollover. The motivation for rollover in this case is not to hide loan losses but rather to take advantage of the deposit insurance put option. Rajan 1994 shows that solvent banks may also choose to roll over loans for reputational reasons.

22. This assumption is not as extreme as it might appear at first glance. G's prior over α may have been established on the basis of earlier monitoring of banks and even the discovery of some level of default in previous periods. Nevertheless, even when regulators have monitored banks and know that some default has occurred, they generally do not have a precise idea of the true amount of bad debt, as witnessed by the number of banks in recent years that have failed after having received favorable ratings from regulators in the previous year.

23. See Mitchell 1998 for a discussion of the effects of including a restructuring decision.

References

Aghion, Philippe, Patrick Bolton, and Stephen Fries. 1996. Financial restructuring in transition economies. University College London. Mimeographed.

Begg, David, and Richard Portes. 1993a. Enterprise debt and economic transformation: Financial restructuring in Central and Eastern Europe. In *Capital markets and financial intermediation*, ed. Colin Mayer and Xavier Vives. New York: Cambridge University Press.

Begg, David, and Richard Portes. 1993b. Enterprise debt and economic transformation. *Economics of Transition* 1, no. 1:116–117.

Blanchard, Olivier, Rudiger Dornbusch, Paul R. Krugman, Richard Layard, and Lawrence H. Summers. 1991. *Reform in eastern europe*. Cambridge: MIT Press.

Bolton, Patrick, and David Scharfstein. 1990. A theory of predation based on agency problems in financial contracting. *Amer. Econ. Rev.* 80, no. 1:93–106.

Bolton, Patrick, and David Scharfstein. 1994. Optimal debt structure and the number of creditors. *JPE* 104, no. 1:1–25.

Bonin, John. 1993. On the way to privatizing commercial banks: Poland and Hungary take different roads. *Comparative Econ. Studies* 35, no. 4:103–119.

Bonin, John, and Mark Schaffer. 1995. Banks, firms, bad debts, and bankruptcy. Discussion paper no. 234, CEPR, Washington, D.C.

Boot, Arnoud W., and Anjan Thakor. 1993. Self-interested bank regulation. *Amer. Econ. Rev.* 83, no. 2:206–12.

Boycko, M., A. Shleifer, and R. Vishny. 1993. Privatizing Russia. *Brookings Papers on Economic Activity* no. 2:139–192.

Brada, Josef C. 1996. Privatization is transition—Or is it? *Journ. Econ. Perspectives* 10, no. 2:67–86.

Brainard, Lawrence. 1991a. The financial sector in the transition to a market economy: How to reform Eastern Europe's banking system. Manuscript, Goldman Sachs, New York.

Brainard, Lawrence. 1991b. Strategies for economic transformation in Central and Eastern Europe: Role of financial market reform. In *Transformation of planned economies: Property rights reform and macroeconomic stability*, ed. Hans Blommestein and Michael Marrese. Washington, D.C.: Organization for Economic Cooperation and Development.

Calvo, Guillermo, and Jacob Frenkel. 1991. Credit markets, credibility, and economic transformation. *Journ. Econ. Pers.* 5:139–148.

Caprio, Gerard, and Ross Levine. 1992. Reforming finance in transitional socialist economies. Policy Research Working paper no. 898, World Bank, Washington, D.C.

Coricelli, Fabrizio, and Alfredo Thorne. 1993. Dealing with enterprises' bad loans. *Economics of Transition* 1, no. 1:112–115.

Dewatripont, Mathias, and Eric Maskin. 1993. Centralization of credit and long-term investment. In *Market socialism: The current debate*, ed. Pranab K. Bardhan and John E. Roemer. New York: Oxford University Press.

Dornbusch, Rudiger. 1991. Strategies and priorities for reform. In *Transition to a market economy*, ed. Paul Marer and S. Zecchini. Washington, D.C.: Organization for Economic Cooperation and Development.

Estrin, S., P. Hare, and M. Suranyi. 1992. Banking in transition: Development and current problems in Hungary. Discussion paper no. 68, CEPR, Washington, D.C.

Grossman, Sanford J., and Oliver D. Hart. 1982. Corporate financial structure and managerial incentives. In *The economics of information and uncertainty*, ed. John McCall. Chicago: University of Chicago Press.

Harris, M., and A. Raviv. 1990. Capital structure and the informational role of debt. *Journ. Fin.* 45, no. 2:321–349.

Hart, Oliver, and John Moore. 1990. A theory of corporate financial structure based on the seniority of claims. Working paper no. 560, Massachusetts Institute of Technology, Cambridge, Mass.

Hart, O., and J. Moore. 1996. Debt, default, and renegotiation. Massachusetts Institute of Technology. Manuscript.

James, Christopher. 1991. The losses realized in bank failures. *Journ. Fin.* 46, no. 4:1223–1242.

Jensen, Michael C. 1986. Agency costs of free cash flow, corporate finance, and takeovers. *Amer. Econ. Rev.* 76:323–329.

Levine, Ross, and David Scott. 1992. Old debts and new beginnings: A policy change in transitional socialist economies. Policy Research Working paper no. 876, World Bank, Washington, D.C.

Lipton, David, and Jeffrey Sachs. 1990. Privatization in Eastern Europe: The case of Poland. *Brookings Papers on Economic Activity*, no. 2:293–334.

Mailath, George J., and Loretta J. Mester. 1993. When do regulators close banks? When should they? Working paper no. 93-10, Federal Reserve Bank of Philadelphia.

Mailath, George J., and Loretta J. Mester. 1994. A positive analysis of bank closure. *Journal of Financial Intermediation* 3, no. 3:272–299.

Marrese, Michael. 1994. Banking sector reform in Central and Eastern Europe. International Monetary Fund. Manuscript.

Mitchell, J. 1993. Creditor passivity and bankruptcy: Implications for economic reform. In *Capital markets and financial intermediation*, ed. Colin Mayer and Xavier Vives. Cambridge University Press.

Mitchell, J. 1997. Strategic creditor passivity, regulation, and bank bailouts. Discussion paper no. 1780, CEPR.

Mitchell, J. 1998. The problem of bad debts: Cleaning banks' balance sheets in economies in transition. Discussion paper no. 1977, CEPR.

O'Hara, Maureen. 1993. Real bills revisited: Market value accounting and loan maturity. *Journ. Finan. Intermed.* 3, no. 1:51–76.

Perotti, Enrico. 1993. Bank lending in transition economies. *Journ. Bank. and Fin.* 17, no. 5:1021–1032.

Rajan, R. 1994. Why bank credit policies fluctuate: A theory and some evidence. *Quart. Journ. Econ.* 109, no. 2:399–442.

Rajan, R., and M. Petersen. 1994. The benefits of lending relationships: Evidence from small business data. *Journ. Fin.* 49:3–37

Saunders, Anthony, and Andrea Sommariva. 1993. Banking sector and restructuring in Eastern Europe. *Journ. Bank. and Fin.* 17, no. 5:931–957.

Schaffer, Mark E. 1998. Do firms in transition economies have soft budget constraints: A reconsideration of concepts and evidence. *Journ. Compar. Econ.* 26, no. 1:80–103.

Shleifer, Andrei, and Robert Vishny. 1992. Liquidation values and debt capacity: A market equilibrium approach. *Journ. Fin.* 47, no. 4:1343–1366.

Slovin, Myron, Marie Sushka, and John Polonchek. 1993. The value of bank durability: Borrowers as bank stakeholders. *Journ. Fin.* 48, no. 1:247–266.

Thorne, Alfredo. 1993. Eastern Europe's experience with banking reform. *Journ. Bank. and Fin.* 17, no. 5:959–1000.

3   On the Design of Bank Bailout Policy in Transition Economies

Philippe Aghion, Patrick Bolton, and Steven Fries

3.1   Introduction

A key challenge in the transition to a market economy is to expand the depth and breadth of financial activity. Although factors outside the financial sector can have a significant impact on its development, such as the degree of macroeconomic stability and progress in privatization, it is important to consider those conditions *within* the financial sector that foster its stable expansion. One such condition is the creation of a suitably competitive market structure in banking, starting from the monobank systems that used to prevail in all socialist economies. But fostering competition and entry in the banking sector in turn requires an adequate *exit policy*, and in particular a realistic and effective approach to resolving bank failures.

In sharp contrast with the nonfinancial sector, however, in which a detailed bankruptcy law governs the liquidation or reorganization of insolvent firms, in the case of banks it is often up to the central bank or other bank regulators to improvise a solution to a banking crisis once it occurs. And in transition economies, where the need for financial discipline in the banking sector is greater than in developed market economies, if only to enforce hard budget constraints on enterprises, several obstacles have stood in the way of setting up and implementing a consistent policy to deal with bank failures.

First, regulators in transition economies often invoke the too-big-to-fail principle: letting a large bank go under may be detrimental to the whole financial system, in particular because the larger the bank, the larger its interbank exposure, and also because a large bank has a large number of depositors, so that a run on a highly visible troubled bank can easily generate a wider banking panic. Somewhat surprisingly, the too-big-to-fail principle has been invoked in transition economies where even the largest banks are small relative to the economies in which they operate. As an illustration of the wide application of the too-big-to-fail principle, in Bulgaria, for example, the seven largest insolvent state banks were recapitalized in 1996, and only very small banks were liquidated. Similarly, the failure of the fifth-largest bank in Croatia in April 1998 elicited a government bailout, despite possible evidence of fraud.

Second, regulators have expressed concerns about the risk of contagious bank failures: namely, that the failure of one bank (even if that bank is small) can sometimes spread through the banking sector as a whole. Such contagion can arise from the web of interbank deposits that exist naturally in banking activity and from depositors' perceptions about the liquidity and stability of the overall banking system (see Aghion, Dewatripont, and Rey 1999 for a theoretical analysis of optimal bailout policy in a multibank context with inter-bank lending).

Third, political constraints have made it difficult for regulators in transition economies to act decisively. In particular, strong political pressures have been exerted on banks to sustain large loss-making enterprises, especially given the governments' concerns about unemployment and the associated fiscal costs. As a consequence banks have been reluctant to foreclose on state-owned firms when they have defaulted on their debt repayment obligations, and they have generally been slow to shift their lending away from these declining enterprises into new private businesses. This, in turn, has contributed to the emergence of a "bad-loan" problem in all transition economies. The factors contributing to this problem of accumulating nonperforming loans, however, extend beyond the political pressure exerted on banks and on banking regulators, which brings us to the main focus of this chapter, namely, the effects of different types of bailout policies on the incentives for bank managers to simply misreport their nonperforming assets.

The idea explored here, first put forward by Janet Mitchell (1993), is that, even in the absence of political pressures, banks themselves often have the incentive—and also the ability—to roll over bad loans to conceal the extent of their problems, rather than to seek to recover nonperforming assets. Managers of troubled banks, for example, may engage in this type of "creditor passivity" to preserve their positions in otherwise failing institutions. Then the question is: does the particular nature (tough, soft, conditional or unconditional) of bank bailout policies affect bank managers' incentives to misreport the true extent of loan losses? If so, how, and can an efficient bailout scheme be designed to mitigate or partly overcome the creditor passivity problem?

For example, once it is recognized that bank managers can delay insolvency by hiding the extent of their bank's losses and that they may refrain from liquidating bad loans in an attempt to hide loan losses, it should be clear that strict bank closure rules requiring the closure of any insolvent bank may be counterproductive. Such rules may simply induce bank managers to hide the size of their loan losses for as long as they can. Such behavior can result in huge misallocations of investments as well as massive bank failures.

Thus, this chapter analyzes the effects of various bank bailout rules on both ex ante incentives to lend and ex post incentives to disclose the size of a bank's nonperforming loan problem. The basic setup considered here includes three types of agents: firms, banks, and bank regulators. Firms and banks are controlled by their managers, who derive private benefits from their continued operations. The main source of discipline on managers' behavior is the possibility of dismissal associated with bank insolvency. The regulators' objectives are to induce efficient ex ante investments, avoid the deadweight costs associated with excessive bank recapitalizations, and promote the efficient restructuring or liquidation of firms that have defaulted on their bank loans.[1]

Banks are assumed here to have private information about the quality of their loan portfolios and the continuation value of firms in default. The regulators know only the probability distribution over the fraction of nonperforming loans across banks in the economy. They therefore face an *adverse selection* problem in the design of bank recapitalization.

Our analysis leads to a number of interesting results. First, a tough recapitalization policy in which the manager of a failing bank is always dismissed results, as already suggested, in bank managers' rolling over bad loans to conceal the extent of their loan losses and therefore in the *softening* of the firms' budget constraints. Vice versa, a soft approach to recapitalization (in which the manager of a failing bank is not dismissed) encourages bank managers to take an overly tough approach to firm liquidations while exaggerating their own recapitalization requirements.

The most socially efficient outcome, however—and this is the second main conclusion of the chapter—can generally be achieved through a soft bailout policy combined with the carving out of bad loans at a suitable *nonlinear transfer price*. In other words, our analysis suggests that insolvent banks should be recapitalized by buying out nonperforming loans rather than through injecting capital by buying subordinated bonds. Our key insight here is that a *nonlinear* transfer pricing mechanism for bad loans can be used to combat effectively the adverse selection problem, and in particular to avoid overreporting of nonperforming loans by the healthier banks at the time of the bailout.

The existing theoretical literature on financial restructuring and bank recapitalization in transition economies comprises only a handful of papers. The most closely related paper is the chapter by Mitchell in this volume, which sets up a formal model of a bank restructuring in which banks must incur a (convex) cost of effort to avoid asset dissipation by firms. Like the current chapter, Mitchell's paper also emphasizes that when a bank manager suffers in some way when the bank he manages gets into trouble, he will roll over loans in default to postpone facing the cost of financial distress. However, Mitchell develops a different formal setup and considers different policy options than those we examine in this chapter.

Also taking a moral hazard approach to bank restructuring, Berglöf and Roland (1995) argue that governments' ex ante recapitalization of banks can limit the extent to which banks will take on additional risky loans and then gamble for resurrection. These studies do not provide a complete characterization of all possible bailout schemes and of the optimality of different bailout policies under different circumstances. Although moral hazard considerations (and in particular the problem of excessive risk taking in banks' choice of portfolios) are reasonably well understood and arise in transition and developed market economies alike, informational asymmetries of the kind emphasized in this chapter are more likely to be relevant in the context of transition economies, where the institutions for evaluating and disclosing the creditworthiness of both firms and banks are inherently weak.

Two other related papers are worth mentioning here. Suarez 1995 studies bank closure rules and recapitalization in a dynamic complete-information model. Given the informational assumptions stressed in Suarez's paper, it is not entirely surprising that it finds that the closure of insolvent banks has good ex ante incentive properties. Povel 1986 deals with bankruptcy of nonfinancial firms but emphasizes a similar tension between ex ante incentives to avoid bankruptcy and ex post incentives to file for bankruptcy in a timely fashion.

The remainder of the chapter is organized as follows. Section 3.2 sets out the basic model, specifying the objectives of and constraints on firms, banks, and regulators. Section 3.3 compares "tough" and "soft" bank recapitalization policies taken in isolation. Section 3.4 derives necessary and sufficient conditions for the existence of an efficient nonlinear pricing mechanism for the carving out of bad loans. Finally, section 3.5 briefly summarizes the main lessons of our analysis.

3.2 The Model

The model presented in this chapter builds on that of Bolton and Scharfstein (1990) by enlarging their framework to allow for three types of agents: firms, banks, and regulators. We consider each in turn.

3.2.1 Firms

For simplicity, we assume that all firms are run by self-interested managers. Whether the firms are state-owned or privatized, their shareholders play no significant governance role; rather, the focus is on bank debt as a disciplining device. A firm is represented by an asset, which yields a random return. In the first period, the return is either high ($\pi > 0$) or low ($\pi = 0$). The probability of a particular firm's receiving a high return is $p \in (0, 1)$. In theory, the manager's actions could control this probability, but we take it here to be exogenously given. In the second period, the firm also has a random continuation value, which is the discounted stream of future returns.

Each firm has an outstanding stock of bank debt and, for simplicity, no other liabilities. This stock of debt imposes a repayment obligation on the firm of $D \in [0, \pi]$. When a firm defaults, the bank can either liquidate the firm, making the manager redundant, or it can allow the firm to continue. The certain liquidation value of the firm is L. The continuation value is either high, $v > 0$, or low ($v = 0$), with $v > L > 0$. The probability of a high continuation value is $(1 - \beta)$, where β is the probability of the firm's being liquidated. In the event of default, the firm's continuation value can be costlessly observed.

For simplicity, we assume that the *private* continuation value of firms' managers is sufficiently large that they will always honor their debt repayment obligations if they can. This assumption rules out strategic defaults by firms.[2]

3.2.2 Banks

As with firms, we assume that self-interested managers run banks. On the asset side of their balance sheets, banks have a portfolio of loans to firms, each of which has a scheduled debt service payment of D. As specified above, each firm may default on its loan with probability $(1 - p)$. In the event of a default, and in the absence of strategic behavior by the bank manager, the bank liquidates the firm with probability β and obtains L. The alternative to liquidation is firm continuation with a realized return v. If all firms have independently and identically distributed returns, and each bank holds a large and well-diversified portfolio of loans, then each bank has approximately a fraction $(1 - p)$ of nonperforming loans.

On the liability side of their balance sheets, banks issue deposits in the amount d to fund each loan. The net worth of a bank per loan is thus

$$W = (1 - p)[\beta L + (1 - \beta)v] + pD - d. \tag{3.1}$$

For the bank to have a positive net worth, the weighted average payoff from nonperforming and performing loans must thus exceed the value of deposits issued to fund the representative loan.

The fact that banks do fail in reality suggests that they cannot build completely diversified portfolios and that they are exposed to aggregate shocks. To introduce the possibility of bank failures we suppose that firms' returns are correlated to some extent so that the fraction of a bank's loans that are performing is a random variable that takes on a range of values, $p_1 > p_2 > p_3 > p_4 > 0$, with respective probabilities $\mu_1, \mu_2, \mu_3, \mu_4 > 0$. We denote the expected fraction of performing loans to be $p = \sum_{i=1}^{4} \mu_1 p_1$. The bank's realized net worth under each realization is then given by equation (3.2), but p_i $(i = 1, \ldots, 4)$ now substitutes for p. Thus, under the four possible outcomes p_i, the bank's realized net worth is equal to

$$W_i = (1 - p_i)[\beta L + (1 - \beta)v] + p_i D - d, \tag{3.2}$$

where we assume that

$$W_4 < W_3 < W_2 = 0 < W_1. \tag{3.3}$$

That is, only banks in states 1 and 2 are solvent; banks in states 3 and 4 are insolvent. (As will become clear in the next section, we need at least four different states of nature to compare alternative bank bailout policies.)

We also suppose that a bank's manager can expend effort ex ante to reduce the probability of its failure. That is, by being more diligent in evaluating the distribution of firms' period 1 cash flows and in structuring efficient loan portfolios, bank managers can reduce the likelihood that a large fraction of the projects they fund will fail. For simplicity, a bank manager's decision to expend effort is an all-or-nothing choice, $e \in \{0, 1\}$. The cost to the bank manager of expending this effort is $c(e)$, where $c(0) = 0$ and $c(1) = c$. We assume that when $e = 1$ the probability distribution $\mu_i(1)$ (first-order) stochastically dominates the probability distribution $\mu_i(0)$ when $e = 0$:

$$\sum_{i=1}^{j} \mu_i(1) > \sum_{i=1}^{j} \mu_i(0), \tag{3.4}$$

for all $j = 1, 2, 3$.

Finally, to simplify notation, we let $\phi_I = (1 - p_i)\beta$ denote the fraction of liquidated loans. We then obviously have $\phi_1 < \phi_2 < \phi_3 < \phi_4$.

When a firm defaults, the manager of the bank that holds its loan must decide whether to allow the firm to continue or to seek its liquidation. We assume that the sale of a firm's assets can be observed costlessly, so that any liquidation decision is observable and verifiable. Loan continuation and write-down decisions, however, are entirely at the discretion of the bank manager and cannot be verified. In other words, unless a nonperforming loan is actually liquidated, it is not possible for anyone outside the bank or the firm, such as a regulator, to verify that it is not performing. This limited verification of a bank manager's behavior in turn allows for strategic behavior on her part.

For example, a bank manager may want to inefficiently refinance bad loans to hide (or understate) the overall extent of her nonperforming loans problem. This seems to be a widespread banking practice, particularly in transition economies, but also in developing and industrialized market economies. Similarly, when a bank is to be bailed out, its manager may want to overstate the proportion of its loans that are nonperforming to elicit a greater recapitalization from the government. The core analysis of this chapter focuses on these two forms of strategic behavior by bank managers.

A bank manager's objective function involves both a monetary and a private-benefit component. The monetary component is the sum of a fixed salary (which we normalize to zero) and, in the case of a high-powered incentive scheme, a share of the bank's (reported) net worth, equal, say, to b. The private-benefit component reflects the facts that (a) bank managers like power and (b) bank managers, like firm managers, would rather retain their job than be fired. In addition, the bank manager's objective function includes the cost of effort, if any, that she expends in managing the bank's loan portfolio.

Formally, we can express the bank manager's objective as

$$U_B = b \max(0, \hat{W}_i) + \tilde{B}[1 + \max(0, W_i + R)] - c(e), \tag{3.5}$$

where $\tilde{B} = B$ if the bank manager retains her position and $\tilde{B} = 0$ if she is fired. $\hat{W}_i$ is the bank's reported net worth (absent recapitalization), and W_i is its true net worth. Any additional resources accruing to the bank in period 1, in particular as a result of recapitalization, are given by R.

To keep the analysis simple, we assume that a bank manager has only a low-powered incentive scheme, so that $b = 0$, and, therefore, that

$$U_B = \tilde{B}[1 + \max(0, W_i + R)] - c(e). \tag{3.6}$$

The analysis can be extended straightforwardly to consider the effects of high-powered incentive schemes. The main effect of such schemes is to create even stronger incentives for managers to hide bad loans but mitigate incentives to overstate losses so as to maximize the size of the recapitalization offered in the event of bank failure.

3.2.3 The Regulator

The regulator's decision problem is to form a policy concerning the recapitalization of banks with announced negative net worth. A constraint on this policy is that any bank that declares its net worth as negative must receive a recapitalization to bring its declared net worth back to zero. In other words, in our model all depositors are fully insured.[3] Our results and analysis do not critically hinge on this assumption. If only a fraction of deposits $\hat{d} < d$ are insured, our analysis remains unchanged when d is replaced by $\hat{d}$.[4]

Regulators' problem is then to design a bank bailout policy to (a) maximize the expected social return of the underlying assets of firms that have defaulted on their loan obligations, (b) induce maximum effort of bank managers in the ex ante evaluation of firms' returns, and (c) minimize the costs associated with any excessive recapitalization of banks. With full information about banks' true net worth, regulators would avoid excessive recapitalizations and the corresponding deadweight losses by simply transferring $-W_i$ to those banks in states $i = 3, 4$ in period 1. It would also maximize bank managers' incentives by committing to a policy of dismissing a manager whenever a bank she is managing is insolvent.

Regulators' problems are made more difficult, however, by the fact that they generally do not know the period 1 net worth of banks. So if the government wants to guarantee that all banks reach at least a minimum reported net worth of zero, it must be prepared to bail out banks up to an amount $-W_4$, the worst possible net worth. Since the government does not know banks' net worth, their managers may be able to get away with claiming to be in the worst possible state. Such misrepresentation by all bank managers would lead to an excessive recapitalization, with an ex ante deadweight of

$$\lambda[\mu_1(W_1 - W_4) + \mu_2(W_2 - W_4) + \mu_3(W_3 - W_4)] = \lambda E. \tag{3.7}$$

Of course, the government has the option of limiting the size of the recapitalization to an amount less than $-W_4$, but then it exposes itself to the possibility that those banks in the worst state will be inadequately recapitalized.

The expected social return on the underlying assets of firms is given by their expected period 1 cash flows, $\bar{p}(e)\pi$ (where $\bar{p}(e) = \sum_{i=1}^{4} \mu_i(e)p_i$), plus their expected continuation values

$$\Omega_i = p_i(1 - \beta)v + (1 - p_i)\{\min[(1 - \beta), (1 - \hat{\beta}_i)]v + \hat{\beta}_i L\}. \tag{3.8}$$

That is, for the proportion p_i of firms with high cash flows, the expected continuation value is $(1 - \beta)v$, since these firms' managers will never liquidate them. For the proportion $(1 - p_i)$ of firms with low cash flows, the manager is forced to default, and the average continuation value per loan is $\min[(1 - \beta), (1 - \hat{\beta}_i)]v + \hat{\beta}_i L$. Here $\hat{\beta}_i$ denotes the fraction of defaulting loans the bank manager chooses to liquidate in each state $i = 1, \ldots, 4$.

Formally, the regulator's objective can be summarized in the following expression:

$$U_G = \bar{p}(e)\pi + \sum_{i=1}^{4} \mu_i \Omega_i - \lambda E - c(e). \tag{3.9}$$

Thus, in our model social efficiency requires fulfillment of three conditions. First, a firm should be liquidated if, and only if, its liquidation value exceeds its continuation value $\tilde{v}$; that is, $\hat{\beta}_i$ should be equal to β for $i = 1, \ldots, 4$. Second, only those banks with truly negative net worth should be recapitalized; that is, E should be equal to zero. Third, bank managers should expend effort in managing their loan portfolio provided that

$$\bar{p}(1)\pi - \bar{p}(0)\pi + \sum_{i=1}^{4} [\mu_i(1) - \mu_i(0)]\Omega_i > c. \tag{3.10}$$

We assume that this condition is satisfied, in other words, that bank managers' ex ante evaluation of firms' returns is socially efficient.

Throughout the remainder of the chapter, we make the (realistic) assumption that the liquidation value, L, of a firm is greater than its manager's private benefit from the firm's continued operation. In other words, it is socially efficient to liquidate the firm whenever the bank's continuation value of the project is zero, even though the firm's manager always prefers not to liquidate. This assumption introduces an ex post inefficiency when firms that are able to service their current debt obligations but have a low continuation value remain in operation because of the private benefits derived by their managers. Although first-best social efficiency would require that these firms be liquidated in period 1, this inefficiency is independent of the form of bank recapitalization and is thus not a factor in evaluating the government's policy alternatives.

3.3 Tough versus Soft Recapitalization Policy

The regulator's goal is to design a bank recapitalization policy that maximizes its objective (social efficiency) subject to the constraint of limited knowledge of banks' true net worth in period 1. Since the banks are managerially controlled, one possible condition that can be imposed with a bank's recapitalization relates to the dismissal of its manager: how "tough" or "soft" should the government be toward the manager of a bank in the event of its recapitalization?

Again, we start with the benchmark case in which the net worth of banks is known to the government in period 1. The optimal bailout policy is then straightforward: restore the net worth of banks in states $i = 3, 4$ to zero after allowing for the expected recovery of nonperforming loans, and dismiss the manager if these recoveries deviate from expectations. This policy satisfies two of the three conditions for first-best efficiency. In particular, it guarantees both that only those banks with truly negative net worth are recapitalized and that firms in default are liquidated if, and only if, their liquidation value exceeds their continuation value. Satisfaction of the third condition for first-best efficiency, the ex ante evaluation of firm returns and the structuring of efficient loan portfolios, depends on the incentives the bank manager faces.

Such a policy would clearly have perverse effects when regulators must rely on bank managers' reports to learn about banks' period 1 net worth. We illustrate these perverse effects in this section by considering two extreme bailout policies often discussed:

1. A tough recapitalization policy, which results in the liquidation of a bank that is found insolvent and the ensuing dismissal of the bank's manager.

2. A soft recapitalization policy, which maintains the insolvent bank's manager in control and fully bails out the bank.

We also consider an "in-between" policy that involves the liquidation of an insolvent bank and the dismissal of its manager only in the worst state, $i = 4$. The government fully bails out any bank in state $i = 3$, leaving the bank manager in control.

3.3.1 Tough Recapitalization Policy

Consider first the case in which the manager of a bank that reports a negative net worth is dismissed. Assuming for the moment that $b = 0$, the manager of a bank with realized p_1 or p_2 has no incentive to manipulate either the bank's accounts or its decisions as to whether to liquidate firms that are in default or to write down their loans. A bank would be insolvent, however, if either p_3 or p_4 were realized. With such outcomes, the bank manager will act as if $p_k = p_2$ has occurred in order to preserve his job. Since the liquidation of firms is verifiable, the bank manager will liquidate a fraction ϕ_2 of firms in its portfolio, where ϕ_2 is defined as the fraction of liquidated loans in the portfolio of a bank with realized p_2 (that is, $\phi_2 = [1 - p_2]\beta$).

In other words, the bank manager in such a situation will liquidate a fraction $\hat{\beta}_k$ of defaulting firms such that

$$(1 - p_k)\hat{\beta}_k = \phi_2 = (1 - p_2)\beta. \tag{3.11}$$

Therefore, in states p_3 or p_4 the bank manager actually liquidates less than the socially efficient proportion of defaulted loans, that is, $\hat{\beta}_k < \beta$. Bank managers' incentive to maintain the appearance of bank solvency under a tough bailout policy thus leads to a softening of debt as a disciplining device on firms and thereby a softening of firms' budget constraints.

More formally, a tough bailout policy leads to an ex ante payoff of

$$U_G = \bar{p}(e)\pi + \sum_{i=1}^{2} \mu_i(c)[p_i(1-\beta)v + (1-p_i)(1-\beta)v + \beta L]$$

$$+ \sum_{i=3}^{4} \mu_i(e)\{p_i(1-\beta)v + (1-p_i)[(1-\beta)v + \hat{\beta}_i L]\}, \tag{3.12}$$

where, from equation (3.11), $\hat{\beta}_i < \beta$ for $i = 3, 4$. A tough bailout policy thus leads to an insufficient number of firm liquidations. The loss in social surplus due to the softness of banks on firms in default is the foregone liquidation value of those firms that are continued even though they have a zero continuation value.[5]

Introducing the possibility of strategic defaults by firms would amplify the loss in social surplus due to banks' hiding the extent of their nonperforming loans. More precisely, suppose that the private continuation value of firms' managers is such that they would choose not to default strategically if the probability of liquidation in case of default is β but might decide to default if they anticipate a lower probability of liquidation by banks. Then not only will the number of firm liquidations be less than is socially optimal, but there will also be a further buildup of nonperforming loans in banks' portfolios.[6]

There is, however, no deadweight cost due to excessive recapitalization under a tough bailout policy. Indeed, no bank recapitalizations take place under this rule, because no bank manager will declare her institution insolvent.

Whether bank managers are induced to expend effort in managing loan portfolios under a tough bailout policy depends here only on the private benefits bank managers derive from this activity. In particular, a bank manager will expend such effort under a tough policy only if

$$E[U_B(1)] = \sum_{i=1}^{4} \mu_1(1)B[1 + \max(0, W_i + R)] - c > E[U_B(0)]$$

$$= \sum_{i=1}^{4} \mu_1(0)B[1 + \max(0, W_i + R)],$$

or equivalently

$$[\mu_1(1) - \mu_1(0)]BW_1 > c. \tag{3.13}$$

Note that no bank manager is ever dismissed in equilibrium under this policy because of the manager's costless ability to misrepresent a bank's net worth. Note also that a manager receives private benefits in all states of nature. The value of private benefits equals B in all states of nature except state 1, when the value of private benefits equals $B(1 + W_1)$. The expected value of private benefits thus rises with managerial effort to the extent that this effort raises the probability that state 1 will occur.

3.3.2   Soft Bailouts

Under a "soft" policy toward bank recapitalization, a bank manager is immune from dismissal, regardless of the reported net worth of the bank he manages. This approach creates an incentive for bank managers to overstate their problem loans so as to increase the amount of recapitalization their bank receives. Bank managers can easily overstate the extent of their anticipated losses by taking excessively high charges.[7] The change in bank manager utility from reporting the worst possible net worth W_4 instead of the true net worth W_i is always positive and equal to

$$\Delta U_B = B(W_i - W_4). \tag{3.14}$$

Soft bailouts do have benefits, however, and one is that they restore bank managers' incentives to impose financial discipline on the firms to which they lend. Indeed, without a hard budget constraint, bank managers' incentive is to liquidate every defaulted loan if and only if the continuation value is less than the liquidation value. Thus, with a soft recapitalization policy, the bank manager hardens the budget constraint on firm managers. The social payoff achieved through a soft bailout policy is then

$$U_G = \bar{p}(e)\pi + \sum_{i=1}^{4} \mu_i(e)\{p_i(1 - \beta)v + (1 - p_i)[(1 - \beta)v + \beta L]\}$$

$$- \lambda[\mu_1(e)(W_1 - W_4) + \mu_2(e)(W_2 - W_4) + \mu_3(e)(W_3 - W_4)]. \tag{3.15}$$

Thus a soft bailout policy has at least two social costs. One is the deadweight costs from excessive recapitalization.[8] The second is an inadequate incentive for bank managers to expend effort in evaluating the investment returns of firms and in structuring efficient loan portfolios. As with the tough recapitalization rule, the only incentive for bank managers to expend such effort under a soft rule arises from the private benefits associated with such effort.

More specifically, under a soft recapitalization policy, note that the amount of government recapitalization of each bank equals the net worth of a bank in the worst state of nature. A bank manager would thus exert effort in structuring efficient loan portfolios only if

$$\sum_{i=1}^{3}[\mu_i(1) - \mu_i(0)]B[\max(0, W_i) - W_4] > c. \tag{3.16}$$

Now since

$$-\sum_{i=1}^{3}[\mu_i(1) - \mu_i(0)] = \mu_4(1) - \mu_4(0),$$

this incentive constraint is equivalent to

$$[\mu_1(1) - \mu_1(0)]B \cdot \max(0, W_1) + [\mu_4(1) - \mu_4(0)]BW_4 > c \tag{3.17}$$

Comparing equations (3.13) and (3.17) reveals that whenever $\mu_4(1) - \mu_4(0) < 0$, the incentive compatibility constraint on managerial effort is looser under a tough than under a soft recapitalization policy provided that $|W_4|$ is not too large.

A tough bailout policy does not necessarily induce more effort among bank managers toward structuring efficient loan portfolios than a soft policy because under a soft bailout policy the benefit of overstating loan losses is an increasing function of the extent of the overstatement. It may thus not always be a good idea for the government to minimize the scope for bank managers' ex post overstatement of their bad loans problems (e.g., by implementing a tough bailout policy) because this may sometimes have adverse ex ante incentive effects.

We summarize our discussion so far in the following proposition:

PROPOSITION 3.1

(a) *ex post efficiency comparison:* When μ_4 is close to 1, that is, when the government knows that the banking system as a whole is in crisis, a soft bailout policy dominates tough bailout. However, when $\mu_1 + \mu_2$ is sufficiently close to 1, that is, when the banking system is basically sound, tough bailout dominates soft bailout.

(b) *ex ante incentives:* A tough bailout policy will generally provide stronger ex ante incentives than a soft bailout policy, except when $|W_4|$ is large.

Although tough (soft) bailout policies dominate ex post when the government knows that the banking system is basically sound (in deep crisis), the comparison between these two extremes become less clear-cut in intermediate situations. For example, when μ_3 is close to 1, then the excessive recapitalization of banks in state p_3 and the excessive liquidation of firms by those banks under a soft bailout policy must be weighed against the insufficient liquidations by banks in state p_3 (and p_4) under a tough policy. The balance depends on the deadweight loss parameter λ and on the cost of excessive liquidation $(v - L)$.

3.3.3   An "In-Between" Policy

Now consider a less extreme approach toward bank recapitalization under which the decision whether to dismiss the manager of a failing bank depends on the amount of required recapitalization. Specifically, if a bank reported that p_3 has occurred, the bank would be recapitalized without its manager being dismissed. But if a bank reports p_4, the bank would be liquidated and the manager dismissed. In other words, a bank manager would be held accountable only for an extremely poor outcome.

Under this policy, banks in states p_1 and p_2 will seek to increase their size by attracting excessive recapitalizations while banks in state p_4 hide the true extent of their insolvency problem. Banks in state p_3, however, accurately reveal their net worth and make efficient liquidation decisions. Thus, although an in-between bailout policy combines inefficiencies present in the two extreme policies, it involves a smaller deadweight cost of excessive recapitalization than under soft bailout and less under-liquidations of defaulted firms than under a tough policy.

Such an in-between policy may provide worse ex ante incentives for bank managers than both the tough and soft bailout policies. Under the in-between recapitalization policy a bank manger would exert effort toward structuring efficient loan portfolios only if

$$\sum_{i=1}^{2}[\mu_1(1) - \mu_i(0)]B(W_i - W_3) > c. \tag{3.18}$$

A comparison of equations (3.18) and (3.16), however, readily reveals that the incentive compatibility constraint on managerial effort is looser under an in-between than under a soft recapitalization policy. Whether the incentive compatibility constraint is looser than under a tough bailout policy depends again on the amount of the recapitalization banks receive. As before, the tough policy is not necessarily looser because recapitalization yields private benefits that increase with the size of the overstatement of loan losses.

Our discussion in this section can be summarized by the following proposition:

PROPOSITION 3.2

(a) *ex post efficiency comparison:*   When μ_3 is close to 1, an in-between bailout policy dominates both tough and soft bailout policies from an ex post efficiency viewpoint.

(b) *ex ante incentives:*   An in-between bailout policy provides weaker effort incentives to bank managers than a tough bailout policy, except when $|W_3|$ is sufficiently large. It provides weaker effort incentives than a soft bailout policy in any circumstances.

Although an in-between policy may under certain circumstances reduce the ex post deadweight cost of recapitalizations of failing banks and the costs of excessive continuation of defaulted firms, other policies may perform as well or better both from an ex post and an ex ante point of view. One such alternative policy is explored in the next section.

3.4 Bank Recapitalizations Conditional on Firm Liquidations

Since one observable and verifiable action of bank managers is their liquidation of firms that have defaulted on their loan obligations, liquidation can be used as a parameter to provide a possible condition for a regulator's policy toward bank recapitalization. This section examines whether a regulator can use such a parameter to achieve its overall objective of first-best social efficiency and, if so, under what circumstances.

We shall show that it is possible for regulators to use bank managers' liquidation activity as a conditioning parameter for bank recapitalizations to achieve two of the three criteria for first-best social efficiency: (a) the efficient liquidation of firms in default so that $\hat{\beta}_i = \beta$ for $i - 1, \dots, 4$, and (b) the absence of any excessive bank recapitalization. A complementary policy, however, may be required to provide a sufficiently strong incentive for bank managers to expend effort in the ex ante evaluation of firms' returns. The next section considers such a policy.

A key issue in the design of a bank recapitalization policy that is conditional on a bank's liquidation of firms in default on their loan obligations to it is the relationship between the liquidation of firms by a bank and the amount, if any, of its recapitalization. Consider first a simple linear transfer scheme under which the government pays to the bank a fixed amount t for any loan it has made to a firm that the bank manager liquidates (with proceeds L). To achieve a zero net worth for banks in the worst state of nature, p_4, the transfer amount t must raise the true net worth of such a bank to the break-even point:

$$\phi_4(L + t) + (1 - p_4)(1 - \beta)v + p_4 D = d. \tag{3.19}$$

Such a recapitalization policy would be too generous, however, for those insolvent banks in state p_3, increasing their net worth beyond zero. Banks with positive net worth, moreover, would be encouraged to participate in the scheme even though they are not in need of recapitalization.

The excessive recapitalization under such a policy can be eliminated, however, if the government introduces a nonlinear transfer scheme. Suppose that the government sets a low transfer amount, t_L, for loans in default that are liquidated, up to a threshold $\bar{m} \geq \phi_2$ of the bank's portfolio and that beyond that threshold, transfers per liquidated loan are increased to $t_H > t_L$. We can then establish the truth of the following proposition:

PROPOSITION 3.3   There exists an $\bar{m} \geq \phi_2$ such that a two-part transfer scheme price $(t_L, t_H, \bar{m})$ implements the level of bank recapitalization that leads to the efficient liquidation of firms in default, that is, $\hat{\beta}_i = \beta$ for $i = 1, \ldots, 4$, and that recapitalizes only those banks that are truly insolvent, if, and only if,

$$p_4 D + (1 - p_4)(1 - \beta)v + (\phi_4 - \phi_2)v + \phi_2 L \geq d. \tag{3.20}$$

Proof   Without loss of generality we can assume $D > v$.

First, to avoid bank managers' excessive liquidation of nonperforming loans, the high transfer price t_H cannot be larger than the minimum possible recovery on a defaulted loan, v. With $t_H > (v - L)$, managers of all banks would have an incentive to engage in excessive liquidation, since doing so would increase their recoveries on nonperforming loans, including the per loan transfer from the government. So we must have $t_H \leq (v - L)$. Without loss of generality, we restrict the analysis to two-part transfer schemes such that $t_H = (v - L)$.

Now, it is sufficient to show that the low transfer price, t_L, and cutoff level, $\bar{m}$, can be chosen so as to deter solvent banks in state p_2 (and a fortiori those in state p_1) from participating in the scheme. This requires that the pair $(t_L, \bar{m})$ satisfy the following condition:

$$(\phi_2 - \bar{m})v + \bar{m}(L + t_L) \leq \phi_2 L. \tag{3.21}$$

The left-hand side of equation (3.21) is the payoff that a bank in state p_2 would receive by participating in the government's recapitalization scheme, and the right-hand side is the bank's revenue from remaining outside the scheme and liquidating those nonperforming loans that have a zero continuation value. One set of parameter values for which this condition is satisfied is $t_L = 0$ and $\bar{m} = \phi_2$.

It is also sufficient to show that the two-part transfer scheme $(t_H = v - L, t_L = 0, \bar{m} = \phi_2)$ succeeds in fully recapitalizing insolvent banks in states p_3 and p_4. Consider in particular a bank in state p_4, the worst possible state. The realized net worth of such a bank under this recapitalization scheme that links the amount of government transfers to the bank's liquidation of insolvent firms is

$$p_4 D + (1 - p_4)(1 - \beta)v + (\phi_4 - \phi_2)v + \phi_2 L - d. \tag{3.22}$$

From equation (3.22), it is clear that condition (3.20) in proposition 3.3 must hold for a bank in state p_4 to be fully recapitalized. This condition is therefore sufficient to ensure the full recapitalization of insolvent banks and to avoid both the excessive liquidation of nonperforming loans and the excessive recapitalization of insolvent banks.

To complete the proof of proposition 3.3, we must show that condition (3.20) is also necessary. This requires showing that the condition cannot be relaxed by allowing a more generous two-part transfer scheme with $t_L > 0$.

Suppose we take $t_L > 0$. The necessary condition on t_L and $\bar{m}$ for banks in state p_4 to be fully recapitalized then becomes

$$p_4 D + (1 - p_4)(1 - \beta)v + (\phi_4 - \bar{m})v + \bar{m}(L + t_L) \geq d. \tag{3.23}$$

In choosing the optimal t_L and $\bar{m}$, the government seeks to ease the above constraint while discouraging solvent banks from participating in the scheme. In other words, the government must choose $(t_L, \bar{m})$ so as to maximize

$$\max[(\phi_4 - m)v + m(L + t_L)]$$

subject to

$$(\phi_2 - m)v + m(L + t_L) \leq \phi_2 L. \tag{3.24}$$

At the optimum the incentive constraint for a bank in state p_2 is binding so that the above problem simplifies to

$$\max_m [(\phi_4 - \phi_2)v + mL + (\phi_2 - m)L], \tag{3.25}$$

for which there is no unique solution. Setting $\bar{m} = \phi_2$ and $t_L = 0$ thus involves no loss of generality, provided that condition (3.23) is satisfied. With $t_L = 0$, this is nothing but condition (3.20) in proposition 3.3. This establishes that condition (3.20) is both necessary and sufficient and therefore completes the proof of proposition 3.3.

Whenever condition (3.20) is satisfied, a bank bailout policy that is conditional on the liquidation of firms in default can meet two of the requirements for first-best social efficiency: efficient liquidation decisions by bank managers and no excessive government recapitalization of banks. Moreover, this result obtains regardless of the government's knowledge (or beliefs) $\mu_i(e)$ about the state of the overall banking system. In particular, it dominates the tough, soft, and in-between policies considered in the previous section, none of which would achieve these requirements for first-best efficiency, except perhaps on a negligible (measure-zero) subset of parameter values for $\mu_i(e)$. If condition (3.20) is not satisfied, this conditional recapitalization policy would lead to excessive recapitalization of solvent banks in state p_2 (and/or of insolvent banks in state p_3), with the associated deadweight costs. In that case, a tough bailout policy may sometimes dominate, in particular if $\mu_1 + \mu_2$ is close to one.[9]

The analysis of this section thus shows that conditioning bank recapitalization on an observable and verifiable action of bank managers can increase the ex post efficiency of bank bailouts and, under certain circumstances, meet the two requirements for ex post efficiency.

As for ex ante effort incentives, it turns out that the tough recapitalization policy analyzed in section 3.3 and the more complicated conditional recapitalization developed in this section provide bank managers with precisely the same incentive to expend effort toward ex ante evaluation of firms to which they make loans. It is straightforward to show that the incentive compatibility constraint for a bank manager to expend such effort under the conditional bank recapitalization policy discussed in this section simplifies to

$$[\mu_1(1) - \mu_1(0)]BW_i > c, \tag{3.26}$$

which is the same as under the tough recapitalization policy. This equivalence arises because the expected value of private benefits rises with managerial effort only to the extent that this effort raises the probability that state 1 will occur, since the bank manager gets exactly B in all other states of nature.

That our conditional recapitalization scheme provides the same ex ante effort incentives as a tough bailout policy should come as no surprise. Both policies give the bank manager the option of distorting his ex post report about loan losses (i.e., about β_i), although our conditional scheme is designed in such a way that bank managers are *indifferent* between distorting (and announcing state 1) and not distorting. This in turn explains why ex ante effort incentives are the same under the two policies, even though our scheme avoids the ex post inefficiencies induced by a tough bailout policy. Our scheme should thus be seen as a strict improvement over a tough recapitalization policy.[10]

To conclude this section, we point to a limitation of our findings and to a possible further extension. The analysis in this section shows that by reducing bank managers' incentive to exaggerate the extent of their bad loans, a suitably designed conditional recapitalization scheme in which government transfers to insolvent banks are linked to their liquidation of firms in default can achieve some of the first-best social efficiency conditions. In somewhat more complex circumstances, however, these efficiency gains could be lost. For example, if we allowed for heterogeneity in the quality of nonperforming loans (such as differences in the liquidation values of each loan) and if the exact quality of bad loans were the private information of bank managers, then the two-part transfer scheme considered above would fail to deliver first-best efficiency, because there would no longer be a simple relationship between the proportion of liquidated loans in a bank's portfolio and its true net worth.

Characterizing a more sophisticated nonlinear transfer scheme that would "solve" this problem and more generally deriving the conditions under which such a scheme could dominate some simpler schemes (such as those analyzed in section 3.3) is left for further research.

3.5   Policy Conclusions

Although mandatory corrective policies such as no-bailout and the liquidation of any insolvent bank can be thought as having positive effects on bank managers in situations of moral hazard in the choice and monitoring of bank investments, such policies also create incentives for bank managers to conceal asset quality problems and to overstate their banks' capital adequacy. If full disclosure triggers regulatory intervention and conservatorship, bank managers will inevitably attempt to under-report the size of their bad-loan problems, thereby undermining the whole purpose of these rules. In Russia, for example, such a policy has motivated banks to move bad loans to a subsidiary to remove them from the parent bank's accounts.

Where the ability of bank managers to misreport their loan losses remains largely unconstrained by reliable information about banks, as in many transition countries, it is desirable to move to a system for bank recapitalization that gives troubled banks an incentive to reveal their asset quality problems and to foreclose on bad loans and other nonperforming assets. Such an incentive can be created by a conditional recapitalization scheme that takes the form of a "purchase" of nonperforming assets at a premium to their market value that is conditional on the amount of non-performing loans a particular bank liquidates. Nonperforming loans would either be acquired at a premium by a special government agency set up for the recovery of bad assets or they would remain on the books of the troubled bank for recovery, in which case the bank would receive recapitalization in the form of a subsidy for asset recoveries. In either case, the subsidy element would help restore the bank's capital adequacy, thereby providing its managers with the appropriate incentives to harden the budget constraints on enterprises.

Whether bad assets should be transferred to a specialized workout agency or kept on the books of the troubled bank for recovery is a complex problem. The main arguments for keeping the responsibility for recoveries with the banks is that they tend to have better information about the loans, that the workout of bad loans builds banking skills, and that individual banks are less vulnerable to political interference than a government-owned agency. For instance, in Poland in 1993 bad loans were kept with the banks, but to receive recapitalization, banks were forced to present a feasible workout strategy, which was supported by a special law on debt restructuring. By 1995, most of the bad loans targeted by the program had been restructured. The main arguments in favor of a specialized agency are that it allows for the concentration of expertise on asset recoveries, quickly eliminates the debt overhang on banks' balance sheets, and allows banks to focus on new lending, thus helping to avoid a credit crunch. Experience with recent banking crises in the United States and the Nordic countries suggests that on the whole special debt resolution agencies have played an important role in speeding up bank restructuring. However, a specialized agency in transition economies may be less effective in recovering on nonperforming assets than the issuing banks themselves because of political pressure to maintain soft budget constraints on enterprises, as was the case in Slovenia.

Another potential advantage of conditional recapitalizations is that, when carefully designed, they can limit the drain on the government's fiscal resources by targeting recapitalizations at only truly insolvent banks. By conditioning recapitalizations on write-downs and restructuring of bad loans, it is possible to distinguish insolvent banks from solvent ones. This discrimination between solvent and insolvent banks can be fine-tuned by implementing a graded subsidy (or pricing) scheme for bad debts. Such a scheme would involve a greater unit subsidy (or price) per loan recovery when the proportion of a bank's written-down loans to its total assets is higher. In this way, more-insolvent banks—with a higher proportion of nonperforming loans—receive a bigger unit recapitalization than less-insolvent banks with a lower fraction of bad loans.[11] In contrast, more standard recapitalization methods based on purchases of subordinated debt or preferred stock cannot provide a mechanism for discriminating between truly solvent and insolvent banks. Although a graded-subsidy scheme offers a potential way of overcoming regulators' limited information about the financial condition of individual banks, its implementation would nevertheless require some general knowledge of how losses are distributed throughout the banking system.

Of course, it may not always be practical or feasible to set up such a conditional scheme on short notice following the outbreak of a banking crisis. We would therefore also advocate the institution of a bankruptcy procedure for banks in anticipation of future banking crises. We believe that, just as with nonfinancial firms, the establishment of such an institution can go a long way toward resolving in an orderly and efficient way most banking crises.

The model in this chapter is, of course, highly stylized and can only serve as a framework to organize our analysis of bank bailouts. Although it does cover most important incentive aspects raised by bank failures and bailouts, it does so only in a highly simplified way. Much additional work is required to design a proper bankruptcy institution for banks, but we hope that this chapter can serve as a first step in this direction.

Notes

This paper, prepared for the William Davidson Institute conference "Financial Sectors in Transition," is part of a wider European Bank for Reconstruction and Development research project on private-sector development. We are grateful to European Bank for Reconstruction and Development for intellectual and financial support and to Patricia Armendariz de Hinestrosa, Sudipto Bhattacharya, John Boyd, Janet Mitchell, and Harald Uhlig for helpful comments.

1. Another objective we consider by extension is to replace inefficient bank managers.

2. It is possible to extend the model to allow for strategic defaults. The results obtained in this extension are qualitatively similar to those reported in this chapter.

3. Banks must have fully insured deposits for two basic reasons. First, the failure of a large institution may have an adverse impact on other banks in the system through the payment system and the interbank market, which can precipitate a generalized loss of confidence. Second, depositors in a large bank may effectively exert political pressure for deposit guarantees. In addition, banks are de facto perceived by depositors as being fully backed by the government.

4. Under partial deposit insurance, however, new issues must be addressed, such as the behavior of uninsured depositors. These issues are undoubtedly important, but they are somewhat orthogonal to our analysis.

5. The loss in social surplus also includes the misallocation of funds that could have been directed to better investments. An important limitation of our model is that it is not set up to account for that cost.

6. For example, suppose that the private continuation value of firms' managers is random, equal to V with probability $(1 - \varepsilon)$ and to zero with probability ε. Assuming that

$$\beta[1 - p_2(1 - \varepsilon)]V < D < \beta V,$$

we then leave it to the reader to verify that in the case of a solvent bank (in state 1 or 2), the pair of strategies ($\hat{\beta}_i = \beta$, strategic default with probability ε) is the unique Nash equilibrium. In the case of a bank in state 4, there exists a Nash equilibrium involving a higher probability of strategic default, namely $\hat{\beta}_4 < \beta$ (strategic default with probability one), where $\hat{\beta}_4$ satisfies

$$[1 - p_4(1 - 1)]\hat{\beta}_4 = \phi_2 = [1 - p_2(1 - \varepsilon)]\beta.$$

7. Note that by taking charges banks only bring forward in their books anticipated loan losses. They do not report actual loan losses. Unless reported anticipated loan losses turn into actual losses for banks, writing down loans is just "cheap talk," and bank managers have every incentive to exaggerate the size of anticipated losses if it results in a bigger recapitalization.

8. In practice, this cost is reduced somewhat, since by purchasing preferred stock or taking a stake in the bank, the regulatory authorities get a cut in all of the bank's future profits. It is not clear, however, that regulators are able to fully recover an excessively generous recapitalization.

9. Another potential problem with this nonlinear pricing scheme is that it may create incentives for solvent banks to sell their bad loans to insolvent banks. To prevent such profitable arbitrage from taking place, a regulator would need to monitor the secondary market for loans and scrutinize net purchasing banks more closely.

10. This conclusion hinges, however, on the fact that the manager is never dismissed in equilibrium under any recapitalization policy. In section 3.7 we consider an extension of the model in which the true state of nature is publicly revealed in period 2.

11. See Aghion, Bolton, and Fries 1998.

References

Aghion, P., P. Bolton, and S. Fries. 1998. Financial restructuring in transition economies. Working paper no. 32, EBRD, London.

Aghion, P., M. Dewatripont, and P. Rey. 1999. Competition, financial discipline and growth. *Review of Economic Studies* 66, no. 4:825–852.

Berglöf, E., and G. Roland. 1995. Bank restructuring and soft budget constraints in financial transition. Discussion paper no. 1250, CEPR, Washington, D.C.

Bolton, P., and D. Scharfstein. 1990. A theory of predation based on agency problems in financial contracting. *American Economic Review*, 80, no. 1:93–106.

Fries, S., and T. Lane. 1994. Financial and enterprise restructuring in emerging market economies. In *Building sound finance in emerging market economies*, ed. Gerard Caprio, David Folkerts-Landau, and Timothy D. Lane. Washington, D.C.: International Monetary Fund and World Bank.

Fries, S., P. Mella-Barral, and W. Perraudin. Optimal bank reorganisation and the fair pricing of deposit guarantees. *Journal of Banking and Finance* 21:441–468.

Mitchell, J. 1993a. Creditor passivity and bankruptcy: Implications for economic reform. In *Capital markets and financial intermediation*, ed. C. Mayer and X. Vives. Cambridge: Cambridge University Press.

Mitchell, J. 1993b. Cancelling, transferring or repaying bad debts: Cleaning banks' balance sheets in economies in transition. Cornell University. Mimeographed.

Povel, P. 1986. Optimal "soft" or "tough" bankruptcy procedures. Financial Markets Group Discussion paper no. 240, London School of Economics.

Suarez, J. 1995. Closure rules and the prudential regulation of banks. Universita Bocconi, Centro di Economia Monetaria e Finanziaria "Paulo Baffi," Milan. Mimeographed.

4 Revisiting Hungary's Bankruptcy Episode

John P. Bonin and Mark E. Schaffer

4.1 Microeconomics for Transition Economies

As many countries move into the latter years of the first decade of transition from state to market economies, microeconomic issues and resource reallocation have taken center stage. Institutional reform, enterprise restructuring, and financial-sector reform have become the focus of attention. The design of institutions that provide proper incentives to induce agents in these transition economies to act in response to market signals, however, has proven to be the most difficult aspect of the transition, as Svejnar (1991) predicted. Efficiency demands the reallocation of resources "frozen" in less-productive uses as measured by market principles. Supply network linkages, however, may induce a ripple effect from firm closures. Because of these interdependencies, imposing strict legislation that promotes enterprise liquidation may take down "good" firms with "bad" firms. Although imposing a hard budget constraint on companies is a necessary condition for financial discipline, it must be supplemented by market-enabling legislation to promote efficient allocation of resources. This chapter takes a retrospective look at Hungary's experiment with a particularly draconian bankruptcy law. For an 18-month period in 1992–1993, the Hungarian bankruptcy code contained an unusual automatic trigger that required the managers of firms that held overdue debt to any creditor to initiate reorganization or liquidation proceedings to avoid prosecution under the civil code. We analyze the impact of this "legislative shock therapy" on the Hungarian economy during the period and examine its effects on resource reallocation and institution building.

To stylize the issue of resource reallocation, we can divide the real sector of transition economies conceptually into three groups of firms. The first consists of firms that are profitable and viable in the new market environment; for these, the financial sector should be developed sufficiently to provide credit on reasonable terms. The second consists of firms that are unprofitable and nonviable; these should be liquidated and their assets should be reallocated as quickly as possible. The third consists of firms that are unprofitable but potentially viable and in need of restructuring to survive and prosper in the new market environment. Our focus in this chapter is on the last two groups, that is, on financially distressed firms. The issue with such firms is how to separate those for which the most efficient outcome is to preserve the firm's going-concern value (by reorganizing or restructuring) from those for which the most efficient outcome is liquidation and reallocation of the firm's assets to other uses. The lack of reliable firm-specific information in transition economies makes this a daunting task.

Bankruptcy legislation is a court-based, market-oriented approach to reallocation that promotes both the release of assets so that they may be transferred to their most productive uses and the restructuring of debt to allow the continuation of viable but illiquid or insolvent companies. In addition to addressing these stock problems, bankruptcy legislation allows creditors to impose financial discipline on debtors because it affords a credible threat of action if the debtor defaults. Thus, it helps to create the proper financial incentives to prevent future bad debts, that is, the flow issue. In 1992, Hungarian policymakers chose this market-oriented approach to resolving the bad debts of firms in 1992. The Hungarian bankruptcy experiment received considerable attention at the time, in part because it included an unusual automatic trigger that required many firms to enter reorganization. This chapter revisits the Hungarian bankruptcy episode to see what lessons hindsight offers. We suggest that, whereas most attention at the time of the experiment was directed at the automatic trigger, other features of the Hungarian bankruptcy framework provide more important lessons. In particular, that framework shows that it is possible to introduce a bankruptcy track in a transition economy that can both transfer control from management to creditors and maintain the firm as a going concern while restructuring and reorganization takes place.

Section 4.2 begins with a discussion of the role of bankruptcy in market economies, focusing in particular on the relationship between the contingent control rights of creditors as they are exercised and the problems of inefficient termination versus inefficient continuation. We then discuss various aspects of bankruptcy reform in transition economies: the deep transition-induced recessions, creditor passivity, and soft budget constraints. In section 4.3, we describe the Hungarian policy response to this economic crisis: the introduction in 1992 of bankruptcy legislation with an automatic trigger plus a new banking act. Section 4.4 discusses the perceived key source of creditor passivity and soft budget constraints, namely interenterprise or trade credit, and argues that concern about such credit was exaggerated in the Hungarian case. Section 4.5 considers whether banks were a source of soft budget constraints in Hungary and argues using evidence from the enterprise level that here too concern about the existence of flow problems was exaggerated. Section 4.6 analyzes the Hungarian experience with the bankruptcy experiment. Section 4.7 concludes with lessons from the Hungarian experiment and policy implications for other transition economies.

4.2 Bankruptcy in Market and Transition Economies

4.2.1 Bankruptcy in Market Economies

Bankruptcy is the legal framework that determines the governance of a firm that has been declared, or declared itself, insolvent and unable to pay its creditors. Bankruptcy allows creditors to exercise their contingent property rights in the event of the firm's defaulting upon its debts. What makes the design of bankruptcy frameworks more complex than simply assigning control of the firm to the creditor(s) is that typically a firm has multiple creditors, with claims of varying seniority (Hart 1995). Faced with a debtor entering financial difficulties, creditors have an incentive to engage in a socially wasteful race to seize their collateral or obtain court judgments against the firm. Bankruptcy frameworks specify collective procedures that spell out how various creditors can exercise control over the defaulting firm and its assets and how they may negotiate or bargain with the debtor and with each other.

A desirable goal for a bankruptcy procedure is ex post allocative efficiency, meaning an efficient (re)allocation of the bankrupt firm's assets (Hart 1995). The direct costs of the procedure (administrative resources needed, speed of the procedure) figure here, of course. Still more important is whether termination or continuation of the firm is the more efficient outcome. Continuation will be inefficient if the bankruptcy process results in a firm that continues as a going concern after reorganization the value of which is less than the liquidation value of the assets following shutdown and asset dispersal. Termination will be inefficient if the loss of the firm's going-concern value is large relative to what can be obtained by shutting the firm down and selling off its assets. This may be the case even if, for example, the firm's assets are currently in best use and all that is really needed is a simple rescheduling of claims: once a firm is shut down, even temporarily, much firm-specific capital can be lost (e.g., relational capital involving the firm and its customers, suppliers, and employees if they abandon the firm, or even physical capital if assets deteriorate rapidly when not maintained).[1]

The nature of limited liability and the assignment of differing priority to claims of different creditors can in principle lead to inefficient termination instead of continuation or inefficient continuation instead of termination. Creditors, for example, may prefer a rapid and cheap but inefficient termination to continuation in which the firm's expected value is high but uncertain if the firm's liquidation value will with certainty be great enough to cover their claims (but leaves little left over for equity holders). By the same reasoning, senior creditors may seek (inefficient) termination because it shares the potential upside gains from continuation with junior creditors and equity holders. On the other hand, inefficient continuation can result when a coalition of senior creditors and management is able to gamble with junior creditors' claims by investing them in a risky activity with uncertain returns, that is, continuation, even though the junior creditors do not participate fully in the upside gains. In general, the greater the uncertainty, the larger this problem (White 1989).

Bankruptcy frameworks typically include features that aim to protect a bankrupt firm's going-concern value while it is in bankruptcy. It is common, for example, to give firms in bankruptcy the ability to reenter credit markets by freezing their debts at the start of bankruptcy and giving new credit subsequently granted to the firm superpriority over frozen prebankruptcy debts. One such set of features aims to reduce inefficient termination through the way the control rights of creditors are specified. Secured creditors are usually prevented from removing their collateral unilaterally from a bankrupt firm, and the law often specifies the responsibilities of the liquidator in charge of the bankrupt firm to be to operate the firm in the interest of all creditors (instead of, for example, only those of senior creditors). One important limitation on the contingent control rights of creditors that is sometimes observed is the right of the firm's management to obtain unilaterally an automatic stay on the claims of creditors—a protection period—while they seek to negotiate a settlement with them.

Some but by no means all bankruptcy frameworks offer this link between measures to allow continuation and measures limiting the rights of creditors, as a comparison of the U.S. and U.K. frameworks shows. In the United States, the link is very clear. Firms that enter liquidation under Chapter 7 of the U.S. Bankruptcy Code are typically shut down and have their assets dispersed under the control of a bankruptcy trustee (the liquidator) who represents the creditors.[2] Under Chapter 11, firms reorganize as going concerns under the control of their management, protected from their creditors and able to operate; this protection can last years. Creditors as well as management may well prefer this protection if the potential losses from inefficient termination via Chapter 7 are substantial enough. By contrast, in the United Kingdom all three main bankruptcy tracks allocate control to the creditors. Receivership and administrative receivership are used to maintain the firm as a going concern while reorganization takes place; the main difference between the two is that the receiver is primarily responsible to the firm's main secured creditor,[3] whereas the administrator is responsible to the creditors generally. The third track, liquidation, is used when the firm is to be shut down and the assets dispersed; it is overseen by a liquidator who is again responsible to the creditors generally.

A bankruptcy framework will also affect ex ante efficiency via the incentives and behavior of creditors, owners, and management. The most obvious of these is that a bankruptcy system should provide creditors with some expectation of being able to get their money back from a firm that defaults; without this basic protection, creditors will be unwilling to offer financing in the first place. The prospect of bankruptcy has a disciplining role on management and can help to align its incentives with those of investors in the firm (Hart 1995); the fear of losing their jobs in bankruptcy should get them to take measures to avoid it. A bankruptcy procedure that is too lenient on management can thus lead to managerial inefficiency; but a procedure that is tough on management can also generate problems, since management may engage in excessive risk taking in the hope of being able to avoid bankruptcy should their gambling pay off (White 1989).

4.2.2   Bankruptcy Reform in Transition Countries

The discussion of bankruptcy above was expressed in general terms. In this section we relate the various aspects of bankruptcy discussed in the previous section to the specific characteristics of transition countries in general and Hungary in particular.

Hungary began the transition from a state to a market-based economy with a combination of macroeconomic shocks: a transition-induced recession, the collapse of the Council for Mutual Economic Assistance (CMEA), and an extreme change in relative prices due to liberalization. This meant, on the one hand, many firms entering financial distress, and on the other hand, potentially large gains through reallocation of assets from inefficient uses in activities determined by socialist planners to uses appropriate to a market-led economy. Implementing an effective bankruptcy framework therefore offered large potential allocative efficiency gains. At the same time, however, implementing a bankruptcy framework brings with it the problem of how to preserve going-concern value where this is efficient. Putting many firms through bankruptcy runs the risk of allocative inefficiency through large-scale inefficient termination of firms. It was precisely the fear of this outcome that led the Czech authorities, for example, to delay implementation of their bankruptcy framework in 1993.

Hungary also started its transition to a market economy with a problem of "creditor passivity" (Mitchell 1993). A bankruptcy law had been enacted in Hungary in 1986, but creditors had rarely used it, for a number of reasons. Bankruptcy was a new and relatively unused procedure, and creditors were deterred by the prospect of large transactions costs involved in filing and the lengthy completion times for the procedure. Banks were also reluctant to pursue liquidation because of their unwillingness to draw attention to nonperforming assets in their portfolios. Furthermore, the aforementioned macroeconomic and transition shocks, plus the legislative shock of the rapid introduction of Western-style financial legislation and regulatory requirements, made the continuation value of financially distressed firms extremely uncertain. Creditors had high levels of exposure to downside risk with limited or no compensating participation in upside return. This uncertainty is likely to have generated a bias toward continuation on the part of the senior creditors, the banks. In some transition economies, policymakers tried to resolve the issue of inefficient continuation by involving major creditors in both decision making and upside gains sharing, for example, the Polish bank-led enterprise restructuring program. Hungarian policymakers took a different approach and stressed a market-based reallocation of resources via bankruptcy.

A problem of particular concern in transition economies is that firms may have soft budget constraints. Soft budget constraints can be defined in a number of ways (Schaffer 1998); for our purposes, we will use Kornai's (1993) "paternalism" definition: soft budget constraints result when a paternalistic agent, typically the state or one under the direction of the state, rescues distressed firms from failure by injecting cash in the form of subsidies or additional credit. Both creditor passivity and soft budget constraints can directly enable loss-making or insolvent firms to continue in operation, but for different reasons. In the case of creditor passivity, inefficient continuation results because liquidating the firm offers an insufficient return to creditors; in the case of soft budget constraints, because the state or creditors value the continuation of the firm for its own sake and are willing to bear the costs of keeping it afloat by providing subsidies or extending new credit even in the absence of a prospect of repayment. Soft budget constraints and creditor passivity may interact, as Mitchell (1998a) notes; if there is the expectation that distressed firms will be rescued, creditors may wait for the rescue rather than pursue immediate liquidation.

The Hungarian authorities were most worried about two sources of soft budget constraints: the state-owned commercial banks and state-owned firms themselves; the volume of bad bank debt and of overdue trade credit ("interenterprise arrears") had been growing since the start of transition. But it was not just the commercial creditors of firms that were not exerting effective corporate governance over firms. Hungary began its economic transition with an enterprise sector that was almost entirely state-owned, and the problems of ineffective control by the state as owner extended beyond merely tolerating inefficiencies within the firm. Asset stripping by incumbent management was a particular problem, as a 1996 survey of crisis managers installed in 37 troubled state-owned firms in the early 1990s illustrates. The survey asked crisis managers to rank the importance of various possible sources of the crisis in the firms they managed. Loss of demand for the firm's products came first in the list, rated as first or second in importance in 13 and 6 firms, respectively.

The next most important factor was the failings of the previous management (first in 9 firms, second in 7), ahead of liquidity problems, debt problems, supply problems, and others. The two main failures of the previous management, in the view of the crisis managers who replaced them, were asset stripping and bad investment decisions.

Finally, as we shall see below, the weakness of the Hungarian state as owner was mirrored in the weakness of the state as creditor: with the start of transition, the Hungarian tax authorities, like those in most other transition countries, began to have problems collecting taxes from firms, and tax arrears started to accumulate.

4.3   Hungary's Legislative Shock Therapy

At the beginning of 1992, Hungary implemented what has been termed "legislative shock therapy" (Abel and Bonin 1994): the statutory frameworks for both bankruptcy and banking were comprehensively reformed. In this section we describe the provisions of the new frameworks and the motivation behind their introduction.

4.3.1   Bankruptcy

The 1992 bankruptcy act (formally, Act IL of 1991) was passed by the Hungarian parliament on September 24, 1991, and took effect on January 1, 1992, superseding Law-Decree No. 11 of 1986 on liquidation and winding up. The introduction of the 1992 bankruptcy act was motivated by a dissatisfaction with the 1986 act and a perceived need for new measures. The 1986 act was a product of the socialist era and unsatisfactory in some respects for a market economy, as it was designed with state-owned legal entities in mind. The 1992 act was meant to establish a uniform bankruptcy procedure comparable to those found in Western countries.

The act applied to legal entities in Hungary regardless of ownership (individual entrepreneurs were not covered). It allowed for three types of bankruptcy procedures: liquidation (winding-up) proceedings in which control of the debtor firm passed to a court-appointed liquidator; reorganization proceedings affording the debtor firm temporary protection from its creditors and leaving incumbent management in control; and final accounting. The 1986 act had introduced liquidation procedures that were broadly similar to those in the 1992 act. The 1992 act's main innovation was its introduction of reorganization proceedings. Final accounting refers to the an economic entity's cessation of activity without a legal successor in cases not covered by liquidation. We do not discuss this last procedure here and instead concentrate only on liquidation and reorganization.

4.3.2 Liquidation

Although the first of the two main tracks in the Hungarian bankruptcy framework is usually referred to as "liquidation",[4] this is a somewhat misleading use of the term. The essential feature of the liquidation track in Hungary's bankruptcy framework is in fact the transfer of *control* away from incumbent management and into the hands of the liquidator, an agent meant to represent the interests of the creditors. With respect to a continuation decision, however, the liquidation track is flexible: firms in liquidation can be closed and the assets sold off, but they can also continue operations during liquidation and after restructuring emerge from liquidation as going concerns. For these reasons the Hungarian liquidation track can be described as resembling a combination of the "administration" and "liquidation" tracks in the U.K. bankruptcy framework.

The liquidation procedure begins when an insolvent firm is unable to meet the claims of its creditors and is under the control of a court-appointed agent, the liquidator. Liquidation proceedings may be initiated either voluntarily by the debtor or by a creditor with a debt past due by application to the court. In the latter case, the court may, upon the request of the debtor, grant a delay of up to 30 days for the settlement of the debt. The law does not require the debtor to file for liquidation under certain circumstances; unlike the reorganization track (see below), there is no "automatic trigger." Liquidation begins formally after the court's declaration that the debtor is insolvent, at which point the claims against the debtor are frozen and the court appoints an official liquidator. The mandate of the liquidator is to dispose within two years of the firm's assets to satisfy as best as possible the claims of the firm's creditors. The liquidator is responsible, however, to the court and not directly to the creditors. If the creditors (or the debtor) object to any action of the liquidator, their only recourse is to complain to the court, which then may or may not set aside the measure and/or instruct the liquidator to undertake a different measure. Only if the liquidator does not comply with this court order can the petitioner then ask for the court to replace the liquidator. More generally, the court has only a limited involvement in the affairs of the firm, and the liquidator has considerable autonomy.

The debts of a firm in liquidation are settled in accordance with the absolute priority rule, which establishes the following order:

1. Liquidation costs. Liquidation costs include the liquidator's fees plus wages and any other costs arising from the continuation of the firm's economic activity following the start of the liquidation procedure. Such costs include debts acquired since the start of the liquidation procedure. The liquidator's fees are 2 percent of the gross revenues derived from turnover and the sales of assets and collected claims, but not

less than H Ft. 250,000 (approximately U.S. $25,000 in 1992 prices). The court may deviate from this payment schedule, however, in complex cases.

2. Secured creditors.

3. Social security and tax debts. (Within this class, social security debts take priority over other tax and taxlike claims.)

4. Claims of other creditors, including trade creditors.

5. Interest, late penalties on taxes, and the like.

If at the end of the liquidation assets remain after satisfying the claims of the creditors, these are distributed among the equity holders of the firm.

The debtor may reach a settlement with its creditors at any time during the liquidation procedure. A settlement constitutes a program designed to restore the debtor's solvency and an agreement between the debtor and the creditors concerning the timing of debt repayments, write-downs of claims, and restructuring measures. The debtor firm's creditors do not necessarily have to agree unanimously to the settlement for it to be approved by the court and implemented. Rather, agreement of half the creditors in each class (corresponding roughly to debt categories 2–5 above) is enough, provided they hold among them at least two thirds of the total value of claims against the debtor.

The liquidation track has two procontinuation features. The first is essential to continued operation of a firm in bankruptcy and is often found in bankruptcy frameworks, namely, the freezing of existing debts and the superpriority given to new debts. The treatment of wages and other current costs, including new borrowing, as priority claims means firms in liquidation are able to employ staff, purchase inputs, sell output, and raise funds from banks or other creditors (e.g., trade creditors). The second procontinuation feature, a Hungarian novelty, is found in the statutory specification of the liquidator's remuneration scheme. By rewarding the liquidator with 2 percent of *all* gross revenues—not just of revenues from sales of assets but revenues from gross sales as well—the law gives the liquidator a strong incentive to maintain the firm as a going concern while in liquidation (Gray, Schlorke, and Szanyi 1996). The relative independence of the liquidator form the creditors, who might otherwise try to pressure the liquidator into choosing early and possibly inefficient termination, reinforces these two procontinuation features.

4.3.3   Reorganization

The second main track of the Hungarian bankruptcy framework is usually referred to as "reorganization" or, sometimes, "bankruptcy".[5] The key distinguishing feature of this track is not, however, that the firm is given an opportunity to reorganize as a going concern—this can happen in the "liquidation" track as well—but rather than control remains with incumbent management while reorganization and negotiation with the creditors takes place rather than being transferred to a liquidator. In this broad sense, the reorganization track resembles Chapter 11 of the U.S. Bankruptcy Code. But the resemblance does not go much deeper than that: unlike Chapter 11, the reorganization track in the Hungarian bankruptcy framework is designed to be a rapid procedure with limited court involvement, has limited attractions to incumbent management, and had, until its modification in 1993, a peculiar form of "automatic trigger" that could send a firm into compulsory reorganization.

In the reorganization procedure outlined in the 1992 act, a debtor firm renegotiates its debts with its creditors while temporarily protected from them. The debtor enjoys a 90-day period of protection (including protection from liquidation proceedings) while negotiating with its creditors. The bankruptcy court can extend this protection for another 30 days upon the joint request of the debtor and the creditors. During the protection period, the debtor remains in control of the firm. At their own expense, the creditors may request that a property supervisor be installed to represent the interests of the creditors and supervise the firm's assets and financial activities. Unlike the liquidation procedure, in the reorganization procedure any settlement agreement reached between the debtor and the creditors requires the approval of *all* creditors present at the creditors' meeting; this is referred to in the bankruptcy literature as unanimous consent procedure (UCP). The debtor and the creditors are allowed very substantial flexibility in drawing up the settlement agreement. If the debtor and the creditors are unable to come to an agreement by the time the deadline expires, the bankruptcy court declares an end to the reorganization procedure and begins liquidation proceedings ex officio. Once the debtor has entered the reorganization procedure, it is prohibited from filing for reorganization again for three years. If, during this period, the debtor is unable to meet its creditors' claims, it enters the liquidation route directly.

The logic of the kind of reorganization procedure implemented in the 1992 act is to give a debtor in financial difficulties a period of protection from creditors during which the debtor can formulate a restructuring plan. Under the 1992 act, only the debtor can file for reorganization; either the debtor or the creditors, however, may file for liquidation of the debtor. Debtors may exercise their option to file for reorganization if they foresee that they will be unable to meet claims on the firm maturing within a year or if they have debts past due that they are unable to pay.

An important feature of the reorganization procedure is the approach, or more accurately, the nonapproach, to debts acquired by the debtor firm during reorganization, while it is protected from its creditors. The act makes no distinction between debts acquired prior to a firm's filing for reorganization and debts acquired during reorganization. In effect, any debts incurred by the debtor firm during the protection period, that is, new lending by banks or trade credit for goods being received from suppliers, are thrown into the pot with prior debts and subject to renegotiation. This can result in these creditors' refusing to deal with the firm while in reorganization, which in turn would be a deterrent against filing for reorganization. By contrast, the liquidation track has special features allowing firms to raise capital while protected from existing creditors.

The main innovation of the 1992 act was an automatic trigger that *required* a firm to file for reorganization if it had a debt that it was unable to repay within 90 days of the debt's becoming due. If a firm had a payable of *any* size, owed to *anybody*, that was overdue 90 days or more, it had to file for reorganization within eight days of the due date on the debt. If the firm did not file for reorganization when it was legally required to do so, the firm's managing director would be held responsible under the civil code for the firm's failure to file. This requirement to file for reorganization could be avoided only if the firm separately filed for liquidation instead.[6]

Bankruptcy frameworks sometimes have automatic triggers, but the Hungarian automatic trigger was novel in two respects. First, the bankruptcy framework required the firm to file for reorganization, though in effect this meant a requirement to file for reorganization or liquidation (since filing for liquidation eliminated the firm's obligation to file for reorganization). In effect, managers were being required to seek protection from creditors who were not actually pursuing them through the bankruptcy courts. Germany and the United Kingdom, for example, have a requirement to file for a bankruptcy procedure in which control is removed from the incumbent management. Second, automatic triggers are typically based on measures of insolvency, for example, liabilities that exceed assets (Germany, the United Kingdom), or a permanent inability to make payments on debts as they come due (Germany). Such triggers are intended to deter a firm's management from trying to gamble its way out of insolvency with the creditors' money. The Hungarian trigger, by contrast, was based on a peculiarly tough measure of illiquidity: the simple existence of overdue payables, without regard to their size or to whether they might reasonably be expected to be paid. The choice of the trigger varied in the Hungarian case from international practice because it was meant to serve a different purpose. It was not meant to prevent excessive risk taking by management, nor was it intended to identify overindebted firms that needed workouts (the approach taken in, for example, the Polish bank and enterprise restructuring program). Rather, the automatic trigger in Hungary was the main mechanism by which the new bankruptcy act was intended to improve the state of payments discipline and harden budget constraints in Hungary. In particular, it was intended to address the perceived problem of growing interenterprise debt and arrears.

4.3.4 Banking Act

The second part of Hungary's legislative shock therapy was a new banking law enacted at the same time as the new bankruptcy law. The banking act (officially, Act No. LXIX of 1991 on Financial Institutions and Financial Institutional Activities) was promulgated on December 1, 1991. It introduced three categories of qualified or "problematic" loans for use in rating Hungarian banks' loan portfolios, mandated banks' accumulation of provisions (loan loss reserves) against loans so qualified, and specified a schedule for meeting capital adequacy targets. Temporary regulations for loan classification were applied retroactively to the balance sheets of the banks for the full year of 1991. According to a subsequent decree from the State Banking Supervision in March 1992, banks must classify assets in their portfolios as "bad" if the borrower is in default for more than one year or the claims are held against a company that is in liquidation proceedings. Provisions equal to 100 percent of a bank's total "bad" debt had to be accumulated by the end of a three-year period. The banking act legislates two other categories of qualified loans, namely "substandard" and "doubtful," requiring banks to accumulate provisions equal to 20 percent of the former and 50 percent of the latter within the same time period. The banking act made the banks recognize the drop in the real value of their assets over a relatively short period of time. It was expected to bring the problem of bad debts into the open and by doing so to discourage banks from further lending to problem borrowers, that is, to harden their budget constraints. It did *not*, however, include any special measures aim at promoting or easing workouts of the stock problem; this was to be covered by the regular routes of liquidation and reorganization as specified in the bankruptcy act.

4.3.5 Summary

Hungary's 1992 legislative shock therapy had a twofold motivation. First, the legislation's liquidation and reorganization procedures were meant to facilitate the restructuring or termination of troubled firms and to bring about the settlement of creditors' claims. In this sense, the bankruptcy act was directed at a stock problem, namely, the liabilities of the debtor. The second motivation, one that distinguishes the bankruptcy act from most other bankruptcy procedures, was the importance given to countering a perceived flow problem, namely, creditor passivity and the lack of payments discipline. The weight given to fighting the perceived flow problem is evident not only from the 90-day automatic trigger, but also from the act's treatment of the stock of bad loans inherited from the previous systems (henceforth referred to as the stock problem). The act did not include any significant measures to promote fast-track workouts of the debts of insolvent firms; the requirement of 100 percent agreement of creditors to the restructuring plan in the reorganization procedure was unusually strict; and the Hungarian Ministry of Finance did not increase funding of the bankruptcy court system despite the flood of bankruptcy filings that followed the act's introduction.[7] The absence of special or accelerating workout procedures in or accompanying the banking act carried a similar message: stopping the perceived flow problem was the top priority. The significance of the flow problem, that is, the perceived problems of the lack of payments discipline between enterprises and of banks providing firms with soft budget constraints, is therefore crucial to evaluating the success of the 1992 Hungarian bankruptcy and banking acts in terms of their own objectives.

4.4   Interenterprise Credit in Hungary: Was It a Problem?

Two measures of interenterprise credit are commonly used in Hungary: data on the so-called queue reported by the National Bank of Hungary (NBH) and collected from Hungarian commercial banks, and data on payables and receivables deriving from enterprise balance sheets. We consider each of these data sources in turn.

The value of payables in the queue is the most commonly cited figure for interenterprise credit in Hungary. The rapid increase in the size of the queue in 1989–1991 was a source of concern for policymakers and was probably the main source of evidence for their assertion that there was a serious payments discipline problem in Hungary. The queuing data have, however, been much misinterpreted.

The queue refers to firms' payables that have been sent to the firms' banks and are waiting to be paid because the firms have insufficient funds in their accounts to cover the payables. The payables wait in a queue for the funds to arrive, hence the name. The NBH collects the data from the commercial banks and reports them. Under the prereform system, banks were legally required to operate queues, but starting in 1990, the queuing procedure became optional. This meant that firms and banks could decide for themselves if they wanted to arrange to queue payables in cases when the firms had insufficient funds in their accounts to cover them. The alternative to queuing was for the banks to return the payment requests to the creditors when there were insufficient funds to pay them. We have no information about the proportion of firms or transactions subject to queuing arrangements following this

Table 4.1
The queue in Hungary, 1987–1993: Payables queued at banks and waiting for payment

Date (end-period)	Million forints	As a percentage of GDP
1987	14.0	1.0
1988	45.5	3.2
1989	72.8	4.3
1990.Q1	67.5	
1990.Q2	75.3	
1990.Q3	82.4	
1990.Q4	90.5	4.4
1991.Q1	119.3	
1991.Q2	130.8	
1991.Q3	139.8	
1991.Q4	158.6	6.8
1992.Q1	187.0	
1992.Q2	168.0	
1992.Q3	106.0	
1992.Q4	104.0	3.7
1993.Q1	94.0	
1993.Q2	90.0	
1993.Q3	103.0	

Source: László and Szakadát 1992; NBH.
Note: Queued payables greater than 25 million forints.

change, although we suspect that most medium and large firms retained their queuing arrangements.

Table 4.1 presents some data on the queue. Between the end of 1989 and the end of 1991 the queue did increase noticeably, from about 4 percent of GDP to about 7 percent. The key fact about the queue, however, is the identity of the queued payables. What most observers and policymakers did not realize at the time is that not one but three types of payables appear in the queue: payables to other enterprises, payables to banks, and tax, social security, and other taxlike payables. In early 1990 the NBH studied the identity of queued payables based on a survey of Budapest firms. It found that queued payables to other enterprises, that is, interenterprise arrears, accounted for only perhaps 20 percent of the total of queued payables in Hungary. Queued payables to banks accounted for a similar fraction. The largest component of the queue was in fact tax and social security payables, at about one-half of total queued payables.

During a trip to Hungary in January 1994, we asked the staff of the commercial bank branches we visited about the composition of the payables in the queues of

Table 4.2
Trade credit extended and trade credit received: Hungary and developed Western economies compared

Country and date	End-year trade credit as a percentage of GDP	
	Trade credit extended (commercial receivables)	Trade credit received (commercial payables)
Hungary		
1988	37	28
1989	35	27
1990	36	29
1991	35	30
1992	29	22
Canada 1990	16	14
United States 1990	17	14
France 1990	38	35
Japan 1990	59	45
Finland 1990	20	23
Sweden 1990	21	20
United Kingdom 1990	20	19

Sources: Hungarian CSO, U.K. CSO, OECD, authors' calculations.

their customers as of early 1992. Their responses were that as of that date, the composition of the queue was similar to what the NBH found in early 1990: less than a quarter for both payables to other enterprises and payables to banks, and about half in tax and social security payables. We conclude from this information that, given the relatively low importance of payables to other firms in the queue, the increase the amount of queued payables in 1989–1991 is less evidence of deteriorating payments discipline between firms than of a deterioration of tax discipline, that is, an increase in tax arrears.

Although the increase in queued payables in 1990–1991 does not necessarily meant that payment discipline between firms was poor or declining, this could still have been the case. We address this question directly using the second source of aggregate data on interenterprise credit, payables and receivables as reported by firms to Hungary's Central Statistical Office (CSO). We begin with several international comparisons of aggregate trade credit. Table 4.2 shows receivables (trade credit extended) and payables (trade credit received) of the enterprise sector as a percentage of GDP in Hungary and in several developed Western countries. Total trade credit in Hungary at the end of 1991 amounted to about 30–35 percent of GDP: less than in some developed Western countries and more than in others. Table 4.2 also shows that the scale of total interenterprise credit had been roughly flat in Hungary

Table 4.3
Trade credit and overdue trade credit in Hungary and selected Western European countries

Country	Total trade credit in months	Overdue trade credit in months	Overdue trade credit as a percentage of total trade credit
Hungary (end-1991)	1.7	0.8	47
Denmark	1.6	0.7	40
Finland	1.8	0.8	45
France	3.5	1.6	44
Germany	1.6	0.6	38
Ireland	2.0	1.0	50
Italy	3.0	1.0	33
Netherlands	1.7	0.7	42
Norway	1.6	0.6	38
Sweden	1.6	0.6	38
Switzerland	2.0	1.0	50
United Kingdom	2.6	1.6	62
Western European average	2.1	0.9	44

Sources: Intrum Justitia, reported in Chittenden et al. 1993; Hungarian CSO; authors' calculations.
Notes: Trade credit is trade credit extended (commercial receivables). Western figures are survey-based; figures for Hungary are based on balance sheet aggregates.

in the period 1988–1991. The stocks of total trade credit were equivalent to an average payment period of roughly two months (table 4.3). Since this stock was approximately constant over the period 1988–1991, in aggregate in Hungary, inflows of trade credit approximately equaled outflows. Nor was the percentage of trade credit overdue unusually high by Western standards. According to Hungarian CSO data, at the end of 1991, 47 percent (by value) of total receivables in the Hungarian enterprise sector were overdue (as defined by the reporting enterprises). This is about the Western European average, as can be seen from table 4.3. Simply put, there was no serious payment discipline problem with respect to trade credit in Hungary prior to the introduction of bankruptcy reform; as in the West, Hungarian firms did pay each other for goods delivered—but just as in the West, they paid each other late.

In our view, dealing with the phenomenon of late payment by forcing late-paying firms to file for reorganization was thoroughly misguided. In a market economy, payment discipline is enforced primarily by *market forces*. When a customer fails persistently to pay a supplier, the supplier will typically learn the obvious lesson and stop shipping to the customer in the future or ship only for cash or payment in advance. We note that the key prerequisite for this lesson to be learned is, very simply, the hard budget constraint. A firm that doesn't learn this lesson is simply throwing

Table 4.4
How Hungarian manufacturing firms control their overdue receivables: Results of a 1994 survey of 200 manufacturing firms

Method used to control overdue receivables	Always or frequently used?	In use?
Require payment in advance from new customers	42%	83%
Require payment in advance from traditional customers	13%	53%
Refuse to supply until past debt is paid or renegotiated	40%	82%
Charge interest on overdue receivables	62%	87%
Informal methods (phone, letter, . . .)	66%	87%
Legal action	17%	71%
Sell overdue receivables on debt market	0%	14%
Average number of methods always or frequently used	2.3	
Percentage of firms with at least one method always or frequently used	100%	
Response rate	189/200	

Source: World Bank Research Project on Enterprise Behavior and Economic Reform.

money away; and if it throws enough away it will cease to be able to stay open. Our interpretation of the existing evidence from transition countries is that most firms do indeed learn this lesson.

The results of a World Bank survey of 200 medium and large Hungarian manufacturing enterprises conducted in early 1994 provide strong evidence that, in fact, Hungarian firms did learn the lessons of what to do about customers who don't pay. In that survey, firms were asked what methods they used to control overdue receivables and how often they used them. Table 4.4 summarizes their responses. Every firm in the survey used at least one method to control their overdue receivables frequently. Payment in advance, charging interest on overdue receivables, refusing to supply until past debts are repaid or renegotiated, and "informal methods" were the most commonly mentioned methods. Note that payment in advance was required substantially less frequently from traditional customers, reflecting the fact that these customers were able to establish themselves as important or reliable customers. Particularly noteworthy for our purposes is the infrequency with which legal methods were used, just as in Western countries; only 17 percent of firms said they used them always or frequently. Since the survey was taken immediately after the trigger episode, the infrequency with which the respondents used legal methods is striking.

As just noted, late payment is endemic in developed Western countries, but in practice only a small fraction of late payments are pursued through the courts. Transactions costs are one important reason for this. Another is that supplier-customer relationships are typically repeated, long-term relationships. Suppliers are not likely to take customers to court in such circumstances; late payments will simply be reflected in the next round of negotiations over price and payment terms. The scale of late payment reflects in part the relative bargaining strength of the partners: customers can extract trade credit in this way from suppliers if their bargaining position is sufficiently strong. Most overdue trade credit, including overdue trade credit in transition economies, is therefore not involuntary credit, as is sometimes claimed; firms readily learn what kind of promptness of payment to expect from their customers, and if they continue to extend trade credit to customers that pay late regularly, they do so voluntarily. If, however, a customer tries to extract more trade credit than the supplier is willing to offer, or if the customer decides not to pay at all, then the supplier will simply stop selling, and only at this point may we reasonably describe the overdue debt as involuntary. At this point the system of contract enforcement, including the bankruptcy framework, becomes relevant, because the supplier has the option of pursuing his claim through the courts.

An effective system for contract enforcement therefore provides a deterrent to nonpayment following "one-off" or "last-time" purchases by customers. In fact, such a system was put in place in Hungary in 1986 (the 1986 liquidation act, mentioned above), and the 1992 act did not introduce major changes into this procedure; as before, a creditor could pursue a debtor through the courts by filing, or threatening to file, for the debtor's liquidation. That the liquidation procedure was not widely used prior to 1992 is best explained in terms of creditor passivity: expected low return to filing, institutional weaknesses in the legal framework for debt collection, and relative novelty and lack of experience with the procedure. Problems with collecting debts make credit both more expensive and more difficult to obtain and thus impose real costs on the economy. If the problem in Hungary lay in the incentives for creditors to pursue debtors through the courts, policy changes should logically have been directed at these incentive problems by making it easier and more profitable for creditors to pursue their debtors. The approach adopted in Hungary essentially forced debtors to pursue their creditors and did not address these underlying incentive problems in any obvious way.

4.5   Were Banks in Hungary a Source of Soft Budget Constraints?

The other group of creditors, aside from firms themselves, about whose behavior the Hungarian authorities were deeply concerned in 1991 was the banks. The banks' bad-debt problems began to emerge in 1990–1991; by the end of 1991, total problematic loans (including interest arrears) as classified under temporary State Banking

Supervision regulations amounted to 88 billion forints, or (adjusting for comparable treatment of interest arrears) about 10 percent of total credit to the enterprise sector. The Hungarian authorities were worried that, as with interenteprise debt, a serious bad-debt flow problem existed in the banking sector, that is, that Hungarian firms were pumping money into their loss-making clients. If banks were indeed providing loss-making firms with soft budget constraints, this would help explain the small number of liquidations banks sought against delinquent firms. Both the banking act and the bankruptcy act, it was thought, would address the flow problem by hardening firms' budget constraints and improving payment discipline: the former by requiring banks to qualify debts and provision accordingly, thus helping to bring the problem into the open and hopefully discouraging further bad lending, and the latter by discouraging firms from running arrears to banks and again by bringing the problem into the open by forcing problem firms into reorganization or liquidation. Workout of the stock problem would be handled through the bankruptcy framework.

Hungarian authorities' concerns about the scale of the bad-debt problem were indeed well-placed, as subsequent events demonstrated. By the end of 1992, total problematic loans in Hungary had ballooned to 289 billion forints, almost two thirds of which was classified in the lowest category of bad. In other words, we estimate (again adjusting for comparability and including interest arrears) that by the end of 1992, banks had qualified about one third of total credit to the enterprise sector, and about 20 percent of total credit was classified as bad. In early 1993 the government implemented a loan consolidation program in which it removed 102.5 billion forints of bad loans from the books of the banks, and then about 20 billion forints more in a related operation. Loans the banks classified as problematic then ballooned again in 1993. We estimate that at the end of 1993, including the bad loans taken from the banks as part of loan consolidation (and again including interest arrears), over half of banks' credit to the enterprise sector had been classified as problematic in some way, and over one third was in the lowest category of bad.

But were Hungarian banks in fact a major source of soft budget constraints in 1991 or subsequently? The empirical problem in determining the answer to this question is that we can make only limited inferences from the fact that problematic loans grew rapidly in the early 1990s in Hungary. Data on problematic loans are based on the banks' own application of the loan classification rules. An increase in loans classified as problematic is an accounting flow and indicates only the banks' recognition of the existence of problem loans (a stock problem) but not necessarily that new problem loans were currently being created by bad lending practices (a genuine flow problem). In the face of a significant shock to the real economy, some lag in "marking to market" the loan portfolio and realizing fully the decrease in

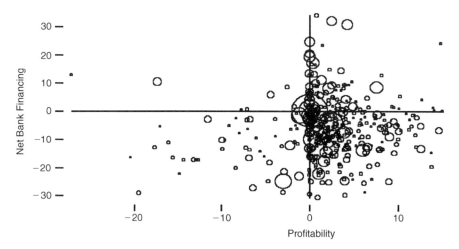

Figure 4.1
1991 net bank financing versus 1990 profitability

asset values would be a natural response in any banking system. For the purposes of this chapter, the question is whether or not, at the time of formulation of the Hungarian legislative shock therapy in 1991, Hungarian banks were providing firms with soft budget constraints. Our approach in this section is to employ data from the borrowers rather than the lenders to try to characterize how bank debt was being allocated.

To see whether Hungarian banks were providing firms with soft budget constraints in 1991, we look at the net bank financing of loss-making firms. Bank financing net of interest charges, that is, the change in nominal bank debt less interest due, is a useful indicator of soft budget constraints because it provides an absolute benchmark. If a bank is providing a distressed firm with a soft budget constraint, then the firm's net bank financing will be positive; cash is flowing from the bank to the firm. Conversely, negative net bank financing of loss makers suggests the banks are imposing hard rather than soft budget constraints.

The scatterplot in figure 4.1 shows the relationship between firm profitability and net bank financing received by the firm. The database used covers all medium and large nonfinancial firms in Hungary in 1991, but to make the scatterplot readable we plot only larger firms, those with an average 1991 bank debt greater than U.S. $1 million. We also exclude firms that were majority foreign-owned at the end of 1992 (we do not have 1991 ownership data) because even a loss-making foreign-owned firm is likely to be a reliable creditor (e.g., a greenfield foreign direct investment just starting up). The size of each firm's average bank debt in 1991 is indicated by the size of the plotted circle associated with it. The figure's vertical axis measures net bank financing in 1991 as a percentage of the firm's end-1991 assets, that is, (end-91 bank debt minus start-91 bank debt minus 1991 interest costs) ÷ (end-91 assets), expressed as a percentage; the horizontal axis measures firm profitability in the previous year, 1990, as a percentage of the firm's end-1990 assets.

Figure 4.1 shows that in 1991, Hungarian banks were apparently presenting unprofitable firms with *hard*, not soft, budget constraints. For nearly all unprofitable firms, net bank financing in 1991 was negative (quadrant II is almost empty compared to quadrant III): interest payments to banks exceeded nominal increases in bank debt, usually by a wide margin. In 1991, prior to the introduction of both the bankruptcy act and the banking act, it appears that the banks were already attempting to withdraw from their uncreditworthy clients.

The continued existence of significant numbers of unprofitable firms in Hungary combined with low numbers of liquidations was considered as evidence of the existence of soft budget constraints. If loss makers were not being kept afloat by injections of either trade credit or bank credit, then how were they financing their losses? We attempt to address this question by calculating the sources and uses of financing separately for Hungarian firms making operating profits and those sustaining operating losses, using the same comprehensive data set of medium and large nonfinancial firms. The contribution of changes in different categories of current assets and debt is calculated as the real change in end-1991 prices normalized by end-1991 total assets; sources of financing are indicated by negative values for changes in assets and positive values for changes in debt. We calculate both weighted averages (i.e., aggregates for the profitable and unprofitable groups) and medians. The results are presented in table 4.5.

The picture that emerges from the data in table 4.5 is consistent with the evidence presented above. Firms having operating losses in 1991 actually decreased their holdings of debt to suppliers and to banks in real terms. The main source of financing for loss makers was on the asset side: in particular, inventory decumulation and reductions in trade credit extended (commercial receivables). The only significant source of financing of loss makers on the debt side was an increase in tax and social security debts. Here we have further evidence, in addition to that on the queue presented above, that if any creditor was presenting firms with soft budget constraints, it was apparently the government, by allowing loss-making firms to accumulate tax arrears instead of pursuing them into liquidation. This pattern—tax arrears as a source of soft budget constraints—is common in transition countries (Schaffer 1998).

Table 4.5
Financing of Hungarian Firms, 1991–1993: Real changes in assets and debt as a percentage of end-year assets

	1991		1992		1993	
	OP	OL	OP	OL	OP	OL
Current assets						
Sources (−) and uses (+) of financing						
Total current assets	−8.4	−23.9	−6.9	−26.2	1.8	−7.2
	(−10.4)	(−22.4)	(−12.6)	(−25.8)	(−1.7)	(−11.1)
Commercial receivables	−0.4	−13.5	−1.8	−8.0	0.0	−2.3
	(−1.0)	(−6.8)	(−4.0)	(−8.2)	(−0.6)	(−1.9)
Inventories	−5.2	−10.4	−5.4	−12.7	−0.2	−4.3
	(7.0)	(−11.9)	(−7.2)	(−13.5)	(−1.5)	(−5.3)
Cash and deposits	−1.3	−1.6	0.1	−1.0	1.5	−1.1
	(−0.7)	(−1.1)	(0.2)	(−0.3)	(−0.1)	(−0.4)
Other current assets	−0.6	1.7	0.2	−4.6	0.4	0.5
	(−0.9)	0.4	(−0.5)	(−1.3)	(0.4)	(−0.3)
Debt						
Sources (+) and uses (−) of financing						
Total debt	−5.8	−4.5	−4.7	−9.7	0.7	−1.1
	(−5.1)	(−1.8)	(−8.5)	(−9.3)	(−2.2)	(−1.8)
Commercial payables	−2.2	−3.4	−2.4	−5.8	0.1	−1.2
	(−1.1)	(0.4)	(−2.4)	(−4.9)	(−0.5)	(−1.0)
Bank debt	−1.4	−1.3	−1.0	−1.1	−0.5	−2.1
	(−1.6)	(−1.9)	(−1.2)	(−1.5)	(−1.5)	(−2.0)
Other debt	−2.1	0.3	−1.3	−2.8	1.2	−2.2
	(−0.9)	0.2	(−3.0)	(−2.4)	(0.0)	(1.2)
Tax and social security debts	0.5	2.2	n.a.	n.a.	n.a.	n.a.
	0.3	1.1				
Miscellaneous						
Operating profit/assets	9.4	−8.4	5.9	−9.2	6.2	−7.0
	(7.8)	(−7.0)	(6.4)	(−7.4)	(7.7)	(−6.9)
Profit/assets	2.4	−17.2	−0.1	−18.4	0.8	−12.8
	(0.9)	(−16.1)	(0.3)	(−17.8)	(1.1)	(−14.9)
Net bank financing/assets	−3.0	−3.5	−1.8	−3.4	−1.5	−4.6
	(−3.8)	(−4.0)	(−2.8)	(−3.4)	(−2.9)	(−3.9)
N	2,067	771	939	733	1,296	555

Notes: Figures are weighted means (aggregates); medians are given in parentheses. Data cover all medium and large nonfinancial Hungarian firms, excluding firms with missing values. Firms are grouped into profit categories according to performance in a given year. Contribution of assets and debts to financing calculated as the real change in opening and closing stocks in end-year prices deflated using the December–December industrial price index (1991: 22.1 percent, 1992: 18.8 percent, 1993: 10.3 percent) and normalizing by end-year assets. Weighted means are aggregates taking all firms in that profit category. OP = Operating profits; OL = operating losses. Operating profit = earnings before interest, taxes, and depreciation. Net bank financing = end-year nominal bank debt minus start-year nominal bank debt minus interest costs.

4.6   The 1992 Bankruptcy Act and the Trigger Episode

4.6.1   Reorganizations and the Automatic Trigger

Hungary's new bankruptcy act went into effect at the start of 1992, and in the first quarter of 1992 there were over 700 filings for reorganization. The act's 90-day automatic trigger started to bite only in April 1992,[8] however, and in that month there were more than 2,000 petitions for reorganization (table 4.6). The April 1992 filings alone amounted to almost half of all filings for reorganization in the period when the automatic trigger was in operation. The number of reorganization filings fell immediately in May to 201, and the rate then gradually declined from about 150 per month in mid-1992 to less than half that by September 1993, when the automatic trigger was removed from the statute books. About 80 percent of filings in the period through September 1993 were compulsory filings, presumably required by the automatic trigger. Most of the overdue debts that caused the trigger to bite were probably overdue trade credits: although the volume of trade credit was comparable in scale to that of bank credit, much more of the former was overdue (47 percent vs. 10 percent at the end of 1991). Voluntary filings were also concentrated in the early part of the bankruptcy experiment: about 1,000 such filings took place in 1992, compared with 137 in all of 1993. Not all filed reorganizations made it as far as the formal announcement by the court; 30–40 percent of all filings terminated in an administrative end, meaning withdrawal from or rejection by the court of the procedure for administrative reasons. The remaining filings went on to the next stage, formal initiation (announcement) of reorganization proceedings by the court.

The size distribution of firms in which the courts formally initiated reorganization reflected that in the economy as a whole. Most firms that filed for reorganization were relatively small, but a substantial number of large firms also filed, and these large firms accounted for the bulk of employment, sales, and exports of all firms that entered reorganization (see table 4.7). By the end of 1993, 3–4 percent of all legal entities in the Hungarian economy were in or had been through court-declared reorganization, but this underestimates the volume of economic activity in firms that entered reorganization, because larger firms were more likely to have done so: for example, more than 10 percent of all firms with employment of more than 300 filed for reorganization in 1992–1993 (table 4.8). We estimate that employment in all firms in which the courts formally declared reorganization in 1992–1993 amounted to 12–13 percent of total enterprise-sector employment. If the size distribution of filed reorganizations that did not go on to formal court initiation is similar to that of those formally started by the courts, employment in all firms

Table 4.6
Reorganizations in Hungary

	1992 Q1	April	Q2	Q3	Q4	1992 Total	1993 Q1	Q2	Q3	Q4	1993 Total	1994	1995	1996
Filings	724	2,259	2,605	418	422	4,169	372	332	195	88	987	189	145	80
Voluntary						1,016					137	136	139	80
Compulsory						3,153					850	53	6	0
Court-announced	285	205	1,152	473	590	2,500	295	257	238	97	887	79	28	14
Closed (including not announced)						2,703					1,924	469	205	89
Administrative end						1,260					740	351	175	76
Agreement with creditors						740					510	90	21	9
Liquidation started						703					674	28	9	4

Sources: Hungarian Ministry of Finance, except for 1994–1996 data, from Mitchell 1998b.

Table 4.7
Employment in firms in court-announced reorganizations in 1992

| | | 1991 employment | |
Size class by employment	Number of firms	Thousands	As a percentage of total enterprise sector employment
All firms entering reorganization	2,294	273	9.7
Those with employment			
>300	233	167	
51–300	656	84	
<50	1,401	22	

Source: Hungarian CSO.
Note: Employment in all entities with legal status was 2,825,000 in 1991. Data differ in coverage from Ministry of Finance data reported in table 4.6.

Table 4.8
Court-announced reorganizations, 1992–1993 (by size of firm)

Size class by employment	Number of firms	As a percentage of all firms with legal status
All firms entering reorganization	3,074	3.6
Those with employment		
>300	174	10.7
51–300	738	12.2
21–50	604	7.9
<20	1,558	2.3

Source: Hungarian CSO.

that filed for reorganization during 1992–1993 would amount to about 20 percent of enterprise sector employment.

The NBH collected data from commercial banks on credit to enterprises in reorganization and liquidation; we present these in table 4.9. In the first few months after the automatic trigger started to bite, about 8 percent of all bank credit was extended to firms in reorganization; this gradually fell to about 2 percent by the end of 1993. Assuming that firms were on average in reorganization 90–120 days, these data suggest that the equivalent of 20–30 percent of the total credit stock in Hungary was in firms that went through reorganization in 1992–1993.[9] There have been suggestions that the banks protected some customers from reorganization by extending credit to enable them to pay off overdue payables and thus avoid having to file; but even if so, the amount of outstanding credit to firms that were not so privileged was very substantial.

Table 4.9
Bank credit to firms in reorganization and liquidation, May 1992–November 1993

Date (end-month)	Total bank credit (billion forints)	Percentage of bank credit to firms in	
		Reorganization	Liquidation
Before-1992 LCP reduction of credit stock			
1992.05	725.0	8.9	4.3
1992.06	727.2	8.4	5.2
1992.07	740.1	8.5	5.7
1992.08	746.3	7.7	6.3
1992.09	750.2	7.7	6.9
1992.10	755.3	6.1	7.4
1992.11	763.8	5.2	7.6
1992.12	763.3	4.3	7.7
1993.01	749.2	4.6	8.2
1993.02	775.9	4.4	7.8
1993.03	n.a.	n.a.	n.a.
After-1992 LCP reduction of credit stock			
1993.04	711.2	2.7	5.0
1993.05	704.9	2.2	4.4
1993.06	711.8	2.2	4.9
1993.07	726.6	2.6	5.0
1993.08	716.6	2.6	5.5
1993.09	738.3	2.2	6.4
1993.10	740.1	1.8	6.3
1993.11	747.2	1.8	6.7

Source: Hungarian CSO.

Data from 1991 on all firms in court-announced reorganizations in 1992 shows that they were financially less healthy than average the year before reorganization but not extraordinarily so (table 4.10). As noted above, the automatic trigger was based on a measure of illiquidity rather than insolvency. Consistent with this, table 4.10 shows that firms in reorganization in 1992 were experiencing large losses in 1991 (equivalent to 13 percent of assets, compared to near-zero profits in the enterprise sector as a whole) and had themselves debtors who were late in paying them (overdue receivables); but they were not actually very highly indebted (as a group, they had a 1991 debt-to-assets ratio of 0.58 compared to 0.39 for all Hungarian firms).[10]

The Hungarian court system apparently dealt with most reorganization filings fairly promptly, as the law required. By the end of 1993, more than 90 percent of the

Table 4.10
1991 indicators of firms in court-announced reorganizations in 1992

	Firms in reorganization	Total enterprise sector
Profit (as a percentage of sales)	−12.7%	0.5%
Debt-to-assets ratio (book value)	0.58	0.39
Receivables-to-assets ratio (book value)		
All receivables to assets	0.19	0.13
Overdue receivables to assets	0.12	0.06
Nonoverdue receivables to assets	0.07	0.07

Source: Hungarian CSO.

reorganization filings had been brought to closure. As noted above, the most common conclusion to a reorganization filing was an administrative end. Anecdotal evidence suggests that sometimes debtor firms would deliberately misfile their reorganization applications to play for time. Using a sample of reorganization filings from the documents of the Budapest court, Mitchell (1998b) finds that about 30 percent of the petitions during this time period were rejected because they were missing required documents. She reports that more than 50 percent of these firms filed for liquidation in subsequent years (Mitchell, 1998b, table 4.6).

Of the reorganization cases formally announced by the court and subsequently completed in 1992, termination via agreement with creditors was initially more common than continuation into liquidation, but in 1993 liquidation became the more common exit route (see table 4.6). Mitchell suggests this may have been because creditors, learning from their experiences in previous reorganization procedures, started to require better-formulated restructuring plans from the debtors. Furthermore, Mitchell found that 70 percent of the firms in her sample that initially came to agreement with their creditors in the reorganization process were in liquidation proceedings within three years. She found this percentage to be the same for all the firms in her sample that filed for reorganization, regardless of the outcome of that filing. As liquidation becomes the final route for financially distressed firms, court dockets obviously become more crowded.

The restructuring plans in the reorganizations that ended in agreement between the debtor and its creditors generally consisted of fairly simple measures (Gray, Schlorke, and Szanyi, 1996). Financial restructuring measures (rescheduling of debt, capitalization of interest, debt write-offs, etc.) were the most common. Separately, Mitchell (1998b) reports that, based on a sample of firms filing for reorganization during the period of the automatic trigger, 70 percent of those whose reorganizations ended in agreement with their creditors subsequently filed for liquidation within the following two years. Thus in terms of real restructuring and freeing up assets to move into other uses, reorganization was not particularly successful. The direct contribution of the automatic trigger to restructuring, via putting large numbers of firms into reorganization, thus appears to have been limited.

After mounting dissatisfaction with the bankruptcy experiment, in September 1993 the Hungarian parliament amended the 1992 bankruptcy act. The automatic trigger was removed, and the UCP was loosened to a requirement similar to that which governed agreements for firms in liquidation. Once the trigger was removed, compulsory filings for reorganization disappeared, leaving only small numbers of voluntary filings, about 100 a year (table 4.6). The infrequency with which debtors filed for voluntary reorganization (in early 1992, before the trigger became a binding constraint, during the trigger period, and after it was removed in late 1993), demonstrates that firm managers did not see reorganization as an attractive option, despite the fact that it temporarily preserved their control of the firm. The reason for this, we argue, is that entering reorganization cut firms off from credit markets; and by forcing many firms to enter reorganization in these conditions, the automatic trigger in effect generated a credit crunch in 1992.

Firms that were thrown into compulsory reorganization, even if they were in arrears on only one kind of credit or even to only one creditor, were cut off from access to all kinds of credit as a result. A supplier will obviously not want to extend trade credit to a firm about to enter reorganization. The absence of any clause in the 1992 bankruptcy act giving priority status to debts incurred during reorganization was a powerful disincentive for suppliers to extend trade credit to firms in reorganization. A supplier, if it ships at all to a firm near or in reorganization, will demand payment in advance or on delivery. The firm will not be able to solve this liquidity problem with the help of bank credit, because a bank will not lend to it for the same reasons. Lending to a firm about to enter reorganization is clearly a mistake, and lending to a firm in reorganization is just as mistaken because of the lack of priority status for new lending.[11] A potential customer may be unwilling to start or remain in a long-term relationship with a supplier in (or about to enter, or leaving) reorganization if it has doubts about whether the firm will still exist as a going concern in a year's time. The economy-wide and coordinated implementation of the automatic trigger in Hungary had the effect of causing many firms to try to repay overdue trade credit in early 1992 so as to avoid having to file for reorganization. Both bank credit and trade credit fell substantially in real terms in 1992 (see table 4.11), and the 1992 bankruptcy act may have been a major factor (in the case of trade credit, the

Table 4.11
The 1992 credit crunch in Hungary

	January 1, 1992	December 31, 1992	Percentage real change
Commercial receivables of medium and large enterprises			
Billion forints	466	449	−18.8
As percentage of GDP	20%	16%	
Commercial payables of medium and large enterprises			
Billion forints	353	311	−25.7
As percentage of GDP	15%	11%	
Bank credit to enterprises (small entrepreneurs excluded; effects of 1992 LCP excluded)			
Billion forints	705.4	695.5	−17.0
As percentage of GDP	30%	25%	

Notes: Data on trade credit derive from the enterprise data set used in the chapter. The data are not directly comparable to those in table 4.2 because of differences in data coverage and data definitions. The percentage real change is calculated using the producer price index (18.8 percent December 1991–December 1992). Percentage of 1991 GDP given for January 1, 1992, figures; percentage of 1992 GDP given for December 31, 1992, figures.

major factor) behind this. This loss of liquidity could have depressed output, perhaps significantly.

Evidence on the impact of Hungary's 1992 bankruptcy act can be culled from a World Bank survey of 200 Hungarian medium and large manufacturing enterprises conducted in early 1994. Firms were asked if, in the period April 1992 to August 1993 when the automatic trigger was active, they were involved in a reorganization procedure as a debtor or as a creditor. If they responded affirmatively, they were asked whether they lost sales or suppliers as a consequence. Table 4.12 reports the survey's results. About one fifth of the survey's sample had actually filed for reorganization during this period, a figure consistent with the aggregate data cited above. About half of these, or 10 percent of the total sample, lost either sales or suppliers as a result (most lost both). What is surprising is how numerous were the firms affected by reorganization as creditors, and how costly they reported the experience to have been. Fully three quarters of the entire sample were involved in reorganization procedures as creditors. About four fifths of these, or 63 percent of the entire sample, reported that they lost either sales or suppliers as a result. As one would expect, nearly all of these creditor firms involved in costly reorganizations said they lost sales as a result. Most surprising of all is the degree to which creditor firms passed on the demand shock of these lost sales to their suppliers: about 70 percent of the

Table 4.12
The costs of reorganization: Results of a 1994 survey of Hungarian manufacturing firms

Were you involved in a reorganization procedure in the period April 1992 to August 1993		
	as a debtor? (as a percentage of responding firms)	as a creditor? (as a percentage of responding firms)
Yes	19%	75%
If yes, as a result, did you lose		
Sales?	9%	58%
Suppliers?	8%	42%
(Sales or suppliers)?	(10%)	(63%)
Response rate	173/200	157/200

Source: World Bank Research Project on Enterprise Behavior and Economic Reform.

creditor firms, or 42 percent of the entire sample, reported that they lost suppliers as a result of being involved in a reorganization as a *creditor*.

It is not clear why more creditors reported reorganization to have been costly than did debtors. One reason may be selection bias; firms with severe difficulties that filed for reorganization may have subsequently entered liquidation (or even closed down) and hence may have been unwilling (or unable) to participate in the survey. Even if we take the lower figure (one half) as the estimate for the proportion of costly reorganizations, the evidence suggests that the automatic trigger experiment was costly because it propagated trigger-induced liquidity problems originating in the debtor firms and spread them to their creditors. The World Bank survey provides fuel for those who argue that forcing reorganization and liquidation too quickly in transition economies will lead to a snowballing effect that will disrupt the countries' real economy significantly.

Finally, what of the so-called queue, the increase in the size of which provided some of the impetus behind the introduction of the automatic trigger? The scale of queuing following the implementation of the bankruptcy act did indeed decrease quite sharply (see table 4.1). It has been suggested that this indicates an improvement in payments discipline, but most of this is actually a statistical illusion. According to an NBH study, 70 percent of the decrease in the queue was due to the debtor protection afforded by the bankruptcy act; when firms entered reorganization, their payables were automatically removed from the queue.

4.6.2 Liquidation

The number of liquidation procedures also increased dramatically in Hungary with the introduction of the new bankruptcy act in 1992. Liquidations outnumbered reorganizations by a substantial margin; in 1992, there were almost 10,000 liquidation filings and, in 1993, there were a further 7,000 (table 4.13). The monthly data for liquidation filings following do not show the same huge spike in April 1992 as those for the reorganization filings: the number of liquidation filings jumped dramatically as soon as the law took effect at the start of the year, with more than 2,000 filings in the first quarter of 1992 and only a modest increase in April of 1,281 filings, compared to an average of about 800 filings per month for the year as a whole. The April 1992 surge in reorganizations far exceeded this number. The main increase in liquidation filings thus took place before the automatic trigger bit, and the automatic trigger made only a very limited direct contribution to the increase in the number of liquidations, via debtors caught by the trigger filing for liquidation rather than reorganization.

Table 4.13 also presents some information about the initiators of liquidation proceedings. Between 15 and 20 percent of liquidations were initiated by the debtor itself; another 10 percent were initiated by state creditors (the tax collection, social security, and customs authorities). Hardly any were initiated by the banks (less than 1 percent in 1992 and only 2 percent in 1993). The bulk of liquidations (about 70 percent or so) were initiated by state enterprises and "other creditors": in other words, by trade creditors. Debtors filing for liquidation to escape having to file for reorganization therefore did not cause the surge in liquidation filings in early 1992. Rather, creditors apparently reacted quickly to the introduction of the new bankruptcy law and started to file in large numbers for liquidation of their debtors. Creditors may initially have been motivated to do this in part by the prospect of their debtors' filing for reorganization because of the trigger, but we have no direct evidence of this one way or the other. Whatever the reason for the very rapid start in widespread use of the liquidation procedure, it has continued to be used in Hungary on a large scale. The removal of the automatic trigger in late 1993 may account for the subsequent moderate fall in annual filings for liquidation in 1994 to not quite 6,000 filings, but filings subsequently increased again to more than 7,000 in 1997.

As in the case of reorganization, a large number of liquidations never really get started and instead terminate in an administrative end; over 4,000 ended this way in 1992. The numbers of court-announced liquidations are still substantial, however, and in fact have risen somewhat over time, from 2,227 in 1992 to over 3,000 in 1996. Exits from reorganization to liquidation accounted for a relatively small proportion of the total number of liquidations.

As with reorganization, most firms in liquidation in 1992–1993 were small, but larger firms accounted for the bulk of economic activity in firms in liquidation. As of the end of 1993, about 7 percent of total bank credit was to firms in liquidation.

Table 4.13
Liquidation in Hungary, 1989–1994

	1989	1990	1991	1992 Q1	April	Q2	Q3	Q4	1992 Total	1993 Q1	Q2	Q3	Q4	1993 Total	1994	1995	1996
Filings				2,436	1,281	3,033	2,197	2,225	9,891	2,180	2,156	1,633	1,273	7,242	5,711	6,316	7,397
By initiator																	
Debtor-initiated									1,760	436	389	281	253	1,359	996	918	1,025
Creditor-initiated									8,131	1,744	1,767	1,352	1,020	5,883	4,715	5,398	6,372
State (tax and taxlike)									~900	146	165	152	145	608			
Banks									~60	44	30	42	43	159			
State enterprises									~1,100	297	209	131	102	739			
Other creditors									~6,100	1,257	1,363	1,027	730	4,377			
Court-announced									2,227	591	683	639	680	2,593	2,484	2,799	3,078
Closed (including not announced)	141	233	526	120	161	529	911	667	4,936	1,206				5,115	4,149	5,457	6,842
Administrative end									4,401					3,975	2,997	3,202	3,844
Completed liquidation									562					1,140	1,152	2,255	2,998

Sources: Ministry of Finance, except Kornai 1993 for 1989–1991, breakdown for creditor-initiated liquidation in 1992 deriving from somewhat different figures in Mitchell 1994, and Mitchell 1998b for 1994–1996.

Allowing for credit to firms in liquidation taken from the banks in the 1992 loan consolidation program and for credit to firms in completed liquidations, we estimate that in excess of 10 percent of the total credit stock was held by firms in liquidation in 1992–1993. Gray, Schlorke, and Szanyi's (1996) survey-based study suggests that firms that entered liquidation were in serious financial difficulties compared with those that entered reorganization: not merely very unprofitable, but also insolvent.

Termination of a liquidation via administrative end is apparently quick, but those liquidations that do proceed however, are fairly time-consuming. Only about 600 liquidations were completed in 1992, and many or most of these were probably started prior to 1992, under the old liquidation law. The rate at which liquidations were closed increased in 1993 and 1994 to more than 1,000 per year, but this was still only about half the rate of court announcements, so a significant backlog developed. Filings continued to exceed completions in 1995 and 1996, and only in 1997 did the number of completions start to approach the number of filings. As noted above, the law allows up to two years to complete a liquidation, and so it appears likely that some liquidations have been missing the two-year deadline.

There are several reasons for the relatively slow pace of the liquidation procedure. It is the liquidator's duty, as set out in the bankruptcy act, to try to recover as much as possible for the firm's creditors, which is an incentive for "slow and correct" rather than "quick and dirty" liquidations. Prices for the assets of liquidated firms have been low, reportedly 20–30 percent of book value.[13] This low yield is due, in part, to the large number of ongoing liquidations and the glut of assets being offered on the market. Evidently, liquidators have been reluctant to accept these prices. Probably just as important are the strong continuation biases built into the liquidation procedure: priority to new debt and ongoing operating costs, the structure of compensation of the liquidator (a percentage commission of not only sales of assets but also current revenues), and the relative independence of the liquidator vis-à-vis the creditors. The Gray, Schlorke, and Szanyi (1996) study shows that about half of the large firms in liquidation, and one quarter to one third of the small firms, operated as going concerns during liquidation. Finally, Gray, Schlorke, and Szanyi report, based on interviews of liquidators, that liquidators see themselves not only as representing creditors' interests but also as agents for restructuring firms. The way the liquidation framework was structured would thus seem to have avoided, at least partially, the problem of inefficient termination on a large scale—a particularly serious danger for a transition economy. If anything, some inefficient continuation may actually have occurred under this framework, but the time limit for completing liquidations would have limited the scale of this.

The Gray, Schlorke, and Szanyi (1996) study indeed suggests that liquidations, unlike reorganizations, lead to major restructuring of firms, including labor shedding, asset sales, privatization, and management change. An important caveat to this is that the study by Gray and colleagues and our survey of crisis managers suggest a substantial number of liquidations were of "shell" firms in which previous management or owners had already stripped assets. For these firms, the transfer of control to the liquidator came too late. Nevertheless, in terms of promoting restructuring and freeing assets to be deployed in more efficient uses, the liquidation procedure, not the reorganization procedure, has been the most successful part of the Hungarian bankruptcy experiment. Moreover, liquidation is now a commonly used procedure in Hungary. As Gray, Schlorke, and Szanyi (1996) argue, the Hungarian bankruptcy reform can be viewed as a success with respect to "institution building." Whether the automatic trigger played a role in establishing liquidation as a working institution is not clear, however. A firm caught by the automatic trigger could avoid reorganization by filing for liquidation instead, since a firm in liquidation was not cut off from new credit, and liquidation could also lead to settlement. In fact, most firms didn't take this route; liquidation filings were indeed higher than normal in April 1992, but not by very much compared to the surge in reorganization filings, and in any case creditors, not debtors, initiated most liquidations in 1992. The contribution of the trigger via this route to the large numbers of liquidations would have been limited at most. The domestic publicity given to bankruptcy reform and the trigger in particular may have increased public awareness of the various possibilities open to creditors who are not paid, including filing for liquidation of the debtor, but we have no evidence of this one way or the other.

4.6.3 Spillovers: The Impact on the Banking Sector

According to the State Banking Supervision's rules for classification of bank debt, credit to firms in liquidation (but not to firms in reorganization) must be rated in the lowest category of bad. During the initial period of bankruptcy reform, Hungarian banks were reluctant to recognize their bad debts openly. Moreover, while the liquidation process is in progress, a debtor firm in liquidation is not required to service or repay inherited debts, including inherited bank debt. Finally, the bargaining power of banks relative to the firms to which they lend money is typically large compared to the bargaining power of trade creditors. While a highly indebted firm is outside reorganization/liquidation procedures, banks have better prospects of extracting money from it than would trade creditors and possibly even than would state creditors. For these reasons, we would not expect to see banks file frequently for the liquidation of their debtors.

The Hungarian bankruptcy experiment contributed to the banking sector's cash flow problems in two ways. First, firms did not service or repay their bank debt while in the 90-day protection period offered by reorganization, depriving the banks of that source of cash flow.[13] Second, the bank debts of firms that left reorganization via liquidation would be classified as nonperforming for the entire length of the liquidation procedure. Thus by putting many firms in a position in which they would not service their bank debt either temporarily (while the reorganization negotiations took place) or for a longer period (while liquidation took place), the bankruptcy experiment exacerbated the banking sector's cash flow and bad debt problems.

That said, the bankruptcy and banking acts do not seem to have generated a very significant change in the hardness of the budget constraints that banks presented to firms. We argued above, based on enterprise-level evidence on net bank financing of firms, that banks were not providing firms with soft budget constraints in 1991. The pattern of financing for 1992 and 1993, after the introduction of the new legislation, was in fact very similar to that in 1991, as figures 4.2 and 4.3 demonstrate: net bank financing of loss-making firms was negative. In 1992 and 1993, too, banks were attempting to withdraw from their bad debtors at the same time that they were declaring large volumes of their lending to be nonperforming.

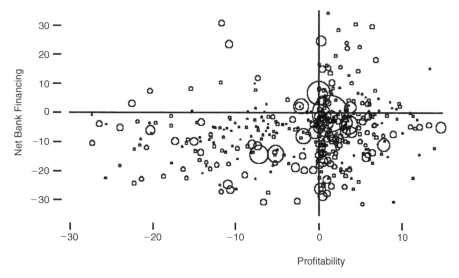

Figure 4.2
1992 net bank financing versus 1991 profitability

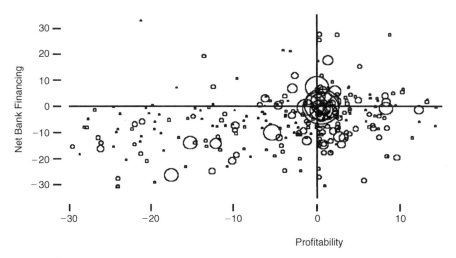

Figure 4.3
1993 net bank financing versus 1992 profitability

The financial distress in which Hungarian banks found themselves in 1992–1993 did not lead to the gambling behavior frequently attributed to banks that have essentially lost their equity because of the liabilities of bad loans. Rather, our data indicate that the banks were acting as if they were "conservative" bankers trying to extract themselves from high-risk, deadbeat clients. Most likely, a primary concern of the bankers in the large state-owned banks during 1992 was the collection of information required to satisfy the new banking regulations and the international auditors. Equally important was the daunting task of creating the internal management structure necessary both to monitor their loan portfolios and to rationalize lending activity in a market economy. The evidence indicates that, as the bankers were scrambling around attempting to adjust, they were also trying to prevent their loan portfolios from deteriorating still further. This is not to say that the large Hungarian banks were well-managed banks throughout this period. Rather, at best, these banks were involved in damage control and, at worst, the requirements of the new regulatory and market environments simply overwhelmed them. The creditor passivity problem noted earlier in the chapter with respect to the large Hungarian banks can be attributed to a lack of expertise and information regarding workouts, to the fact that filing for liquidation of debtors or otherwise attempting a workout required banks to recognize their bad debt openly, and the banks lacked the equity to fully mark to market, because the prospective return to liquidation was low, and probably also because they were playing for time, anticipating some government support. A full analysis of the incentives that generated this conservative behavior would take us too far afield. We note here only that the career prospects of a banker in a Hungarian bank suffer as a result of being seen to bear some responsibility for making bad loans, both because bad loans delay privatization (and subsequent expected salary increases) and because the likelihood of obtaining an attractive new job in alternative employment (e.g., joining a new or foreign-owned bank) declines.

4.7   Policy Lessons for Transition Economies

Transition economies face the problem of reallocating resources in a short period of time after transition begins. Much attention has deservedly been given to macroeconomic stability and enterprise privatization in orchestrating the transition. Somewhat surprisingly, however, the necessity to develop the institutional infrastructure required to thaw resources frozen in unproductive uses for a market economy has been neglected. Although the problem of creditor passivity has been recognized, no satisfactory way has been found to involve creditors in decision making or give them participation in the potential upside gains from restructuring. In capitalist market economies, the involved parties have created such mechanisms without government action: for example, strip financing, debt convertible to equity. But these require well-developed, sophisticated capital markets. Would it be preferable for the governments in transition economies to concentrate on providing the necessary legal (e.g., contract law) and institutional infrastructure for such arrangements to evolve rather than to intervene directly? In our opinion, the transition economies do not have the luxury of an evolutionary strategy. Hungary had in place traditional bankruptcy legislation prior to the implementation of the 1992 policies, but the incentives for creditors to act were lacking. Hence, some government action was necessary to jump-start the reallocation process.

Hungary has made significant progress in developing a strong, market-oriented legal framework to deal with resource reallocation. Yet in the process, Hungarian policymakers experimented with a draconian instrument, the automatic reorganization trigger, designed to deal with flow problems that were for the most part nonexistent, namely, the incentives for firms to continue to accumulate involuntary trade credit and soft budget constraints provided by the banking sector. By 1992 when the trigger was instated, banks were already becoming tough, and firms were already imposing financial discipline on each other. The real source of soft budget constraints in Hungary was the state itself, in its inability to collect taxes and its toleration of tax arrears in loss-making firms, in its inability to act as a tough owner and prevent management of state-owned firms from stripping assets, in its implementation of a series of bailouts of banks and important debtors. The first lesson to be learned from the Hungarian bankruptcy experiment is: policymakers should concentrate on getting taxes collected, avoiding bailouts, and implementing reasonable corporate governance frameworks for commercial banks and should trust market forces to ensure that firms themselves impose hard budget constraints on each other.

The trigger episode enforced a time-compressed quick fix of an inherited stock problem on an underdeveloped infrastructure that was ill equipped to handle the magnitude of the reorganization filings the trigger generated. The trigger was a sledgehammer that caught firms with temporary liquidity problems and effectively cut them off from short-term bridge financing because the reorganization legislation had no provision for superpriority of new borrowing while a firm was in reorganization. Hence, lending to firms in reorganization was a risky venture, and neither banks nor trade creditors were interested in doing so. Furthermore, the 100 percent creditor agreement clause allowed a minor creditor to hold the negotiation process hostage and force a debtor firm into liquidation. The resulting legislated credit crunch exacerbated the output drop in the real economy and prolonged the wait for its recovery. The second lesson from the trigger episode is: don't shake things up unless you are sure of the problem and you have a good idea of the expected outcomes.

From the period April 1992 to September 1993, the trigger certainly shook things. Undoubtedly, as resources were reallocated and more efficient downsized restructured companies emerged, the real economy benefited. Most of the restructuring, however, seems to have taken place via the liquidation route rather than via reorganization. Indeed, it is not at all clear that a reorganization route was even necessary. The usual justification for reorganization is that protecting a firm from its creditors avoids inefficient termination and loss of the firm's going-concern value. The Hungarian experience, however, suggests that the liquidation route does not have an anti-continuation bias necessitating an alternative that is more "continuation friendly," and at the same time it can be structured to remove control from incumbent management and place it in the hands of an agent that is both more likely to engage in major restructuring and more likely to look after creditors' interests. The third lesson of the Hungarian bankruptcy reform episode is: concentrate on getting the liquidation framework right, so that it both transfers control away from incumbent management and favors continuation over shutdown.

The Hungarian bankruptcy reform was indeed successful in establishing liquidation as an operating institution in Hungary, and in this sense can be deemed a success. This suggests that some sort of trigger that increases creditors' use of the liquidation framework may have some use; as liquidation is used more and firms, liquidators, lawyers, and judges accumulate experience with it, the incentives to use it increase. A liquidation trigger, based on insolvency criteria rather than, as in the Hungarian experiment, illiquidity criteria, is sometimes found in Western bankruptcy frameworks. Such a trigger, if introduced in a transition economy in a nondisruptive way, could increase use of the liquidation framework. The fourth lesson of the episode is: not all triggers are alike, and some may actually be useful.

The form of trigger included in the Hungarian bankruptcy framework created a financial externality that the government did not attend to properly. The large number of companies in reorganization and liquidation proceedings exacerbated the already weak cash flow positions and distressed balance sheets of the state-owned banks. Thus the episode contributed to a rapid recognition of the stock of bad debt in the banking system and hence forced the government into several bank recapitalizations. The fifth lesson from the episode is: don't neglect the financial repercussions of shaking up the real sector, especially if the financial sector has yet to be rationalized.

Creditor passivity was rational in Hungary as liquidation values were low because of an underdeveloped and thin secondary market for assets. Banks typically have great bargaining power with respect to their clients, relative to that of other creditors. While a highly indebted firm is outside reorganization or liquidation procedures, banks have better prospects of extracting money from it than do even state creditors. None of the provisions in the 1992 bankruptcy act addressed the basic issue of creditor passivity due to low liquidation values. Indeed, by forcing a rapid resolution of a stock problem, the trigger exacerbated the low resale prices for assets by adding to supply. The final lesson from the episode is: don't try to impose a quick market fix on an inherited stock problem, especially when the underlying market is nascent and thin.

Notes

This chapter is based on a paper presented at the William Davidson Institute conference "Financial Sectors in Transition: A Conference on the Design of Financial Systems in Central and Eastern Europe," held at the University of Michigan, May 14–17, 1998. Financial support from the European Union's Phare-ACE program (project P-95-2052-R) is gratefully acknowledged. The usual caveat applies.

1. For example, a steel foundry that is shut down and cools off will be very expensive to restart.

2. Baird (1986) argues, however, that this need not be the case and that under Chapter 7 the bankruptcy trustee may continue to operate the firm if this is in the best interests of the estate. Nevertheless, this is rarely done in practice.

3. The firm's main bank, the security of which takes the form of a "floating charge" over the assets of the firm.

4. In Hungarian, *felszámolási eljárás.*

5. In Hungarian, *csodeljárás.*

6. In fact, under Section 26 of the act, if the automatic trigger bit (the firm had a payable overdue by more than 90 days) and the firm filed for liquidation instead of bankruptcy, then insolvency (a requirement for the liquidation to proceed) was automatically presumed.

7. On this last point, see Mizsei 1994.

8. Ninety days from when the act took effect on January 1, 1992, plus an eight-day deadline for filing.

9. The scale of this figure suggests that banks were including credit to firms that had filed for bankruptcy, not just to firms in which bankruptcy was eventually formally announced.

10. As a benchmark, the debt-to-assets ratios in firms in the G7 countries, also measured at book value, range from 0.58 (United Kingdom) to 0.72 (Germany); see Rajan and Zingales 1995. The book value of the assets of Hungarian firms filing for reorganization would likely be overestimates of the market value for obvious reasons, but inflation rates of 30-odd percent in 1990 and 1991 would have introduced a bias in the opposite direction.

11. When we inquired at the special division for loans to firms in bankruptcy or liquidation at one of the three major commercial banks, they said that in their experience they never saw any lending to firms in the middle of a bankruptcy procedure. They also said that for the bank to be willing to lend, special conditions would have to be attached to the loan (e.g., a repayment guarantee offered by a third party).

12. OECD 1993, 84. We were quoted a similar figure at a firm in liquidation that we visited in 1993.

13. In a World Bank survey of 200 manufacturing firms, about one fifth of the sample filed for reorganization during this 90-day protection period, a figure consistent with the aggregate data. Of these firms, 40 percent had not failed to repay a bank loan on time in the previous two years. Surprisingly, 18 percent of the firms that had not filed for reorganization during the trigger period had failed to repay a bank loan on time during the same period. In the total sample, 25 percent of the firms had failed to repay a bank loan on time in the prior two years. Of these, 74 percent capitalized the interest and/or rescheduled the loan and 24 percent subsequently repaid the loan. In the sample, 28 percent of the firms had been classified as qualified debtors by a bank during the period 1990–1994. Of these, two thirds were classified as creditworthy by that bank at the time of the survey.

References

Abel, István, and John P. Bonin. 1994. Financial sector reform in economies in transition. In *The development and reform of financial systems in Central and Eastern Europe*, ed. John P. Bonin and István P. Székely, 109–126. Brookfield, Vt.: Edward Elgar.

Baird, Douglas G. 1986. The uneasy case for corporate reorganizations". In *Corporate bankruptcy: Economic and Legal Perspectives*, ed. Jagdeep S. Bhandari and Lawrence A. Weiss. New York: Cambridge University Press.

Bhandari, Jagdeep S., and Lawrence A. Weiss, eds. 1996. *Corporate bankruptcy: Economic and legal perspectives.* New York: Cambridge University Press.

Chittenden, Francis, Anthony Kennon, Suneil Mahindru, and Richard Bragg. 1993. Payment practices, legislation and their effect on SMEs: A comparative study. London: National Westminster Bank.

Gray, Cheryl W., S. Schlorke, and M. Szanyi. 1996. Hungary's bankruptcy experience, 1992–1993. *World Bank Economic Review* 10, no. 3:425–450.

Hart, Oliver. 1995. *Firms, contracts and financial structure.* New York: Oxford University Press.

Kornai, Janos. 1993. The evolution of financial discipline under the postsocialist system. *Kyklos* 46, no. 3:315–336.

László, Géza, and László Szakadát. 1992. Money, banking and capital markets in Hungary. Department of Economics, Budapest University. Mimeographed.

Mitchell, Janet. 1993. Creditor passivity and bankruptcy: Implications for economic reform. In *Financial intermediation in the construction of Europe*, ed. Colin Mayer and Xavier Vives. New York: Cambridge University Press.

Mitchell, Janet. 1998a. Strategic creditor passivity, regulation and bank bailouts. Discussion paper no. 1780, CEPR, Washington, D.C.

Mitchell, Janet. 1998b. Bankruptcy experience in Hungary and the Czech Republic. Davidson Institute working paper no. 11, University of Michigan.

Mizsei, Kálmán. 1994. Bankruptcy and banking reform in the transition economies of Central and Eastern Europe. In *The development and reforms of financial systems in Central and Eastern Europe*, ed. John P. Bonin and Istvan P. Szekely. Edward Elgar.

Organization for Economic Cooperation and Development (OECD). 1993. *OECD economic surveys: Hungary*. Paris: Author.

Rajan, R. G., and L. Zingales. 1995. What do we know about capital structure? Some evidence from international data. *Journal of Finance* 50, no. 5:1421–1460.

Schaffer, Mark E. 1998. Do firms in transition economies have soft budget constraints? *Journal of Comparative Economics* 26, no. 1:80–103.

Svejnar, Jan. 1991. Microeconomic issues in the transition to a market economy. *Journal of Economic Perspectives* 5, no. 4:123–138.

White, Michelle. 1989. The corporate bankruptcy decision. *Journal of Economic Perspectives* 3:129–151. Reprinted in *Corporate bankruptcy: Economic and legal perspectives*, ed. Jagdeep S. Bhandari and Lawrence A. Weiss. New York: Cambridge University Press.

5   Tax Avoidance and the Allocation of Credit

Anna Meyendorff

5.1   Introduction

Despite major progress in the reform of banking sectors in transition economies, including the privatization of many state-owned banks, entry of successful de novo competitors, and the development of regulatory and supervisory capabilities, financial intermediation in most of these economies remains at a very low level. The ratio of bank credits to GDP is 13 percent in Russia, 20 percent in Poland and 23 percent in Hungary, as compared to levels of 120 percent typical of Western economies. Existing literature on financial-sector reform in transition economies focuses on macroeconomic stabilization and continued development of the banking sector, including the promotion of regulatory and supervisory capabilities in the context of consolidation. This approach overlooks endogenous constraints on efficient credit allocation.

There are many possible constraints on efficient credit allocation in transition economies and more generally in economies characterized by weak institutions and macroeconomic instability. Demirgüç-Kunt and Maksimovic (1998) find that firms in countries with a more highly developed legal and financial sector have an increased reliance on long-term external financing. In transition economies, poor accounting standards and short credit histories, severe moral hazard problems due to poor corporate governance in the industrial sector, and alternative profit opportunities for banks created by an inflationary environment all further complicate lending.

This chapter looks specifically at tax evasion and the imperfect monitoring capability of fiscal authorities as they relate to the allocation of credit. There is an extensive literature on taxation as it affects the cost of capital (see Auerbach 1983 for an overview) that looks at the impact of various forms of taxation on a firm's capital structure, assuming that tax payment is enforceable. In contrast, I focus on the incentive effects of taxation in the context of a weakly enforced tax regime.

Fiscal authorities in many transition economies, largely in response to primitive tax collection systems, have resorted to using the banking sector to monitor firms and enforce tax payment. In the context of a well-functioning tax collection system, the method of tax enforcement should not have any secondary effects on economic behavior. When taxes are easily avoided *unless* the banking sector is involved, however—when applying for a loan raises the probability of being monitored by fiscal authorities—distortions in real behavior are likely to occur. In other words, differences in the method and degree of enforcement of tax law lead to distortions in real behavior.

Using Russia as a case study, I investigate in this chapter the effect of tax enforcement policies on the allocation of credit. In an economy in which explicit taxation is relatively new, replacing the implicit taxation that occurred through financial and physical plans, it is reasonable to expect that the government's ability to collect financial information and enforce tax payments will be low. In addition, Russian business culture clearly tolerates tax avoidance, and new institutional arrangements have arisen to accommodate such behavior. Many Russian firms avoid taxation by operating in the "gray" market, either eschewing legal status altogether or conducting most of their activities off the books.

Whereas firms are extremely reluctant to disclose financial information and routinely maintain different sets of books for different audiences, banks demand extensive financial disclosure. The Russian government has attempted to take advantage of this disclosure by putting banks under a legal obligation to serve as agents of the state tax service.

Although not explicitly included in the chapter's analysis, taxation based on financial information derived from banks may come from illegal as well as legal sources. Many Russian firms apparently avoid disclosing information to banks because they feel this is equivalent to disclosing it to the Mafia or organized extortion rackets (see Lotspeich 1996). Thus, although the analysis in this chapter refers to fiscal authorities as the source of taxation, in the Russian context it may be more realistic to think of taxes as being some combination of legal and extortionary payment. Section 5.2 gives a more detailed description of the Russian tax system and its relationship to bank lending.

Section 5.3 presents a simple model of a firm that must decide whether to apply for a bank loan to finance a project. The firm operates in an environment in which the fiscal authorities have a very low ability to monitor and in which tax evasion is therefore common. Given the lack of readily available indicators of financial success and the difficulty of monitoring firms directly, fiscal authorities may turn to banks for valuable information. The process of applying for a bank loan reveals significant information about a firm, yet the bank cannot credibly commit not to reveal this information to the fiscal authorities if requested. Thus applying for external financing raises the probability of paying taxes by some significant amount; in the Russian case, this probability is equal to one. More generally, the model presented in this chapter can refer to the decision of a small and growing firm to enter the official economy when staying in the unofficial economy limits its access to credit but shields it from taxation.

Section 5.4 lays out the central result of the simple model. Faced with a higher expected cost of external capital, where the cost is now both the interest rate and the tax rate with some probability, a profit-maximizing firm will demand a lower interest rate from the bank. More importantly, the less risky is the current project and the more profitable a firm has been in the past, the more sensitive it will be to the increased probability of tax payment and the less likely to apply for bank financing. Section 5.5 concludes and provides some policy implications.

5.2 Banking and the Russian Tax System

This section is not an exhaustive description of the functioning of the Russian tax system. Rather, it contains empirical evidence, based on primary and secondary sources, to support the assumption made in the chapter that interaction with the banking sector will increase a firm's probability of being monitored by the tax authorities and of paying taxes:

• Tax registration is a requirement for opening a bank account, and the bank is subject to administrative fines and possible loss of license if it opens an account without proper documentation. Registration consists of recording the taxpayer's name with the State Tax Service and receiving a taxpayer identification number. This taxpayer identification number must subsequently appear on all payment documents, allowing the authorities to trace all transactions between buyers and sellers.

• The tax authorities require enterprises to present a balance sheet, income statement, other financial statements, and quarterly tax returns in person at the tax inspector's office, making tax payment cumbersome and time-consuming.

• Enterprises pay profit (income) tax, a value-added tax, excise taxes and payroll taxes (the latter go to extrabudgetary funds, e.g., social insurance, unemployment insurance and medical and pension funds). According to current income tax law, a flat income tax of 13 percent goes to the federal budget, and the regional government is allowed to charge from 0 percent to 22 percent more, adding up to a maximum rate of 35 percent. Most transfers between enterprises are subject to withholding taxes and/or the value-added tax, and banks are legally responsible for ensuring that proper payment of these taxes has been made. Specifically, a bank is not allowed to make a transfer between enterprises unless it is given a service contract that shows an order for payment of all required taxes. Noncompliance can result in revocation of the bank's license.

• The low level or even absence of deductions allowed for costs related to investment, including depreciation, capital expenditures, advertising and marketing, and employee training serve as a strong disincentive for firms to engage in these activities.

For example, interest on loans for operating cost is deductible up to a rate equal to the official refinancing rate plus 3 percent. Interest on loans for capital investment is not deductible and must be paid out of profits that are subject to a tax of up to 35 percent. (When this type of investment is undertaken, however, if the loan is greater than 50 percent of the profit of the company, only 50 percent of the profits are taxed.)

• Once a firm is in arrears to either the government or other creditors, the bank is legally obligated to put all of the firm's current revenues into a special account (kartoteka 1 for tax payment, kartoteka 2 for private debt) and close all the firm's other accounts. All revenues that flow into the new account are automatically used for payment of either back taxes or the private debt, resulting in a marginal tax rate of 100 percent.

• Over the past few years, tax inspection and auditing has been focused on high-income taxpayers, according to at least one source, providing obvious incentives to hide income (Korolenko and Klein 1997).

• Lack of institutional support for tax payment includes poor enforcement of property rights, poor corporate governance, and lack of contract enforcement. Institutionalized tax evasion is common, in the form of barter transactions and monetary surrogates including *veksels* (a form of IOU). According to several sources, about 40 percent of sales in Russia were conducted with barter trade in 1997 (Aukutsionek 1997; Gaddy and Ickes 1998).

• According to one estimate, 40 percent of all corporate profits are illegally kept out of the tax base (Lanyi, McMullen, and Polishchuk 1997).

5.3   The Firm's Financing Decision

I model the behavior of a firm that must decide whether to undertake an investment project using bank financing. This firm has no access to outside equity, an assumption that easily approximates reality in countries like Russia with nascent capital markets. The decision is made in the first period and the loan paid off, with interest, in the second period. The expected mean return to the project is $(1+r)B$, where B is the amount of the loan. Using a simple linear version of a mean-preserving spread:

$$(1+r)B = z[(1+r)B+d] + (1-z)\{(1+r)B - [z/(1-z)]d\},$$

where z is the probability that the project is successful. Thus for a given rate of return r, a higher d corresponds to a riskier project. I make the further assumption that when a project fails, the return is insufficient to repay the loan, and the firm must pay collateral in the amount C. The firm faces an interest rate of i that it treats as exogenous.

In the simplest case, the firm has no retained earnings, and the only cost of undertaking the investment is the interest payment on the loan, B, or the collateral payment in the case of failure. The firm's expected profit can be written as:

$$E\Pi 1(i) = z[(1+r)B + d - (1+i)B] + (1-z)[-C]$$

$$= z[(r-i)B + d] - (1-z)C. \tag{5.1}$$

Assuming that the firm will apply for a loan as long as expected profit is greater than zero, $E\Pi 1(i) \geq 0$ when

$$i \leq r + d/B - (1-z)C/zB. \tag{5.2}$$

Differentiating i with respect to d gives the Stiglitz and Weiss (1981) adverse selection result. Firms willing to pay a higher interest rate for a project with a given return are worse risks. As the interest rate increases, less risky firms will choose not to borrow.

Now consider the same firm in the case where applying for a bank loan increases the probability of taxation. The firm is monitored by the government with probability p, and there is an exogenous tax rate of t. Since the investment project is the firm's only source of income in this simple model, there is no taxation if the project fails.

The firm's profit can be written as

$$E\Pi 2(i) = z\{p(1-t)[(1+r)B + d - (1+i)B]$$

$$+ (1-p)[(1+r)B + d - (1+i)B]\} + [1-z](-C)$$

$$= z\{(1-pt)[(r-i)B + d]\} - (1-z)C. \tag{5.3}$$

Assuming that this firm will apply for a loan as long as profit is greater than zero, $E\Pi 2(i) \geq 0$ when

$$i \leq r + d/B - [(1-z)C]/[z(1-pt)B]. \tag{5.4}$$

For a given project, the reservation interest rate is lower, since the tax increases the cost of borrowing for the firm. In addition, the adverse selection effect is aggravated, since riskier firms are less sensitive to the threat of taxation. This follows from solving for d and differentiating with respect to t. The tax rate creates a wedge between the price the bank charges and the price the firm pays. Adverse selection as described in Stiglitz and Weiss 1981 is reversible if the bank has full information and can charge lower interest rates to less risky firms. Adverse selection caused by the tax wedge would not be reversible unless the bank absorbed the cost of the tax.

Now assume the firm has retained earnings of R, which earn an exogenous rate of return $\underline{r}$. To focus attention on the effect of the tax, I assume that retained earnings cannot readily be turned into cash to finance the new project and that the return to their use is known with certainty. The firm's profit if it does not undertake the project is simply the return to retained earnings and can be written as

$$\Pi 3(i) = (1 + \underline{r})R. \tag{5.5}$$

In the absence of taxation, if the firm does undertake the project, its expected profit is the return to retained earnings and the expected return on the project minus the cost of the loan:

$$E\Pi 4(i) = z[(1 + \underline{r})R + (1 + r)B + d - (1 + i)B] + (1 - z)[(1 + \underline{r})R - C]$$

$$= (1 + \underline{r})R + E\Pi 1(i). \tag{5.6}$$

The firm will then apply for a loan as long as the expected profit from doing so is greater than the profit earned from retained earnings only: $E\Pi 4(i) \geq \Pi 3(i)$ when

$$(1 + \underline{r})R + E\Pi 1(i) \geq (1 + \underline{r})R \quad \text{or} \tag{5.7}$$

$$i \leq r + (d/B) - [(1 - z)C]/[zB] \tag{5.7a}$$

Since retained earnings cannot be used to finance the project, the firm's decision about whether to borrow from a bank and undertake the project is unaffected by their presence. The reservation interest rate is identical to that in the first example.

In the case where the firm has retained earnings and may be monitored by the tax authorities, I assume that tax liability is generated by the return on both retained earnings and the externally financed project. In other words, once the fiscal authorities choose to monitor a firm, they are able to acquire a fairly accurate assessment of the firm's actual tax liability. The expected profit function of this firm is

$$E\Pi 5(i) = z\{p(1 - t)[(1 + \underline{r})R + (1 + r)B + d - (1 + i)B]$$

$$+ (1 - p)[(1 + \underline{r})R + (1 + r)B + d - (1 + i)B]\}$$

$$+ (1 - z)\{p(1 - t)[(1 + \underline{r})R - C] + (1 - p)[(1 + \underline{r})R - C]\}$$

$$= z\{(1 - pt)[(1 + \underline{r})R + (r - i)B + d]\}$$

$$+ (1 - z)\{(1 - pt)[(1 + \underline{r})R - C]\}. \tag{5.8}$$

As before, the firm applies for a loan if the expected profit of doing so exceeds the profit earned from using retained earnings alone: $E\Pi5(i) \geq \Pi3(i)$ when

$$z\{(1 - pt)[(1 + \underline{r})R + (r - i)B + d]\}$$

$$+ (1 - z)\{(1 - pt)[(1 + \underline{r})R - C]\} \geq (1 + \underline{r})R, \quad \text{or} \tag{5.9}$$

$$i \leq r + (d/B) - [(1 - z)C]/[zB] - [pt(1 + \underline{r})R]/[zB(1 - pt)] \tag{5.9a}$$

The reservation interest rate is clearly lower than in the case without the tax and is also lower than the case with taxation but without retained earning. If the probability of monitoring is zero, if the tax rate is zero or if the amount of retained earnings is zero, equation (5.9a) reduces to equation (5.2).

5.4   Taxation and the Firm's Credit-Seeking Behavior

The distorting effect of taxation through monitoring of the banking sector occurs when firms have retained earnings. Firms are then trading off the amount they pay in taxes as a result of applying for a loan against the extra income earned from undertaking the project the loan is intended to finance. This can be made clearer by rewriting equation (5.9) as follows:

$$(1 + \underline{r})R - (1 - z)C - pt(1 + \underline{r})R + (1 - z)ptC$$

$$+ z(1 - pt)[(r - i)B + d] \geq (1 + \underline{r})R \tag{5.9}$$

where $pt(1 + \underline{r})R + (1 - z)ptC$ is the additional tax liability generated by applying for a loan and $z(1 - pt)[(r - i)B + d]$ is the additional profit net of taxes the project will generate.

The following propositions can be derived from this analysis:

• An increased probability of taxation when borrowing from a bank decreases the interest rate that a firm is willing to pay to finance a given project. To put this another way, at a given interest rate more firms avoid bank financing and reduce their investment activities than at the same interest rate in the absence of a taxation risk. This result has two significant consequences. First, the overall level of investment is lower. Second, disintermediation results from less funds flowing through the banking sector.[1]

• When taxation is associated with applying for a loan, the tax rate will adversely affect the quality of the borrower pool.[2]

· When the firm has taxable retained earnings and faces taxation with probability p when applying for a loan, the maximum interest rate at which it would borrow

· falls as the tax rate t increases.

· falls as the probability of taxation p increases.

· rises as the rate of return r on the investment project increases.

· rises as the probability of success z in the investment project increases.

· rises as the size of the loan, B, increases.

· falls as the rate of return $\underline{r}$ on retained earnings, that is, the profitability of the firm, increases.

· falls as the level of retained earnings R, or the net worth of the firm, increases.

This follows from differentiating equation (5.9a).[3]

The last two results are noteworthy. The probability of taxation in the presence of retained earnings leads more profitable firms to drop out of the borrower pool and decrease their total investment. The intuition is as follows. In all cases the firm will earn the rate of return $\underline{r}$ on its retained earnings R. If it also undertakes a new investment project, applying for a loan and increasing the probability of paying taxes, a higher $\underline{r}$ or R simply increases its tax liability. In other words, the extra profit it will earn from undertaking the project decreases, making it less attractive to use bank funds. The empirical prediction that emerges from this analysis is that the relationship between firm profitability and outstanding debt or investment should be different for firms that exist under this type of tax regime than for firms in economies with more effective fiscal regimes.

From the bank's perspective, the quality of the borrower pool decreases at any given interest rate. First, less risky firms are more sensitive to the probability of taxation. Second, holding the (expected) quality of the new project constant, the more demonstrably profitable a firm has been in the past, the less likely it will be to apply for new loans. Thus an increased probability of taxation when applying for a bank loan aggravates the adverse selection described by Stiglitz and Weiss (1981).

From a social welfare point of view, not only is the overall level of investment decreased, but those firms that have been the most successful in generating a profit on previous investments are less likely to undertake new investment. An extension of the model can investigate the possibility that the interest rate that good firms are willing to pay, given the additional cost of taxation, is so low as to be unprofitable for the bank. In such a case, banks would charge high interest rates to more risky firms, while less risky firms would choose not to borrow, a story that seems familiar in the Russian context.

5.5 Conclusions

Several policy implications can be drawn from this approach to financial intermediation in transition economies and should be transferable to other economies
with underdeveloped financial systems and high rates of either legal or extortionary
taxation. The first concerns the effect of fiscal policy on bank credit decisions. If
firms are reluctant to apply for bank financing because of distortions in tax incidence, then further development of the banking sector will have only a limited impact on the level of lending. Reformers should concentrate on improving both tax
policies and other government functions that influence a firm's decision to enter the
formal economy. Although this chapter focuses on only one benefit of joining the
formal economy, access to bank credit, and compares this to the accompanying tax
burden, the model could be extended to include benefits such as legal protection and
access to capital through domestic and international capital markets.

The second policy implication regards financial system development. Alternative
mechanisms for financial intermediation, despite clear inefficiencies, are likely to arise
in response to an environment that discourages arm's-length financial transactions.
Specifically, this model of the relationship between tax avoidance and credit-seeking
behavior is consistent with the presence of bank-led financial-industrial groups
(FIGs). Firms will seek sources of financing that do not expose them to the threat of
taxation. In general, as the availability of such sources increases or the cost of capital
from them decreases relative to the bank interest rate, banks will be less likely to act
as intermediaries. One of the functions of FIGs, as argued in Johnson 1997 and elsewhere, is to redistribute profits among member firms so as to decrease tax liability.
An FIG's bank will have inside information about the quality and profitability of
member firms and will lend to them even if their accounts make them look unprofitable. Thus tax payments are minimized even if the fiscal authorities monitor the
firm. It is also likely that the FIG's bank can credibly commit to conceal financial
information, decreasing the risk of monitoring altogether. The empirical prediction
that emerges from this analysis is that the relationship between firm profitability and
outstanding debt or investment should be different for firms that are members of
FIGs than for firms that are not.

This argument is consistent with the empirical findings in Perotti and Gelfer 1997,
which show that investment is less sensitive to internal liquidity for members of bank-
led FIGs. One interpretation of these findings is that FIG member firms are more
willing to apply for bank loans, indicating a lower sensitivity to the possibility of
taxation. The presence of FIGs should then reverse some of the distortion to credit
markets described above and raise the overall level of investment in the economy.

Notes

This chapter is part of a research project funded by a grant from the National Council for Eurasian and East European Research. I would like to thank Klaas van't Veld, Michael Keren, Jan Svejnar, Raghu Rajan, Anjan Thakor, Jeffery Abarbanell, and Guido Freibel as well as participants at economics seminars at the University of Michigan and Indiana University for valuable comments and advice. All errors are, of course, my own.

1. When the model is adapted to allow for the use of retained earnings to finance the project, retained earnings are preferred as a source of investment funds, a result familiar from the theoretical and empirical literature on the firm's financing choice. All other substantive results remain the same.

2. Empirical work by Fan, Lee, and Schaffer (1996) finds indication of adverse selection in the Russian credit market.

3. I am making the simplifying assumption that all the equity in the firm is generated as prior earnings; in other words, there is no initial capital contribution. In this case, the firm's retained earnings are equivalent to the net worth or book value of equity, and the rate of return on retained earnings is equivalent to the return on equity. Since capital contribution is not taxed, this assumption does not alter the results of the model.

References

Auerbach, A. 1983. Taxation, corporate financial policy and the cost of capital. *Journal of Economic Literature* 21:905–940.

Aukutsionek, S. 1997. Industrial barter in Russia. *Russian Economic Barometer* 6:3–17.

Demirgüç-Kunt, A., and V. Maksimovic. 1998. Law, finance and firm growth. *Journal of Finance* 53, no. 6:2107–2137.

Fan, Q., U. Lee, and M. Schaffer. 1996. Firms, banks and credit in Russia. In *Enterprise restructuring and economic policy in Russia*, ed. S. Commander, Q. Fan, and M. Schaffer. Washington, D.C.: Economic Development Institute/World Bank.

Gaddy, C., and B. Ickes. 1998. To restructure or not to restructure: Informal activities and enterprise behavior in transition. Washington, D.C.: The Brookings Institution and Pennsylvania State University.

Johnson, J. 1997. Understanding Russia's emerging financial-industrial groups. *Post-Soviet Affairs* 13, no. 4:333–365.

Johnson, S., H. Kroll, and M. Horton. 1992. New banks in the former Soviet Union: How do they operate? In *Reforming the Russian economy*, ed. Anders Aslund and Richard Layard. London: Pinter.

Korolenko, D., and S. Klein. 1997. Russian tax barriers. *International Tax Journal* 23:62–75.

Lanyi, A., N. McMullen, and L. Polishchuk. 1997. Technical assistance for Russian fiscal reform. A Study for USAID-Moscow. IRIS Center, University of Maryland, College Park.

Lotspeich, R. 1996. An economic analysis of extortion in Russia. Unpublished paper, Indiana State University, Terre Haute.

Perotti, E., and S. Gelfer. 1997. Investment and financing in Russian financial-industrial groups. Unpublished paper, University of Amsterdam and Central European University.

Stiglitz, J., and A. Weiss. 1981. Credit rationing in markets with imperfect information. *American Economic Review* 71:393–410.

6 Franchise Value and the Dynamics of Financial Liberalization: The Use of Capital Requirements and Deposit Rate Controls for Prudential Regulation

Thomas Hellmann, Kevin Murdock, and Joseph Stiglitz

6.1 Introduction

Over the last three decades, financial market policy has shifted significantly toward the promotion of financial liberalization. Policymakers around the globe have been preoccupied with deregulating interest rates, lifting restrictions on bank portfolios, and enticing competition in financial services.

Financial deregulation in a given country is typically accompanied by a change in its system of prudential regulation. As the volume and complexity of financial transactions has increased, there has been movement away from monitoring individual transactions, and more emphasis has been placed on evaluating the systems banks use to monitor risks. As a part of this trend, the use of capital requirements as a tool of prudential regulation, typically using the Bank for International Settlements (BIS) standards developed in the Basle Accord, has been more strongly emphasized. Although this trend in financial regulation has led to some notable improvements in the provision of financial intermediation, it has also been marred by a surprisingly large number of banking crises. Caprio and Klingebiel (1996) count 80 major financial crises in 69 countries for the period 1974–1995, most of them systemic crises. They argue that although the trigger events of these crises tend to be some macroeconomic events, they typically uncover some serious structural problems in the financial sector. The recent crises in East Asia are a case in point.

Strong empirical evidence now exists on the link between financial liberalization and banking crises. Demirgüç-Kunt and Detragiache (1997, 1998) show that countries that have liberalized their financial system are significantly more likely to face a financial crisis and that the seeds of the crisis tend to develop relatively soon after liberalization.[1] It may, however, take somewhat longer before structural weaknesses of banks in the crisis economy become apparent. The question then is whether there is a causal link between financial liberalization and banking crises? Do particular difficulties created during the process of liberalization make it more likely that crises will follow in the aftermath of a liberalization episode? In this chapter, we argue that the announcement of liberalization in the future causes an immediate decline in franchise value today with a potential adverse effect on bank incentives to invest prudently.

Obviously it is not enough just to note the problems of banking crises. The main policy question is what kind of regulation will be effective in combating the underlying problems such crises reveal. At the center of these problems are the banks' incentives to engage in prudent investment behavior. In particular, banks present a well-known moral hazard problem: they may choose to invest their assets in a gambling portfolio, where they can reap the benefits in case of success, but because of limited liability, they can pass on the losses to others, such as the government in its role as deposit insurer.

In principle, capital requirements are meant to prevent banks from engaging in such gambling behavior. The idea can be easily shown in a static framework, where a higher level of capital makes banks act more like residual claimants, thus encouraging them not to engage in wasteful gambling activities. We note, however, that capital requirements are actually less effective than such a static analysis suggests. Using only the assumption that capital is costly for banks, we show in this chapter that there is also a negative incentive effect associated with capital requirements, stemming from the fact that a higher capital requirement depresses banks' future profits. This reduces their "franchise value," that is, the net present value of their future profits, and the net impact of capital requirements is less than that implied by a simple static analysis because of this adverse impact on franchise value.

This argument suggests that an excessive reliance on capital requirements can become costly for banks. Regulators either need to rely on very high levels of capital requirements to encourage banks to invest prudently, or they need to seek other instruments. In line with our previous line of research we emphasize the usefulness of deposit rate controls as an instrument that can create franchise value for banks.[2] Deposit rate controls can credibly create an environment in which banks will earn profits in the current period and out into the future. The capitalized value of these profits then contributes to the bank's franchise value.

The argument that franchise value affects banks' incentives to behave prudently then directly allows us to address the questions of liberalization and banking crisis. First, banks may be more prone to gambling in an environment in which they have lower franchise value. But this is precisely the effect of interest rate liberalization and greater competition in the financial markets. As a consequence, we should not be surprised by the incidence of banking crises in liberalized economies.

The problem, however, may become even more severe in the transitional period toward liberalization. Although the actual steps of liberalization may be gradual, the announcement of a financial liberalization has an immediate impact on banks' franchise. Even if banks are told only that they will face more competition in the future, their behavior may change immediately, because of the immediate impact of the announcement on their franchise value. After all, a bank's franchise value is the capitalized value of the bank's future profits. The announcement of increased future competition implies that future profits will fall, which implies in turn that the *current* franchise value will fall as well. Interestingly, this announcement effect implies a seemingly counterintuitive policy recommendation. To stem banks' greater incentives for gambling in the early days of liberalization, regulators need first to tighten their regulation of banks before they relax the regulations at some later point. In particular, it may be necessary to first lower the deposit rate ceiling before subsequently relaxing it or lifting it. This will counteract the adverse effect of lower future profits with higher present profits. It also will make it more difficult for a bank to pursue a gambling strategy by growing rapidly because it will preclude the bank from offering high deposit rates to attract new funds. Furthermore, if the policy of lower deposit rates is implemented with short-run restrictions on dividend payments, banks will be able to grow their capital base and more readily meet the more stringent capital requirements necessary to promote prudent behavior in the liberalized environment. Similarly, it may be necessary to phase out restrictions on asset classes only gradually during liberalization, allowing banks to invest in new areas only in pace with the development of appropriate controls and capabilities of the regulatory oversight.

The main objective in this chapter is to provide an intuition the mechanics into of capital requirements and deposit rate controls that we have explored elsewhere and to explore the implication of these dynamics for the particular problem of transitions to a more liberalized system. In section 6.2 we explain the logic of capital requirements and deposit rate controls in a steady state, that is, where banks expect continuity of the policy regime. We note that in a sufficiently competitive system freely determined deposit rates are inconsistent with prudent banking. In particular, banks are tempted to raise their deposit rates to attract more resources. But the high interest rates they pay on these deposits makes it worthwhile for banks to invest in a gambling portfolio. Without any regulation, competitive banking systems have a tendency to gyrate toward unsound lending. We then show that because capital is costly, capital requirements are a fairly blunt instrument of prudential control. In addition to the well-understood bonding role of capital, it also has less obvious effects. Because capital is costly, capital requirements lower banks' franchise value, partly undermining capital's static bonding role. Further, because capital requirements force banks to hold more capital as they attract incremental deposits, this reduces the marginal return to deposits, and as such capital requirements have the indirect effect of lowering equilibrium deposit rates.

But if capital requirements only work if they indirectly lower deposit rates, why not lower deposit rates directly? Indeed, we show that a deposit rate control naturally complements a policy of capital requirements and that regulators can gain control over the incentive to gamble at a much lower level of capital if they also use deposit rate controls. Because capital requirements are in effect an indirect instrument for reducing equilibrium deposit rates, the *endogenous* lowering of interest rates associated with capital requirements is greater than what would be required if deposit rate ceilings were applied directly. The standard criticism of deposit rate controls—that by lowering interest rates they discourage savings—is thus turned on its head. The regulator can actually implement higher deposit rates using deposit rate ceilings than it can using capital requirements alone.

In section 6.3, when we examine transitional dynamics, the importance of deposit rate controls becomes even more evident. Capital is not only costly, it is also sticky; that is, banks cannot markedly increase their levels of capital in a short period of time. If in the process of liberalization regulators were to enforce a higher standard of capital immediately, banks would be forced to reduce their lending and sell off assets, which would cause a credit crunch and asset deflation. As a consequence, regulators tend to allow banks to build up their capital more gradually over time. We show that in the transitional period when banks have not yet attained the desired level of capital, deposit rates would need to be particularly low to counteract both the lack of capital and the immediate reduction of franchise value due to the effect of the liberalization announcement. The lower deposit rate would also allow banks to accumulate capital more rapidly, which would shorten the duration of the transition period. The key insight to be gained from an analysis of transitional dynamics is thus that a policy of "regulatory overshooting" (where the regulator temporarily imposes stricter regulations) ensures that the transition to a liberalized banking sector is both faster and safer.

6.2 Prudential Regulation in a Steady-State Environment

This section analyzes instruments of prudential regulation in an environment in which banks may be tempted to engage in morally hazardous behavior. The underlying issue is that banks have discretion in how they allocate their investment portfolio and that a government regulator cannot perfectly observe their actions. Because of the limited-liability nature of deposit contracts, banks may have incentives to engage in excessive risk taking, exploit the imperfect supervision of the banking regulators, and put together an excessively risky asset portfolio. We consider a bank to be engaged in gambling when it puts together an asset portfolio that is privately optimal, but only because the depositors (and the government insurer) bear the downside risk. The goal of prudential regulation is to create an environment in which banks will choose to invest in a prudent asset portfolio that involves lending decisions predicated on the full social costs and benefits of the investment, rather than exploiting the limited-liability nature of deposit contracts.[3]

There are two main classes of instruments available to combat moral hazard: those that create constraints and those that affect incentives. In the case of banks' lending practices, direct supervision and restrictions on lending activities are examples of the former. Their main role is to limit the degrees of freedom available to banks within which they can pursue excessively risky strategies.[4] In contrast, policies such as capital requirements and deposit rate controls are aimed at affecting bank incentives. In an environment in which direct supervision is imperfect, banks will always have some ability to distort their portfolios and gamble. It is then incumbent upon this latter class of instruments to create an environment in which the banks choose instead to invest in a prudent portfolio of assets.

This chapter focuses on the analysis of instruments of prudential regulation aimed at altering bank incentives. It is well understood how capital requirements affect bank incentives. The more of its own capital a bank places at risk, the greater proportion of the downside risk of the asset portfolio it internalizes. Only after losses on the portfolio exceed bank capital will those losses be imposed on the bank's depositors (and their insurer). If the bank has sufficient capital at risk, then the bank will choose to invest in a prudent portfolio.

Less widely understood is the role of deposit rate controls as an instrument of prudential regulation. The main idea is that deposit rate controls provide a mechanism for creating franchise value for the bank. When the government imposes a binding deposit rate ceiling, banks will capture an economic profit due to their lower cost of funds. Provided that the government will credibly maintain the rate ceiling in the future, banks will expect to continue earning this rent. The bank's franchise value is the capitalized value of this future stream of rents. Of course, for the bank to earn this rent stream, it must stay solvent. This imposes a hefty opportunity cost on gambling, because if the bank gambles and fails, it will be shut down and lose its claim on this future rent stream. In contrast, by investing in a prudent portfolio, the bank can largely ensure that it will retain its franchise value.[5]

It is interesting to note that these seemingly disparate instruments of prudential regulation affect bank incentives in a qualitatively similar manner: by raising the opportunity cost of gambling. Capital requirements force banks to place their own capital at risk so that if a gamble results in an adverse outcome, the bank bears the cost up to the amount of capital at stake. Deposit rate controls create a franchise value for the bank that is really just a form of intangible capital. If a bank gambles and fails, the bank forfeits its franchise value, so that it again bears the cost up to the amount of its franchise value.

Even though these two instruments may affect bank incentives in qualitatively similar ways, they are different instruments with differing mechanisms for making those incentives effective and with potential issues that would affect their implementation. As a consequence, it is worthwhile to develop a more concrete framework within which these two policy instruments can be evaluated.[6] One of the main results that we will derive our results within this framework is within it the regulator can implement *Pareto-superior outcomes when capital requirements are implemented in conjunction with deposit rate ceilings compared to the best outcome that can be achieved using capital requirements alone.*

As a starting point for our analysis, we begin with three assumptions:

1. *Direct supervision is imperfect.* This implies that banks do have some scope for diverting their investment portfolios into gambling activities. Obviously, with perfect direct supervision, the bank regulator could simply preclude banks from gambling.

2. *Banks have either explicit or implicit deposit insurance.* Depositors will therefore not play a strong disciplinary role in monitoring banks.[7]

3. *Capital is costly.* Capital has an opportunity cost, so that banks would prefer to mobilize deposits rather than increase their own capital at stake. If capital had no opportunity cost, prudential regulation would be simple and straightforward: banks could be required to hold an arbitrarily large capital base and thus would never have any incentive to gamble. Because this is not observed in practice, this assumption seems both practical and relevant.[8]

We can think of banks as engaging in two primary activities: mobilizing deposits and allocating investments. For simplicity, we can think of banks as choosing between two investments: a prudent asset and a gambling asset. In reality, of course, banks invest in a mixture of assets in their portfolio. We can think of the prudent asset as the bank's optimal portfolio given that the bank is not trying to exploit its limited liability. In contrast, we can think of the gambling asset as the optimum portfolio that the bank chooses when the bank engages in excessive risk to maximize its private returns at the expense of depositors. These two assets (portfolios) differ in two important respects. The prudent asset has higher expected return than the gambling asset, but the gambling asset has a higher return if the gamble succeeds. The bank may choose to invest in the gambling asset despite its lower expected return, however, because the depositors, rather than the bank, bear the cost if the gamble fails.

We begin by considering how the bank would choose to invest its assets, *taking the deposit rate and the amount of assets it has available as a given.* Once we understand how banks will invest a given portfolio, we then consider how that affects the manner in which banks compete for deposits. Finally, we can compare how the two instruments of prudential regulation can be implemented to ensure that the prudent outcome is selected.

When a bank is investing a given portfolio of assets, it faces a simple trade-off. If it gambles, it will earn a higher expected return in the current period than if it invests prudently. If the gamble fails, however, the bank will be shut down and lose its franchise value. A number of factors determine whether the bank will choose to gamble or invest prudently: the expected return on the prudent asset, the gambling return when the gamble succeeds, the probability that the gamble succeeds, the opportunity cost of bank capital, the discount factor at which the bank values future earnings, the deposit rate, and the ratio of bank capital to deposits. The environment in which the bank is investing determines most of these factors, but the last two are determined by the two policy instruments we are presently considering: deposit rate controls and capital requirements.

We would like to summarize the bank's trade-off by considering the threshold deposit rate at which the bank would switch from prudent investment to gambling. It should be evident that when the deposit rate is sufficiently low the bank will invest prudently, and if it is sufficiently high, the bank will gamble. (Consider the case in which the deposit rates are so high that the bank earns no profit by investing prudently. By gambling, the bank has a positive probability of earning a positive profit.) In our previous work (Hellmann, Murdock, and Stiglitz 1998b) we derived this critical level of deposit rates, denoted by $\hat{r}$. The level of $\hat{r}$ is determined by the following expression:

$$\hat{r} = [(1 - \delta) * \text{capital-at-risk effect}] + [\delta * \text{franchise value effect}]. \tag{6.1}$$

This threshold is important for our subsequent analysis, so it bears some further discussion. Two main components determine the threshold: the capital-at-risk effect and the franchise value effect. The capital-at-risk effect is largely a result of the bonding role of capital. As the bank has more capital at stake, it internalizes more of the static inefficiency of investing in the gambling asset, and so the bank is more likely to invest prudently. The more capital the bank has invested, the more of the downside risk the bank will bear when a gamble fails. This increases the deposit rate the bank can pay before its incentives switch to gambling. The franchise value effect follows directly, because the bank values the future stream of rents it will capture if it invests prudently. The higher the future return on invested deposits, the greater the deposit rate that the bank can pay before it switches to gambling. The δ term in equation (6.1) is the discount factor. When δ is zero, the bank is myopic, and the

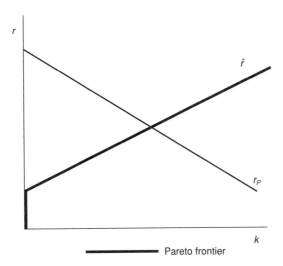

Figure 6.1

capital-at-risk effect determines the bank's incentives, whereas as δ goes to one, the bank becomes perfectly farsighted, and franchise value is all that matters.

As shown in figure 6.1, this threshold will in general be upward sloping in the capital requirement. When a bank holds more capital, it can pay a higher deposit rate and still choose to invest in the prudent asset. This is consistent with the traditional analysis of capital requirements: that they reduce a bank's incentives to gamble.

This threshold defines the Pareto frontier. All gambling outcomes are socially wasteful, so it is Pareto efficient to implement prudent outcomes. Along the $\hat{r}(k)$ line, depositors can capture a higher return only if banks also hold a higher level of capital. The next part of our analysis is designed to determine what prudent outcomes each instrument of prudential regulation can implement.

We still need to analyze how capital requirements affect the deposit rate paid in equilibrium. To analyze deposit rates, we begin by assuming that banks will invest prudently, then determine what policies of prudential regulation are necessary to make sure that banks do not gamble in equilibrium. Assuming that banks are investing prudently, they will offer deposit rates such that the marginal benefit of increasing rates equals their marginal cost. The marginal benefit is the amount of incremental deposits that the bank will capture times the profit margin the bank gets from investing those deposits in the prudent asset. *Capital requirements, however, adversely affect the bank's profit margin.* A capital requirement forces the bank to

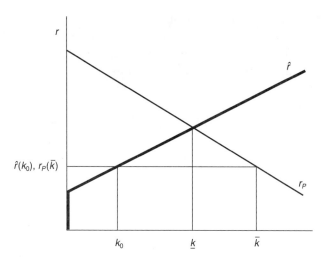

Figure 6.2

hold capital in some proportion to its deposits. Because capital is costly (relative to deposits), a higher capital requirement reduces the profit margin on incremental deposits.

As shown in figure 6.1, this implies that the deposit rate is downward sloping in the level of the capital requirement. Interestingly, this implies that *capital requirements are an indirect instrument for reducing deposit rates.* An increase in a bank's capital requirement results in a lower deposit rate because the marginal return on deposit falls. Note that capital requirements lower deposit rates by raising the bank's cost structure.

One further issue with capital requirements can be understood by examining our current framework: capital requirements can only implement outcomes strictly inside the Pareto frontier. When deposit rates are freely determined, the only outcomes that could potentially be equilibrium outcomes are those along the r_P line. The only Pareto-efficient outcome in that situation is $(\underline{k}, r)$ (see figure 6.2). But even that outcome is not feasible, because banks would have an incentive to deviate to gambling. Consider a capital requirement of $\underline{k}$. If prudent investment were the equilibrium outcome, then banks would offer a deposit rate of r and a Pareto-efficient outcome would be implemented. Unfortunately, with a capital requirement of $\underline{k}$, banks have an incentive to deviate to gambling because they will offer a higher deposit rate, collect more deposits, and thus earn a higher total return from gambling than from prudent investment. To understand why, recall that along the $\hat{r}(k)$ line, banks are just indifferent between prudent investing and gambling, *given a fixed amount of assets to invest*. But banks have a higher marginal return from gambling than they do from prudent investing, so at the deposit mobilization stage, they have an incentive to offer higher deposit rates, capture more deposits, and gamble. With freely determined deposit rates, banks always have the option of offering a high deposit rate and gambling. An effective capital requirement must then force banks to hold sufficient capital such that the best possible gambling deviation is less attractive than investing prudently. This forces the government to impose a capital requirement that is strictly greater than k. For concreteness, let's assume the minimum feasible capital requirement is $\bar{k}$.

We have identified three issues involved in using capital requirements in the context of freely determined deposit rates:

1. Capital requirements are an indirect instrument for lowering deposit rates.

2. Capital requirements reduce bank franchise value because they increase the bank's cost structure.

3. Capital requirements can only implement outcomes strictly inside the Pareto frontier.[9]

In contrast, deposit rate controls directly lower deposit rates, increase franchise value by creating future rents for banks, and can implement outcomes along the Pareto frontier.

In particular, consider a deposit rate ceiling of $\hat{r}(k_0)$ combined with a capital requirement of k_0. This outcome yields the exact same deposit rate while lowering the capital requirement from $\bar{k}$ to k_0. Depositors are indifferent, and banks are much better off, because they are forced to hold substantially less costly capital. Thus it is possible to implement a Pareto-dominant outcome by using a deposit rate ceiling in conjunction with a lower capital requirement.

6.3   Transitional Dynamics and the Need for Regulatory Overshooting

Our analysis so far considers the trade-offs a policymaker faces in a dynamic environment that is in a steady state. In the context of financial liberalization, however, policymakers are concerned not only with the regulation of the steady state system, but also with the question of how to get the banks to safely attain this liberalized steady state. In the period of transition the regulator may have some constraints on what regulation can be implemented immediately. In addition, the regulator may need to be particularly sensitive to the incentives and the behavior of banks in the period of transition. In this section we therefore examine some of the transitional challenges associated with financial liberalization.

We have already seen that in a steady-state dynamic environment the fact that *capital is costly* limits the usefulness of capital requirements. If we consider the problem of policy transitions, we are faced with an additional problem, namely, that *capital is sticky*. In general it is difficult for banks to increase their capital rapidly. Finding new sources of capital is time consuming, and raising the additional capital is expensive on the margin. Apart from the information problems of moral hazard and adverse selection, discussed extensively in the large literature on credit and equity rationing (see, for example, Stiglitz and Weiss 1981; Myers and Majluf 1984; Hellmann and Stiglitz 1999), there may be additional market liquidity problems, because a number of banks may all be trying to raise capital at the same time. And these problems may be further compounded if a country also has a legacy of underdeveloped stock markets and/or a financial system that is relatively closed to foreign investors.

At the beginning of financial liberalization, a bank may thus typically not be able to satisfy a regulator's desired capital requirement with its existing assets. Suppose now that it is also unable to raise the required amount of capital in short time. If the regulator were to strictly enforce the steady-state capital requirement immediately, then the only option for a capital-constrained bank would be to sell off a substantial part of its assets and to reduce the amount of its lending, recalling old loans and refusing new loans. Both of these policies would have severe consequences. If many assets are all sold off at the same time, asset prices are likely to fall, as assets markets respond to the sudden increase in supply (Shleifer and Vishny 1992). This means that banks receive fewer proceeds from the asset sale, thus weakening their capital base. Falling asset prices may also weaken the bank's existing loan portfolio, leading to further deterioration of its balance sheet. The reduction in lending might have even more serious implications, as it can have disastrous effects on economic activity, especially if a number of banks do this simultaneously. If no new loans are made, and existing loans are recalled or not renewed, the economy experiences a credit crunch; industrial investment falls and economic activity is severely affected.

With the understanding that a credit crunch would undermine the liberalization policy itself, policymakers tend to be understanding toward the problems of banks not being able to satisfy immediately the capital requirement imposed by regulators as part of the liberalization process. The critical question then becomes whether it is acceptable for a regulator to settle for a compromise in which banks phase in capital requirements over time, but all other elements of the financial liberalization program remain unchanged? The answer is no, as there is an important trap here in the adjustment process of moving toward a new steady state. In fact, for a number of reasons, regulators temporarily need *stricter* regulation to ensure an orderly transition to a liberalized steady-state banking equilibrium.

In fact, regulators and policymakers need to be particularly careful about bank behavior in the adjustment process and to guard against the possibility that banks may be tempted to gamble, especially in the early days of liberalization. The problem can be reduced to one simple but profound observation: *the announcement of financial liberalization creates an immediate shock to banks' franchise value*, even if the process of liberalization and the adjustment path to a new steady state are very gradual. The incentives a bank faces change in a discontinuous fashion the moment that a liberalization policy is announced. Even if the environment will change only gradually, and even if actual competition is several years away, the incentive for a bank to engage in gambling appears immediately at the announcement of the liberalization process.

Why does the announcement of financial liberalization matter so much for banks' incentives? This is where the dynamic analysis of the previous section comes in. A bank's incentive to gamble is governed largely by its franchise value, that is, the discounted net present value of the future profit streams. Even if nothing else has changed today, bank actions are guided by the benefit of still being in operation tomorrow. The announcement of future liberalization thus reduces the current franchise value of an incumbent bank.[10]

What is the implication of the sudden fall in franchise value? We can see from the equation derived in the previous section that the highest possible interest rate consistent with a prudent investment strategy (given by $\hat{r}$) falls. Supposing that the economy had previously been in equilibrium with a deposit rate at $\hat{r}$, the announcement of liberalization means that at the old deposit rate banks now have an incentive to gamble. Now consider that in the short run the amount of capital of the bank is sticky. To induce a bank to invest in a prudent portfolio in the period of transition, the regulator now needs to lower deposit rates, essentially to counteract the sudden decline in franchise value caused by the announcement of financial liberalization.

This is a striking result. To get to a steady-state regime of liberalization with higher deposit rates, an economy needs to go through a transitional period in which deposit rates are particularly low. This stringency is actually necessary for two reasons. First, it provides the appropriate incentives for banks not to gamble in the short run, as the system moves toward the steady state. And second, lower deposit rates allow banks to accumulate capital more quickly, which speeds up the adjustment process, as banks can build up internal capital to ready themselves for the higher capital requirement under liberalization. This is the irony of transitional dynamics: *to get to the liberalized banking equilibrium, it is faster and safer to enforce temporarily stricter deposit rate controls.*

This type of regulatory overshooting does not just apply to interest rate controls. To transition toward a regime of more competitive banking, it may be necessary to go through a period of more stringent regulation overall. One can think of a number of other policies that might help bridge the period of transition, during which banks are particularly prone to gamble and during which they still have only relatively modest levels of capital. First, there might be a temporary moratorium on all dividend payments of banks to their shareholders. This would ensure that retained earnings go toward building the capital base. It would also prevent shareholders from looting their banks by taking out the bank's value through high dividend payments before letting the bank go under, with the government bearing the liabilities to depositors (see Akerlof and Romer 1993). Another way of curtailing imprudent bank behavior is to be careful with lifting restrictions on the asset classes in which banks are allowed to invest. For example, it might be argued that banks should not be allowed to invest immediately in real estate or financial derivatives, asset classes that are particularly prone to gambling behavior. The problem here is not only that certain asset classes are inherently more risky than others, but also that it is more difficult to account for the true risk involved in investing in these assets.

The lack of understanding about the true risks of certain asset classes suggests an even broader problem, namely, the quality and intensity of regulatory oversight in the transition period. Banks' greater freedom after financial liberalization necessitates a closer regulatory scrutiny. During the transition period the need for prudential supervision is greatest: as banks experience falling franchise value, and as an industry shakeout occurs, greater desperation among the banks leads to greater incentives to gamble on resurrection. In addition, banks intending to invest prudently may make mistakes or seek high returns without fully appreciating the risks involved, exacerbating the need for sound regulation. The greater need for prudential oversight of banks in the transition period is unfortunately typically coupled with a great difficulty in providing effective supervision. In the early stages of liberalization there is usually a scarcity of experienced regulators and greater uncertainty about the type of supervision required. Furthermore, private-sector demand for such well-trained individuals increases tremendously at the same time. The public sector cannot meet the salaries the private sector offers, so typically at precisely the time when there needs to be greater strength in the public sector, its capabilities are weakened. These difficulties thus further point to the need to control the speed at which banks are allowed to invest in new, poorly understood asset classes.

In summary, examining the dynamic incentives of banks to invest prudently, we note that there is a particular danger of banks' engaging in gambling behavior in the early stages of financial liberalization. Even if the liberalization program is gradual— and we have seen that to avoid a credit crunch, the imposition of increased capital requirements on banks needs to be gradual—the announcement of financial liberalization reduces banks' franchise value immediately. This implies that stricter policies are needed in the transition period. In particular it is necessary to reduce deposit rates to a particularly low level and maintain them there. Moreover, restrictions on banks' investing in certain asset classes should be lifted only gradually, keeping in mind that such investments require better prudential oversight at a time when the regulatory institutions themselves are typically in the process of being revamped. Only once banks have accumulated sufficient levels of capital should deposit rate controls be relaxed. Obviously, as we have seen in the previous section, even then an argument might be made for mild deposit rate controls.

6.4   Conclusion

In this chapter we have argued that one can understand why financial liberalization has often led to banking crisis if one applies a dynamic framework of analyzing bank incentives. Banks may have incentives to invest in an inefficiently risky portfolio when they see their franchise value erode. Capital requirements alone are inadequate to check these incentives, since the high cost of holding capital may actually harm banks' franchise value and may thus undermine incentives for prudent investing. Instead, a policy of deposit rate controls may be more beneficial, as it allows regulators to lower the burden of capital requirements. In a period of transition the problems of bad banking tend to become more severe, as banks are experiencing significant declines in franchise value. Even if the liberalization process is gradual, the announcement of financial liberalization may affect bank behavior immediately. In these circumstances, a regulator may first want to tighten deposit rate controls before relaxing them. Especially if banks have difficulty in raising external capital, a lower deposit rate will also allow them to build up internal capital at a faster rate. This suggests that to have a faster and safer transition to a liberalized banking system, regulators need to accompany an announcement of liberalization with a temporarily stricter regime of regulation.

Notes

We would like to thank Jerry Caprio and seminar participants at the William Davidson Institute at the University of Michigan. All remaining errors are our own. This chapter represents the views of the authors and does not necessarily represent that of any organization with which they are or have been affiliated. The third author is on leave from Stanford University.

1. See Fischer and Chénard 1997 for some further evidence.

2. See Hellmann, Murdock, and Stiglitz 1996, 1997a, 1997b, 1998a, 1998b, and Stiglitz 1992, 1993.

3. See also Besanko and Kanatas 1996; Bhattacharya 1982; Dewatripont and Tirole 1994; Genotte and Pyle 1991; Gianmarino, Lewis, and Sappington 1993; and Rochet 1992.

4. Restraints on lending activities can also have an adverse effect on franchise value by limiting the bank's opportunity set for investment. The important issue is that these restrictions have two effects. First, they limit the bank's ability to invest in gambling assets, but second, they also reduce the bank's expected future profits, reducing franchise value and potentially increasing the bank's incentives to gamble. Restrictions on lending make sense as an instrument of prudential regulation only if they succeed in deterring gambling without significantly interfering with prudent investment.

5. See Caprio and Summers 1996 for a discussion of franchise value. Keeley 1990 and Demsetz, Saidenberg, and Strahan 1996 also provide some empirical evidence.

6. In Hellmann, Murdock, and Stiglitz 1998b we develop the formal model.

7. This assumption seems to reflect reality: most countries that do not have explicit deposit insurance tend to have some implicit insurance, especially for those banks that are too large to fail. We note, however, that deposit insurance is not necessary for the results obtained here; in Hellmann, Murdock, and Stiglitz 1998b we derive the same qualitative results in a model in which the government can credibly commit to a regime of no deposit insurance.

8. Gorton and Winton (1995) develop a general equilibrium model and derive from it that bank capital has positive opportunity cost. Further, Hellmann, Murdock, and Stiglitz (1998b) derive that provided that capital requirements are a binding constraint on bank behavior, capital has a positive opportunity cost.

9. There are additional problems with capital requirements. For example, it is exceedingly difficult to define adequate risk classes. And because capital is an accounting-based measure (unlike deposit rate controls, which are price-based), there may be many creative ways to circumvent the regulation. This implies that the quality of supervision itself affects the effectiveness of capital requirements. For example, banks may satisfy those requirements by selling off assets that have increased in value and while retaining those that have decreased in value. This has no real effect on the economic value of the bank's capital, but it increases the accounting measure of capital. Over time, this can result in a significant distortion in the book value of capital. Furthermore, in anticipation of the future need to dispose of assets selectively, banks may invest more in assets with high variability and with less reliable market indicators of value.

10. Note that in some instances there may be a few stronger banks that might benefit from liberalization, if they are expected to take market share away from other banks. The point, however, is, that many or most of the existing banks do not benefit from the increased competition. The decline in franchise value may be particularly dramatic for the weakest bank in the system, and the "average" incumbent is also hurt, as there will be more competition both among the existing banks and from potential new entrants.

References

Akerlof, G., and P. Romer. 1993. Looting: The economic underworld of bankruptcy for profit. *Brookings Papers on Economic Activity* 2:1–73.

Besanko, D., and G. Kanatas. 1996. The regulation of bank capital: Do capital standards promote bank safety? *Journal of Financial Intermediation* 5:160–183.

Bhattacharya, S. 1982. Aspects of monetary and banking theory and moral hazard. *Journal of Finance* 37, no. 2:371–384.

Caprio, G., and L. Summers. 1996. Finance and its reform: Beyond laissez-faire. In *Stability of the financial system*, ed. D. Papadimitriou, 400–421. New York: MacMillan.

Caprio, J., and D. Klingebiel. 1996. Bank insolvency: Bad luck, bad policy, or bad banking? Paper presented at The Annual World Bank Conference on Development Economics, World Bank, Washington, D.C., April.

Demirgüç-Kunt, A., and E. Detragiache. 1997. The determinants of banking crises: Evidence from developed and developing countries. World Bank, Washington, D.C. Mimeographed.

Demirgüç-Kunt, A., and E. Detragiache. 1998. Financial liberalization and financial fragility. Paper presented at The Annual World Bank Conference on Development Economics, World Bank, Washington, D.C., April 20–21.

Demsetz, R., M. Saidenberg, and P. Strahan. 1996. Banks with something to lose: The disciplinary role of franchise value. *Economic Policy Review* (Federal Reserve Bank of New York), 2, no. 2:1–14.

Dewatripont, M., and J. Tirole. 1994. *The prudential regulation of banks*. Cambridge: MIT Press.

Fischer, K., and M. Chénard. 1997. Financial liberalization causes banking systems' fragility. Working paper no. 97-12, Centre de recherche en économie et finance apliqueés, Université Laval, Quebec City, Quebec, Canada.

Genotte, G., and D. Pyle. 1991. Capital controls and bank risk. *Journal of Banking and Finance* 15:805–824.

Gianmarino, R., T. Lewis, and D. Sappington. 1993. An incentive approach to banking regulation. *Journal of Finance* 48, no. 4:1523–1542.

Gorton, Gary, and Andrew Winton. 1995. Bank capital regulation in general equilibrium. Working paper no. 5244, National Bureau of Economic Research, Cambridge, Mass.

Hellmann, T., K. Murdock, and J. Stiglitz. 1996. Deposit mobilization through financial restraint. In *Financial development and economic growth: Theory and experiences from developing economies*, ed. N. Hermes and R. Lensink, 219–246. London: Routledge.

Hellmann, T., K. Murdock, and J. Stiglitz. 1997a. Financial restraint: Toward a new paradigm. In *The role of government in East Asian economic development: Comparative institutional analysis*, ed. M. Aoki, M. Okuno-Fujiwara, and H. Kim, 163–207. Oxford: Oxford University Press.

Hellmann, T., K. Murdock, and J. Stiglitz. 1997b. Financial sector development policy: The importance of reputational capital and governance. In *Development strategy and management of the market economy*, vol. 2, ed. R. Sabot and I. Skékely, 269–323. Oxford: Oxford University Press.

Hellmann, T., K. Murdock, and J. Stiglitz. 1998a. Institutional foundations of East Asian economic development. In *Proceedings of an International Economic Association Round Table Conference*, ed. M. Aoki and Y. Hayami. London: Macmillan.

Hellmann, T., K. Murdock, and J. Stiglitz. 1998b. Liberalization, moral hazard in banking, and prudential regulation: Are capital requirements enough? Graduate School of Business research paper no. 1466, Stanford University, Stanford, Calif.

Hellmann, T., and J. Stiglitz. 1999. Credit and equity rationing in markets with adverse selection. *European Economic Review* 44, no. 2:281–304.

Keeley, M. 1990. Deposit insurance, risk, and market power in banking. *American Economic Review* 80, no. 5:1183–1200.

Myers, S., and N. Majluf. 1984. Corporate financing and investment decisions when firms have information that investors do not have. *Journal of Financial Economics* 13:187–221.

Rochet, J. 1992. Capital requirement and the behavior of commercial banks. *European Economic Review* 36:1137–1178.

Shleifer, A., and R. Vishny. 1992. Liquidation values and debt capacity: An equilibrium approach. *Journal of Finance* 47, no. 4:1343–1466.

Stiglitz, J. 1992. Introduction—S&L Bail-Out. In *The reform of the federal deposit insurance: Disciplining the government and protecting the taxpayers*, ed. J. R. Barth and R. D. Brumbaugh, Jr. New York: Harper Collins.

Stiglitz, J. 1993. The role of the state in financial markets. In *Proceedings of the Annual World Bank Conference on Development Economics*, 19–52. Washington, D.C.: World Bank.

Stiglitz, J., and A. Weiss. 1981. Credit rationing in markets with imperfect information. *American Economic Review* 71, no. 3:393–410.

7   Bank Liquidity Provision and Capital Regulation in Transition Economies

Gary Gorton and Andrew Winton

7.1   Introduction

Consider the structure and regulation of a transition economy's banking system. In most market economies, banks play important roles channeling savings to borrowers and providing a liquid medium of exchange through demand deposits and the payments system. Precisely because of this importance, banks are usually heavily regulated, and in developed countries this regulation has become increasingly focused on capital requirements, that is, the level of equity capital relative to deposits and other debt in a bank's financing mix. Bank equity capital is deemed important because bank failure is socially costly, and higher levels of capital in a bank reduce the chance that the bank will fail. Thus, given the relatively greater risk of loans and other bank assets in transition economies, a well-intentioned observer such as *The Economist* might well advocate bank capital requirements that match or even exceed those imposed in developed countries.[1]

We argue that this view is too simplistic, because it neglects the costs of bank capital, costs that are likely to be much higher in transition economies than in developed ones. Formal analysis of these costs can be found in Gorton and Pennacchi 1990, Qi 1993, and Gorton and Winton 1998a; in this chapter, we give the intuition behind the models presented in those analyses and pursue their policy implications for the specific case of transition economies.

Bank equity capital is a costly funding source because, unlike demand deposits and other bank liabilities, it is a poor vehicle for meeting liquidity needs. Being a junior claim to the bank's assets, bank equity bears most of the bank's risk and is thus very sensitive to information about the bank's situation. If someone has to liquidate her shareholdings to meet a sudden need for funds, for example, potential buyers may well be concerned that the seller is selling, not for liquidity reasons, but instead because she has private information that the shares are "lemons," that is, worth less than the going price.[2] By contrast, deposits have lower risk, making their value relatively insensitive to information about the bank and thus relatively immune to lemons concerns. Thus, deposits are a better hedge against potential liquidity needs.

In general equilibrium, a system-wide increase in bank equity capital forces individuals to hold more bank equity, decreasing aggregate bank deposits; thus, individuals are more likely to be forced to draw on equity holdings to meet their liquidity needs, increasing overall liquidity costs. If the costs are high enough, it may be socially optimal to choose bank capital levels that leave banks with a significant risk of failure.

Transition economies have a number of features that intensify these liquidity costs of bank capital. Bank asset quality is low in such economies, making bank equity more risky, more subject to lemons concerns, and thus a worse liquidity hedge. Low levels of disclosure by banks and relatively small and illiquid stock markets exacerbate these problems. Banks and bank assets are a large fraction of the financial system, wealth is low, and liquid assets are few, increasing the relative impact of a system-wide increase in bank capital. As a result, aggregate liquidity costs of increased bank capital are likely to be quite significant in transition economies.

In addition to aggregate liquidity concerns, the private objectives of the existing bank shareholders may constrain regulators in a transition economy. The shareholders' private costs of additional capital are higher than social costs, both because additional capital creates a transfer to depositors (by making their deposits safer) and because issuing additional capital requires a net transfer to new shareholders that exceeds the overall increase in social liquidity costs. At the same time, to the extent that bank failure involves negative externalities, the social costs of bank failure exceed its private costs; since the value of bank capital is that it reduces the chance of bank failure, the social benefit of additional capital exceeds the private benefit to existing shareholders. Since their costs of raising capital are higher and their benefits from raising that capital are lower, shareholders prefer a lower level of capital than the social optimum.

Thus, faced with a higher capital requirement than they would choose on their own, bank shareholders may either refuse to comply or else shrink the size of their bank rather than raise additional capital. In the first case, the regulator must either close the bank—thus putting the bank out of operation and shrinking the banking system—or else back down, so that bank capital levels and the chance of failure are what the shareholders would freely choose. In the second case, banks themselves shrink the banking system.

Shrinking the banking system is likely to be quite costly in transition economies. Recall that bank capital requirements are aimed at preventing bank failure and ensuing social costs. One social cost is that borrower-specific information the bank has gathered through its lending relationships may be lost, damaging borrowers' liquidity; another is that there may be harmful spillovers from one bank's failure to other banks and the payments system itself: the so-called domino effect. Regulatory bank closures can create similar effects, and even reductions in bank balance sheets can be costly: some borrowers will lose critical funding sources, and reductions in scale can hamper the efficiency of the payments system as a whole. Both issues loom large in transition economies, in which borrowers typically have few alternative sources of funds, and payments systems are small and struggling with efficiency problems to begin with (Gorton and Winton 1998b). Indeed, the costs of shrinking the banking system in such economies may further undermine regulators' credibility in enforcing higher capital requirements, since banks know that regulators will be tempted to back down ex post rather than enforce requirements that lead to such a costly outcome.

Given this state of affairs, regulators have three options. They can try to encourage foreign equity investment, since foreign investors may have relatively lower liquidity demands than domestic investors. They can subsidize incumbent banks by restricting entry, since higher profit margins may reduce banks' risk of failure and may increase banks' incentives to raise additional bank capital so as to further reduce the odds of losing high future profits. Finally, regulators can aim for capital levels that banks will go along with, accepting that banks may have significant chances of failure.

Although regulators should certainly work toward the long-run goals of increasing bank disclosure and stock market efficiency and liquidity, in the short run, the third of these alternatives, forbearance, may dominate. Until better disclosure and stock markets are in place, attracting foreign equity investment will be difficult, and it is likely to be politically costly. Furthermore, the existing inefficiency in scale and expertise of banking systems in transition economies makes entry restrictions a costly choice. As we argue in Gorton and Winton 1998b, regulators in transition economies may simply be unable to achieve both efficient and stable banking systems in the short run, and efficiency may be the better short-term goal.

The rest of this chapter is structured as follows. Section 7.2 discusses costs of bank failure and to what degree they apply to other reductions in the size of the banking system. Section 7.3 gives a fuller account of the liquidity costs of bank equity capital, and section 7.4 gives a fuller account of the potential conflict between regulatory and bank objectives in this setting. Finally, section 7.5 discusses the three alternative policy responses just outlined.

7.2   Costs of Bank Failure

As mentioned in the previous section, bank failure can have significant costs above and beyond direct losses to bank shareholders and depositors. One source of these costs is the disruption of bank-borrower relationships; another is the domino effect, in which one bank's failure causes difficulties for other banks and the payments system as a whole. We now discuss the nature of these costs, how they apply to situations in which regulators or banks themselves choose to shrink the banking system, and why it is likely that bank shareholders do not fully internalize them, creating a gap between social and private costs of bank failure.

Evaluating, financing, and monitoring borrowers are key functions banks perform.[3] Moreover, banks tend to finance borrowers with limited access to public securities markets; thus, most of the information a bank obtains by evaluating and monitoring borrowers is not publicly available. Now suppose that the bank faces financial distress. Borrowers that depend on this bank must now find other financing sources, but these new sources will be concerned that the borrowers are not creditworthy; after all, the bank's distress suggests that its borrowers are generally in bad shape, and borrowers in relatively good shape are less likely to need additional financing. Free access to the bank's information about its borrowers would mitigate these lemons concerns among the new financing sources, but such information may be hard to transmit credibly and cheaply: because it is in trouble, the bank has an incentive to claim that *all* its loans are in good shape, regardless of the truth. Thus, a bank's financial distress causes liquidity costs for its borrowers.

There is evidence that these costs are significant. Slovin, Sushka, and Polonchek (1993) study the collapse of Continental Illinois Bank (at that time one of the top 10 banks in the United States) in 1984. The share prices of publicly traded firms for which Continental was a major funding source dropped significantly when Continental failed in May 1984; when the Federal Deposit Insurance Corporation (FDIC) resolved the situation in July 1984 by nationalizing the bank, share prices of these firms recovered, suggesting that the market felt that this would revive a significant source of funds for these firms. Similarly, Kang and Stulz (1997) show that, during Japan's ongoing banking crisis of the 1990s, the shares of firms that depended on banks for financing significantly underperformed those that did not depend on banks. Since firms with publicly traded stock are less dependent on bank finance than are those firms without any public market access, these results understate the likely effect of bank financial distress on bank borrowers as a whole. This should be especially true in transition economies, where public securities markets are relatively weak and few firms have access to them.

Another cost of bank failure is the domino effect, in which one bank's distress causes other banks to topple. In part, this could reflect banks' exposures to one another, since banks rely on interbank borrowing and lending to correct their own funding imbalances. In addition, one bank's failure could inflame concerns among investors that all banks are in trouble: because bank loans involve considerable private information, bank balance sheets are relatively opaque to investors, and a bank's failure may loom large in the absence of credible information about other banks' quality. Studying the U.S. bank holiday declared during the Great Depression, Bernanke (1983) finds evidence of significant domino effects. Again, these concerns are particularly strong in transition economies: with small numbers of banks, any interbank exposures are relatively concentrated, and with poor public disclosure, bank balance sheets are especially opaque.

A further spillover cost of bank failure concerns the payments system. Payments systems exhibit strong economies of scale, both because transaction systems' higher volumes allow their fixed costs to be spread more widely, and because there are diversification gains (with more transactions, the relative variance of imbalances falls). As we discuss and detail in Gorton and Winton 1998b, payments systems in transition economies are relatively small and inefficient, so the sudden collapse of one or more banks could worsen an already poorly performing system.

Regulatory bank closure may generate many of the costs associated with bank failure. Since a closed bank's failure to comply with capital requirements is likely to be viewed as a signal of the bank's poor quality, its borrowers may find it hard to get alternative funding. This will cause more failures among the closed bank's borrowers, which in turn will increase the risk of any other banks that have exposures to the closed bank. Relatively uninformed investors may view the bank's closure as a bad signal about the state of the banking system in general, leading to further difficulties for other banks. To the extent that there is a short-run disruption in the closed bank's operations, the scale of the payments system will also decrease. Thus, although bank closure may be a somewhat less negative signal than outright bank failure, it is still likely to cause problems for the bank's borrowers and other banks.

Some of these costs can be reduced if regulators can get another bank to take over the closed bank's business and assets. However, acquirers will have the same lemons concerns as other market participants, so they may be reluctant to take on this potential exposure; the FDIC was unable to find a buyer for Continental Illinois Bank between May and July 1984. Also, acquisitions take time and effort to digest even when the target is a healthy institution; they are harder still when the target is troubled, and even harder yet if managerial expertise is in short supply, which may well be the case in a transition economy. Thus, some disruption in the closed bank's operations seems inevitable.

Suppose now that a bank chooses to comply with regulators' increased capital requirements by shrinking its loans rather than by raising additional capital. Clearly, some of its borrowers will find it more difficult to get necessary funding; thus, the shrinkage will have some negative impact on bank borrowers, though less than outright closure or failure would probably cause. Again, the negative effects will be relatively greater in transition economies, in which financing alternatives are relatively few.

Thus, bank failures, closures, or balance sheet reductions are all likely to have significant social costs. Bank shareholders are likely to internalize some, but not all, of these costs. For example, Sharpe (1990) and Rajan (1992) show that a bank may be able to capture much of the value of its relationship-specific information by charging existing borrowers higher rates (if a borrower balks and goes elsewhere, new lenders will be concerned that the borrower may be a lemon that the old bank has cut off); thus, bank shareholders themselves will lose valuable future rents if the bank fails or is closed. The same analysis, however, shows that shareholders won't capture all of this value unless the borrower has no bargaining power at all. One factor that influences bargaining power is the degree to which the legal system protects creditor rights: more protection strengthens lenders' bargaining power, since they can threaten to go to court and enforce their claims. Since such legal protections are weak in many transition economies, transition economy banks may not be able to appropriate a large fraction of these potential informational rents. Furthermore, unless the bank has total monopoly power, damage to other banks and the payments system will be shared with shareholders, borrowers, and depositors at other banks and with society at large.

Costs of a bank's failure or closure can also be viewed as benefits of the bank's continued operation. Following common practice, we refer to these benefits as the value of a bank charter, or "charter value" for short. Thus, the preceding discussion suggests that a bank's social charter value exceeds the private charter value that shareholders can capture and that the difference between the two may be particularly large in transition economies.

7.3   The Liquidity Costs of Bank Equity Capital

We now turn to the costs of bank equity capital. As discussed in section 7.1, equity is a worse hedge against liquidity needs than bank deposits because equity is subject to greater lemons concerns. After discussing how this comes about, we discuss how these lemons concerns create social costs and how changes in the economic environment are likely to affect these costs.

As a junior claim to the bank's assets, equity bears more relative risk for any given change in these assets' value than do deposits. In turn, greater relative risk means that any private information about a bank's asset quality has greater relative impact on its equity's value than on its deposits' value. To see how this causes lemons problems, consider the market for a particular bank's equity.[4] Suppose some individuals are privately informed about the bank's stock value: half the time, they find out the bank stock is worth $9 per share; half the time, it is worth $11 per share. By contrast, the best guess of uninformed investors is that the bank's stock is worth $10 per share on average.

From time to time, any investor may have a sudden need for funds (a "liquidity need"). If shareholders with liquidity needs were the only sellers, the selling price would be $10, less any transactions costs; after all, the liquidity need itself is unlikely to be highly correlated with inside information on the bank's true value. However, at this price, investors with private information that the shares are worth only $9 will also wish to sell. Since uninformed buyers don't know if they are dealing with an informed investor selling strategically or an investor selling to meet liquidity needs, the actual selling price will be between $9 and $10, depending on the buyer's best guess as to the relative numbers of liquidity-driven sellers and informed strategic sellers. Greater numbers of strategic sellers will cause the price to drop, since the stock is more likely to be coming from someone who knows it is only worth $9; conversely, greater numbers of liquidity-driven sellers will cause the price to rise. Similar arguments can be used on the buying side to show that, so long as some buyers are driven by strategic concerns and others by concerns unrelated to the bank's value, the buying price must be between $10 and $11, and this price will rise or fall with the relative number of informed strategic buyers.

Thus, the presence of informed traders causes a spread between selling and buying prices, and this spread rises or falls as relatively more or fewer trades are due to strategic behavior by investors with private information. This creates a cost for an investor with liquidity needs: after all, since the investor's need is uncorrelated with the stock's true value, the bank's shares could be worth either $9 or $11 with equal probability, yet buyers pay a price below $10 because of their concern that they may be getting a "lemon."

Some authors suggest that these costs to liquidity sellers are not a social problem, since the liquidity seller's loss is the strategic seller's gain (the informed strategic seller gets a price above $9 even though she knows the shares are only worth $9). These zero-sum transfers, however, lead to other costs. Leland (1992) shows that the additional risk that informed trading imposes on liquidity traders may hurt overall welfare when investors are risk averse. Qi (1993) shows that, by increasing banks' cost of capital, informed trading reduces aggregate investment. Finally, in Gorton and Winton 1998a, we show that the presence of liquidity sellers means that there are gains to gathering costly private information about the bank's asset value; these gains increase if the relative volume of liquidity trades increases (there are more liquidity traders to take advantage of) or if the inherent risk of bank equity increases (equity will be more sensitive to private information about the bank's condition). All else equal, resources spent in this fashion are a deadweight loss.

Clearly, *some* information gathering is useful, since more-accurate share prices may have beneficial effects on resource allocation. If many investors are all chasing the same information, however, making a profit only because of the presence of liquidity-driven trades, duplication of effort will quite probably occur, so that the marginal *social* benefit of additional information gathering is small relative to the marginal cost. As Hirshleifer (1971) pointed out, additional information production is not always socially beneficial. This seems particularly relevant to banks, since one of their key functions is to provide a liquid means of payment that requires little information gathering. Moreover, more information gathering means more informed trading, which increases the costs analyzed in Leland 1992 and Qi 1993.

Since bank deposits are much less risky than bank equity, their value is less sensitive to information. This reduces the lemons problems investors face when using deposits to meet liquidity needs.[5] Also, since deposits are less sensitive to information about the issuing bank's situation, holders of deposits have much less incentive to gather such information; this means that parties using deposits for transactions are less likely to be informed, further reducing the incidence of lemons costs. Lower lemons costs are most attractive to investors with a high chance of facing liquidity needs; conversely, since high liquidity needs leave little freedom to trade strategically, these are the investors least interested in acquiring costly private information for trading purposes. Thus, deposits' lower risk creates a "virtuous circle," making them a better payment vehicle and attracting investors most interested in holding such a vehicle to meet their liquidity needs.

Just as deposits are most attractive to investors with high liquidity needs, bank equity is most attractive to those with relatively low liquidity needs: these investors are most able to trade strategically, and equity's greater risk allows them to leverage the value of any information that they acquire. In equilibrium, bank shares will be concentrated in the hands of investors with relatively low liquidity needs and deposits in the hands of those with higher liquidity needs.

Now suppose that banks throughout the system issue shares so as to raise additional equity capital. By definition, buyers of shares must either use bank deposits to pay for the shares or else sell other financial assets; if other assets are sold, the buyers of *those* assets must either use bank deposits to pay, or sell yet other assets, etc. In general equilibrium, one of two things must happen: either nonbank financial assets are transferred to the banking system, or else the level of deposits falls to offset the increase in bank capital.

If other risky assets are transferred to the banking system, the increase in capital resulting from their transfer won't have as much effect in reducing the risk of bank failure, which is the goal. On the other hand, if the assets transferred are low-risk substitutes for deposits (such as currency), there is still a drop in aggregate liquid assets held by economic agents other than banks, and the effects are similar to those in the case where deposits drop. Moreover, deposit levels are more likely to drop as bank assets are a greater fraction of total financial assets, which is often the case in transition economies. For simplicity, consider the case in which aggregate deposit levels drop to offset an increase in bank capital.

Since all banks are raising additional capital, there is a significant jump in the supply of bank equity. To absorb this, either individuals already holding bank equity will draw down any liquidity reserves of deposits that they hold, or individuals with higher expected liquidity needs who previously held only deposits will now buy bank equity. Either way, liquidity reserves decrease, and on the margin individuals will now more likely be forced to sell bank shares to meet liquidity needs. This in turn implies that more equity trades will be motivated by liquidity needs, but this makes gathering information for use in trading more attractive. The net result is that costly gathering of information increases; additional bank capital has a social cost.[6]

Next, consider some factors that increase incentives to gather information for speculative purposes. A deterioration in the quality of a bank's assets makes equity more risky, increasing its sensitivity to private information about the bank's condition and thus making informed trading more attractive. Similarly, a decline in the quality or availability of public information about banks increases the trading advantage conferred by private information, making such information more attractive. Since the quality of bank loans and of banks' public disclosures is lower in transition economies than in developed economies, it follows that the social costs of additional bank capital will be especially great in transition economies.

A capital increase will also be more expensive as its size increases relative to the overall supply of financial assets or as the demand for liquid assets is relatively greater. Thus, if the banking sector makes up a large fraction of the economy's financial assets, a capital increase represents a large relative shift from liquid to illiquid assets. Also, if individual wealth in the economy is relatively low, liquidity needs may represent a greater fraction of individual wealth, increasing the costs of holding illiquid bank equity. Again, both issues seem particularly relevant in transition economies, in which banks are a critical part of the relatively small financial sector, wealth levels are low, and the supply of liquid assets is also low.[7]

To summarize, in this section we have argued that, because it is riskier and thus more sensitive to information, bank equity is inferior to bank deposits as a vehicle for meeting liquidity needs. Forcing investors to hold more bank equity increases the incidence of lemons problems and related costs, creating a social cost of increasing bank capital requirements. These costs are greater as bank loan quality is worse, public information about banks is less revealing, banks' share of overall financial assets is larger, or wealth levels relative to likely liquidity needs are lower—all of which are characteristics of transition economies in comparison with developed economies such as that of the United States. Thus, the social costs of additional bank capital are likely to be high in transition economies.

7.4   The Conflict between Regulatory and Private Objectives

In section 7.1, we suggested that the net gain to a bank's existing shareholders from additional capital is typically less than the net gain to society: private benefits are lower than social benefits, and private costs are higher than social costs. After motivating this point more fully in this section, we explore the implications it has for socially minded regulators' choice of bank capital requirements.

In section 7.2, we discussed why continued bank operation is likely to have a social charter value that exceeds its private value to the bank's shareholders, particularly in transition economies. Since bank capital reduces the chance of bank failure and subsequent loss of charter value, it follows that the social benefit of any given capital increase is greater than the private benefit.

Turning to the question of costs, to raise capital, bank shareholders must attract new shareholders. At a minimum, they must reimburse these new shareholders for expected liquidity costs, so they internalize the social cost of additional capital. Raising capital, however, creates two transfers from existing bank shareholders to other agents. Since these transfers make existing shareholders worse off without directly affecting aggregate welfare, they increase the private costs of additional bank capital relative to the social liquidity cost.

The first transfer is a variant of the "debt overhang" or "underinvestment" problem of Myers 1977. Higher levels of capital absorb more of any losses a bank may suffer on its assets, reducing expected shortfalls on bank deposits. This is a windfall to depositors: the risk to their deposits is lower, yet the nominal rate on deposits has not changed, so they are better off. Of course, this gain to depositors is a loss to the bank's existing shareholders.[8] Since this transfer increases with the risk of the bank's assets (deposits are more risky to start, so additional equity causes a greater reduction in risk), and bank loans in transition economies are generally more risky than those in developed economies, this suggests that the debt overhang transfer can be quite high in transition economies.

The second transfer reflects the nature of the liquidity costs of bank capital. If additional shares are to be issued, they must be priced so that the marginal new shareholder is willing to buy them. In making the decision on whether to buy the shares, the marginal new shareholder takes into account her chance of facing liquidity needs that force her to sell her shares and incur the lemons-related liquidity costs already discussed. Given that all banks in the system are raising substantial amounts of additional capital, this marginal new shareholder will have significantly higher expected liquidity needs than the average new shareholder. (To see this, consider what would happen if shares were sold piecemeal: as more and more shares were issued, buyers would be more likely to be either existing shareholders digging deeper into liquidity reserves or investors who formerly held no shares at all because of liquidity concerns.) Since the share price bears a discount that reflects the marginal shareholder's expected liquidity costs, new shareholders with lower expected liquidity costs get a bargain. Once again, this comes at the expense of the old shareholders.

As is the case with social liquidity costs, the liquidity cost transfer to new shareholders is likely to be especially significant in transition economies. Lemons-related liquidity costs are likely to be high, both because the risk of bank assets makes bank equity more risky and prone to lemons problems and because public information about banks is of relatively poor quality. Aggregate wealth and liquid assets are low, suggesting that the supply of funds for new shares is likely to be rather inelastic. Finally, to the extent that banks account for a large fraction of all financial assets, a system-wide increase in bank capital will represent a significant shift in asset holdings.

In sum, the private costs of additional bank capital are higher than the social costs because of both the debt overhang transfer to depositors and the liquidity cost transfer to new shareholders, and the difference between private and social costs is likely to be particularly high in transition economies. Since private benefits from additional capital are smaller than social benefits, the net effect is that bank shareholders are much more reluctant to raise additional capital than are socially minded regulators.

Of course, regulators can simply tell banks to raise additional capital or be closed. If this threat is credible, banks will be more willing to raise capital: after all, if they don't, they lose their bank's private charter value with certainty, which increases the downside of not raising capital. If private charter values are low, however, even this threat won't have much weight relative to the private costs of raising additional capital. Again, the discussion in section 7.2 suggests that private charter values may be relatively low in transition economies (banks' bargaining power vis-à-vis borrowers is limited), whereas private costs are likely to be high. Thus, regulators that make credible threats to close banks for noncompliance with increased capital requirements may well find themselves closing banks, with all the attendant social costs discussed in section 7.2; if these costs are high enough, the regulators will prefer to choose weaker capital requirements with which banks will comply.

On a similar note, since capital requirements are typically expressed as ratios of capital to some risk-weighted sum of bank assets, banks that view raising additional capital as costly may prefer to comply with increased capital requirements by reducing their assets. Since the Basle Accord guidelines give loans the highest risk weight among typical bank asset classes, loans are an obvious place for such reduction.[9] Concern that higher capital requirements may have led to such a lending cutback or "credit crunch" in the United States in the early 1990s led to a great deal of empirical work. As summarized by Sharpe (1995), the evidence suggests that capital concerns did affect bank loan growth during that time period, although other forces that reduced bank capital levels in the late 1980s and early 1990s were probably more important than any one change in banking regulation per se. However, this was in the United States, where capital markets are far more active and liquid and banks are a much smaller part of the financial system than they are in transition economies. With banks in transition economies being much more reluctant to raise capital and cutbacks in lending being much more disruptive, regulators in those economies may well prefer looser capital requirements over stricter ones that induce a credit crunch.

This leads to a further problem: the threat of closing banks for noncompliance may not be credible in transition economies precisely because the social costs of bank closure are likely to be very high. Suppose that a bank refuses to raise any capital beyond the level that bank shareholders would freely choose themselves. Faced with the prospect of closing the bank and incurring the costs of closure for certain, regulators may well back down: after all, the social costs of certain bank closure may exceed the expected costs of letting the bank continue and fail with some probability below one. Knowing that regulators will behave in this fashion, banks will ignore regulatory capital requirements that they would not freely choose themselves, and the credibility of regulators is nil.

Even if the cost of closing a single bank does not exceed the cost of letting the bank continue with significant risk of failure, the costs of closing most banks in an already small and fragile financial system likely exceed the costs of letting them continue with significant risk of failure. In this case, if most banks believe that regulatory threats of closure are not credible, their belief is self-fulfilling: large numbers of banks will refuse to raise capital to the socially desired level, and regulators will back down rather than close much of the banking system.[10]

7.5 Policy Implications

Although the risk level of banks in transition economies suggests that additional bank capital would be very helpful in reducing the risk of bank failure, our discussion suggests that raising bank capital in these economies is especially costly: social costs linked to bank equity's illiquidity are high, bank shareholders' private incentives to raise capital are low, and regulators' ability to credibly enforce strict capital guidelines are limited. Given these constraints, what can regulators do to bolster bank capitalization? Below, we consider three alternatives: attracting foreign equity capital, imposing entry restrictions so as to subsidize domestic banks, and "forbearance."

7.5.1 Foreign Equity Capital

Since capital markets in developed economies are better developed than those in transitional economies and wealth levels are higher, investors from these countries may be better able to commit equity capital over the long term, reducing the likelihood that they will be forced to sell their equity holdings and incur lemons-related costs. Recall that these costs are the key social cost of bank capital and are an important component of private costs to existing bank shareholders; at first glance, cheap, "patient" foreign capital would seem to resolve both issues, leaving only the potential debt overhang cost to be overcome.

This ignores a number of likely complications, however. First, foreign investors will demand safeguards: better disclosure, better corporate governance procedures, and legal protections for minority shareholders. If these features were fully developed, the illiquidity of bank equity capital in transition economies would be a lesser issue to start with.

Also, foreign sources of capital may be limited in practice. Given the risk and illiquidity of transition economy stock markets and the necessity of having specialized country knowledge for investment in that country's banks to be profitable, equity investment from foreign sources is likely to come from institutional investors rather than individuals and from institutions interested in taking stakes large enough to compensate for the required investment in specialized information. A further reason for taking large stakes would be to maintain clout with bank management, incumbent shareholders, and regulators in the transition economy, especially given the relative weakness of investor safeguards in such economies. Many institutions, however, have regulatory limits on their ability to take large illiquid stakes, and institutions that are subject to investor withdrawals (such as mutual funds, or pension managers under contracts that are subject to frequent performance review) may balk at tying up large sums in illiquid markets from which exit is difficult. Perhaps the best source of capital would be foreign banks looking for entry into the market: their goal would give them a longer-term horizon, their banking expertise would make it easier for them to evaluate the target bank's situation, and, as suggested by Caprio and Levine (1994), their expertise might also be a source of useful skills needed by the target bank.[11]

A third concern with this source of finance is that, when capital is most needed—when the transition economy is troubled and bank asset quality is weak—even institutional investors may balk at investing in transition economies. Weaker bank assets increase the risk of bank equity, magnifying the informational problems previously noted, and the increased risk of bank failure may increase the risk of exploitative behavior by bank managers, incumbent shareholders, or even the government. The flight of capital from East Asia in the fall of 1997 illustrates some of these issues.

Finally, foreign ownership of banks may create political problems for the government: during a downturn, even domestic banks tend to be unpopular with borrowers and others, and foreign ownership will only intensify this backlash. Also, since foreign shareholders have less at stake in the country, they may be less subject to governmental pressure to make concessions in a downturn.

7.5.2 Entry Restrictions

If the costs of domestic or foreign equity are great enough, another alternative is to restrict entry, increasing incumbent banks' market power and profitability. One advantage of this approach is that higher profit margins reduce a bank's chance of failure, serving as a direct substitute for costly additional bank capital.[12]

Entry restrictions may also reduce banks' reluctance to raise additional capital. First, since the bank loses future profits if it fails, subsidies increase the bank's private charter value (see Marcus 1984); with higher charter value at stake, bank shareholders benefit more from raising additional capital and reducing the bank's chance of failure. Second, higher profit margins can reduce the relative risk of bank profits and thus the relative risk of bank equity. Since less risky equity means lower lemons costs, this reduces the discount demanded by the marginal new shareholder, thus reducing the liquidity cost transfer from old shareholders and making additional equity more attractive to them. Also, less-risky equity reduces investors' incentives to spend resources gathering costly information, lowering the social costs of bank capital.

The drawback to entry restrictions is the accompanying distortion in bank incentives. Market power may lead to a smaller banking system: higher loan rates will discourage borrowing, and lower deposit rates will discourage saving. As shown in Gorton and Winton 1998b, incumbent banks may have excessive incentives to lend to inefficient state-owned enterprises (SOEs) and former SOEs rather than newer, more efficient firms. Finally, to the extent bank management is not fully aligned with bank shareholders, market power would allow bank management to become lax, eroding expense and risk controls. Since transition economy banking systems are already inefficiently small, allocate large amounts of credit to SOEs, and lack managerial expertise and controls, the costs of a policy of discouraging entry could be quite high.[13]

7.5.3   Forbearance

A third alternative is simply to allow banks to raise the amount of capital they desire, pushing for additional capital only to the extent that this request is credible and will not shrink the banking system. This means accepting a banking system that is riskier than the social optimum, even including social costs of additional capital.

In the short run, this forbearance strategy may be the best of the three alternatives. Encouraging foreign equity investment is likely to be difficult, in terms both of attracting foreign investors and of political costs. Also, attracting foreign investors requires better bank disclosure than exists in most transition economies and more efficient, liquid stock markets; although these changes should be pursued, it must be recognized that they will take years to achieve. Restricting entry to subsidize domestic banks is likely to have high costs because transition economy banking systems are extremely inefficient to begin with. Given the high costs of additional bank capital and the need to expand the scale and efficiency of the banking sector, regulators in transition economies may be better off sacrificing some degree of bank stability in favor of improved efficiency.

Notes

We are grateful to the institute for its support and to Anna Meyendorff, Anjan Thakor, and Sharon Nakpairat for organizing both the conference and this volume. We would also like to thank the conference participants and especially our discussant, Steven Fries, for their comments.

1. See Valencia 1997.

2. Akerlof (1970) gives the classic formulation of the "lemons" problem, while Glosten and Milgrom (1985) apply this to the secondary stock market.

3. For theoretical models of such "delegated monitoring," see Campbell and Kracaw 1980, Diamond 1984, Ramakrishnan and Thakor 1984, and Boyd and Prescott 1986.

4. This is a simple example of the model of Gorton and Pennacchi (1990).

5. Indeed, Gorton and Pennacchi (1990) and Qi (1993) argue that one benefit of government deposit insurance is that it further reduces the risk of bank deposits and thus the size of potential lemons costs.

6. If equity levels are very low, deposits may be so risky that even depositors gather information for use in trading; in this case, additional equity capital may make *deposits* a better liquidity hedge by reducing their

risk. However, once a critical level is reached, deposits won't be risky enough for depositors to become speculators. Also, any government guarantee (explicit or otherwise) will reduce incentives of depositors to gather costly information.

7. See Gorton and Winton 1998b for evidence on liquid-asset levels.

8. Since new shareholders won't buy shares for more than they think the shares are worth, shares are issued at a price that reflects this transfer to depositors, causing a capital loss to the old shareholders. This debt overhang problem occurs even if deposits are insured, though in this case the reduction in the risk to deposits benefits the deposit insurer rather than the depositors.

9. See Committee on Banking Regulations and Supervisory Practices 1987.

10. This "too-many-to-fail" argument mirrors Mitchell's (1997) analysis of the problem regulators may face in trying to force banks to adopt tough policies toward borrowers.

11. One example of such a partnership is that between International Nederlander Group and Bank Śląski, studied in Abarbanell and Bonin 1997.

12. Another form of subsidy is underpriced deposit insurance, but without entry restrictions this would be dangerous. Such insurance makes entry easier (see Winton 1997), and subsequent competition drives down profit margins, reducing private charter values and encouraging excessive risk taking (see Marcus 1984); the savings and loan crisis in the United States in the 1980s is a case in point.

13. For details on these issues, see Gorton and Winton 1998b and Meyendorff and Snyder 1997.

References

Abarbanell, Jeffery, and John Bonin. 1997. Bank privatization in Poland: The case of Bank Śląski. *Journal of Comparative Economics* 25:31–61.

Akerlof, George. 1970. The market for "lemons": Quality uncertainty and the market mechanism. *Quarterly Journal of Economics* 84:488–500.

Bernanke, Ben. 1983. Nonmonetary effects of the financial crisis in the propagation of the Great Depression. *American Economic Review* 73:257–276.

Boyd, John, and Edward Prescott. 1986. Financial intermediary coalitions. *Journal of Economic Theory* 38:211–232.

Campbell, Tim, and William Kracaw. 1980. Information production, market signalling, and the theory of financial intermediation. *Journal of Finance* 35:863–882.

Caprio, Gerard, and Ross Levine. 1994. Reforming finance in transitional socialist economies. *World Bank Research Observer* 9:1–24.

Committee on Banking Regulations and Supervisory Practices. 1987. *Proposals for international convergence of capital measurement and capital standards*. Basel: Bank for International Settlements.

Diamond, Douglas W. 1984. Financial intermediation and delegated monitoring. *Review of Economic Studies* 51, no. 3:393–414.

Glosten, Lawrence, and Paul Milgrom. 1985. Bid, ask, and transaction prices in a specialist market with heterogeneously informed traders. *Journal of Financial Economics* 13:71–100.

Gorton, Gary, and George Pennacchi. 1990. Financial intermediaries and liquidity creation. *Journal of Finance* 45:49–72.

Gorton, Gary, and Andrew Winton. 1998a. Liquidity provision and the social cost of bank capital. Finance Department working paper no. 236, Northwestern University, Evanston, Ill.

Gorton, Gary, and Andrew Winton. 1998b. Banking in transition economies: Does efficiency require instability? *Journal of Money, Credit, and Banking* 30:621–650.

Hirshleifer, Jack. 1971. The private and social value of information and the reward to inventive activity. *American Economic Review* 61:561–574.

Kang, Jun-Koo, and René Stulz. 1997. Is bank-centered corporate governance worth it? A cross-sectional analysis of the performance of Japanese firms during the asset price deflation. Dice Center working paper no. 97-6, Ohio State University.

Leland, Hayne. 1992. Insider trading: Should it be prohibited? *Journal of Political Economy* 100:859–887.

Marcus, Alan. 1984. Deregulation and bank financial policy. *Journal of Banking and Finance* 8:557–565.

Meyendorff, Anna, and Edward Snyder. 1997. Transactional structures of bank privatizations in Central Europe and Russia. *Journal of Comparative Economics* 25:5–30.

Myers, Stewart. 1977. Determinants of corporate borrowing. *Journal of Financial Economics* 5:147–175.

Qi, Jianping. 1993. Efficient investment and depository intermediaries. Working paper, University of South Florida.

Rajan, Raghuram. 1992. Insiders and outsiders: The choice between informed and arm's-length debt. *Journal of Finance* 47:1367–1400.

Ramakrishnan, Ram, and Anjan Thakor. 1984. Information reliability and a theory of financial intermediation. *Review of Economic Studies* 51:415–432.

Sharpe, Steven. 1990. Asymmetric information, bank lending and implicit contracts: A stylized model of customer relationships. *Journal of Finance* 45:1069–1087.

Sharpe, Steven. 1995. Bank capitalization, regulation, and the credit crunch: A critical review of the research findings. Working paper, Federal Reserve Board of Governors, Washington, D.C.

Slovin, Myron, Marie Sushka, and John Polonchek. 1993. The value of bank durability: Borrowers as bank stakeholders. *Journal of Finance* 48:247–266.

Valencia, Matthew. 1997. Capital punishment. *Economist*, April 12, pp. S12–S17.

Winton, Andrew. 1997. Competition among financial intermediaries when diversification matters. *Journal of Financial Intermediation* 6:307–346.

8

Financial System Reform in Emerging Economies: The Case of Romania

Anna Meyendorff and Anjan V. Thakor

8.1 Introduction

The Romanian economy has entered its second decade of transition from a centrally planned economy to a free-market economy. Its financial system is currently mixed, with nascent capital markets, privately owned brokerage houses, a combination of state-owned and private domestic banks and insurance companies, and branches and subsidiaries of foreign banks and insurance companies. At the same time, the actual level of financial intermediation in Romania is low, with bank lending only 10 percent of GDP. What steps should the Romanian government take to reform its financial system and guide its future evolution?

This is an important question because a large body of research has shown that financial-sector growth is positively correlated with an increase in economic growth over long periods of time (see DeGregorio and Guidotti 1995; King and Levine 1992, 1993a, 1993b; and Johnston and Pazarbasioglu 1995). Moreover, Levine and Zervos (1995) show that both the banking sector and equity market variables make significant independent contributions to GDP growth, and Johnston and Pazarbasioglu's (1995) results demonstrate the crucial importance of having a sound, well-regulated financial system to foster growth. Thus, taking steps to reduce the fragility of the Romanian financial system is important for sustained economic growth in that country.

Schwartz (1995) defines *financial fragility* as a state in which "the ability of the financial system to withstand economic shocks is weak," which implies that such fragility will result in financial system failure. Commercial banks are generally viewed as the most fragile and the most important of all financial institutions. Thus, the majority of the space in this chapter is devoted to the Romanian banking system.

Our research on the Romanian financial system has allowed us to generate a set of reform recommendations. Although these recommendations are specific to Romania, the framework within which we developed them is not: it is broad enough to be applied to many other emerging markets. Our study has focused on two main questions:

1. What are the key problems at present that Romanian financial system reform should address?

2. What specific action steps are needed to address these problems and achieve the desired financial system reform?

Our key findings and conclusions on these two questions are as follows:

• The major problems facing the Romanian financial system at present are inadequate restructuring of and weak corporate governance in both enterprises and banks, a lack of an appropriate credit culture, poor credit skills among banks, legal and regulatory ambiguities, weak banking supervision, and missing markets and institutions.

• The process of restructuring and privatizing the industrial (real) sector has yet to be completed. Since 1991, state-owned enterprises have been subsidized through negative real interest rates, government-guaranteed bank loans, and administratively determined prices. (The interest rate subsidies were discontinued in 1994, although they occasionally reappeared in 1997. See Daianu 1996). There is weak corporate governance in both state-owned and newly-privatized enterprises. This has profound implications for Romanian banks as well as capital markets, as it lowers the credit qualities of bank loan portfolios and retards capital market growth.

• Banks have only minimally changed the structure of their loan portfolios and have continued to roll over loans to traditional clients (see Perotti and Carare 1996 and Croitoru 1997). Even though bank balance sheets look healthy in book value terms, this is partly because banks were reluctant to extend credit in 1997, choosing to focus on fee income rather than interest rate income. In part, banks behaved this way because of a shrinking economy, causing repayment behavior on the part of borrowers and corruption to deteriorate. A moral hazard problem resulting from past bailouts is apparent as the banks anticipate further resolutions of loans extended to old clients with government guarantees. The situation has not changed significantly since 1997. The current reluctance to extend new credit is in sharp contrast to the climate in 1995–1996, when there was extensive lending. The proportion of credit (as well as overdue credits) accounted for by the emerging private sector increased during this time.

• Privatization is a necessary first step to improving bank performance. Significant progress has been made with the privatization of several state-owned banks in the past 5 years. However, the largest bank, BCR, remains in state ownership, and continues to lend to the state sector. In the meantime, increasing globalization of financial services means that Romania cannot contemplate remaining isolated from international banking.

• The Romanian legal system is both incomplete and inconsistent, with ambiguities that impede banks' ability to collect their debts and the central bank's ability to close financially troubled banks. Both the independence and the credibility of the central bank are called into question as a result.

• Bank regulation is plagued by lack of clarity and weak supervision. Central bank supervisors focus too much on accounts rather than risks and have an inadequate understanding of international banking. At the same time, banks are subject to intervention from several other government bodies, including the fiscal authorities and the Court of Accounts, in a way that seriously distorts their lending behavior.

Our major recommendations for reform are as follows:

• Effective bank privatization should be implemented and impediments to foreign ownership removed. In light of the Chilean experience, we are particularly concerned about effective bank privatization in Romania. We suggest in this chapter numerous steps that can be taken to increase the interest of significant foreign banks and thereby improve postprivatization bank performance.

• Although outside the scope of financial-sector reform, both macroeconomic stability and improvements in corporate governance, management skills, and capitalization in the industrial sector are necessary for the ultimate success of such reform. Indeed, we strongly believe that unless the industrial sector in Romania is reformed *simultaneously* with the financial sector, it is very likely that financial-sector reform, no matter how well thought out, will fail. Privatization of state-owned enterprises is a good start but may not be enough to ensure success. There should be more of an emphasis on selling at least the large state-owned enterprises to foreign multinational corporations, which can put in place their own managers. Where this is not possible, an attempt should be made to sell large ownership blocks to foreign institutional investors, which would exert the desired corporate control on managers and ensure that the enterprise is managed competently. Moreover, there should also be a focus on improving the net worth positions of firms in the industrial sector. This depends in an important way on a macroeconomic policy that leads to stable and sustainable growth.

• If Romania fully adopts the European Union (EU) model of universal banking, a great deal of care will have to be taken to ensure that problems of internal governance, conflicts of interests, and misallocation of risk capital do not become serious impediments to successful development of basic commercial banking functions.

• The legal environment, bank regulation, and supervision should be improved. Although prudential bank regulation in Romania is well *designed*, problems with implementation remain. We suggest in this chapter specific initiatives that deal with bank closure policy, capital requirements, deposit insurance, and on-site supervision.

• Creating missing markets and institutions should be a focus of the reform efforts. For example, we suggest the creation of a government or quasi-government agency to facilitate mortgage securitization, providing appropriate incentives for internationally renowned bond rating agencies and brokerage houses to participate more actively in the Romanian capital markets, and strengthening the role of the Romanian National Securities Commission in enforcing stricter information disclosure requirements on the country's securities exchanges.

We cannot overemphasize the urgency or the importance of these reform initiatives for Romania. A recent empirical study by Demirgüç-Kunt and Detragiache (1997) found that systemic banking crises are most likely to erupt in economies with the following attributes:

- a weak macroeconomic environment, especially with low growth and high inflation
- high real interest rates
- vulnerability to balance-of-payments crises
- weak institutions
- weak law enforcement.

Many, if not all, of these factors are present in the Romanian economy.[1] Expeditious implementation of reform initiatives is an imperative that cannot be ignored.

The remainder of this chapter is divided into four sections. In section 8.2 we describe the present state of the Romanian financial system to provide a backdrop against which to examine our reform proposals. We provide some fast facts about the economy and the financial system, describe the real (industrial) sector, summarize key facts about banks and bank regulation, explain how privatization works in Romania, and discuss the salient features of Romanian capital markets and its insurance industry. Section 8.3 offers an analysis of the major problems in financial-sector reform in Romania. Section 8.4 describes our reform recommendations. Section 8.5 concludes the chapter.

8.2 The Present State of the Romanian Financial System

In this section we briefly describe the present state of the Romanian economy, with special focus on its financial system, to provide a proper backdrop against which to examine our proposals for financial system reform. An initial subsection provides some facts about the Romanian economy and its financial system, and the remaining subsections take up, in turn, the Real Sector, banking and bank regulation, bank privatization, securities markets, and insurance.

Table 8.1
Basic Romanian macroeconomic indicators (in percentages)

	1991	1992	1993	1994	1995	1996	1997	1998	1999
Real GDP growth rate	−12.9	−8.7	1.5	3.9	7.1	3.9	−6.1	−5.4	−3.2
Inflation rate (annual average)	161.1	210.4	256.1	136.7	32.3	38.8	154.8	59.1	45.8
Unemployment rate (end of period)	2.4	7.4	9.5	9.5	7.4	4.6	6.6	8.1	n/a
Share of private sector in GDP	24	26	35	39	45	55	61	61	61.5
Share of agriculture in GDP	18.9	19	21	19.9	19.8	19.2	18.0	14.6	13.9

Sources: World Bank, European Bank for Reconstruction and Development.

8.2.1 Fast Facts about the Romanian Economy and Its Financial System

The Romanian economy has undergone important political and economic changes since 1989, when the country began the transition from a centrally planned communist system to a democratic political system with free markets and private ownership. This transition has been somewhat slow and has been fraught with both economic failures and recurring lapses of determination to forge ahead full steam and to transform the economy rapidly.

Romania has numerous advantages in its struggle toward a market economy. A country of about 23 million people, it is rich in natural resources and situated strategically in the geographic heart of Europe. It has a fairly large potential market, an educated workforce, and a liberal government that seems to be seriously committed to a largely privatized economy in which large foreign multinationals play a significant role.

Table 8.1 displays basic macroeconomic indicators in Romania for 1991 to 1999. On several fronts, progress has been made and creates a favorable environment for ongoing reforms. The share of the private sector in GDP has grown from 24 percent to 61 percent.

There are also numerous structural and attitudinal impediments to reform in Romania, however. On the structural front, Romania's GDP experienced positive growth from 1993 to 1996, but then declined by 6.7 percent in 1997 by more than 5 percent in 1998 and by 3.2 percent in 1999. Inflation is high and volatile. The annual rate of inflation for 1997 was about 154.8 percent, falling to 45.8 percent in 1999.

In addition, unemployment is over 8 percent and would be a lot higher were it not for the fact that about half of all assets in the economy are still state-owned and many of these state-owned businesses are bloated with excess labor. As more of the economy comes under the control of the private sector, the unemployment rate could rise as high as 14 percent.

The agricultural sector in Romania is significant, accounting for 14 percent of the country's GDP. Farmers receive interest rate subsidies, and the reform/elimination of this subsidy structure is politically constrained. Another key problematic sector is energy. Both the agricultural and energy sectors expose other sectors to risks as well. For example, Banca Agricola is exposed significantly to agricultural risks and Bancorex to energy risks; both banks have serious financial problems.

Furthermore, the Romanian legal system is creaky and biased very heavily in favor of borrowers. Moreover, issues related to the central bank's legal authority to close problem banks have yet to be resolved.

There are missing institutions within existing industries. For example, the absence of significant venture capital means that small companies, which generally lack access to bank financing, are starved for capital. This impedes the development of vibrant small firms and diminishes the economy's adaptive ability of the economy to respond to shocks, increasing its fragility.

The present French-based accounting system used in Romania lacks transparency, which increases informational frictions and both increases the cost of capital as well as limits its availability for firms. The Central Bank of Romania is starting to introduce International Accounting Standards for all commercial banks.

The high inflation rate invites firms to speculate in raw materials inventories. In 1996–1997, inventories accounted for 12 percent of GDP, with raw materials inventories representing almost 60 percent of all inventories. Firms also possess little liquidity and use very high financial leverage, largely because the equity capital needed to build net worth is in limited supply. This low capitalization (high leverage) makes firms very vulnerable when inflation is high. Moreover, the poor capitalization of privatized and emerging private enterprises affects the quality of bank portfolios as well as the dynamics of the interactions between banks and borrowers.

A number of impediments to reform remain on the attitudinal front as well. There seems to be a widespread belief that privatization of state-owned enterprises by itself will attenuate the many ills of the past. The real problems in Romania, however, are poor corporate governance and lack of borrower net worth, and the mass privatization program has not adequately addressed these problems. There is also a lack of general understanding of business ethics and the meaning of contractual obligations. As senior executive in a major foreign bank told us, "signing a contract in Romania merely seems to be a license to carry on negotiating."

Conflicting opinions among Romanians about the role and objective function of banks are another problem. Not everybody believes that the main goal of (private) banks should be to maximize value for the bank's shareholders. Many believe that banks should also view the serving of social needs and government industrial priorities as important goals. Romania is among Europe's poorest countries: according to a World Bank estimate, 22 percent of the population lived below the poverty line in 1994, and there has not been much improvement since then. Average annual after-tax wages are a little over $990, and the average pension is only 60 percent of that. This means that the government will be constantly pressed to meet the social needs of the poor, and the view that banks and the newly privatized enterprises have a responsibility to help the government meet this social agenda may continue to frustrate economic reform. The 1998 unemployment rate was about 8.1 percent.

8.2.2 The Real (Industrial) Sector

Early reform of the enterprise sector in Romania consisted of a nominal change in the ownership of enterprises with no real effect on their governance. Most Romanian enterprises were transformed into so-called commercial companies in 1990. In 1991, their ownership was temporarily transferred to the newly created state ownership fund (SOF) and several private ownership funds (POFs) in anticipation of privatization. Although the SOF was required by law to privatize 10 percent of its holdings every year, in fact privatization was carried out more slowly. By the end of 1999, only 30 percent of Romania's large commercial companies were privatized, with total cumulative privatization accounting for 35 percent of the shares owned by the SOF. Of these companies, the majority were privatized through a program of management-employee buyout (MEBO).

This new ownership structure was ineffective in assisting with real enterprise restructuring. Managers felt little accountability, and in the face of an irrational price structure and recession, clung to their preexisting commercial relationships. This contributed to the spiraling problem of interenterprise debt, which the Romanians call "financial blockage." Fears that financial instability would spread to the banking sector, along with disappointing results of privatization, led the government to bail out loss-making enterprises several times and ultimately to get directly involved in corporate restructuring. The largest loss-making state-owned enterprises (SOEs) in the metallurgical, chemical, and machine-building sectors, nicknamed the "dirty 30" were put into a surveillance program in 1993 intended to isolate them from the rest of the economy while assisting with reorganization and restructuring. Recent empirical work on this program shows that its objectives were not met (Djankov and Ilayperuma 1997 and Croitoru 1997). A majority of the "dirty 30" companies were neither restructured nor privatized.

By law, the SOF is required to help identify at least 50 companies per week for privatization. A significant impediment to privatization has been the valuation of companies. There is a feeling that many state-owned enterprises were sold in the past at artificially low prices. A law enacted in March 1997 governs the prices at which SOEs can be sold. Clearly, valuation is going to be more of an issue if privatization involves selling to a foreign company than to Romanian citizens. However, selling state-owned Romanian enterprises to foreign multinationals will not be easy, as most state-owned companies are worth less (in economic value terms) than their book values. With the valuation sensitivity being heightened in potential transactions with foreign buyers, management buyouts and sales to Romanian citizens are more likely than purchases by foreign companies. If this continues, the goal of reforming corporate governance through privatization will remain elusive.

8.2.3 Banking and Bank Regulation

Romania's prereform banking system consisted of the National Bank of Romania (NBR), which played the role of both central and commercial bank, and specialized banks for investment, foreign trade, agriculture, and savings. A two-tier banking system was created in 1991, when the commercial banking activities of the NBR were spun off into the new Romanian Commercial Bank. The remaining specialized banks were not reconfigured, however, and Romania's banking sector remains dominated by the five state-owned banks, which initially had complete monopoly power in their respective sectors. Two significant new pieces of bank legislation, the Law on Banking Activity (Law No. 33/1991) and the law regarding the statute of the NBR (Law No. 34/1991), were enacted in 1991 to achieve consistency with EU banking directives.

Along with most other state-owned enterprises, the Romanian state-owned banks were turned into joint-stock companies under privatization, and in 1991 70 percent of their shares were transferred to a newly established SOF and 6 percent to each of five POFs, which held the shares in the name of Romanian citizens. Simultaneously, new banks entered the market in response to relatively liberal licensing requirements, and foreign banks were allowed to establish operations on an equal basis with domestic banks. Although Romanian banks are universal in their scope of activities according to the legal framework set up in 1991, securities laws passed in 1994 prohibit banks from conducting brokerage activities.

Table 8.2 summarizes the ownership structure of the Romanian banking sector from 1996 to 2000. Almost 45 percent of the country's total assets remain in state-owned banks. The remaining 55 percent of the country's assets are divided among 31 private domestic banks, and seven branches of foreign banks.

The NBR is directly accountable to the Romanian legislature. Its governor and board of directors are appointed by the prime minister and parliament for renewable eight-year terms. The NBR's responsibilities are to (1) conduct monetary policy, (2) supervise banks, and (3) act as a lender of last resort. The NBR has licensing stan-

Table 8.2
Major state-owned banks in the Romanian banking sector, 1996–2000

	1996	1997	1998	1999	June 2000
(Number of banks)					
All commercial banks	35	37	45	41	42
Romanian incorporated banks	29	31	36	34	35
State-owned	7	7	7	4	4
Saving banks	1	1	1	1	1
Private	22	24	29	30	31
Joint venture with foreign investors	8	11	15	19	22
Branches of foreign banks	6	6	9	7	7
Banks under special treatment (under suspension, in court, etc.)	1	1	3	3	3
(Share of total banking sector assets)					
All commercial banks	100	100	100	100	100
Romanian incorporated banks	96.1	93.4	94.3	92.9	92.5
State-owned	77.8	74.7	71.0	46.8	44.3
Private	18.4	18.7	23.3	46.2	48.2
Joint venture with foreign investors	4.3	6.4	10.4	40.5	44.1
Branches of foreign banks	3.9	6.6	5.7	7.1	7.5
Banks under special treatment (under suspension, in court, etc.)	3.7	1.7	2.5	1.8	2.0

Sources: NBR and IMF Country Report No. 01/16.

dards for banks, and their objective is to ensure quality in banking rather than to limit competition. Selected key bank regulations in Romania are discussed below.

8.2.3.1 Minimum Capital Requirements

The minimum capital requirement for a Romanian bank to commence operations is Lei 250 billion, roughly $9 million; Beyond that requirement, there are risk-weighted capital requirements in the spirit of the Basle guidelines. Different asset risk categories are established for on–balance sheet items, and off–balance sheet items (such as standby letters of credit) are also classified into different risk groups for capital computation purposes. The minimum capital requirement is 12 percent of risk-weighted assets.

8.2.3.2 Prudential Regulations

The design of prudential regulations in Romania is quite good. The key elements of these regulations are as follows:

• A loan to a single borrower cannot exceed 20 percent of a bank's capital and reserves.

• Total loans to insiders cannot exceed 20 percent of a bank's capital and reserves.

• Investments by banks in nonbanking companies cannot exceed 20 percent of the capital of the nonbanking company.

• Open foreign exchange (forex) positions by a bank cannot exceed 10 percent of the bank's capital and reserves.

• The NBR must approve ownership of a bank by a nonbank exceeding 5 percent of the bank's capital.

• Specific rules exist for loan classifications (e.g., standard, watch, substandard, doubtful, and loss) and provisioning (loss reserves).

8.2.3.3 Payments System

A new net multilateral clearing system was established in Romania in April 1995. This new system has reduced both float and duration of interbank payments.

8.2.3.4 Deposit Insurance

A May-June 1996 Romanian law made deposit insurance mandatory for banks. The only two banks currently not in the country's deposit insurance system are the two ailing banks (Dacia Felix and Credit Bank).

Deposit insurance coverage is available only to individuals in Romania, not corporations. The deposit insurance coverage ceiling per depositor per bank was raised to Lei 20 million in August 1997. The ceiling is indexed to the CPI and adjusted twice a year.

The deposit insurance fund in Romania is currently financed by banks, but it is a public law fund, with financing provided from initial contributions by banks (1 percent of the bank's social capital at the time it joined the system) plus an annual premium of 0.8 percent of all deposits. The fund may ask for an additional "special contribution," raising the maximum effective annual premium as high as 1.6 percent, if there is a deficiency in the fund in the sense that its payouts to the depositors of failed banks exceed the reserves it has to make the payouts.

The deposit insurance fund is managed by a seven-member board with three members from the NBR, two from banking associations, and one each from the Ministries of Finance and Justice.

8.2.3.5 Reserve Requirements

For both their individual and corporate deposit accounts, banks must hold minimum reserves equal to 30 percent of lei deposits as deposits with the NBR. The requirement is 20 percent for dollar deposits.

8.2.3.6 Bank Supervision

The NBR relies on both off-site and on-site supervision of banks, coordinated by a Supervision Department newly established in September 1999. Off-site supervision consists of reports submitted by banks on solvency ratios, balance sheet accounts, forex deposits, sizes of their largest loans, and loan classifications and provisioning for losses. Since September 1999, the Supervision Department has been developing a Bank Rating and Early Warning System based on accepted international standards. In addition, the NBR is increasingly employing on-site inspections of both state-owned and private banks. A *Manual of Supervision* is available to bank examiners for use in on-site supervision and the NBR has conducted extensive training with the technical assistance of the U.S. Agency for International Development (USAID). The NBR is also in the process of developing a central credit risk register that will provide banks with information about the total level of indebtedness of their borrowers, thereby facilitating improved management of their credit risk.

8.2.3.7 Bank Closure

According to current law, judicial authorities determine the outcome of bankruptcy proceedings against banks. Initiating such proceedings, while clearly spelled out in the Law on Bankruptcy Procedures, remains difficult and ineffective.

After several failed attempts to restructure Bancorex, the former foreign trade bank collapsed in April 1999. Recapitalization, without adequate restructuring of its nonperforming loans, and without a change in the policy of subsidizing the energy and heavy industry sectors, could not turn the bank around. Fearing a systemic banking crisis, the Romanian authorities put in place a liquidation plan. A newly formed Asset Recovery Agency (AVAB) absorbed all of Bancorex's bad loans for workout and liabilities were transferred to other banks (mostly to BCR). The bank's license was withdrawn in July 1999.

Since, before its closure, Bancorex had accounted for about one quarter of all banking assets in the economy, its closure greatly improved the soundness of the banking system. The cost of closure was absorbed by an increase in public debt on the order of 4.5 percent of GDP.

8.2.3.8 Main Problems in Bank Supervision

A number of problems plague the current system of bank supervision in Romania. The following offer particular cause for concern:

1. On-site supervision needs to be considerably strengthened.

2. The NBR needs to have increased enforcement powers. In particular, it currently has no effective intermediate sanctions to address problems in bank behavior short of withdrawing a bank's license.

3. The founders of a bank have disproportionately large voting rights relative to those of other shareholders. This works against corporate governance and increases the burden on regulatory supervision to resolve issues arising from failures of corporate governance. For example, 80 percent of the loans at the financially troubled Dacia Felix and Credit Banks were to insiders (executives and large shareholders), and this saddled the banks with a huge concentration risk.

4. Many of the banks we interviewed felt that the NBR supervisors were ill equipped to supervise a modern banking system with international transactions. NBR supervision is perceived as focusing on accounts rather than risks.

5. State-owned banks are under the authority of the Court of Accounts as well as the central bank, distorting the incentive structure of individual bank employees, who fear prosecution from government officials who are not familiar with banking practices.

8.2.4   Bank Privatization

In 1997, the Romanian parliament approved Law No. 83 for privatizing the financial services industry. Since then, significant progress has been made in privatizing or closing some of the large state-owned banks.

As a result, more than half of banking sector assets are now in the private sector. The first bank to be privatized was the Romanian Development Bank, which in 1991 accounted for about 9 percent of total lei deposits in the economy. A significant strategic foreign investor, Societe Generale France, purchased 51 percent of the shares, with the European Bank for Reconstruction and Development purchasing an additional 5 percent. Banc Post, an even smaller bank, subsequently went through privatization in 1999, with partial ownership retained by the state.

By the end of 1999, privatization plans were also in place for Romania's two largest banks, the Romanian Commercical Bank and Banca Agricola, the agricultural bank. Each of these banks had been used extensively to subsidize the industrial and agricultural sectors respectively, and had large portfolios of bad loans. The AVAB was charged with absorbing and working out the bad loans of the state-owned banks.

While delays have attended the proposed privatization of the RCB, Banca Agricola has undergone an aggressive restructuring program. Initial efforts included recapitalization of the bank, and some labor-shedding in 1997. In 1999, with failure of the bank imminent, all bad assets were transferred to the AVAB in exchange for government bonds, and existing management was replaced by an administrative board that effectively put the bank under the direction of the NBR. Banca Agricola was officially offered for sale in April 2000. As of June 1, 2001, a deal had been concluded with a consortium of foreign banks including Raiffeisenbank, although several outstanding issues remained to be settled.

The government has announced plans to privatize the Romanian Commercial Bank, the largest bank in the system, in 2002. RCB has a 40 percent market share of banking business, and its sale to strategic foreign investors would put about 80 percent of Romania's banking assets under foreign control. Even if the government is able to overcome political opposition to domination by foreign banks, it may have problems attracting yet another foreign investor, especially for such a large bank.

8.2.5   Securities Markets

The securities markets in Romania consist primarily of two markets where corporate equities are traded: the Bucharest Stock Exchange (BVB) and an over-the-counter market called RASDAQ that was set up with the help of USAID and is patterned after the NASDAQ. There is no corporate bond market, and the government (Treasury) bond market is in the process of being established.

The BVB, established with the help of Canadian advisors, is the older of the two equities markets and is an exchange that has an order-driven system. It has about 128 stocks listed as of June 2001, of which 23 are first-tier (blue chip) companies, 88 are second tier and 17 are on the TNQ (traded not quoted) market. The turnover per trading session is between a quarter and a half million US dollars. The exchange has two strategic priorities at present: developing indices, with one index for the first-tier companies and one overall index; and encouraging more companies to list on the exchange. About 60 percent of the total money invested in the BVB is foreign capital (through mutual funds and other financial institutions).

By law, every state-owned company that privatizes is required to list on RASDAQ, and RASDAQ thus has 5,452 listed companies as of March 2001. RASDAQ has a quote-driven system. The turnover per trading session is usually below a quarter million US dollars. In addition to the BVB and RASDAQ, Romania also has a commodities exchange.

Both the BVB and RASDAQ are supervised and regulated by the National Securities Commission (NSC), an autonomous public body appointed by the Romanian parliament. The commodities exchange is currently unregulated, but under a new law, the NSC will regulate all spot and derivatives (options and futures) transactions, including commodities.

In our opinion, the Romanian capital markets are facing a number of challenges. Perhaps the most readily apparent is that competition between the BVB and

RASDAQ is distorting the strategies of these two institutions. In particular, the RASDAQ's listing requirements, by the very mandate of its charter, are relatively minimal. Moreover, its information disclosure requirements are also fairly lax. To compete with the RASDAQ for listings, the BVB has fairly lax disclosure requirements as well, even though there is recognition in the BVB that its comparative advantage over the RASDAQ lies in the greater price transparency it offers investors, and this calls for more stringent, rather than less stringent, disclosure requirements. Moreover, the BVB has fairly minimal listing requirements because one of its primary objectives is growth.

A further problem is that many firms do not understand the benefits of listing on a stock exchange. They do not use the capital market to raise capital, since they rely on bank debt for external financing. Since the availability of bank credit is limited, however, the reluctance of firms to use the stock market as a viable alternative source of funds is puzzling. Nonetheless, it appears that firms view information disclosure in the capital market as imposing a cost on them without any associated benefits. This makes the BVB's task of obtaining the necessary information disclosure more difficult.

Finally, an insufficient number of real blue chip companies are available for listing on either the RASDAQ or the BVB. This makes it almost impossible for any exchange to satisfy the dual goals of growth in listings and stringent listing requirements.

8.2.6 Insurance

The Romanian insurance market was started in 1991. Although there are 53 insurance companies in Romania, the market is dominated by the largest player, a state-owned insurance company named Asirom that has 270 branches and more than 50 percent of the insurance premium business in Romania. Asirom offers third-party automobile liability insurance, automobile collision insurance, life insurance, and property and casualty insurance.

The insurance industry in Romania accounts for a relatively small fraction of the country's GDP, although it is growing. Moreover, the market is very incomplete. There is virtually no health insurance available in Romania, although Asirom plans to offer this in the future. There is also no mortgage insurance, and even though life insurance is offered, the total premium inflow from this business is very small.

Insurance companies in Romania are supervised and regulated by a body that resides in the Ministry of Finance. Banks are allowed to offer insurance products, and many (e.g., Bancorex) do. However, they are limited in this business to 20 percent of their capital. An important issue is how banks will be regulated in non-banking activities like insurance and securities market brokerage. Will the regulation evolve to be functional or institutional? The NBR has proposed that it regulate *all* activities of banks. The NSC and the insurance regulator, however, feel that bank regulation should be functional, so that bank brokerage activities, for example, should be regulated by the NSC.

Like the nation's capital markets, the Romanian insurance industry faces a number of significant challenges. For example, the existing insurance law is outdated and lacks clarity, which has discouraged strategic foreign investors from participating more actively in the Romanian insurance industry. Although some foreign companies such as AIG and Canadian Capital have representatives in Romania, their overall participation in the market is small. The Romanian parliament is currently discussing a new law dealing with insurance regulation and supervision.

The current insurance market in Romania has tapped into only 10 percent of the potential market, and all the existing players are competing for this 10 percent. Missing or underdeveloped markets such as those for life, health, and mortgage insurance as well as corporate insurance may fail to emerge quickly because of gaps elsewhere in the economy. For example, it is unlikely that there will be a significant demand for life insurance until per capita incomes rise significantly. Similarly, the absence of liquidity in the residential mortgage market and the lack of an effective reinsurance market for mortgage insurance are likely to frustrate the growth of mortgage insurance.

Supervision of the Romanian insurance industry presents another set of challenges. The duties and responsibilities of the supervisory body regulating insurance companies in Romania need to be more clearly defined. Perhaps this body needs to be accountable directly to the Romanian parliament rather than to the government. This might help to provide a clearer legal framework for foreign investors.

Another challenge involves capitalization and infrastructure (both in the industry and in the nation at large). Romanian insurance companies are undercapitalized and have information systems problems as well as facility constraints. These problems will impede the development of new products and the opening of new markets. Furthermore, there needs to be greater investments in ports, highways, buildings, and other infrastructure to stimulate the growth of the insurance industry. Such investments expose the firms involved in building the infrastructure to risks that must then be insured. Moreover, the employment generated by the building of infrastructure elevates individual incomes for workers and creates a demand for various sorts of insurance at the individual level.

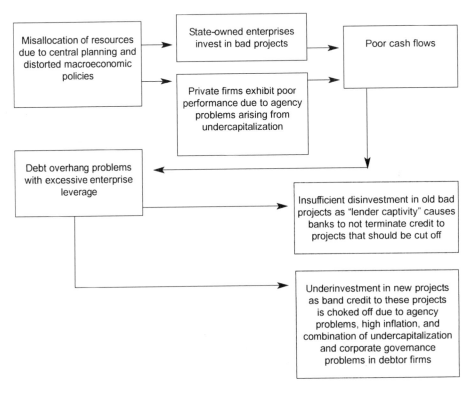

Figure 8.1
Major problems in banking

8.3   Anaylsis of Major Problems in Financial-Sector Reform

Figure 8.1 highlights the most pressing problems arising from the current state of the Romanian economy. The figure suggests a perverse feedback loop. Poor performance by state-owned enterprises and private firms in the real sector has spillover effects into banking, leading to deterioration in the credit qualities of bank portfolios. Lack of experience and talent in the loan workout departments of banks, in combination with political pressures brought to bear on banks by state-owned borrowers, results in the continued availability of credit to projects that should be terminated. To make matters worse, there is a rising share of overdue credits from the new private sector. This insufficient disinvestment in bad projects by banks has two perverse effects.

First, it reinforces the fundamental lack of project investment discipline in both state-owned and private enterprises and perpetuates inefficient capital management in the real sector. Second, it siphons off the credit that should have gone to good new projects that remain unfunded as a result of capital's being tied up in investments that are known to be unproductive. The result is a lack of sustainable economic growth and hence impeded growth in the financial services industry (capital markets and insurance, for example) as well. For example, there was a spurt of economic growth in 1995–1996, but it could not be sustained.

The financial services industry in Romania must overcome a number of significant hurdles to make a successful transition. Weak corporate governance in both the state-owned and the newly-privatized enterprises in the real sector of the Romanian economy is a pervasive problem. Privatization has resulted in mostly diffused ownership of these enterprises by individual citizens who represent a highly fragmented ownership block with neither the will nor the monitoring skills to ensure effective corporate governance. The managers of these former state-owned enterprises are still, by and large, the same people who were running these enterprises *before* privatization. Little has happened to change either their skills or their incentives. Without improved corporate governance, many of the agency problems that existed in state-owned companies exist in the privatized companies as well.

Another problem is that most enterprises (including private ones) are undercapitalized, leading to higher agency costs of debt (see Jensen and Meckling 1976) and inviting borrowers to behave in ways that increase lenders' credit risk. For example, borrowers may increase their business risk by investing in riskier projects or speculating in raw materials inventories, or they may expend insufficient effort to improve cash flows, or their managers may consume excessive perquisites. The thrift industry in the United States in the 1980s provides a good example. Most savings and loan associations had very low net worths, and many blatantly exploited the federal deposit insurance system by significantly increasing their risks.

The combination of macroeconomic instability, debt-related agency problems, and weak corporate governance in the real sector has profound implications for banks as well as capital markets in Romania. For banks it means greater credit analysis and postlending monitoring responsibilities as well as elevated credit risk. For Romanian capital markets, it means less activity, since managers who are used to weak corporate governance and lax shareholder monitoring are unlikely to expose themselves to heightened shareholder scrutiny by directly accessing these markets. Thus, weak corporate governance and the associated managerial inefficiencies in the real sector lead to potential problems in banking and also retard the growth of capital markets.

Corporate governance in the current state-owned Romanian banks is also weak, with a few exceptions. In most cases, current bank management is interested only in very diffused ownership after privatization. Much of the current focus of privatization is on internal teams suggesting restructuring measures to current management. Consequently, real restructuring initiatives in the state-owned banks have been few and far between. Many current bank managers think of restructuring as the acquisition of new technology, new investments, duty exemptions, new holidays, and government-sponsored subsidies, rather than cost cutting, layoffs, wage reductions, and asset divestitures. State-owned banks believe that privatization is desirable mainly because it will bring in foreign capital and the "brand equity" of foreign institutions to help attract human capital and expertise.

Most Romanian banks also need to improve their risk management skills. Loan workout departments should be organized as separate entities within banks, with employees adequately trained. Fortunately, this is already beginning to happen. The RCB has a special workout division established with assistance from foreign advisers. Similarly, the RDB has also set up a distinct workout group with the help of the European Commissions Phare Program and European consultants.

Credit skills and culture in state-owned banks are still weak. The lack of reliable product market prices (energy, grain, etc.) makes it difficult for banks to determine credit risks and price them. Exacerbating this difficulty is the old relationships banks have with their state-owned borrowers and the political pressures often brought to bear on banks.

It is difficult to ascertain the credit quality of even the so-called good loans. Many of them could be quite bad, given the overall poor quality of management in the borrowing enterprises and largely illiquid collateral. Moreover, Romania has an economic austerity plan in place, and it calls for industrial restructuring that is likely to increase the number of borrowers who will be forced to liquidate and be unable to repay their loans in full. For example, Sorin Dimitru, chairman of the SOF, announced in 1997 that 222 enterprises had been identified as making sufficient losses that they were slated for liquidation. At least five are large companies.

Mortgage lending is virtually nonexistent in Romania. One significant disincentive to such lending is that if the borrower defaults, the collateral with which she has secured her loan may be worth little. Buyers are mostly local homeowners, and default by one homeowner is likely to have been triggered by a local calamity that affects everybody. This kind of systematic (nondiversifiable) risk limits banks' diversification opportunities, and the lack of mortgage securitization means the absence of a secondary market for banks to manage these risks.

Bank regulation is ambiguous and too "paper based." That is, there is too much focus on accounting documentation and on getting banks to micromanage the economy. Moreover, banks are subject to intervention by the Court of Accounts in ways that seriously distort their lending behavior. For example, rescheduling a loan may be considered a criminal offense because by rescheduling, the bank prevents the state from receiving penalties from the borrower.

8.4 Reform Recommendations

8.4.1 Improve Corporate Governance and Capitalization in the Industrial (Real) Sector

Although the issue of real-sector reform is outside the scope of this chapter, it must be recognized that reform of the financial and real sectors should be closely linked in order for either to be successful. For example, a recent World Bank study shows that in many Central European countries, increased bank lending in the absence of enterprise privatization is associated with declines in productivity and profitability (see Pohl et al. 1997). For this reason, we include here a brief discussion of the real-sector reforms we feel are necessary for the success of the financial-sector reforms proposed above.

A major problem in the emerging free-market economies of the former communist countries is the widespread failure of enterprise debtors to make scheduled payments of principal and interest to creditors, as well as creditor passivity or lack of aggressiveness in pursuing their claims (see Mitchell 1993 and Begg and Portes 1993). In Romania, this problem has manifested itself somewhat differently. Enterprise debtors have, in many instances, been repaying banks, but only by increasing their debts to the state budget. Thus, examining bank balance sheets and income statements fails to reveal the magnitude of the problems in the real sector of the Romanian economy. The effect on capital discipline and investment efficiency is the same, however: managers in the borrowing firms do not behave as if enterprise budget constraints are binding. When this happens, the price mechanism loses much of its meaning. Just as importantly, as Begg and Portes (1993) suggest, simply privatizing the real sector and the banking sector may not suffice to resolve this problem.

Corporatization and privatization of Romanian state-owned enterprises has apparently not resulted in desired improvements in corporate governance. In many instances, these enterprises are still being run by trade unions and managers who were in control prior to privatization. Private ownership is so diffuse as to be ineffective in monitoring and controlling management. As Jensen (1986) points out, failure of corporate governance leads to an abundance of agency problems and economic inefficiency.

These difficulties in the real sector engender numerous effects that spill over into the financial sector:

• Bank loan portfolios deteriorate in credit quality.

• Promising new investments get choked off as banks struggle to cleanse their loan portfolios and improve or maintain credit quality by limiting new credit availability. This sacrifices both growth in the real sector and growth in banking.

• Capital market growth is retarded. Because managers in many privatized enterprises are relatively incompetent and very much used to weak corporate governance, they have no desire to raise capital in the most cost-effective manner, particularly if doing so means they must expose themselves to the harsh glare of capital market scrutiny. Consequently, even credit-starved firms that are unable to expand their credit availability from banks are not tapping Romanian capital markets for finance, which limits those markets' growth. Moreover, without the threat of losing business to the capital market, banks face less pressure to lower funding costs for their borrowers than they do in economies with greater market pressures. This means lower levels of investment by banks in initiatives that focus on cost efficiencies and financial innovation.

The other difficulty in the industrial sector is that borrowers have inadequate net worths. Combined with informational problems, this can lead banks to ration credit to these borrowers (Stiglitz and Weiss 1981). Dittus (1994) points out that this may well have been what happened in Czechoslovakia, Hungary, and Poland in 1991 and 1992. Solving this problem in Romania will require numerous simultaneous steps. First, corporate governance and management skills in the industrial sector must be improved. Second, macroeconomic policy should be stabilized in a way that improves enterprises' profit prospects. Greater government investments in infrastructure and eliminating distortive subsidies may accomplish this for at least some of these enterprises. Third, Romania could try creating support programs for small businesses such as those in Germany (Kerditanstalt für Wiederaufbau, or KfW), the Czech Republic (Czech-Moravian Guarantee and Development Bank), or Hungary (the Credit Guarantee Corporation). This is particularly important because the emergence of viable and vibrant small businesses could go a long way toward creating a built-in adaptive ability in the economy to external shocks; small firms typically adapt to shocks better than large firms.

8.4.2 Carefully Consider the Range of Issues and Safeguards Needed to Adapt the EU Universal Banking Model Effectively to Romania

The Romanian parliament is currently discussing an increase in the scope of permissible activities for Romanian banks, including securities brokerage, that would move Romania closer to the EU universal banking model. As this transition occurs, particular care will have to be taken regarding three main issues. First, what are the possible ramifications of expanding banking scope for the focus of reform efforts? Second, what kinds of internal governance problems are likely to arise as a result of expanding banking scope? Third, what effect do bank ownership stakes in debtor firms have on economic efficiency?

Where Should Reform Attention Be Focused?

In most of the developed countries, borrowers typically follow the credit life cycle suggested by figure 8.2. In countries without a well-developed venture capital industry, borrowers begin with internal finance, then go to banks, and then finally begin to access the capital market directly. Unfortunately, it appears that at present in Romania, there is little internal finance, only an embryonic venture capital industry, and insufficient access to the capital market. This leaves borrowers with mainly bank credit. But their low net worth positions lead to agency problems that cause banks to ration credit to them. Economic growth is thus unsustainable.

The question is: Should borrowers in developing countries like Romania follow the steps in figure 8.2 as the financial system develops? On both theoretical and institutional grounds, the answer is yes (see Boot and Thakor 1997a; Blommestein and Spencer 1994; Mayer 1989; Singh and Hamid 1992; and Repullo and Suarez 1995). Contemporary research points strongly to the desirability of first developing an efficient banking sector and then concentrating on capital markets. The danger for an emerging financial system is that universal banking could create an unfocused agenda in which concerns about banks' securities activities could divert attention from basic commercial banking activities. Moreover, expanding banking scope also

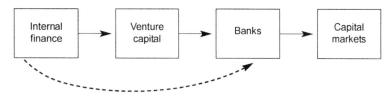

Figure 8.2
Typical borrower credit life cycle

raises questions about being able to maintain an effective deposit insurance safety net that can be confined to banking activities without having to cope with potentially porous Chinese walls separating commercial banking from nonbanking activities (see Kaufman 1996 for a discussion of the importance of an effective safety net for banks in emerging economies). Thus, expanding banking scope will place even greater demands on NBR supervisors, who are already quite challenged by the existing banking issues in Romania.

There are many reasons why Romania should focus first on banking and only later on capital markets:

- Capital markets generally depend on well-functioning banks to provide key services (see Blommestein and Spencer 1994).

- Banks are key providers of payment services and help create the necessary liquidity for the capital markets (see Diamond 1996). A well-functioning payments system greatly expands the opportunities for capital market trading.

- As experts in resolving a variety of borrower-related moral hazards through credit analysis and postlending monitoring, efficient banks help improve the overall credit quality of the borrower pool. This has two effects. First, those borrowers who still remain relatively high in credit risk tend to borrow exclusively from banks. And second, banks improve the creditworthiness and credit transparency of some borrowers who borrow both from banks and the capital market. Both effects serve to enhance the transparency and credit quality of the pool of borrowers who seek financing from the capital market. This improves the functioning of the capital market, encourages its growth, and lowers the cost of capital for a variety of borrowers (see Boot and Thakor 1997a).

- Participation in the wholesale payments system gives banks privileged access to "good funds" from the central bank and allows banks to provide other financial and nonfinancial institutions with liquidity at short notice.

What Internal Governance Issues Does Expanding Banking Scope Raise?
Greater scope in banking activities means that the actions of bank managers become more difficult to ascertain, possibly making corporate governance worse and making these institutions more opaque. In turn, investors may raise the cost of capital for banks to compensate for the greater opaqueness. In this environment, regulation has to become more sophisticated and regulatory supervision more intense.

In addition to potentially worsening corporate governance, expanded scope also increases the likelihood of conflicts of interest (e.g., if a borrower's loan is overdue, the bank may underwrite the borrower's public debt issue to help repay the loan) and errors in allocating risk capital. The Barings fiasco as well as other recent failures illustrate the point that even Western banks are often not very efficient in determining the relative risks of capital market trading activities vis-à-vis bank lending. This leads to errors in pricing and determination of prudent capital reserves and could potentially distort the allocation of resources by banks.

Finally, in a recent paper, Boot and Thakor (1997b) have shown that financial innovation and the rate of growth of capital markets are both slower in economies with universal banking than in economies with functionally separated banking. Their reasoning is that financial innovation and capital market development typically come at the expense of traditional banking. Thus, a universal bank in an oligopolistic financial services industry will wish to invest lesser resources in financial innovation and in facilitating capital market growth because it will internalize the potentially pernicious effect of such innovation on its traditional commercial banking business. The implication is that universal banking may retard capital markets; consider the example of functionally separated U.S. banking compared to universal-banking continental Europe.

What Effect Do Bank Ownership Stakes in Debtor Firms Have on Economic Efficiency?

In the Czech Republic, bank ownership in debtor firms has significantly distorted bank lending practices, the problem being that banks reallocate credit away from financially strong borrowers to weaker borrowers to ensure that their ownership stakes in the weaker borrowers are not jeopardized. This is a variant on the previously mentioned classic conflict-of-interests problem in universal banking that has been rather extensively researched.

This kind of problem should be expected in Romania as well. Its most serious consequence is that it could distort resource allocation to such an extent that the government could not feasibly delegate credit allocation to market-based mechanisms and expect this allocation to be efficient. Unfortunately, neither bankruptcy laws nor privatization can be relied upon to ameliorate the situation. The only viable alternative may be to separate banks from industrial ownership, as in Poland. This initiative is also currently being considered in the Czech Republic. In the Romanian context, there should be a serious discussion about the upper bound on bank ownership in debtor firms.

Though the global trend even in the United States, is toward universal banking, market forces in well-developed financial systems may resolve many of the problems we have discussed here. In Romania, however, market forces may be far less efficient

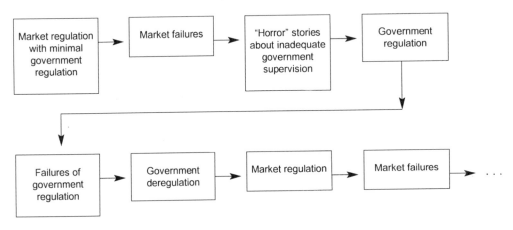

Figure 8.3
Interplay between government and market regulation

for some period of time, which places a greater burden on regulators. Thus, in light of the fact that Romania is likely to adopt the EU universal banking model, we urge that sufficient attention be devoted to discussing these issues from the standpoint of designing regulatory safeguards.

8.4.3   Improve the Legal Environment, Bank Regulation, and Supervision

Kaufman (1996) suggests that in economies in which both government and market regulations exist, a tension between these two forms of regulation simultaneously protects the system against both excessive government regulation and insufficient market regulation. The tension plays out as shown in figure 8.3. This interplay assures a fairly efficient regulatory dynamic. Such beneficial interplay is missing, however, in transition economies like Romania's because many banks are state-owned and do not face market pressures. Thus, the onus shifts even more to government regulation to foster a healthy operating environment for banks.

Another lesson for Romania in the context of figure 8.3 is that a vicious regulatory cycle can develop. If privatization and deregulation are implemented ineffectively, then failures will result. This will invite a new wave of government regulation that may lead to significant backsliding in financial system reform. Something similar happened in Chile after its state-owned banks were privatized. Because this privatization was not effective, there were failures in banking, which then led the government to renationalize these banks. For Romania, then, the key question is: how can the country effectively privatize? The answer, we believe, lies in focusing on the most reputable and capable strategic foreign investors and their commitment to Romanian banking, rather than the price at which the bank is sold.

Regulatory reform in Romania should take as its first task the minimizing of ambiguities in the legal framework of banking. This is particularly important since Demirgüç-Kunt and Maksimovic (1996) find that the efficiency of a country's legal system is an important determinant of its economic growth rate. Moreover, Demirgüç-Kunt and Detragiache (1997) have shown that systemic banking crises are more likely in countries with weak law enforcement. Specific initiatives to improve the legal system should include tightening bankruptcy laws so that they are more creditor-friendly, permit collateral to be collected at lower cost from delinquent borrowers, and provide positive incentives to creditors to enforce debt contracts. Reform should also clearly provide the NBR with the authority to close insolvent banks expeditiously without fear of being overruled by the courts. Bank supervisors' ability and willingness to close financially troubled banks in a timely fashion is central to having a healthy banking system. Regulatory tardiness in closing insolvent institutions was a major factor in driving up the social cost of resolving thrift insolvencies in the United States in the late 1980s (see Kane 1989, 1990). The Federal Deposit Insurance Corporation Improvement Act of 1991 provided the regulatory reform necessary to permit U.S. regulators to close financially troubled institutions even before their book net worth becomes zero or negative.

Along the same lines, as much ambiguity as possible should be eliminated from Romanian bank regulations, and all sanctions therein should be made explicit. Most of the banks we interviewed felt that there was considerable vagueness in the NBR's regulatory guidelines related to loan risk classifications, among other things. We strongly believe that at this stage of development, the Romanian banking system would benefit greatly from greater precision in its regulatory guidelines (see also Kaufman 1996).

The NBR needs to focus on well-designed prudential regulation that is concerned with providing an incentive-compatible safety net for depositors and deposits. Elements of such a safety net would include:

• Deposit insurance protection for small depositors, but not for large ones, to preserve the incentives of large uninsured depositors to monitor the bank (this means the current coverage may be adequate and there should not be any great haste to raise it to EU levels)

• An appropriately risk-sensitive deposit insurance premium structure (see Chan, Greenbaum, and Thakor 1992 for issues related to the design of such a structure)

• On-site inspections of banks, with the frequency of inspections inversely related to the bank's capital, so that scarce auditing resources can be focused where they are most needed.

Romania should also seek to minimize nonprudential regulation that focuses on political, social, or other objectives. Banks should be viewed as profit-maximizing institutions that lubricate the market mechanism–based engine for efficient credit allocation rather than as vehicles for implementing sociopolitical agendas. In particular, the role of the Court of Accounts in monitoring banks should be reduced or eliminated. Although this Court has jurisdiction only over state-owned banks, the credit behavior of these banks prior to privatization will improve if individual loan officers do not feel criminally liable for their lending decisions.

Steps should be taken to ensure that all banks have adequate *economic* capital. As Kaufman (1996) points out, inadequate economic capital in banks means that privatization and prudential regulation will be less effective, and inappropriate prudential regulation and lack of privatization will make it more difficult to effectively recapitalize banks. Although the Basle capital standards are correct in spirit, Romania has far greater macroeconomic instability, narrower financial markets, and less effective supervision than the countries for which these standards were developed. Neither the 12 percent minimum nor the specific Basle risk weights are necessarily appropriate for Romania. We recommend an in-depth study to investigate how the Basle capital standards should be adapted for the Romanian banking system.

Finally, functional rather than institutional regulation should be adopted in Romania. This means that banks' securities activities—if universal banking is continued—should be regulated by the NSC, for example.

8.4.4   Focus on Creating Missing Markets and Institutions

The key missing and underdeveloped financial markets in Romania are capital markets and those for mortgages and insurance. To provide the necessary impetus for the development of these markets, we suggest the following actions:

• Focus strongly on macroeconomic stabilization, the industrial restructuring process, and improving corporate governance in the newly privatized enterprises to create more blue chip companies that want to list on the BVB.

• Continue efforts to develop the government bond market, which in turn will potentially provide banks with additional collaterizable assets.

• Have the NSC play a more active role in enforcing stricter disclosure requirements on firms listing on the BVB and possibly also those listing on RASDAQ.

• Invite international bond-rating agencies and brokerage houses with experience in evaluating and rating companies to help set up rating agencies in Romania; this should improve the dissemination of information about firms and help these firms raise capital in the market.

• Establish a government or quasi-government agency to help develop a secondary market for securitized mortgages, along the lines of Fannie Mae, Ginnie Mae, and Freddie Mac in the United States.

• Accelerate the industrial restructuring process and infrastructure investments to create new opportunities for insurance companies.

• Privatize state-owned insurance companies to attract new capital, information technology, and infrastructure investments.

• Continue revising insurance regulations to provide greater clarity.

8.5   Conclusion: An Integrated Plan for Reform

We have made numerous recommendations for financial system reform in Romania. If they are implemented, we believe that these action steps will help reduce the fragility of the Romanian financial system. We conclude with a brief discussion of an integrated plan for reform that addresses the question of the appropriate sequencing for the changes we have recommended. The sequence we present is related to our earlier discussion that the most urgent problems in Romania involve improving corporate governance and borrower net worth in the industrial sector and reforming the banking sector. Attention can be focused on the capital market at a later stage. We believe these changes should be implemented in three phases, with each new set of reforms building on the success of the previous phase:

Phase 1

• Take steps to improve corporate governance and capitalization in the industrial sector and continue emphasis on macroeconomic stabilization.

• Privatize the remaining state-owned banks effectively and structure privatization transactions so as to increase bank's franchise value to strategic foreign investors.

• Carefully examine the regulatory safeguards associated with universal banking.

• Improve the NBR's on-site supervisory skills and link frequency of on-site inspections to levels of bank capital.

• Remove the legal ambiguities that obstruct the NBR's supervisory ability.

• Continue development of the government bond market.

Phase 2

• Focus on developing well-designed prudential regulations for the NBR that provide an incentive-compatible safety net, including a revised set of capital guidelines and a reexamined deposit insurance pricing scheme.

• Gradually dismantle as many nonprudential regulations as possible that are motivated by sociopolitical agendas.

• Focus on developing functional (rather than institutional) regulation of different financial institutions.

• Set up an agency to provide support programs designed to encourage small business growth.

Phase 3

• Focus on the development of the capital market by inviting internationally renowned bond-rating agencies and brokerage houses to participate more actively in the market and by enforcing stricter disclosure requirements.

• Establish a government or quasi-government agency to facilitate the development of a secondary market for securitized mortgages.

• Privatize insurance companies and continue the process of developing clearer insurance regulations.

Notes

1. Moreover, Levine (1999) has shown that the legal system is an important determinant of both financial system development and real economic growth.

2. In part this was because the NBR, for political reasons, initially sought judicial liquidation rather than administrative liquidation. Once court proceedings began, the NBR was powerless to invoke administrative liquidation.

References

Abarbanell, J., and J. Bonin. 1997. Bank privatization in Poland: The case of Bank Slaski. *Journal of Comparative Economics* 25:31–61.

Begg, D., and R. Portes. 1993. Enterprise debt and economic transformation: Financial restructuring in Central and Eastern Europe. In *Capital Markets and Financial Intermediation*, ed. C. Mayer and X. Vives, 230–255. Cambridge: Cambridge University Press.

Blommestein, H. J., and M. G. Spencer. 1994. The role of financial institutions in the transition to a market economy. In *Building Sound Finance in Emerging Market Economies*, ed. G. Caprio, D. Folkerts-Landau, and T. Lane, 139–189. Washington, D.C.: International Monetary Fund.

Boot, A. W. A., and A. V. Thakor. 1997a. Financial system architecture. *Review of Financial Studies* 10, no. 3:693–733.

Boot, A. W. A., and A. V. Thakor. 1997b. Banking scope and financial innovation. *Review of Financial Studies* 10, no. 4:1099–1131.

Chan, Y., S. I. Greenbaum, and A. V. Thakor. 1992. Is fairly priced deposit insurance possible? *Journal of Finance* 47:227–246.

Croitoru, L. 1997. Enterprise restructuring in Romania. Unpublished paper, Institute of Industrial Economics, Bucharest.

Daianu, D. 1996. Stabilization and exchange rate policy in Romania. *Economics of Transition* 4:229–248.

DeGregorio, J., and P. Guidotti. 1995. Financial development and economic growth. *World Development* 23:433–448.

DeLong, B. 1990. Did J. P. Morgan's men add value? A historical perspective on financial capitalism. Working paper, Natural Bureau of Economic Research, Cambridge, Mass.

Demirgüç-Kunt, A., and E. Detragiache. 1997. The determinants of banking crisis: Evidence from developing and developed countries. Working paper no. 106, International Monetary Fund, Washington, D.C.

Demirgüç-Kunt, A., and V. Maksimovic. 1996. Financial constraints, uses of funds, and firm growth: An international comparison. Working paper, World Bank, Washington, D.C., and the University of Maryland, College Park.

Diamond, D. 1996. Liquidity, banks and markets: Effects of financial development on banks and the maturity of financial claims. Working paper, University of Chicago.

Dittus, P. 1994. Corporate governance in Central Europe: The role of banks. *Bank for International Settlements Economic Papers* no. 42. Basel, Switzerland.

Djankov, S., and K. Ilayperuma. 1997. The failure of the government-led program of corporate reorganization in Romania. Working paper, World Bank, Washington D.C.

European Bank for Reconstruction and Development. 1996. *Transition Report 1996*. London: Author.

International Monetary Fund. 1997. *Romania—Recent economic developments*. Staff country report no. 97/46, International Monetary Fund, Washington, D.C.

Jensen, M. C. 1986. Agency costs of free cash flow, corporate finance, and takeovers. *American Economic Review* 76:323–329.

Jensen, M. C., and W. H. Meckling. 1976. Theory of the firm: Managerial behavior, agency costs, and ownership structure. *Journal of Financial Economics* 3:305–360.

Johnston, B. R., and C. Pazarbasioglu. 1995. Linkages between financial variables, financial sector reform, and economic growth and efficiency. Working paper WP/95/103, International Monetary Fund, Washington, D.C.

Kane, E. J. 1989. Changing incentives facing financial-services regulators. *Journal of Financial Services Research* 2:263–272.

Kane, E. J. 1990. Principal-agent problems in S&L salvage. *Journal of Finance* 45:755–764.

Kaufman, G. G. 1996. Bank fragility: Perception and historical evidence. Working paper WP-96-18, Federal Reserve Bank of Chicago.

King, R. G., and R. Levine. 1992. Financial indicators and growth in a cross-section of countries. Working paper WPS 819, World Bank, Washington, D.C.

King, R. G., and R. Levine. 1993a. Finance and growth: Schumpeter might be right. Working paper WPS 1083, World Bank, Washington, D.C.

King, R. G., and R. Levine. 1993b. Financial intermediation and economic development. In *Capital Markets and Financial Intermediation*, ed. C. Mayer and X. Vives, 156–189. Cambridge: Cambridge University Press.

Levine, R. 1999. Law, finance, and economic growth. *Journal of Financial Intermediation* 8:8–35.

Levine, R., and S. Zervos. 1995. Stock markets and banks: Reviving the engines of growth. Unpublished paper, World Bank, Washington, D.C.

Mayer, C. 1989. Myths of the West: Lessons from developed countries for development finance. Working paper WPS 301, World Bank, Washington, D.C.

Meyendorff, A., and E. Snyder. 1997. Transactional structures of bank privatizations in Central Europe and Russia. *Journal of Comparative Economics* 25:5–30.

Mitchell, J. 1993. Creditor passivity and bankruptcy: Implications for economic reform. In *Capital markets and financial intermediation*, ed. C. Mayer and X. Vives, 197–225. Cambridge: Cambridge University Press.

Perotti, E., and O. Carare. 1996. The evolution of bank credit quality in transition: Theory and evidence from romania. Working paper no. 49, William Davidson Institute, Ann Arbor, Mich.

Pohl, G., R. Anderson, S. Claessens, and S. Djankov. 1997. Privatization and restructuring in Central and Eastern Europe: Evidence and policy options. Technical paper no. 368, World Bank, Washington, D.C.

Repullo, R., and J. Suarez. 1995. Credit markets and real economic activity: A model of financial intermediation. Unpublished paper, London School of Economics.

Romanian Financial Almanac 1996. Bucharest, Romania: Cosmos Development S.R.L.

Schwartz, A. J. 1995. Coping with financial fragility: A global perspective. *Journal of Financial Services Research* 9, no. 3/4:445–451.

Singh, A., and J. Hamid. 1992. Corporate financial structures in developing countries. Technical paper no. 1, International Finance Corporation, Washington, D.C.

Stiglitz, J. E., and A. Weiss. 1981. Credit rationing in markets with imperfect information. *American Economic Review* 71:393–410.

Tsantis, Andreas. 1996. Romania: Restructuring of the banking sector. Background paper prepared for joint Organization for Economic Cooperation and Development/Vienna Institute for International Economic Studies joint seminar "The Progress of Bank Restructuring in Bulgaria, Romania, Slovakia and Slovenia", Vienna, December.

9   Should Banks Have the Power to Enter All Financial Businesses?

Raghuram G. Rajan

In recent years, there has been considerable interest, both in developed and nascent economies, as to whether commercial banks should have extended powers, that is, whether commercial banks should be allowed to become universal banks providing a variety of additional services to customers. Some economists debate whether banks will be more, or less, efficient than existing producers when they provide a new service. For example, Saunders (1985) argues that commercial banks will be better at underwriting than investment banks (the existing producers of underwriting services) because they can realize the scope economies between lending and underwriting.[1] Others have focused on the costs of combining lending and underwriting. For instance, a bank's ability to certify a firm to public markets—a primary function of underwriting—is compromised by its concern about the value of its outstanding loan to the firm. So a firm will not be able to get as good a price for its public securities issues from that bank as it would if they were underwritten by an independent investment bank.[2] Given that there might be both costs and benefits, whether a universal bank is more efficient than specialized producers at providing the new services it undertakes is an empirical issue.

Yet other economists question whether there is any need to debate the issue of institutional efficiency. Using a logic that one could term "institutional Darwinism," they argue that if institutions are allowed to compete freely, efficient institutions will emerge. Reverting to our example of underwriting, if combining lending and underwriting under one roof creates significant conflicts of interest, banks will not be able to attract underwriting business away from independent investment banks. So they will simply not adopt underwriting powers. Absent externalities, the argument goes, there is no need to limit bank powers. It does not really matter if regulators can determine empirically whether conflicts of interest or economies of scope are more important: they should just let the banks decide.[3]

The laissez-faire argument just enunciated assumes that a free market will necessarily lead to the emergence of efficient institutions. By contrast, I argue in this chapter that the laissez-faire argument requires not only unrestricted competition among institutions, but also competitive markets. If the markets in which institutions compete are not competitive, it is possible that it is a dominant strategy for institutions to choose inefficient structures.

9.1   A Sketch of a Model

Although I consider a specific example (see Rajan 1998 for the formal model), the point this chapter makes is quite general. Consider two related services A and B that can be provided to customers either by specialized institutions or by a universal bank. Customers use the services in a natural sequence. They first use A, then some of them go on to use B. The services are not naturally competitive. I assume that if producers were all specialized, they would get ex ante rents from offering each service. In this situation, let a producer have the ability to integrate forward from A to B. In such a situation it is typically argued that allowing integration (universal banking) would increase competition and make consumers better off.

I make one assumption to show that this need not be true. Since the services are related, let the integrated producer get an ex post rent in producing service B for a customer if it produced service A for him. Such a rent may stem from some source of advantage the producer obtains over downstream producers, and it may not be entirely efficiency related. For instance, a producer that acquires an informational advantage over a customer generally captures ex post rents that exceed the cost of acquiring the information (see Sharpe 1990 and Rajan 1992 for an application of this idea to banking). With this assumption, I can show that producers may integrate forward from A to B even if they are less efficient than specialized producers in producing service B.

The intuition is simple. In producing service A for a customer, the integrated producer obtains the possibility of an ex post rent in producing B. So long as this ex post rent is greater than the inefficiency the integrated producer brings to B, he can still drive away competition and capture the customer's downstream business, B. Of course, ex ante, the customer will be aware of the possibility of capture. Will the inefficient integrated producer be able to survive in the ex ante competition with specialized producers for the customer's business? The answer could well be yes. In the ex ante competition for a customer, the specialized producer of A can agree to forego only its own rents but has no control over the rents the downstream producer will extract. By contrast, the integrated producer will be able to sacrifice both rents in an attempt to capture business. As a result, the integrated producer can capture a greater market share than the specialized producer (and can even make a greater rent off of each customer if the downstream rents are greater than its inefficiency). Since integrated production is more profitable than being a specialized producer of A, all producers will become integrated. Downstream specialized producers of B will not get any customers (since the integrated producer siphons them all off). As a result, there will be no specialized producers competing with the integrated producers.

Unfettered by competition, the integrated producers can then pass on the cost of their inefficiency to customers. In summary, all producers are integrated even though it is an inefficient organizational form and even though there is competition ex ante among organizational forms (albeit in oligopolistic markets).

The assumptions behind the model are not wholly implausible. Service *A* could be lending and service *B* be underwriting. Firms typically borrow from banks when young and are underwritten in the public markets when mature. A bank that lends initially obtains a variety of sources of ex post advantage over a client even though its lack of specialization in the specific client's business, or its conflicts of interest, may imply that it is not the best underwriter for that client's business. Finally, perhaps because of the nature of the business and the regulations surrounding them, neither market is competitive.

In this setting, following the lines of the argument above, universal banks may deter the emergence of other specialized organizational forms. In comparison to using a sequence of specialized intermediaries, the all-in cost of being financed by the universal bank can be higher, because the bank monopolizes all the firm's avenues of finance. Also, because the universal bank imposes additional costs on accessing the public markets, firms will be forced to rely more on bank loans and less on stock issue. Public markets can be illiquid and small when banks adopt underwriting powers.[4]

In fact, a government policy of first banning universal banks, allowing a variety of specialized banks to emerge, and then allowing the entry of universal banks may result in a more efficient and robust financial system. Sequencing of institutional regulations matters, according to the model!

Let us be careful about what this chapter says. It simply suggests a plausible scenario in which institutions do not evolve in the socially optimal way. Whether the conditions do, in fact, apply is an empirical question that can be answered in different ways depending on an economy's history and current state of development. For example, if underwriting markets in a particular economy are competitive, commercial banks will be forced to internalize the costs of the structure they choose. In this case, it does not really matter if regulators know whether commercial banks are better at underwriting than independent investment banks: they can rely on the commercial banks to make the right decision about whether to enter the business. But politicians and regulators appear to advocate extending bank powers to services and economies the markets for which do not have the appearance of being competitive, with the intent of making them more competitive. This chapter indicates caution in precisely these situations and suggests that more empirical work be undertaken to determine what kinds of bank powers—taking deposits, making loans, holding equity in firms, underwriting, making markets, managing trust funds, etc.—can reasonably and efficiently be combined.

9.2 The Empirical Evidence

Another way of stating the point of this chapter is that the fact a certain kind of institution exists is not evidence that it is efficient. The nature of competition may be such that the rents associated with an inefficient structure outweigh the cost of inefficiency. The theory simply suggests a possibility. The detailed model (Rajan 1998) shows that a number of conditions are necessary to make even a plausible case for a social planner to restrict the power of banks to underwrite (and, of course, it is quite possible that regulators, while intervening, would increase the rents and the inefficiency that are the source of the market failure). Evidence for (or against) the existence of these conditions is perhaps more easy to obtain than evidence for the model's conclusions.

Some economists (Hayes and Spence 1983 and Pugel and White 1985) have argued that even in the extremely competitive U.S. financial sector, investment banks have market power. More recently, Cosimano and McDonald (1998) provide evidence of market power at the level of individual commercial banks. Finally, Petersen and Rajan (1995) report that in a sample of small firms, more than half are within two miles of their primary lending institution. Taken together, this evidence suggests that even in a developed market like that in the United States, neither the investment banking market nor the local loan market is fully contestable. This supports an important assumption in the model.

I have stressed conflicts of interest as one source of potential inefficiency of universal banks. There could be others: for example, the possibility that the universal bank would inflict its services on the client firm even though it is not the best at providing them. But are conflicts of interest economically important? Kroszner and Rajan (1994) compare the underwriting activities of commercial banks and independent investment banks (investment banks without a lending arm) in the United States before the Glass-Steagall Act of 1933.[5] As predicted by their theory, and contrary to the allegations that prompted the act, they do not find that the banks systematically fooled investors. Ang and Richardson (1994) and Puri (1993) have since confirmed these findings. But this does not mean that there is no evidence of conflicts of interest. Kroszner and Rajan find that relative to comparable investment banks, the securities affiliates of commercial banks underwrote safer securities (debt rather than equity) for older, larger, and relatively less indebted firms. Kroszner and

Rajan argue that these activities are consistent with the market's discounting the risky issues underwritten by commercial banks because of the potential for conflicts of interest and forcing banks to move to safer issues. Kroszner and Rajan's findings indicate that because commercial banks did not typically bring junior issues like equity, or small and risky firms, to market, any scope economies in information may be relatively unimportant.[6]

Further evidence of potential conflicts when activities are combined emerges when Kroszner and Rajan (1997) examine the different structures through which commercial banks underwrote prior to Glass-Steagall. Banks could underwrite either through separately capitalized affiliates or directly through in-house departments. Presumably the potential for conflicts of interest, or any scope economies in information gathering, should be higher in the latter structure. Kroszner and Rajan find that issues underwritten by in-house departments were discounted more (had higher yields) than comparable issues underwritten by affiliates.

Packer (1994) examines initial public offerings in Japan of firms in which venture capitalists have substantial stakes. He finds that, in general, a higher stake owned by the venture capitalist is correlated with lower underpricing of the offering. This suggests that venture capitalists play some kind of certification function. However, issues underwritten by an investment bank in which its own venture capital affiliate has a significant stake tend to be underpriced significantly *more* than the average issue (the effect is economically important also). Consistent with Kroszner and Rajan's findings, fears of conflicts of interest tend to outweigh any benefits from more informed certification when the investment bank has an interest in the proceeds of the issue. All these studies suggest that universal banks are not particularly effective at underwriting informationally sensitive issues.[7] Other studies, however, find the opposite. More recent evidence from the United States suggests that commercial banks play a certification role while underwriting (Puri 1996; Gande et al. 1997). Evidence from Israel suggests that they play a certification role but that conflicts of interest demonstrate themselves in other ways (Ber, Yafeh, and Yosha 1998). More work in this area is clearly needed.

Another important assumption/prediction of the model is that the existence of a prior lending relationship between a bank and a firm enables the universal bank to capture the firm's future financing business. Peach (1941) states that commercial banks moved into underwriting during the 1920s in part because lending officers could use their prior information about a firm's need for public finance to secure its underwriting business. More recently, Merrill Lynch and C.S. First Boston have set up lending affiliates as a way of securing the other business, including underwriting, that firms generate.[8] There is more direct evidence from other countries. Edwards and Fischer (1993, 118) show that "the underwriting of new share issues by domestic firms [in Germany] is concentrated in the hands of the big banks." They cite the Gessler Commission's report on the German banking system as stating that "access to syndicates, especially those for new share issues, was not easy for other banks even if these banks had adequate capital market and placement power."[9] Germany also illustrates a peripheral implication of our model; by capturing the underwriting business of firms (and perhaps diverting them toward bank loans), universal banks may starve independent investment banks of a profitable clientele and force them to exit the market. Consistent with this, the Gessler Commission reports that private bankers lead-managed only 8.6 percent of share issues in Germany between 1966 and 1975. There is evidence from Japan as well that those who lend have an advantage in securing underwriting business. Packer (1994) states that it is widely held in Japan that "venture capitalists affiliated with securities firms have as their primary motive the obtaining of the lead underwriter position for the parent if and when the company goes public." He finds that "a company [one of] whose top ten shareholders is a securities company affiliated venture capitalist is far more likely to choose that securities company as its managing underwriter." This finding is especially remarkable given the underpricing to which these firms are subject (see above).

There is mixed evidence that universal banks may reduce financing efficiency. Calomiris (1992) argues that American industry evolved at a slower, less capital-intensive rate than did German industry around the turn of this century, and he attributes the difference to the positive effect of German universal banks. By contrast, Weinstein and Yafeh (1994) study the effects of close bank ties on firm performance in Japan.[10] They find that firms with close ties to a bank have not enjoyed higher profits despite their preferential access to capital. These firms pay a higher than average interest rate on debt. Finally, firms with a main bank suffered from low profitability and growth rates even as early as the 1960s. Weinstein and Yafeh conclude that their evidence casts doubt on "the existence of growth-inducing and other beneficial effects of universal banking."

There seems to be some evidence that powerful commercial banks retard the growth of public markets. There were only 25 initial public offerings on the German stock market between 1959 and 1979. By comparison, Loughran and Ritter (1993) report 269 initial public offerings in the United States in 1960 alone.[11] Hoshi, Kashyap, and Scharfstein (1990) report the onerous requirements that firms in Japan had to satisfy in order to issue public debt before the liberalizations during the 1980s. This kept the public debt markets underdeveloped. La Porta et al (1996) show that bank-dominated economies typically have poorer disclosure requirements than economies with well-developed markets. Taken together, this evidence certainly suggests a tension between extending banking powers and expanding the efficiency of public markets.

Finally, commercial banks and investment banks themselves recognize the problems with combining lending and underwriting. Kroszner and Rajan (1997) note that some banks in the era before Glass-Steagall recognized that an internal department that underwrote and distributed securities could compromise the integrity of their investment advice, and such institutions proudly advertised that they did not have such a department. Kroszner and Rajan show that over the 1920s, commercial banks moved predominantly to underwriting securities through an arm's-length affiliate structure and away from using in-house departments. This suggests that the affiliate form may have been more efficient, perhaps because it reduced the possibility of conflicts of interest. Interestingly, the slowest to adopt the affiliate (instead of department) structure were small state-chartered banks even though, as Peach (1941, 81) suggests, the costs of setting up an affiliate were minor. One explanation, consistent with our model, is that these were the banks that enjoyed the greatest local monopoly power in lending and were willing to live with an inefficient structure provided it enabled them to control more easily the underwriting decisions of their client firms.

This section has presented evidence from a variety of sources consistent with the assumptions and conclusions of my model. Most of this evidence is peripheral. But taken together with the theoretical foundations I have provided, it suggests that the case for extending bank powers to underwriting merits further investigation, not so much in countries with competitive financial systems, where banks can self-select efficient structures, but in countries with nascent institutions or concentrated markets, where one cannot be so sanguine.

9.3   Conclusion

Although I have made my point in this chapter in the context of extending bank powers to underwriting, I could just as well have made it in the context of other activities. To summarize, this chapter emphasizes that in the financial sector, there are large fixed investments in information gathering. Because of the consequent increasing returns to scale, most financial services have elements of natural monopoly associated with them. Regulatory actions in these environments may have very different effects from regulatory actions in more competitive environments. Allowing banks to enter a business like underwriting because the incumbents in the business enjoy market power may actually reduce the amount of competition in the business and reduce welfare. Unless regulators understand the forces that create the market power in the first place, their actions may have consequences opposite to those intended. At the same time, the chapter argues that to the extent incumbents in a business compete away most of the rents in that business, there may be little danger in allowing banks to enter it.

I conclude by indulging in a little speculation. It has always puzzled me that the United States, which has imposed the strongest strictures on its banks (see Roe 1994 for a political rationale for these restrictions), has what is arguably the economy with the most variety and vitality in its financial markets and institutions. Although I do not want to imply cause and effect (there are many other ways in which the United States differs from other countries), the model should give us pause. Maybe restricting bank powers does give other institutions the space to grow. Moreover, it seems to me that removing the restrictions on U.S. commercial banks at this point would be relatively easy, should have little adverse effect, and would potentially offer some benefit. By contrast, some countries (like Germany and France) have allowed their banks maximum leeway right from the outset. These countries have to travel a much longer road than the United States to improve the transparency and innovativeness of their financial systems. All this suggests that transition and developing economies should pause a while before embarking on full-fledged universal banking systems. More research is clearly needed to take these thoughts beyond the realm of speculation.

Notes

Research support from the National Science Foundation and the Center for Research on Securities Prices of the University of Chicago is gratefully acknowledged. I thank Randall Kroszner, Stewart Myers, Mitchell Petersen, David Scharfstein, Jeremy Stein, and Luigi Zingales for helpful comments. This chapter summarizes material contained in a working paper entitled "An Investigation into the Economics of Extending Bank Powers."

1. See the excellent surveys in Benston 1990; Saunders 1985; and Walter 1985.

2. Benston (1990) and Saunders (1985) argue that rational investors will take the bank's incentives into account and price the issue accordingly. Even though Congress passed the Glass-Steagall Act (prohibiting commercial banks from underwriting corporate securities) to protect the "naive" investor, economic theory (and the evidence) suggests that investors were not hurt by the commercial banks' underwriting activities. But as I argue later, this does not mean that conflicts of interest are costless, just that in this case, they hurt the issuer rather than the investor.

3. Kanatas and Qi 1994.

4. Illiquidity of the public markets is a clear externality that banks will not have to face up to. Another externality ignored is the effect of implicit and explicit deposit insurance. Finally, I do not consider the effect of new activities on perceptions of the safety and soundness of banks. These are important questions, but they are not the focus of this chapter.

5. The Glass-Steagall Act, among other things, prohibited commercial banks from underwriting corporate securities either directly or through affiliates.

6. Their finding does not rule out the possibility that there are scope economies in combining businesses stemming from other sources. For instance, less capital may be needed if two businesses are conducted by the same firm than if they are conducted by separate firms. In fact, the banks' focus on larger issues that Kroszner and Rajan find could partly be explained by the fact that the banks could afford to take on more distribution risk with the same capital base.

7. There is also anecdotal evidence on the importance of conflicts of interest in a somewhat different context. For instance, in describing the lessons from Mexico's privatization program in the late 1980s, the administrator in charge of it said, "Another problem emerged when I selected the banks as our sales agents, and these very institutions were the main creditors of the enterprises being sold. Naturally, there was a conflict of interest for the banks, and selling the company became less important for them than recovering their credit." (Wall Street Journal, May 15, 1992).

8. *Wall Street Journal*, June 16, 1994. There have also been allegations of forced tie-ins. For example, consider the following in a recent lead article in the *Wall Street Journal* (November 11, 1991) on the underwriting activities of J. P. Morgan's securities affiliate: "Even worse [than the advantages banks possess from deposit insurance] Wall Streeters contend, is the perhaps-illegal strong-arm that some banking companies put on corporate borrowers to lead and co-manage their stock issues. They say they know of implicit, and sometimes explicit, suggestions that a company wanting consideration of a loan or better terms should give the bank's securities affiliate a manager role in underwriting deals."

In an attempt to deal with this, the banking bill of 1991 that was ultimately not passed by the U.S. Congress explicitly forbade "bank lending arrangements 60 days before or 90 days after a securities offering managed by a bank's affiliate unless rigorous provisions were met, including a written statement from the company that it was not coerced."

9. A statement by the chairman of Deutsche Bank as to why it is always picked to lead-manage issues by Daimler Benz reveals one source of tie in—information asymmetries—that I have alluded to: "of course we must lead manage that ... because if we didn't, the world would say 'Daimler is cross with us.' That wouldn't be good for Daimler-Benz's business, as much as it is not good for us."

10. Until recently, banks in Japan did not have the power to underwrite corporate securities. So this evidence relates to my more general point about extending bank powers than my specific point about combining lending and underwriting.

11. There is some further anecdotal evidence on Germany. The *Wall Street Journal*, May 12, 1994, states that

[c]orporations, encouraged by board members from the big banks, often borrow directly from banks rather than issuing stock or bonds, although those alternatives are usually less expensive. The total capitalization of the German stock market is only 27% of the country's gross domestic product, compared with 61% in the U.S., 62% in Japan, and 143% in the U.K. As a result, the biggest German banks increasingly are being blamed for crimping the growth of the country's capital markets. The relative lack of competition means German companies often pay more than their counterparts abroad to borrow money or issue stock. This in turn could hurt Germany's industrial base by making expansion more expensive than it is in other countries.

References

Ang, J., and T. Richardson. 1994. The underwriting experience of commercial bank affiliates prior to the Glass-Steagall Act: A re-examination of evidence for passage of the act. *Journal of Banking and Finance* 18:351–395.

Benston, G. 1990. *The separation of commercial and investment banking.* Oxford: Oxford University Press.

Ber, Hedva, Yisha Yafeh, and Oved Yosha. 1998. A conflict of interest in universal banking: Bank lending, stock underwriting and fund management. Hebrew University, Jerusalem. Mimeographed.

Calomiris, C. 1992. The costs of rejecting universal banking: American finance in the German mirror, 1870–1914. University of Illinois at Urbana-Champaign. Mimeographed.

Cosimano, Thomas, and Bill McDonald. 1998. What's different among banks? *Journal of Monetary Economics*, 41:57–70.

Edwards, J., and K. Fischer. 1993. *Banks, finance and investment in Germany*. Cambridge: Cambridge University Press.

Gande, A., M. Puri, A. Saunders, and I. Walter. 1997. Bank underwriting of debt securities: Modern evidence. *Review of Financial Studies* 10:1175–1202.

Hayes, S., and M. Spence. 1983. *Competition in the investment banking industry*. Cambridge: Harvard University Press.

Hoshi, Takeo, Anil Kashyap, and David Scharfstein. 1990. Bank monitoring and investment: Evidence from the changing structure of Japanese corporate banking relationships. In *Asymmetric Information, Corporate Finance and Investment*, ed. R. Glenn Hubbard, 105–126. Chicago: University of Chicago Press.

Kanatas, G., and J. Qi. 1994. Underwriting by commercial banks: Conflicts of interest vs. scope economies. University of South Florida, Tampa. Mimeographed.

Kroszner, R., and R. Rajan. 1994. Is the Glass-Steagall Act justified? A study of the U.S. experience with universal banking before 1933. *American Economic Review* 84:810–832.

Kroszner, R., and R. Rajan. 1997. Organization structure and credibility: Evidence from commercial bank securities activities before the Glass-Steagall Act. *Journal of Monetary Economics* 39, no. 3:475–516.

La Porta, R., F. Lopez de Silanes, A. Shleifer, and R. Vishny. 1996. Law and finance. University of Chicago. Mimeographed.

Loughran, T., and J. Ritter. 1993. The timing and subsequent performance of IPOs: The U.S. and international evidence. University of Illinois at Urbana-Champaign. Mimeographed.

Packer, F. 1994. Venture capital, bank shareholding, and the certfication of IPOs: Evidence from the O.T.C. market in Japan. Research paper no. 9401, Federal Reserve Bank of New York.

Peach, W. N. 1941. *The security affiliates of national banks*. Baltimore: Johns Hopkins University Press.

Petersen, M., and R. Rajan. 1995. The effect of credit market competition on lending relationships. *Quarterly Journal of Economics* 110:407–443.

Pugel, T., and L. White. 1985. An analysis of the competitive effects of allowing commercial bank affiliates to underwrite corporate securities. In *Deregulating Wall Street: Commercial bank penetration of the corporate securities market*, ed. I. Walter, 93–139. New York: John Wiley and Sons.

Puri, M. 1993. The long term default performance of bank underwritten securities issues. *Journal of Banking and Finance* 18:397–418.

Puri, M. 1996. Commercial banks in investment banking: Conflict of interest of certification role? *Journal of Financial Economics* 40:373–401.

Rajan, R. 1992. Insiders and outsiders: The choice between informed and arm's length debt. *Journal of Finance* 47:1367–1400.

Rajan, R. 1998. An investigation into the economics of extending bank powers. University of Chicago. Mimeographed.

Roe, M. J. 1994. *Strong managers, weak owners: The political roots of American corporate finance*. Princeton, N.J.: Princeton University Press.

Saunders, A. 1985. Conflicts of interest: An economic view. In *Deregulating Wall Street: Commercial bank penetration of the corporate securities market*, ed. I. Walter, 207–230. New York: John Wiley and Sons.

Sharpe, S. 1990. Asymmetric information, bank lending and implicit contracts: A stylized model of customer relationships. *Journal of Finance* 45:1069–1088.

Walter, I. 1985. Summary and implications for policy. In *Deregulating Wall Street: Commercial bank penetration of the corporate securities market*, ed. I. Walter, 293–302. New York: John Wiley and Sons.

Weinstein, D., and Y. Yafeh. 1994. On the costs of universal banking: Evidence from the changing main-bank relations in Japan. Harvard University, Cambridge, Mass. Mimeographed.

10 Effects of Ownership by Investment Funds on the Performance of Czech Firms

Andrew Weiss and Georgiy Nikitin

10.1 Introduction

Closed-end investment funds in the Czech Republic have generated considerable controversy.[1] The Czech government encouraged the formation of closed-end investment funds as a means accomplishing a very difficult objective: transferring ownership of companies from the state to the Czech citizenry while still providing a means for shareholders to exercise control over management. The government feared that simply distributing shares of companies to individuals would result in such diffuse ownership that there would be no constraints on management. By allowing individuals to own shares in investment funds that would in turn buy shares in operating companies, the government hoped to solve this problem. The investment companies would, the government hoped, own enough shares of operating companies to be able to influence management. Unfortunately, as it turned out, the interests of the managers of the investment funds did not coincide with the interests of their own shareholders. The personal rewards to the managers of investment funds were in fact far greater if they either colluded with the managers of the operating companies or used financial chicanery to divert the funds' assets to themselves.

From 1996 to 1998 there were several scandals involving investment funds in the Czech Republic, and the funds sector fell into disrepute. The funds were trading at enormous discounts to their net asset value: their prices were typically less than half the value of the assets they held and in some cases less than 20 percent of the value of their assets. This disenchantment with the funds sector led to legislation that will gradually force all the investment funds to convert to open-end mutual funds. The intent of this legislation was to provide a means of removing assets from the worse-managed funds and increasing the asset base of the better-managed funds.

Although the investment fund program fell into disrepute in the Czech Republic, this disrepute was based largely on anecdotes and on the huge discounts at which the shares of the funds traded. It was not known whether the funds had had a positive or negative overall effect on the performance of the operating companies in which they invested. The purpose of this chapter is to try to answer that question.

The data we obtained on investment fund performance through 1996 suggest that from 1993 to 1996, ownership concentration in the hands of investment funds did not improve the performance of operating companies. Performance may have improved recently, however. Starting in 1996–1997, several of the most notorious investment funds disappeared from our data set. For example, in 1996, the largest fund group, Harvard Capital, merged its funds into an industrial holding company that does not report its assets.[2] Trend Fund, the largest fund from the second wave of privatization, had no assets by 1997. The means by which all the assets of Trend were "tunneled" is related in appendix 10.1. Other funds were placed under forced administration. The funds that remained active may have been pressured into improving their performance by the threat of forced conversion to open-end status unless their discounts narrowed.

10.2 Brief History of Czech Privatization

Under communism, 97 percent of the GDP in Czechoslovakia was produced by state-owned enterprises. With the possible exceptions of East Germany and Albania, this was the highest proportion of any country in Eastern Europe or the former Soviet Union. Currently less than one third of the Czech Republic's GDP is produced by state-owned firms, the smallest percentage of any of the former Communist countries (Dyba and Svejnar 1994, 45). This rapid transformation was accomplished by allowing citizens to buy vouchers (at a nominal cost) that they could either use to bid for shares in previously state-owned companies or exchange for shares in publicly traded investment funds, which would in turn use the vouchers to bid for shares in companies. Roughly 70 percent of Czech citizens exchanged their vouchers for shares in these closed-end investment funds. Both individuals and funds then used the vouchers to bid for shares in companies.[3] The bidding process had multiple rounds. At the beginning of each round the government would announce a price, and voucher holders would submit their vouchers for shares in a company. If supply exceeded demand, all shares were allocated at the asking price. On the other hand, if demand exceeded supply by more than 25 percent, the price would be adjusted upward, and there would be another round of bidding; otherwise the shares would be distributed pro rata among the bidders. The bidding stopped when demand did not exceed supply by more than 25 percent (Van Wijnberger and Marcincin 1995, 4–5).

During this first wave of mass privatization, in 1992, 965 Czech companies were available for purchase through vouchers. These companies had a combined book value of approximately $7 billion (Lastovicka, Marcincin, and Mejstrik 1995, 201). The mean book value of companies in this offering was approximately $7 million, but the median book value was considerably lower. The market capitalization of the median publicly traded firm in the Czech Republic was probably below $1 million. By international standards, it is quite extraordinary for such small firms to be publicly traded. In the United States, for example, there is roughly one publicly traded company per billion dollars of GDP. In the Czech Republic, the ratio in 1997 was 30 publicly traded companies per billion dollars of GDP.[4] Regulation of these companies was impossible for a number of reasons. The law itself was vague. There were no precedents to guide prosecutors or judges. The Czech Republic had no securities commission. Judges had no experience with securities law. The capital markets division of the Ministry of Justice was understaffed and underfunded, and none of its personnel had any experience with securities law.

It was difficult even for the private sector to monitor more than a small fraction of these firms adequately. Analysts at brokerage firms had no incentive to cover the many illiquid firms, and the lack of civil discovery, combined with clogged courts and lack of trained lawyers, precluded effective supervision by minority shareholders.

The recent economic history of the Czech Republic also exacerbated problems associated with separation between ownership and control. Publicly traded Czech firms came into existence with assets inherited from the state. Corporate statutes ensuring that management would be responsive to shareholder interests were not needed to attract capital; Czech companies typically do not have such statutes. Threats to control management either through hostile takeovers or through appeals to the courts have not proved credible, as hostile takeovers have been notably unsuccessful in the Czech Republic. Takeover bids have often been tied up in the courts for long periods while the incumbent management continued to run the companies for their own benefit. Appeals to the courts for protection of minority shareholder rights are even less promising. There is a large backlog of court cases, and there are few precedents to guide the judiciary, which lacks expertise in securities law. Furthermore, the ownership structure of Czech firms affects the credibility of these threats. If ownership is diffuse or if investment funds hold major ownership positions, then there may be no owner with sufficient incentives and capabilities to replace ineffective management. For bank-managed funds, the parent bank may find it more profitable to maintain good relations with the managers of the operating companies than to try to displace these managers. The managers of operating companies can secure their own positions by maintaining banking relationships with the parent companies of bank-managed funds.

Under these circumstances, we would expect an exceptionally large difference between the performance of companies with diffuse ownership and companies with concentrated ownership. We would also expect that when ownership of a firm is concentrated in the hands of a few closed-end investment funds, its performance would be worse than when strategic investors control it. The closed-end funds are themselves acting as agents of the true beneficiaries of good performance by the operating companies: the shareholders of the funds. Ownership of shares in the funds was exceptionally diffuse during much of this period.[5] Managers of investment funds had little incentive to improve the performance of the companies they managed. Their fees were less than 2 percent of assets under management, with no bonus for performance, and funds were not allowed to own more than 20 percent of any particular company.[6] Thus if they were able to improve by a million dollars the value of a company in which their fund owned 20 percent the value of the fund would rise by $200,000 and their compensation would rise by at most $4,000. By contrast, in an open-end fund an increase in the fund's value could attract new capital that could have a major effect on the compensation of managers. Thus, when closed-end funds are the major owners of firms, we would expect more severe problems because of the separation between ownership and control than when the major shareholders are operating companies, open-end funds, or individuals.

Managers of closed-end funds have different incentives than the managers of open-end funds. Managers of open-end funds almost always lose assets if their portfolios perform poorly: shareholders simply redeem their shares. This redemption process automatically reduces ineffective fund managers' influence on the economy. By contrast, managers of closed-end funds have little incentive to improve the performance of the operating companies in which their funds have invested. Their fees are independent share prices.[7]

Given these different incentives, it is not surprising that in the United States there are fewer than 40 closed-end funds investing in U.S. securities. Closed-end funds in the United States are much smaller than the open-end funds: the proportion of U.S. assets managed by closed-end funds is a trivial fraction of the assets managed by open-end funds. By contrast, in 1997 there were several hundred closed-end funds in the Czech Republic that invested primarily in Czech equities (160 of them were actively traded). There were few open-end funds in the Czech Republic, however, and the amount of assets managed by open-end funds was insignificant compared to the assets managed by the closed-end fund industry.

Managers of closed-end funds in the Czech Republic were motivated to improve the performance of the operating companies in which they invested only if they planned to market a new fund, raise additional capital for existing funds, or forestall attempts by shareholders to change managers. There were only two waves of voucher privatization, one in 1992–1993 and another in 1994–1995, in which vouchers were used to bid for shares in operating companies. Prior to each of these waves, vouchers were distributed to Czech citizens, and investment funds were established to attract vouchers. Funds established during the first wave of privatization could not bid for vouchers in the second wave. Managers of first wave-funds could, however, establish second-wave funds. Therefore, investment companies that were managing funds established in the first wave had a financial incentive to perform well in 1993, since that performance would affect their ability to attract vouchers for the funds they intended to establish in the second wave. Subsequent to marketing the second-wave funds in 1993–1994, there have been no opportunities to market new funds.

Throughout the period of this study, Czech funds all sold at substantial discounts to their net asset value and have done so since they were founded, effectively eliminating the possibility of raising additional funds through secondary offerings or through marketing a new fund.[8] There have been few attempts to remove fund managers. Most have long-term contracts. Share ownership is diffuse, and proxy voting is both difficult and expensive, because it requires notarization. Finally, in a case in which a major shareholder (Czech Value) removed the managers of an investment fund (Trend), by the time the new managers gained control, there were almost no assets left in the fund. Since that fiasco, there have been no attempts at hostile removals of fund managers, and therefore, fund managers have little incentive to increase the value of the fund's portfolio.

Although this chapter is concerned with the effects of ownership on the performance of operating companies, perhaps an equally important aspect of voucher privatization is its effect on the psychology of the populace. Voucher privatization was intended to build support for the market economy by making the populace the shareholders of privatized firms.[9] Instead, in the Czech Republic, public opinion polls find large majorities reporting that they believe the voucher privatization program was a means of enriching a few individuals at the expense of the rest of society. As major shareholders of companies, the investment funds not only did not stop the diversion of the funds from the companies to managers but often colluded in that process.

A 1997 report of the capital markets division of the Czech Ministry of Finance strongly condemned the administration of closed-end funds. The report found that fund mangers often enrich themselves at the expense of the fund's shareholders. They divert monies from the investment funds into other joint stock companies that they control, or these companies share the gains from the diversion of funds with the fund manager. Some of the mechanisms by which funds are diverted include

- Writing contracts to deliver securities with large fines for failure to deliver or for not complying with the terms of the contract. The fund manager then fails to comply, and the fund pays the fine, which eventually accrues to the manager.

• Manipulating prices of illiquid securities to very high levels and then either selling them to the fund or trading them for fairly valued liquid securities. In some cases these securities were originally purchased from the fund.

• Writing contracts on derivatives with terms that are highly unfavorable to the investment fund. In some cases the other party can choose whether to exercise the contract with no cost for this option.

• Transferring cash from the investment fund to non-interest-bearing uninsured accounts at a securities dealer as advanced payment for securities. The dealer then speculates with these funds.

• Selling securities with payments due several years in the future or spread over periods as long as 30 years. The party owing the money then sells the securities, distributes the revenue, and declares bankruptcy.

• Purchasing of secondary issues of stocks at above-market prices. (Veverka 1997)

Other techniques fund managers use to enrich themselves include that employed in a case in which a bank-managed fund sold all the securities the fund owned and deposited the cash in a non-interest-bearing account at the bank. In other cases, fund managers had enough shares to be able to vote to convert the fund into an industrial holding company, which effectively gave them complete control over the assets, which they then diverted to their own use.

In 1994, one of the authors of this chapter was involved with a team that intended to buy the management contracts of Czech funds that were selling at huge discounts. When we asked one fund manager why he was demanding such a high price for the contract, he explained to us that "[he] could take the shares owned by the fund to a bank and borrow personally against them." Under those circumstances honest investors could never outbid crooks for management contracts.

The typical Czech citizen had a large fraction of his assets invested in these funds, so that these thefts inflicted great hardship. The worst long-term consequence of this mismanagement and theft, however, is that for many Czech citizens free-market capitalism became associated with tolerance of embezzlement and fraud. The greatest financial gains in the Czech Republic were made by people who have made no noticeable contribution to Czech society but were associated with the investment funds. Viktor Kozeny, the founder of the largest fund group, began with less than $15,000 and was estimated to have amassed a fortune in excess of $500 million dollars by using the monies invested in his funds for his own benefit. Kozeny is now an Irish citizen living in the Bahamas and has not been in the Czech Republic for more than five years.

10.3   Previous Research

Several studies have examined the effects of investment funds' ownership on firm performance in the Czech Republic. Economists at the World Bank have been responsible for much of this research (Claessens 1995; Pohl, Jedrzejczak, and Anderson 1997; Pohl, Anderson, Claessens, and Djankov 1997). Several problems exist with the research, however. The most serious shortcoming is that performance has usually been measured in levels without controlling for firm-specific effects.

Lastovicka, Marcincin, and Mejstrik 1995 uses stock market prices to measure performance. The authors find that ownership by investment funds is correlated with high ratios of price to book value. This accords with the previous hypothesis that funds are buying shares in well-managed companies. If shares are owned by funds, however, this likely means that the funds were bidding against one another during the voucher privatization auction, inflating share prices.[10] Shares owned mainly by employees are less likely to have been the object of bidding wars. Also in the Czech Republic, firms' book value is far different from their market value, since the book value reflects the value of raw materials used to construct plant and equipment rather than the usefulness or productivity of these assets. Even if we were to ignore these statistical problems, there is a fundamental problem with the overall approach of the study by Lastovicka and his colleagues. If the ratio of share price to asset value of stocks in the portfolios of the investment funds is a useful measure of the performance of the fund managers, then the low ratio of prices to funds' net asset value should be taken as prima facie evidence of poor performance by the fund managers.[11]

10.4   Research Strategy

The goal of our research is to analyze the relationship between the composition of ownership of Czech enterprises and their performance. Our main problem is the endogeneity of the composition of share ownership. If the criteria used by different types of owners to decide which shares to hold are correlated with the measure of performance being used, then we could be falsely imputing a causal relationship between ownership and performance. Several reasons exist why ownership composition could differ across firms.

Some potential owners might believe that they have private information about the present or future performance of an operating company that is not fully reflected in the price of the company's stock, whether on the stock exchange or in the initial auction. This private information would affect a potential shareholder's decision as to whether to buy shares in that company (either on the stock market or by using vouchers to bid for shares in the auction). We would expect that private information would be most important during the auction stage of the voucher privatization program, before shares were publicly traded or followed by analysts. The bidders at the auction stage were the investment funds and individuals using their assigned vouchers. In general, we would expect the investment funds to have been better informed than the general public (no other large institutions or wealthy investors were participating in the auction). Therefore, the investment funds were likely to have been overrepresented among the initial owners of the better-performing firms, and this effect would be strongest in the first auction, when fund managers sought to establish a reputation that would enable them to attract vouchers for the second auction. Since initial ownership composition is highly correlated with ownership composition several years later, we would expect that the relationship between initial ownership composition and performance would bias any observed relationship between performance and ownership composition during our sample period.

Another reason for different ownership compositions across firms is that preferences differ among classes of investors. If these preferences are correlated with ownership type and with either performance of firms or changes in performance of firms, we may find that certain types of owners choose to invest in either high- or low-performing firms. (This effect is probably weaker than the effect of differences in information about performance, since taste differences would not be expected to affect the decisions of portfolio investors significantly.)

The impact that different types of owners have on the performance of different firms could vary across owner types and could also explain differences in ownership composition. If certain types of owners believe that they can positively affect the performance of low-productivity firms, then these owners will find it most profitable to buy shares in such firms. Similarly, if a particular type of owner is especially capable of slowing the decline in performance of firms whose productivity is falling, then owners of this type will find their most profitable investments in firms with falling productivity.

On the other hand, certain owners may favor investments in firms from which they can most readily divert funds into their own pockets. For instance, developers may try to acquire controlling interests in banks to obtain cheap loans without putting up substantial collateral. In the most extreme cases, a controlling position in a firm can be used to steal from the firm.

Whether certain types of owners are helping or hurting the performance of the firms in which they invest, it would be a mistake to assume that the same effects on performance would occur if these same owners invested elsewhere. The direction of the bias, however, is not clear. Suppose ownership by funds has the same effect on 90 percent of firms and a significantly greater positive effect on the other 10 percent, and other owners have the same effect on all firms. The investment funds will then be more likely to invest in firms in which they do the most good or least harm. If the investment funds improve productivity by more than other investors in all firms, then the endogeneity of ownership choice will increase the difference in performance relative to random assignment. If other investors improve productivity in all firms by more than the investment funds, differential ownership will reduce differences in performance.

The sources of bias that are probably most important and can be most readily addressed are differences in access to information about firms and differences in the abilities of potential shareholders to process that information. Regressing *changes* in performance on *changes* in ownership composition addresses these problems while avoiding the most severe selection biases that would be present if we regressed levels of performance on levels of ownership composition. This is the appropriate model specification if there are firm-specific fixed effects and if random shocks to performance follow a random walk, that is, permanently affect performance. (Even if the effect of random shocks on performance dissipates over time, for the time scales we are using, the estimates may be more precise if the errors are modeled as following a random walk rather than being independent.)

Using changes in ownership composition, however, as an explanatory variable presents its own difficulties. Since all the firms in our sample were privatized after 1993, it is conceivable that ownership in 1993 had a greater effect on the change in performance from 1995 to 1996 than did the change in ownership from 1994 to 1995. A shareholder who increases his stake from 1 percent to 6 percent is likely to have far less control over the company in subsequent years than a shareholder who maintains a constant ownership of 51 percent of the shares, or even one whose ownership share decreased from 51 percent to 46 percent after having established control.

One of the reasons a shareholder may want to increase the proportion of shares she owns in a company would be to gain control of the company. Once a shareholder has gained control over a company, she has less motivation to continue buying shares in it. She may even sell shares if outside threats weaken after control has been established and rivals for control have sold their shares, creating more diffuse outside ownership. A controlling shareholder who is reducing her stake in a company is likely to have greater control over the company's performance than she had while accumulating shares to gain control. Large owners who are reducing their shareholdings because they no longer face threats to their control of the company may thus be the owners with the greatest control. To limit the effects of these biases, we treated cases in which there was a majority owner separately when regressing changes in ownership on changes in performance.

In addition, using first differences amplifies the effects of measurement error and thus reduces the precision of the estimates. On the other hand, using the change in ownership composition as an explanatory variable removes biases arising from the *initial* auction in which potential buyers bid for firms. It does not, however, eliminate all the biases present when levels of ownership shares are used as explanatory variables. In both cases purchase and sale decisions after the initial auction affect the explanatory variable, and those decisions are endogenous. They can be based on private information about future changes in performance, on private information about the owner's ability to affect performance, or on differences in preferences regarding changes in performance. Some types of owners may favor firms with good future prospects for productivity improvements, whereas other types may favor firms with poor future prospects.

In our analysis we used ownership data from 1993, 1994, and 1995 and annual performance data from 1993, 1994, 1995, and 1996. Table 10.1 describes the data set. All data were purchased directly from Aspekt, a Czech publishing company. Aspekt obtained data from questionnaires it mailed to firms. No ownership data existed for the Fund for National Property in 1993. We calculated the following performance measures from Aspekt's data (see table 10.2):

Table 10.1
Data and empirical results. Description of ownership data: restricted pooled data set

	Number of observations in pooled data set	Percentage of total
Largest owner is fund (including bank funds and holdings)	38	30.40
Holdings	6	4.80
Bank funds	19	15.20
Largest owner is not a fund	82	65.60
NPF and federal	28	22.40
Municipal	7	5.60
Domestic corporation	15	12.00
Foreign corporation	6	4.80
Investment company	16	12.80
Others	10	8.00
Ownership is dispersed among small owners (less than 5%)	5	4.00
Total	125	100.00

1. value added per worker
2. value added per unit of capital
3. operating profit per worker
4. operating profit per unit of capital
5. the Solow residual

Each of these performance measures was modeled as a linear function of a firm-specific constant term, ownership composition in the previous year, a year-industry interactive dummy variable, and a cumulative error term. When we took first differences we eliminated the firm-specific constant term and the effects of lagged errors in the cumulative error term.

In the first four measures in the list, the numerator was intended to capture total producer surplus, whereas in the final approach, the Solow residual was used to measure the contribution of management expertise to firm performance. Thus all the

Table 10.2
Description of performance data

	Change in years	Mean	*SD*	Min.	Max.
Change in value added per worker	93–94	33.20	151.19	−1244.01	777.67
	94–95	1.97	28.32	−244.97	356.72
	95–96	−1.74	120.35	−1700.92	940.66
	All years	13.47	156.99	−1700.92	940.66
Change in value added per unit of capital	93–94	−0.41	3.24	−17.18	27.54
	94–95	−0.03	1.07	−8.59	19.48
	95–96	−1.02	16.93	−449.95	20.89
	All years	−1.21	17.07	−449.95	27.54
Change in operating profit per worker	93–94	−3.03	106.54	−332.25	704.02
	94–95	−1.96	29.06	−454.02	319.06
	95–96	−4.70	142.48	−1265.29	2977.42
	All years	−7.87	160.09	−1265.29	2977.42
Change in operating profit per unit of capital	93–94	−0.54	2.40	−8.38	21.49
	94–95	−0.07	0.58	−6.73	2.92
	95–96	−0.42	4.21	−89.43	34.85
	All years	−0.69	4.48	−89.43	34.85
Change in Solow residuals using ordinary-least-squares estimation of production function	93–94	0.15	0.68	−1.34	5.28
	94–95	0.00	0.11	−1.16	0.87
	95–96	−0.02	0.25	−3.21	0.81
	All years	0.04	0.52	−3.21	5.28
Change in Solow residuals using robust estimation of production function	93–94	0.18	0.71	−1.32	5.37
	94–95	0.00	0.11	−1.18	0.71
	95–96	−0.02	0.28	−3.25	0.90
	All years	0.05	0.55	−3.25	5.37

measures of performance combine price effects with output effects. Changes in value added, operating profits, or the Solow residual could be due either to efficiency gains in production or to changes in the prices of goods sold or of inputs. We are implicitly assuming that the ownership structure is affecting the efficiency of production rather than the prices of the goods produced or the cost of inputs. In this case, differences in price changes simply introduce noise into the measurement process. This assumption seems reasonable in cases in which control lies with financial firms. Where control is in the hands of operating companies who are customers or suppliers of the firms in question, noneconomic considerations could affect the prices of goods traded. (If the price changes refer to prices of exports, then these price changes may properly be included as efficiency gains for the Czech economy.)

Each of these measures has specific drawbacks. Using either labor or capital in the denominator ignores the effect of the other factor. Hence, if the change in the measured performance was due to an increase in the other factor of production, our results would be seriously distorted. Ownership structure might plausibly affect the cost of capital so that changes in the capital-to-labor ratio could be associated with changes in the ownership structure. This would lead us to infer mistakenly that the ownership structure had affected performance when it had actually affected the capital-to-labor ratio.

This problem is less severe in our data than in other firm-level data, because during this period there was little investment of new capital in existing Czech firms. We obtained rough estimates of the magnitude of this bias by measuring producer surplus (operating profits) per worker as well as per unit of capital. Thus, if changes in the capital-to-labor ratio were driving our results, we would find that the results would move in opposite directions depending on whether capital or labor was used in the denominator. In deciding whether to place greater weight on the results measured in terms of units of labor or units of capital, the most important considerations are which factor is more scarce and which factor is more accurately measured. If one of the factors is in excess supply, the other factor should be used for measures of performance. The value of capital reported by firms often bears little relationship to its market value, because the accounting values are frequently based on the value of physical materials used in production of the capital. Much of that physical capital has no market value. After the fall of communism, investment in capital goods in the Czech Republic was low. Thus, the capital that exists is imprecisely measured, and in many cases it is useless. Because education levels in the Czech Republic are relatively uniform, labor is probably more accurately measured than capital. (See table 10.A.1 for data on the distribution of education levels in the Czech Republic.)

In addition, low unemployment rates indicate that labor is in scarce supply. On the other hand, many Czech firms had (and probably still have) tremendous over-staffing. Anecdotal evidence suggests that in some firms the marginal product of labor is close to zero, or even negative when we include the social costs of employing a worker.

Returning to the choice of numerators in performance measures 1–4 above, we used two different measures of producer surplus: value added and operating profits. If wages were equal to the opportunity cost of labor and if operating profits were correctly measured, then operating profits would be our best measure of producer surplus and thus should be used in the numerator. However, neither of these conditions holds. In many cases, workers have considerable influence or potential influence on the firm for which they work. Diffuse stockholder ownership and a "stakeholder ethic" may cause managers to be more responsive to the interests of workers than to the interests of shareholders. Consequently, wages may rise or fall with economic profits (producer surplus) generated by the firm. Moreover, in over-staffed firms a decrease in economic profits may cause a decline in employment. Hence, changes in the wage bill may reflect changes in economic profits. In addition, operating profits are extremely difficult to measure correctly. Many of the accounts receivable on firms books are past due and will probably never be collected. Yet firms often do not write off these losses. For the transitional years used in this study, it is unrealistic to expect uniform or accurate accounting practices.

Our measure of capital was depreciation, which is a better measure than book value, because it avoids problems of including land holdings and other assets that do not enter into the production process as capital inputs. It does not, however, avoid the problem that the imputed values of capital may bear little relationship to their market values.

We dropped several observations from the pooled data set, believing them to be erroneous or not feasible.[12]

We assume that performance of each firm in period t was a linear function of time-invariant characteristics of the firm, ownership composition of the firm in period $t - 1$, an industry-specific year effect to capture differences in economic conditions across industries and years, and an unobserved but persistent shock to performance. The structural equation is

Performance of firm i in period $t = \text{constant} + \alpha S_{i,t-1} + \beta X_{i,t} + \varepsilon_{i,t}$, where performance can be measured by value added per worker or per unit of capital or by operating profits per unit of labor or per unit of capital.

The equations we estimated were

$$(VA/L)_{i,t+1} - (VA/L)_{i,t} = \alpha(S_{i,t} - S_{i,t-1}) + \beta\mathbf{X}_{i,t} + \varepsilon_{i,t+1}; \tag{10.1}$$

$$(\pi/L)_{i,t+1} - (\pi/L)_{i,t} = \alpha(S_{i,t} - S_{i,t-1}) + \beta\mathbf{X}_{i,t} + \varepsilon_{i,t+1}; \tag{10.2}$$

$$(VA/K)_{i,t+1} - (VA/K)_{i,t} = \alpha(S_{i,t} - S_{i,t-1}) + \beta\mathbf{X}_{i,t} + \varepsilon_{i,t+1}; \tag{10.3}$$

$$(\pi/K)_{i,t+1} - (\pi/K)_{i,t} = \alpha(S_{i,t} - S_{i,t-1}) + \beta\mathbf{X}_{i,t} + \varepsilon_{i,t+1}; \tag{10.4}$$

where

VA denotes value added

π denotes operating profits

L denotes the number of workers

K denotes capital depreciation

S denotes the ownership share of different types of owners

$\mathbf{X}$ is a vector of other variables, including 36 year-industry dummy variables

ε denotes a persistent shock

The subscript i, t in the above equations refers to firm i in year t. We don't require that $\varepsilon_{i,t}$ be normally distributed; regressions are estimated using both robust regression techniques and ordinary least squares (OLS). Note that if ε is independently distributed, the coefficients estimated for equations (10.1–10.4) remain unbiased but inefficiently estimated. The true error term would be $\varepsilon_{i,t+1} - \varepsilon_{i,t}$ rather than $\varepsilon_{i,t+1}$.

Our final approach was to estimate changes in Solow residuals. Computing Solow residuals with data from the Czech Republic, however, is problematic. When we estimated production functions by taking first differences at the firm level, we found that changes in labor were negatively correlated with changes in output. These spurious estimates of a negative marginal product of labor may arise because firms that failed to reduce their labor force are inefficient in other ways. For instance, their capital stock may be obsolete, or their product mix may be inappropriate to the market economy, or they may be choosing economically inefficient suppliers of other inputs. The magnitude of staffing reductions may be correlated with managerial efficiency.

Instead of taking first differences to estimate production functions and changes in Solow residuals, we measured changes in Solow residuals by first estimating Cobb-Douglas production functions, computing the error term for each firm in each year, and then using the change in this error term as a measure of the change in the Solow residual. This change in the Solow residual was used as a proxy for the change in firm productivity.

In particular, we estimated Solow residuals for each firm in an industry by using data from all firms in that industry to estimate an industry-specific unconstrained Cobb-Douglas production function in which value added was used as the measure of output. We did not allow for firm-specific effects. We then calculated changes in the error terms for each firm from 1993 to 1994, 1994 to 1995, and 1995 to 1996. These differences were used as dependent variables to measure the effect of ownership composition on performance. Formally, we estimated the Solow residuals for each firm in each year as follows:

$$\ln VA_{i,t} = \text{Constant} + a \ln K_{i,t} + b \ln L_{i,t} + \varepsilon_{i,t}. \tag{10.5}$$

Equation (10.5) was estimated separately for each of the 18 industries.

We assume that $\varepsilon_{i,t} = \text{Constant} + \alpha S_{i,t} + \beta \mathbf{X}_{it} + \eta_{i,t}$, where $S_{i,t}$ denotes the ownership share of firm i in period t, $\mathbf{X}$ is a vector of industry-year dummies, and we assume that $\eta_{i,t}$ is an i.i.d. error term. From equation (10.5) we derived estimates of $\varepsilon_{i,t}$. We then estimated

$$\varepsilon_{i,t+1} - \varepsilon_{i,t} = \alpha(S_{i,t} - S_{i,t-1}) + \beta Z_{it} + \eta_{i,t},$$

where Z_{it} is the difference between the industry effect for firm in period t and period $(t-1)$.

Although in the context of the Czech Republic this formulation is an improvement over using first differences to compute Solow residuals, serious problems remain. For example, changes in accounting conventions could cause measured capital to increase even if actual capital was unchanged. In this case, we would find spurious *decreases* in Solow residuals for those firms that have high capital-to-labor ratios. If ownership composition is correlated with changes in the measurement error of factor inputs or with changes in the use of mismeasured inputs (perhaps because different types of owners demand different accounting standards), then there may be spurious correlation between ownership composition and estimated changes in the efficiency of the firm's production.

To see how such distortions may affect our results, consider the following scenario. Assume that particular types of investors are more likely to use inaccurate accounting values, rather than the economic value, of the capital stock when making decisions as to whether to shut down a particular division in a firm in which they hold shares. Now suppose that the capital in any division of a firm is useless, that is, it does not add value to the production process of *any* firm (the economic obsolescence of capital could be due to changes in the demand for quality, stricter environmental regulations, or increases in energy costs, all problems that are especially severe in postcommunist economies). Additionally suppose that the labor employed in that division is producing goods that are worth more than the opportunity cost of labor used in their production. Hence, the firm is using labor efficiently. If the firm were to shut down the division, then the firm-specific error term in the industry production function would increase. Economic efficiency would have decreased, however, since labor would now be employed in less productive ways and capital would not be employed in a better way: *its productivity is zero everywhere.*[13] Owners who shut down divisions of this sort would appear to have increased productive efficiency even though they had actually decreased it.

Because of the difficulty in estimating production functions in an economy in which investment decisions have been made according to political rather than economic considerations, we do not have great confidence in estimates of changes in productive efficiency that are derived from residuals of a production function. As we discussed above, our best measures of the effect of ownership on performance come from using robust estimates of the relationship between changes in ownership composition and several different measures of changes in performance.[14] No single result by itself would be decisive; our hope is that together they will be informative.

The OLS results are reported to facilitate comparison between our results and those of other researchers who typically report only results derived from OLS estimation. The popularity of OLS derives partly from its theoretical advantage given "ideal" data. If errors are normal i.i.d., then OLS is more efficient than any other unbiased estimator. However, the efficiency of OLS degrades quickly in the face of heavy-tailed (outlier-prone) error distributions, such as those present in our data. Using a Jarque-Berra test we were able to reject normality of each of the dependent variables at confidence levels above one in a million. In figures 10.1 and 10.2, we plot dependent variables using value added as our measure of producer surplus. By inspection, it is obvious that these data are far from normally distributed.

The terms in bold in table 10.3 denote coefficients statistically significant at the 10 percent level. Aspekt supplied ownership shares of the "largest shareholders" of each firm but never included data on more than six shareholders and in most cases included data on fewer than six shareholders. Consequently, we use ownership shares only among the six largest shareholders to measure ownership concentration. The two key independent variables in table 10.3, for the purpose of this chapter, are the change in squared ownership shares by funds and the change in squared ownership shares by nonfunds in firms where no single owner owns more than 50 percent of the shares. Other independent variables included 36 industry-year dummies. In table 10.3 we report results using changes in squared ownership shares as our measures of concentration. The disproportionate weight given to the largest owners is intended to reflect their disproportionate influence on management. For example, we would

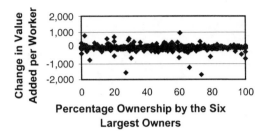

Figure 10.1
Ownership composition and change in value added per worker

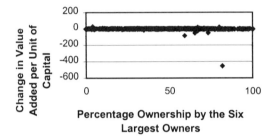

Figure 10.2
Ownership composition and change in value added per unit of capital

expect one owner with 60 percent of a firm's shares to have more effect on the firm's management than three owners with 20 percent of the shares each. Although we present the results derived using both robust and OLS regression techniques, for the reasons discussed above, we would urge readers to pay more attention to the results derived from robust regression.

Because we did not have ownership data for 1992, we could not use changes in performance from 1993 to 1994 in our analysis. In addition, whenever we were measuring changes in performance from year t to $(t+1)$, we could include only firms for which ownership data was available for years t and $(t-1)$.

In our previous discussion of the suitability of using changes in ownership as an explanatory variable for changes in performance, we pointed out the problems that arose if an owner had at least 50 percent control of a firm and then increased or decreased her share holdings while retaining control. In table 10.3 we address this issue by separately estimating the effect of the change in ownership when in period $(t-1)$ there was an owner with than 50 percent or more of the firm's shares. We focus on the effect of changes in squared ownership shares when no owner had 50 percent or more of the firm's shares in period $(t-1)$.

Table 10.3

Change in performance from 1994 to 1995 and 1995 to 1996		Change in value added per worker		Change in value added per unit of capital × 100		Change in operating profit per worker		Change in operating profit per unit of capital × 100		Change in Solow residuals × 100	
		Robust	OLS	Robust	OLS	Robust	OLS	Robust	OLS	Robust	OLS
Constant	Coeff.	-22.24	-16.67	-79.64	-120.33	-17.53	-89.64	-53.46	-41.21	-9.80	-22.52
	t	-0.43	-0.12	-0.60	-0.34	-0.40	-0.87	-0.46	-0.22	-0.41	-0.66
	$P > |t|$	0.67	0.90	0.55	0.73	0.69	0.39	0.65	0.82	0.69	0.51
Change in squared percentage ownership share by funds (including bank funds and holdings) among the six largest owners/100, if none of the owners owns more than 50%	Coeff.	-0.12	**-4.05**	**-3.11**	-3.80	-0.35	**-4.57**	**-3.88**	-4.08	-0.24	**-1.00**
	t	-0.15	-2.00	-1.69	-0.79	-0.63	-3.44	-2.42	-1.59	-0.78	-2.30
	$P > |t|$	0.88	0.05	0.10	0.44	0.53	0.00	0.02	0.11	0.44	0.02
Change in squared percentage ownership share by nonfunds among the six largest owners/100, if none of the owners owns more than 50%	Coeff.	0.13	0.03	-0.08	**6.34**	-0.04	0.24	-0.04	-1.97	0.10	0.13
	t	0.27	0.02	-0.07	2.07	-0.11	0.30	-0.04	-1.22	0.51	0.48
	$P > |t|$	0.79	0.98	0.95	0.04	0.91	0.76	0.97	0.23	0.61	0.63
Change in squared percentage ownership share among the six largest owners/100, if one of them owns more than 50%	Coeff.	-0.36	-0.58	0.19	0.68	0.19	0.05	0.25	-0.80	0.16	0.09
	t	-0.50	-0.31	0.10	0.14	0.36	0.04	0.16	-0.32	0.57	0.21
	$P > |t|$	0.62	0.76	0.92	0.89	0.72	0.97	0.88	0.75	0.57	0.84
p value of F-test on the equality of the coefficients on changes in ownership for funds versus nonfunds when funds own less than 50% of the company	F-test	0.95	0.14	0.24	**0.08**	0.82	**0.00**	**0.06**	0.16	0.62	**0.06**
R^2 (for OLS estimation only)			0.1919		0.1646		0.3450		0.1250		0.2632
Number of observations		113	113	124	124	112	112	123	123	110	110

The results in table 10.3 provide the strongest evidence that share ownership by funds fails to improve the performance of operating companies. In each of the regressions in table 10.3, the coefficient on percentage change in squared ownership by a fund, if it owns less than 50 percent of the shares, is negative. In 5 out of 10 regressions these coefficients are statistically significant at the 5 percent confidence level and at less than the 2 percent level for a one-sided test. These levels of statistical significance are surprising given the small sample sizes and the high levels of measurement error associated with first differences. In every regression the coefficients on changes in squared ownership by nonfunds are larger than the coefficients for changes in squared ownership by funds, and in four of the regressions we can reject the hypothesis that the coefficients on changes in squared ownership by funds and nonfunds are equal. Similar results were obtained when changes in ownership shares, rather than changes in squared ownership, were used as explanatory variables and dummies were used instead of the change in squared percentage change in ownership to control for the ownership in excess of 50 percent. Those results are presented in appendix 10.2.

Preliminary research using performance data after 1996 suggests that these effects may have vanished. This could be due to conversion of some of the least reputable investment funds into industrial holding companies, including the funds managed by Harvard Capital, the largest fund management organization. These conversions took place during the first half of 1996, before legislation restricting those conversions took effect in July 1996. Other major changes were the passage of an amendment to the investment funds legislation in April 1998, the establishment of a securities and exchange commission in the Czech Republic, a highly visible crackdown by the finance ministry that credibly threatened the fund managers with the loss of their contracts, and the imprisonment of fund managers. Although among these actions the jailing of fund managers may have had the greatest effect on behavior, from our viewpoint the most interesting factor was the amendment to the Investment Funds Act, which mandated terms under which all closed-end investment funds would be converted into open-end mutual funds. The anticipation of the effects of this amendment may have led the investment fund managers to try to improve their performance so as to stay viable as managers of open-end funds.

10.5 Conclusion

We have established in this chapter that the data from the Czech Republic are consistent with our economic intuition concerning the effect of ownership composition on economic performance. Ownership concentration and the composition of ownership jointly affect the performance of operating companies.

Concentration of ownership in the hands of large shareholders other than investment funds and investment companies is associated with increases in performance. This result held for all our measures of performance. These shareholders would typically have strong financial incentives to improve the performance of the operating companies in which they have invested. To the extent that these shareholders have large positions in operating companies, they can use their ownership power to exert control and thus improve the performance of the operating companies.

We could not find any evidence that concentrated ownership share by funds improves the performance of operating companies. This negative result holds both for bank-managed funds and funds not managed by the subsidiaries of banks.

We conjecture that conversion of closed-end funds into open-end funds would improve the performance of operating companies, because managers of open-end funds have more incentive to improve the performance of the companies in which they invest, and ineffective managers of open-end funds will lose assets. Besides that, the sale of shares in operating companies due to redemptions from poorly managed closed-end funds will make it easier for outside investors to accumulate controlling positions in operating companies in which they believe they can improve performance.

The 1998 amendment to the Investment Funds Act in the Czech Republic requires that funds whose discounts exceed a certain level (starting at 40 percent and declining to 20 percent by December 1999) convert to open-end status. All funds must be open-end by 2002. Thus, we will soon have a real-world experiment against which to measure our results. We would anticipate that this process would cause investment funds to exert pressure on operating companies to improve performance. Investment funds will care more about the performance of their portfolio, first to reduce the discount so as to delay forced open-ending, and second to establish a good track record that would enable the fund to retain assets, or even grow, after conversion to open-end status.

Appendix 10.1   How 95 Percent of Trend Fund's Assets Disappeared

The Cast

Trend V.I.F., a.s. Investment Fund (hereafter "Trend" or "the Fund"):   One of approximately 450 investment funds established during two waves of voucher privatization in the Czech Republic. Trend's management company controls its assets, and that company was sold to KHB, in November 1996, a brokerage company controlled by Miroslav Halek.

Trend Investment Company a.s.:   The investment management company established by to manage Trend.

Table 10.A.1
Employment in Czech Republic by education level, in percentages

Sector	No formal education	Grammar school	Trade/high school	University	Companies in sample	Share of sample
Agriculture	0.1	18.7	76.7	4.5	40	5.3
Mining	0.0	12.3	82.9	4.9	15	2.0
Manufacturing	0.0	13.4	80.7	5.9	401	53.1
Utilities	0.0	8.1	84.4	7.5	53	7.0
Construction	0.0	8.0	86.5	5.4	70	9.3
Trade and services	0.0	8.1	86.2	5.7	126	16.7
Transportation	0.0	9.9	85.5	4.6	30	4.0
Other/unknown	.	.	.	.	20	2.6
Total	0.0	11.2	83.3	5.5	755	100.0

Source: Czech Statistics Office and authors' calculations.

Cesky Investicni Holding a.s. (CIH): Originally an investment fund established by Creditanstalt, CIH_ was "acquired" by a group of individuals accused of being in the business of "tunneling" funds. CIH was converted to a holding company and allegedly paid more than 700 million CZK for an option to purchase shares in the Czech department store, Kotva from Forminster.

Miroslav Halek: A Czech national who was the economic director of a state company that manufactured musical instruments before buying Trend Investment Company. Released from prison in May 1999 after a two-year detention period, Halek has been charged by the Czech police with numerous criminal and civil violations, including racketeering (the first such case in the Czech Republic), misuse of business information, and conspiracy, in connection with defrauding Trend of 95 percent of its assets.

Consult Invest s.r.o.: A Czech company used to buy Trend Investment Company.

IFM Melodia, s.r.o.: A Czech company allegedly controlled by Halek.

Firex a.s.: A leasing company of which Halek was a director. It founded KHB (see below).

Mercia a.s.: An investment fund controlled by Halek.

Kralovehradecka brokerska a.s. (KHB): Originally owned by Firex, KHB was a brokerage firm controlled by Halek. It handled most of Trend's share transactions and is accused of making substantial profits by churning and artificial pricing. KHB's securities license was suspended and then revoked as a result of these activities.

Forminster Enterprises Ltd.: A Cyprus-based company that now holds 56 percent of Kotva's shares. Halek used Forminster as a vehicle to launder Kotva shares and launder profits from a number of other share transactions.

The Story

During the period under discussion the exchange rate ranged between 25 and 28 CZK per dollar. The exchange rate is currently 35 CZK per dollar.

Chapter 1: How Halek Used Trend's Assets to Buy Trend Investment Company

Trend Investment Company had a number of shareholders and intermediary companies but was ultimately controlled by Kocab and Kratochvil. They sold the management company in August 1995 to KHB, a brokerage company controlled by Halek, for a public price of 197 million CZK, which was paid

Table 10.A.2
Description of ownership data: Unrestricted pooled data set

	Number of observations in pooled data set	Percentage of total
Largest owner is fund (including bank funds and holdings)	361	47.81
Industrial holding companies[a]	22	2.91
Bank-managed funds	108	14.30
Largest owner is not a fund	303	40.13
NPF and federal	109	14.44
Municipal	18	2.38
Domestic corporation	94	12.45
Foreign corporation	32	4.24
Investment company[b]	36	4.77
Others	14	1.85
Diffuse ownership: No owner is listed among six largest owners	91	12.05
Total	755	100.00

[a] Industrial holding companies typically started as closed-end funds, then changed their charter to avoid restrictions placed on the behavior and fees of fund managers. They also lost the favorable tax status given to funds. For our purposes, there is no substantial difference between industrial holding companies and closed-end funds.
[b] An investment company is a fund manager.

to shareholders and a number of managers and employees. It is alleged that the actual purchase price was approximately 317 million CZK, with the additional 120 million CZK going to four individuals (who also received part of the 197 million CZK). At this time, the Fund had assets valued at 1.1 billion CZK, so the management company was officially sold for nine times its revenues, or less than 20 percent of the asset value. If the information about the extra money in the sale price is correct, the control of Trend actually cost Halek 15 times revenues, or a third of the value of Trend's assets. Note that the maximum management fee allowed under Czech law at the time of the sale was 2 percent of assets. There was no requirement to have the transfer of ownership of a management company approved by any regulatory agency at the time of the transaction.

Halek appears to have funded the purchase by entering into a share sale/purchase agreement with a regional electricity distribution company, Electrarny Opatovice (EOP), which had recently been acquired by National Power. In what appears to have been a somewhat unusual deal, EOP placed a purchase order with KHB to purchase 500 million CZK of blue chip shares and advanced KHB—unsecured—500 million CZK to fund the trade. EOP claims it did not know how Halek would obtain the shares. The 500 million CZK was used by Halek to fund the purchase of Trend's management company.

All the money transfers were made to purchase Trend Investment Company on the same day. Power of attorney was issued in favor of a Mr. Vlastnik, the Chairman of KHB, and a Mr. Pav to allow the new purchasers to trade the Fund's assets immediately, since it would have taken between three and six months to remove the existing Board. This power of attorney gave Halek immediate control of Trend's assets.

At the same time, Consult Invest s. r. o. entered into an agreement with Trend to purchase approximately 500 million CZK of blue chip stocks. Consult Invest paid a 25 percent deposit (135 million CZK) to KHB, the broker executing the trade. Consult Invest in turn contracted to sell the same shares to Firex, a leasing company Halek owned. The price for this second trade, however, is believed to have been only 135 million CZK. Firex then transferred the shares to EOP against its 500 million CZK advance.

Fine for Late Delivery

The net result of this exercise was that Consult Invest owed Trend some 365 million CZK but had received a payment of approximately the same amount from the share sale to Firex. A fine of 100 million CZK per day was put into the contract for the late delivery of the shares. As could be expected, Trend released the shares late and incurred a fine of some 1 billion CZK that was due to Consult Invest, which was dissolved on May 29, 1997.

Chapter 2: How the Remainder of Trend's Assets Were Removed

Sales at Below Market Price

One month after Trend Investment Co. was sold, 112 million CZK was transferred from Trend to KHB, allegedly to prepay KHB for the purchase of Kotva shares on the market. (Advance payments to affiliated brokers were not uncommon at that time, although a revised law has subsequently prohibited this activity.) KHB used the money to buy 70,000 Kotva shares, which it registered in its own name rather than Trend's. On December 1, 1995, when the prevailing market price of Kotva shares was 1,475 CZK per share, Trend sold 108,000 of the 109,000 Kotva shares it owned for 1,080 CZK per share. The justification for this lower price was that the purchase had been agreed upon one month earlier when 1,080 CZK was the market price. This trade caused a loss of 43 million CZK for the fund. A number of other trades were made for less than the market price on the date of transfer, with back-dated contract notes to justify a lower price.

Payment Delayed 30 Years

Trend sold 327,000 shares of Sokolovsky Ulehna to IFM, a Halek-controlled company. IFM paid Trend a 10 percent deposit, with the remainder of the sale price due in 30 years.

Overpayment for Services

Trend then entered into a six-year advertising agreement for 90 million CZK and paid 75 million CZK in advance. Halek was chairman of the advertising company with which Trend contracted.

Use of Fines (Again)

Trend had borrowed 30 million CZK due at the end of 1995 and secured by Kotva shares. Trend failed to repay the loan, and its creditor tried to claim its collateral on January 12, 1998. An agreement dated January 10 was produced, under the terms of which 200,000 Kotva shares were to be sold to IFM at 1,800 CZK. The sales agreement contained a late-delivery clause that fined Trend 35 percent of the purchase price if Trend delivered the shares more than a month late. Since the shares were blocked under the security agreement with its creditor, Trend could not deliver the shares. To settle the fine, IFM agreed to accept 60,000 Kotva shares as settlement.

Price Manipulation

In a series of trades between Trend and Mercia on May 28, 1996, some 12,000 of Mercia's shares in Kotva were sold to drive the price down from 950 CZK to 350 CZK per share. When the price was low enough to justify a sale at this "market price," Trend sold 152,000 Kotva shares for more than $3 million less than its value earlier that day. These were all the remaining Kotva shares Trend owned.

30-Year Deferred Payment (Again)

Halek signed a contract on behalf of Trend to sell 248 million CZK of assets to IFM on a 30-year deferred-payment contract. Halek transferred the assets on July 21, 1996, three days before Trend's securities account was frozen.

Appendix 10.2

All variables presented in this appendix are scaled by revenue.

Descriptive Statistics: Trading Volume of Shares

Statistics	Firms		
	Group/low liquidity	Group/high liquidity	All nongroup and group/high liquidity
Stock of cash–revenue	0.02	0.02	0.02
Debt–revenue	0.08	0.04	0.03
Net income–revenue	0.11	0.15	0.11
IBT–revenue	0.17	0.22	0.2
Cash flow–revenue	0.08	−0.03	0.03
Market–book	0.19	1.07	0.64
Investment–revenue	0.71	0.95	0.54
Growth of debt	0.82	1.07	3.07
Number of cases	24	13	48

Descriptive Statistics: Consideration of State Ownership

Statistic	Firms		
	Group/no gov.	Group/yes gov.	All nongroup and group/yes government
Stock of cash–revenue	0.02	0.01	0.02
Debt–revenue	0.1	0.03	0.02
Net income–revenue	0.09	0.17	0.12
IBT–revenue	0.15	0.24	0.21
Cash flow–revenue	0.12	−0.07	0.01
Market–book	0.24	0.87	0.6
Investment–revenue	0.92	0.6	0.45
Growth of debt	0.89	0.59	2.95
Number of cases	24	15	50

Notes

The data for this paper were supplied by Aspekt, a Prague-based firm that provides balance sheet and disaggregated revenue and cost data for Czech firms. The data were obtained through surveys conducted by Aspekt and checked for inconsistencies by Aspekt. We also checked the data and asked Aspekt to verify the accuracy of data with unusual entries.

Funding for this research was provided by the World Bank. We are grateful to participants at seminars at the William. Davidson Institute at the University of Michigan, the World Bank, and CERGE-EI in Prague, as well as to Gerard Caprio, for helpful comments and suggestions.

1. A closed-end investment fund is a publicly traded company whose only assets are the shares of other companies. The shares of the fund can trade at prices above or below the value of the shares they own. The number of shares in a closed-end fund is fixed. After the initial offering, shares can be bought only from other investors, unless the fund makes a secondary offering.

2. The story of Harvard Capital is illuminating. It attracted vouchers (discussed below) in the first wave of Czech privatization by promising that they could be redeemed for 10,000 koruna. Harvard had no assets to support that promise; indeed Viktor Kozeny, the founder of Harvard Capital, apparently boasted that he had only $15,000 when he set out to make his fortune at the start of the privatization program. (His net worth is currently estimated at more than $500 million.) His fortune was based on his personal control of all the assets of the Harvard funds, which he gained in a series of actions that began with his announcement, in an obscure newspaper, of a general meeting of the shareholders, to be held three days after the announcement at a relatively inaccessible location. In order to vote at a general meeting, one's shares must be notarized; since there were few large shareholders of the Harvard funds, attendance at the meeting was predictably low, and there was not a quorum. In such a circumstance, 10 percent of the shareholders are entitled to call an emergency general meeting (EGM); since the shareholders in attendance amounted to more than the required 10 percent of the total, an EGM was immediately convened. At an EGM, shareholders representing 15 percent of the shares have the power to do almost anything. The management of Harvard Capital held such a controlling block of shares in Harvard Capital, and at the EGM they approved the merger of all the Harvard investment funds into an industrial holding company called Harvard Holdings, incorporated in Cyprus. Harvard Holdings combined its assets with those of another company, Stratton, in a new joint venture that became the only asset of Harvard Holdings. No information about that venture was or is available to shareholders of Harvard Holdings. At the time of the merger each share in Harvard Holdings was backed by assets valued at around 2,000 koruna; its shares now trade for around 160 koruna. The perception is that all the assets have been diverted to Kozeny's personal use. The Harvard Holdings story even makes a mockery of the idea that voucher privatization would prevent foreigners from buying up Czech companies: Kozeny is now an Irish citizen. He lives in the Bahamas and Aspen, Colorado, and has not visited the Czech Republic in more than five years.

3. Fund managers were inexperienced, and the funds themselves could be established with a very small capital base. Fund managers could choose either to be paid a fixed percentage (not to exceed 2 percent) of the assets under management or to share in the fund's profits. Almost all managers chose to receive a fixed share of assets. The market price of funds rapidly fell to large discounts to the value of the assets owned by the funds.

4. GDP data are from International Financial Statistics, IMF; the traded companies' data are from International Finance Corporation 1997.

5. The ownership of European corporations is far more concentrated than is the ownership of Czech investment funds.

6. This restriction was occasionally evaded but was often a binding constraint in our data.

7. Performance-based fees are rare in the Czech Republic and are severely limited even in the United States. In Poland, fund managers are reimbursed a percentage of the assets under management control. They also receive 15 percent of the fund's assets after 10 years. Hedge fund managers in the United States are typically reimbursed for the share of funds under management control and for the share of profits.

8. From 1996 to 1999, the average discounts on sale of funds in the Czech Republic and Slovakia were the largest in the world. The funds in Slovakia were founded during the first wave of privatization when the two countries were parts of Czechoslovakia, and thus the Slovak funds have exactly the same management terms and genesis as the Czech funds.

9. The intentions of privatization were similar in Russia (see Boycko, Shleifer, and Vishny 1995 for a view of the intentions and hopes of the some of the principal designers of Russian privatization). Black, Kraakman, and Tarassova (1999) offer horrifying accounts of the consequences of privatization in Russia.

10. Even in a market as liquid as that in the United States, exogenous increases in the level of demand have major effects on share prices. This suggests that the demand for shares of individual companies is inelastic. One example of such an exogenous increase could be that which results from inclusion of the company in the S&P 500.

11. Recently, discounts have narrowed in anticipation of legislation mandating the open-ending of funds trading at discounts above a given level. The legislation passed the lower house on April 17, 1998.

12. These deleted observations can be divided into two categories:

1. All observations in which operating profits are larger than value added. Such a situation is possible in Czech accounting, since calculation of operating profits in the Czech Republic includes gains (losses) from the sale of a company's assets. We do not want such nonproductive operations to affect our results.

2. A variable was created [(*value added – operating profit*)/*number of employees*] as a proxy for average salary in each company for each period under consideration. The one smallest and one largest numbers were extreme outliers and did not look realistic. In those two cases we supposed that either the data were reported incorrectly or some extreme exogenous circumstances distorted measurement of the performance data.

13. Regardless of whether we had used value added or operating profits per unit of labor as our measure of performance, if the division in question was more productive than the rest of the firm, then according to either of these measures, productivity would decrease from closing this economically efficient division. This is the result we want. On the other hand, if we used producer surplus per unit of capital as our measure of productivity, then the results could have been even more seriously distorted than if we used the Solow residual approach. By using both labor and capital as denominators in approaches 1–4, we can bound the impact of these distortions.

14. The specific robust regression estimates we used were provided by (Stata). They were generated by an iteratively reweighted least squares (IRLS) procedure. On each iteration, the econometric program estimates regression parameters, calculates the residuals, and down-weights cases with large residuals. The process repeats until weights no longer show much change. It employs a combination of Huber and biweight functions. These are standard robust estimation techniques and are particularly appropriate for our data, in which we think measurement error is important. For data for which measurement error is not as serious a problem, there is less need to down-weight or eliminate outliers. In this case, minimum absolute deviation might be a better approach for dealing with model misspecification or absence of normality in the error terms.

References

Anderson, Robert E. 1994. Voucher funds in transitional economies: The Czech and Slovak experience. Policy research working paper no. 1324, World Bank, Washington, D.C.

Bebchuk, Lucien, and Mark Roe. forthcoming. A theory of path dependence in corporate governance and ownership. *Stanford Law Review* 52, no. 1:127–170.

Berglof, Erik, and Ernst-Ludwig von Thadden. 1999. The changing corporate governance paradigm: Implications for transition and developing countries. Working paper for World Bank Conference on Development Economics, Washington, D.C., June 28–30, 1999.

Berle, Adolf, and Gardiner Mean. 1932. *The modern corporation and private property.* New York: MacMillan.

Black, Bernard, Reinier Kraakman, and Anna Tarassova. 1999. Russian privatization and corporate governance: What went wrong. Working paper, Stanford University Law School, Stanford, Calif.

Boycko, Maxim, Andrei Shleifer, and Robert Vishny. 1995. *Privatizing Russia.* Cambridge: MIT Press.

Burkhart, Mike, Denis Gromb, and Fausto Panunzi. 1997. Large shareholders, monitoring and fiduciary duty. *Quarterly Journal of Economics* 112:693–728.

Claessens, Stijn. 1995. Corporate governance and equity prices: Evidence from Czech and Slovak Republics. Policy research working paper no. 1427, World Bank, Washington, D.C.

Claessens, Stijn, and Simeon Djankov. 1997. Managers, incentives and corporate performance: Evidence from Czech Republic. Paper prepared for the WDI conference "Labor Markets in Transition Economies," Ann Arbor, Mich., October 17–19.

Claessens, Stijn, Simeon Djankov, and Gerhard Pohl. 1998. Ownership structure and corporate performance: Evidence from the Czech Republic. The World Bank, Washington, D.C. Unpublished manuscript.

Demsetz, Harold, and Kenneth Lehn. 1985. The structure of corporate ownership: Causes and consequences. *Journal of Political Economy* 93, no. 6:1155–1177.

Desai, Raj M. 1995. Financial market reform in the Czech Republic, 1991–1994: The Revival of Repression? Working paper series 86, Center for Economics Research and Graduate Education, Prague.

Desai, Raj M. 1996. Reformed banks and corporate governance in the Czech Republic, 1991–1996. *Post-Soviet Geography and Economics* 37, no. 8:463–494.

Dyba, Karel, and Jan Svejnar. 1994. An overview of recent economic developments in the Czech Republic. Working paper series 61, Center for Economics Research and Graduate Education, Prague.

European Union Delegation of the European Commission to the Czech Republic. 1997. Agenda 2000—Commission opinion of the Czech Republic's application for membership in the European Union. Luxembourg: European Union.

Frydman, Roman, Cheryl W. Gray, Marek Hessel, and Andrzej Rapaczynski. 1997. Private ownership and corporate performance: Some lessons from transition economies. Policy research working paper no. 1830, World Bank, Washington, D.C.

Hayri, Aydin, and Gerard A. McDermott. 1995. Restructuring in the Czech Republic—Beyond ownership and bankruptcy. Working paper series 66, Center for Economics Research and Graduate Education, Prague.

International Finance Corporation. *Emerging Stock Markets Factbook 1997.* Washington, D.C.: International Finance Corporation.

International Monetary Fund. 1997. *International Financial Statistics Yearbook.* Washington, D.C.: International Monetary Fund.

Klipper, Miriam Z. 1995. Governance of privatized firms: Problems of power and control. Working paper series 71, Center for Economics Research and Graduate Education, Prague.

Kyn, Oldrich. 1995. Eastern Europe in transition. Paper prepared for "Economic Transition of Baltic Countries" conference, Norway, Sept.

La Porta, Lopez-de-Silanes, and Andrei Shleifer. 1998. Corporate ownership around the world. Working paper, Harvard University, Cambridge, Mass.

Lastovicka, Radek, Anton Marcincin, and Michal Mejstrik. 1995. Corporate governance and share prices in voucher privatized companies. In *The Czech Republic and economic transition in Eastern Europe,* ed. Jan Svejnar. Burlington, Mass.: Academic.

Lízal, Lubomír, Miroslav Singer, and Jan Svejnar. 1995. Manager interests, breakups and performance of state enterprises in transition. In *The Czech Republic and economic transition in Eastern Europe,* ed. Jan Svejnar. Burlington, Mass.: Academic.

Mondshean, Thomas S., and Bruce R. Scott. 1998. Economic reform in the Czech Republic: Velvet revolution or velvet blanket? Working paper. Harvard Business School Case Study, Boston, Mass.

Morck, Randall, Andrei Shleifer, and Robert Vishny. 1988. Management ownership and market valuation: An empirical analysis. *Journal of Financial Economics* 20:293–315.

Pohl, Gerhard, Robert E. Anderson, Stijn Claessens, and Simeon Djankov. 1997. Privatization and restructuring in Central and Eastern Europe. Technical paper no. 368, World Bank, Washington, D.C.

Pohl, Gerhard, Gregory T. Jedrzejczak, and Robert E. Anderson. 1997. Creating capital markets in Central and Eastern Europe. Technical paper no. 295, World Bank, Washington, D.C.

Schwartz, Andrew. n.d. The Czech approach to the management of residual Shares. Unpublished manuscript.

Schwartz, Andrew, and Stephan Haggard. 1997. Privatization, foreign direct investment, and the possibility of cross-national production networks in Europe. Paper prepared for "Foreign Direct Investment and Trade in East-Central Europe: The Creation of a Unified European Economy," Vienna, June 5–6.

Shleifer, Andrei, and Robert Vishny. 1996. A theory of privatization. *Economic Journal* 106:309–319.

Shleifer, Andrei, and Robert Vishny. 1997. A survey of corporate governance. *Journal of Finance* 52:737–783.

Van Wijnbergen, Sweder, and Anton Marcincin. 1995. Voucher privatization, corporate control and the cost of capital: An analysis of the Czech Republic Privatization Programme. Research discussion paper no. 1215, Centre for Economic Policy.

Veverka, Jan. 1997. Current aspects of the Czech capital market. Working paper, Ministry of Finance of the Czech Republic, Prague.

Zemplinerova, Alena, and Josef Stibal. 1995. Evolution and efficiency of concentration in manufacturing. In *The Czech Republic and economic transition in Eastern Europe*, ed. Jan Svejnar. Burlington, Mass.: Academic.

11 Financial Conditions and Investment during the Transition: Evidence from Czech Firms

Lubomír Lízal and Jan Svejnar

11.1 Introduction

Since investment determines the quantity and quality of one of the two most important factors of production and greatly affects macroeconomic activity, studies of investment behavior have always occupied a pivotal place in Western economics. On the demand side, much of the literature has focused on establishing the relative merits of the Tobin Q, neoclassical, and accelerator models of investment demand, for the most part assuming that the supply of investment finance is perfectly elastic. In recent years, some of the literature has concentrated on the supply side, examining the effects of potential market imperfections on the supply of capital to different types of firms.[1]

In view of Stalin's and other communist leaders' preoccupation with overtaking capitalist economies by carrying out massive capital formation, studies of investment have also constituted a key area of comparative economics.[2] Centrally planned economies (CPEs) indeed reported very high rates of investment during most of their existence, although these rates declined somewhat in the 1980s as the growth of these economies slowed and popular demand for consumption goods became harder to ignore (EBRD 1995). The high pre-1980s investment rates in CPEs also generated large stocks of capital whose vintage became gradually older in the 1980s. Finally, the CPEs increasingly lagged in terms of technical progress, and the Coordinating Committee for Multilateral Export Controls (COCOM) embargo, imposed in the 1980s by Western countries on exports of advanced technology to the CPEs, further hampered the ability of these economies to reduce the rate of growth of their relative technological obsolescence.

As the transition from central planning to a market system started to unfold in the 1990s, it became clear that the transition economies needed to invest heavily to modernize their obsolete capital stock and become competitive in world markets. The issue of how best to restructure and modernize the state-owned firms has been a focal point of a major policy debate about what constitutes an optimal type of ownership and legal form in these new market economies. Interestingly, although a small number of studies have provided valuable partial surveys of investment in the transition economies,[3] detailed analytical studies of the investment behavior of firms in these economies are just being performed.

In this chapter, we carry out an in-depth analytical study of investment behavior using data from most industrial firms located in the Czech Republic in 1992–1995.

The Czech Republic is one of the pioneering transition countries, having carried out the most widespread privatization and commercialization of firms, attracting significant foreign direct investment and maintaining relatively high rates of investment in general. Our study is hence of interest because it analyzes investment behavior in one of the leading transition economies that has served as a model for the countries that have launched their transitions since.

Although our study is naturally of interest to the analysts, policymakers, and observers of the transition process, the fact that we are able to use a very large panel of quarterly firm-level data makes our work relevant in the context of recent investment literature in general. In particular, by using micro panel data we are able to eliminate bias introduced by aggregation (see, e.g., Abel and Blanchard 1986), reduce measurement error, and take into account heterogeneity across firms and over time (see, e.g., Bond and Meghir 1994).

Unlike in many Western studies, we are fortunate to have data on both depreciation and net investment. Our empirical strategy has therefore been to examine the behavior of these two components of gross investment separately. Since our results about the behavior of depreciation parallel the earlier findings by Lizal (1999a), in this chapter we extend this work but focus primarily on the behavior of net investment. Moreover, since the degree of imperfection of capital markets and the relationship between enterprise ownership and investment (strategic restructuring) are key issues in the transition literature, we examine the relationship between net investment and the availability of internal finance, using data from 13 principal ownership/legal form categories of firms.

The switch from central planning to a transition period has made firms that traditionally received centrally allocated investment funds face the emerging commercial banks and other financial institutions. Operating in a highly protected and concentrated environment, the new commercial banks usually imposed high spreads between deposit and lending rates to increase their low initial capitalization. They also had to develop from scratch their project appraisal capability and establish international accounting standards. In this context, many of the new and existing firms likely faced expensive external finance for investment or were denied such finance. The data from transition economies hence lend themselves to testing the financing hierarchy and credit rationing hypotheses advanced in the Western literature.[4]

In this chapter we present estimates of the financing hierarchy (credit rationing) models of net investment. We focus on these supply side models because there are strong beliefs among observers of the transition economies that capital markets are highly imperfect and that verifying the extent of this imperfection is an important task for empirical research. Moreover, our pretests revealed that models that stem form the neoclassical literature do not get much support from the net investment data.[5]

11.2   The Data and Basic Statistics

11.2.1   Comparative Macroeconomic Indicators

Since 1991, the national statistical offices of the Czech Republic, Hungary, Poland, and Slovakia have been collecting comparable data on major macroeconomic indicators in their countries. In table 11.1, we present aggregate time series data from this source on GDP, gross investment, and the investment-to-GDP ratio for these four economies. The corresponding plots of the investment/GDP ratio are shown in figure 11.1. The data in table 11.1 and figure 11.1 reveal two striking features: the Czech and Slovak Republics have since 1991 uniformly invested a higher proportion of GDP than Hungary and Poland, and the investment behavior displays a very strong and regular seasonal character in all four economies.

With respect to the rates of investment across the four economies, between 1991 and the fourth quarter of 1996, the investment-to-GDP ratio in the Czech Republic averaged 30 percent and fluctuated in the 14–54 percent range. In Slovakia, the ratio averaged 32 percent, with the range being 16–67 percent. In Hungary, investment-to-GDP averaged 19 percent and moved between 9 and 32 percent. Finally, in Poland, the investment-to-GDP ratio averaged a mere 10 percent, with the range being 5–19 percent.

The question that naturally arises is why the four Central European countries display such different propensities to invest. In the case of Poland, the data cover only larger firms (those in industry with more than 50 workers and 20 workers elsewhere). It is hence possible that this omission of smaller firms accounts for the low investment figures for Poland. As Gomulka and Jasinski (1994) have shown, small private firms accounted for most of the growth in the Polish economy in the early 1990s, and they are likely to have invested significantly to produce this growth. In the Czech Republic, unlike in the other three countries, the investment data exclude intangible assets. The Czech investment-to-GDP ratio would hence be even higher if this type of investment were included. The greatest puzzle is perhaps Hungary, which is reported by the World Bank (1996) to have received $10.6 billion in foreign direct investment (equivalent to 31 percent of its 1994 GDP) between 1989 and 1995. In contrast, in the same period, the Czech Republic, with a similar population, received only $4 billion (13 percent of its 1994 GDP), Poland $6.5 billion (7 percent of its 1994 GDP), and Slovakia $0.5 billion (4 percent of its 1994 GDP). Hungary's

Table 11.1
Macroeconomic indicators

Date	Czech Republic		Hungary		Poland		Slovak Republic	
	I	I/GDP	I	I/GDP	I	I/GDP	I	I/GDP
1991	154.4	0.22	491.9	0.21	12.3	0.15	69.8	0.25
1992/1	28.1	0.14	80.9	0.11	2.3	0.08	16.3	0.22
1992/2	39.8	0.20	129.1	0.18	2.9	0.10	20.3	0.27
1992/3	40.8	0.20	159.4	0.22	2.7	0.09	20.3	0.27
1992/4	92.2	0.46	186.2	0.26	5.4	0.19	34.2	0.45
1993/1	33.3	0.15	78.1	0.09	2.0	0.05	15.2	0.16
1993/2	58.4	0.26	140.1	0.16	3.3	0.08	22.7	0.25
1993/3	64.2	0.28	202.8	0.23	3.4	0.09	27.0	0.29
1993/4	100.2	0.44	204.0	0.23	5.1	0.13	40.1	0.43
1994/1	40.0	0.15	109.3	0.10	2.9	0.06	20.4	0.18
1994/2	70.7	0.27	171.6	0.16	4.0	0.08	26.6	0.24
1994/3	81.4	0.31	234.2	0.21	4.5	0.09	29.4	0.27
1994/4	126.7	0.49	337.8	0.31	8.0	0.15	48.4	0.44
1995/1	55.3	0.18	139.4	0.10	4.0	0.06	24.1	0.19
1995/2	91.5	0.30	230.8	0.17	5.9	0.08	35.8	0.28
1995/3	101.0	0.33	241.3	0.18	7.1	0.10	39.1	0.30
1995/4	163.3	0.54	391.5	0.29	11.9	0.17	63.8	0.49
1996/1	80.2	0.21	177.1	0.10	5.1	0.06	39.1	0.27
1996/2	133.4	0.35	268.5	0.16	8.9	0.10	55.1	0.38
1996/3	142.5	0.37	313.1	0.18	9.0	0.11	57.9	0.40
1996/4	202.8	0.53	578.9	0.34	17.4	0.19	90.2	0.63
1996	558.9	0.36	1337.6	0.20	41.3	0.11	242.3	0.42

Source: CESTAT (former Statistical Bulletin of Czech, Hungarian, Polish, Slovak, and then Slovenian Statistical Offices).
Notes: All figures in billions of current (nominal) national currencies (Czech Crown, Slovak Crown, Polish Zloty, Hungarian Forint) as of 1997. All figures are comparable since the same methodology is used, whereas Hungary and Poland use the system of national accounts (SNA) methodology. Investment includes tangible and intangible fixed assets (with the exception of figure for the Czech Republic, which includes only tangible fixed assets). With the exception of Poland, all investment data are for the whole national economy, including estimates for entities not monitored by statistical offices. Investment data for Poland reflect entities with more than 20 (50 for industry) employees. I = Investment; I/GDP = Investment-to-GDP ratio.

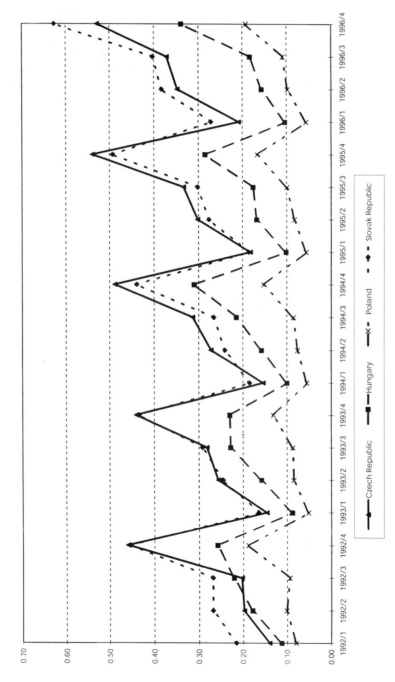

Figure 11.1

domestic investment is hence particularly low compared to that of the other three countries.

The striking aspect of the seasonal pattern is that investment rises continuously each year from the first to the fourth quarter, and in the fourth quarter it is almost twice as high as in the second and third quarters. The pattern is most clearly visible in the Czech and Slovak data, but it exists in the investment series of all four countries. As we will show presently, the same seasonal pattern is visible in the Czech firm-level data.

11.2.2 The Czech Enterprise-Level Data

The principal data set that we use in the present analysis was collected by the Czech Statistical Office (CSO) and covers all industrial firms employing more than 25 people in 1992–1994 and more than 100 people in 1995. The data were collected in quarterly or monthly intervals, depending on the size of the enterprise and the reported variables. We have combined the monthly and quarterly data so as to maximize the sample size. In some parts of our analysis, we also treat the 1995 data separately because of the change in the composition of firms in that year.

Although the CSO was careful in collecting the data, the data set contains a number of errors and inconsistencies. Moreover, when coding data the CSO does not distinguish between missing values and zeros. In an attempt to assemble a reliable data set (approximately 50,700 quarterly observations), we have used various consistency checks.[6]

As a result of these consistency checks, about 10 percent of the observations in the data set had to be dropped, leaving us with a sample comprising about 90 percent of all industrial firms in the Czech Republic.[7] In terms of total number of firms (quarterly observations), our data set covers 2,860 firms (2,252–2,738 quarterly observations) in 1992, 3,231 firms (2,657–3,009 quarterly observations) in 1993, 4,133 firms (3,503–3,867 quarterly observations) in 1994, and 2,271 firms (2,205–2,261 quarterly observations) in 1995. The number of firms and quarterly observations declined between 1994 and 1995 because the CSO switched from covering firms with 25 or more employees to covering those with 100 or more employees. A detailed description of the data is provided in the appendix.

As may be seen from table 11.2, our data set contains detailed information about the ownership and legal form of the firms it tracks. The ownership categories reflect majority ownership of each firm (e.g., a firm is classified as privately owned if it is more than 50 percent privately owned). When no single type of owner (private, cooperative, state, or foreign) holds a majority stake in the firm, the firm is classified as

Table 11.2
Cross-tabulation of known ownership and legal form

Legal Form	Ownership						
	Private	Cooper-ative	State	Foreign	Mixed	Other	Total
Entrepreneurship	**1,845**	0	0	4	0	0	1,849
Limited liability (ltd.)	**13,927**	9	**441**	**2,091**	**298**	22	16,716
Societé Commandité	134	0	0	51	0	0	185
Joint stock company	**2,480**	0	**11,475**	**707**	**766**	51	15,479
Other cooperative	4	**3,063**	0	0	0	0	3,067
Producer cooperative	0	**587**	0	0	0	0	587
State-owned enterprise	0	0	**6,835**	0	0	0	6,835
Subsidized institution	0	0	22	0	0	0	22
Other	12	3	0	26	0	**11**	52
Total	18,402	3,662	18,773	2,807	1,064	84	44,792

Notes: Boldface numbers denote the major ownership/legal form categories of firms that we analyze. All firms with ownership or legal form types other than those categorized are placed in the Other/Other category. Firms with unknown ownership and/or legal form are also included in the Other/Other group.

having mixed ownership. Ownership was categorized by the CSO after the two massive waves of privatization in the Czech Republic in 1992 and 1993. Since the mass privatization of 1992–1993 constituted the principal reallocation of majority ownership stakes in the Czech Republic, there is little variation in the ownership of any given firm during our 1992–1995 sample period.

The legal form of a firm as categorized in table 11.2 denotes the type of legal registration of the firm and reflects the legal obligations and liabilities associated with each form of registration. It also captures the relative financial and bureaucratic ease of establishing a given type of firm. Thus, individual (family), cooperative, and limited liability categories tend to capture smaller firms that were started with a relatively low initial capital base. In contrast, joint stock companies tend to be larger in size. The exceptions to this rule are the state-owned and mixed-ownership firms, each of which has a similar average firm size in both the limited liability and joint stock legal form. Finally, state-owned/state-registered firms tend to be relatively small, averaging less than one half the number of employees of other state-owned firms.

From table 11.2 it is clear that the most important ownership/legal form categories are privately owned/limited liability companies (13,927 quarterly observations) and state-owned/joint stock companies (11,475 quarterly observations). These are followed by state-owned/state-registered enterprises (6,835 quarterly observations), cooperatively owned/rural cooperatives (3,063 observations), privately owned/joint stock companies (2,480 observations), foreign-owned/limited liability companies (2,091 observations), privately owned/individual or family businesses (1,845 observations), mixed-ownership/joint stock companies (766 observations), foreign-owned/joint stock companies (707 observations), cooperatively owned/producer cooperatives (587 observations), state-owned/limited liability companies (441 observations), and mixed-ownership/limited liability firms (298 observations). These 12 categories plus the remaining "other" firms category constitute the 13 categories that we analyze in this chapter.

Tables 11.A.1 and 11.A.2 give the evolution over time of the number of observations in the legal form and ownership categories, respectively. As may be seen from table 11.A.1, between 1992 and 1994 joint stock companies maintained their share in the total number of observations at around 30 percent, but their share jumps to 46 percent in 1995, when only firms with 100 or more employees are considered. The share of limited liability companies rose from 27 percent in 1992 to 47 percent in 1994 and then dropped to 36 percent in 1995, when only firms with 100 or more employees are included. The share of firms registered as having state-owned enterprise legal form declined from 25 percent to 6 percent and those registered as individual or family (entrepreneur) legal form remained at about 4 percent in 1992–1994 period but dropped to less than 2 percent when only larger firms were counted in 1995. In terms of ownership (table 11.A.2), the share of privately owned firms rose from 31 percent in 1992 to 51 percent in 1994 and then receded to 41 percent in the sample of larger firms in 1995. The share of state-owned firms declined from 53 percent in 1992 to 31 percent in 1994, but then rose again to 41 percent in 1995. Between 1992 and 1995 cooperatively owned firms' share decreased from 10 percent to 7 percent, whereas that of foreign-owned firms jumped from 4 percent to 8 percent and that of mixed companies rose from 2 percent to 4 percent. Overall, while the trend has not been in all cases monotonic, since 1992 there has been a definite increase in the share of domestic private, foreign and mixed ownership, together with the limited liability legal form.

Table 11.A.3 gives the distribution of observations across industries. Firms are quite broadly distributed across industries, with the largest share of firms (16 percent) being in the food production industry, 13 percent in the machinery industry, 11 percent in the metal product industry, 7 percent each in the processing of nonmetallic minerals and the furniture industry, and 6 percent in the textile industry. Each of the remaining industry groups has less than 5 percent of all firms.

Table 11.3 presents summary statistics of variables relevant to our analysis. As the table shows, although both net investment and depreciation follow the same seasonal pattern with a fourth-quarter peak that was observed in the aggregate data, the pattern is much more pronounced in net investment than in depreciation. Profit is relatively steady across all quarters in 1992 but shows a strong downward trend across quarters in 1993, 1994, and 1995. In 1993 and 1995 profit reaches negative values in the last quarter and shows relatively low overall levels in comparison to 1992 and 1994. The elimination of the small firms from the data set between 1994 and 1995 increased the average size of the labor force and capital stock dramatically between the last quarter of 1994 and the first quarter of 1995.

To start understanding the micro foundations of the cyclicality of aggregate gross investment, characterized by the peak in the fourth quarter of each year (tables 11.1 and 11.3), we examine the behavior of net investment as well as depreciation in each of the 13 categories of firms. Table 11.4 presents the quarterly evolution of the ratio of net investment to total production for each of the 13 principal ownership/legal form categories of firms. As can be seen from the table, the aggregate cyclical nature of the gross investment behavior is reflected regularly in the net investment behavior of state-owned/joint stock companies, foreign-owned/joint stock companies, and mixed-ownership/joint stock companies. In three out of the four years, this behavior is also detected in private/joint stock companies, state-owned/state-registered firms and foreign-owned/limited liability companies. Finally, cooperatives, state-owned/ limited liability companies, mixed-ownership/limited liability companies, and other firms display this pattern in two of the four years. In sum, the strong aggregate seasonal pattern of gross investment is reflected primarily in the net investment behavior of joint stock companies of all ownership types and to a lesser extent in the net investment pattern of state-owned/state-registered and foreign-owned/limited liability firms. Privately owned/individual (family) businesses and limited liability companies show this pattern in only one of the four years.

In examining the behavior of the ratio of depreciation to production in the various types of firms, we find virtually no reflection of the aggregate cyclical pattern in gross investment (table 11.5). The quarterly depreciation-to-production ratio data of the various types of firms vary but do not display the strong upward trend with a peak in the fourth quarter previously observed in tables 11.1, 11.3, and 11.4. At the level of the specific categories of firms, the seasonal behavior of the aggregate gross investment-to-GDP ratio is hence primarily accounted for by the pattern of net investment described earlier.

Finally, in table 11.6 we present calculations of the ratio of net investment plus depreciation to depreciation for each type of firms (i.e., investment/depreciation). Examining this ratio is useful, because values of less than unity identify firms that are not replacing existing capital stock, whereas values significantly in excess of unity indicate firms that are substantially increasing their capital stock. As may be

Table 11.3
Means (standard deviations) of principal variables

Ownership/ Form	Investment/ Capital	Deprec./ Capital	Investment/ Labor	Investment/ Production	Profit	Labor
1992/Q1	na	na	9.95 (72.30)	0.14 (1.66)	5,913 (34,295)	626 (1,818)
1992/Q2	na	na	12.87 (95.63)	0.17 (2.26)	5,195 (28,505)	552 (1,660)
1992/Q3	na	na	12.06 (52.00)	0.15 (0.97)	4,267 (27,974)	520 (1,584)
1992/Q4	na	na	20.60 (82.07)	0.20 (1.14)	5,265 (74,644)	494 (1,527)
1993/Q1	0.029 (0.094)	0.022 (0.044)	7.61 (29.31)	0.08 (0.27)	4,577 (37,346)	494 (1,536)
1993/Q2	0.041 (0.118)	0.025 (0.052)	13.57 (54.77)	0.15 (1.64)	3,159 (27,386)	457 (1,415)
1993/Q3	0.040 (0.110)	0.025 (0.053)	12.23 (43.43)	0.99 (43.27)	1,577 (33,231)	433 (1,352)
1993/Q4	0.054 (0.132)	0.035 (0.076)	19.46 (67.58)	0.18 (1.22)	−3,800 (45,994)	417 (1,312)
1994/Q1	0.031 (0.096)	0.022 (0.044)	11.38 (93.28)	0.14 (1.67)	5,150 (29,255)	347 (1,086)
1994/Q2	0.039 (0.101)	0.023 (0.039)	13.99 (48.84)	0.10 (0.51)	4,432 (30,952)	337 (1,056)
1994/Q3	0.036 (0.098)	0.024 (0.047)	13.84 (47.68)	0.11 (0.46)	3,392 (34,164)	332 (1,032)
1994/Q4	0.061 (0.132)	0.038 (0.075)	23.51 (98.29)	0.19 (1.37)	1,271 (29,555)	131 (991)
1995/Q1	0.029 (0.097)	0.019 (0.028)	12.47 (51.68)	0.16 (2.89)	5,581 (47,196)	506 (1,242)
1995/Q2	0.034 (0.09)	0.022 (0.041)	16.16 (48.20)	0.13 (0.87)	4,931 (34,482)	500 (1,227)
1995/Q3	0.032 (0.081)	0.021 (0.044)	15.31 (41.83)	0.13 (0.67)	3,172 (41,884)	496 (1,212)
1995/Q4	0.046 (0.100)	0.028 (0.057)	24.26 (62.51)	0.16 (0.51)	−1,884 (35,192)	493 (1,201)
Overall	0.040 (0.107)	0.026 (0.053)	15.06 (66.54)	0.19 (10.96)	3,190 (38,283)	442 (1,326)
Obs.[a]	34,779	34,779	44,879	42,936	44,879	44,879

[a] Number of observations is the sum of all quarterly observations with nonmissing values.
[b] Maximum number of observations is the maximum of all quarterly observations with nonmissing values.

Table 11.3
(continued)

Investment	Production	Depreciation	Capital	Wage	Max. no. of obs.[b]
4,851 (21,288)	76,746 (267)	4,629 (21,660)	na	4.06 (0.98)	2,252
6,113 (28,147)	71,087 (259)	4,791 (23,316)	na	4.4 (1.13)	2,484
5,904 (31,109)	62,763 (235)	4,075 (18,824)	na	4.43 (1.06)	2,626
10,868 (57,006)	67,753 (258)	4,914 (22,750)	na	5.14 (1.38)	2,738
4,278 (30,115)	70,715 (273)	4,440 (19,677)	347 (1,522)	5.00 (1.22)	2,657
6,452 (32,831)	65,880 (273)	4,365 (19,310)	328 (1,469)	5.52 (1.51)	2,841
6,264 (36,822)	56,979 (224)	4,281 (23,792)	315 (1,447)	5.51 (1.40)	2,940
9,488 (56,153)	61,305 (265)	5,154 (33,444)	311 (1,451)	6.16 (1.77)	3,009
3,520 (20,835)	53,363 (227)	3,642 (19,366)	279 (1,350)	5.76 (1.50)	3,503
5,633 (40,038)	57,962 (270)	3,546 (18,740)	278 (1,352)	6.28 (1.72)	3,613
5,685 (45,034)	52,619 (216)	3,549 (17,684)	274 (1,331)	6.46 (1.73)	3,653
8,319 (66,621)	56,160 (221)	3,826 (19,562)	261 (1,329)	7.21 (2.17)	3,867
5,936 (27,955)	105,557 (448)	6,021 (26,858)	445 (1,759)	6.81 (1.69)	2,205
8,262 (37,561)	108,143 (437)	6,455 (30,794)	452 (1,803)	7.51 (2.01)	2,261
8,965 (48,508)	97,267 (389)	6,356 (27,164)	453 (1,784)	7.56 (1.91)	2,234
14,463 (66,746)	120,059 (501)	7,574 (23,887)	459 (1,815)	8.41 (2.50)	2,243
7,033 (43,544)	70,895 (299)	4,673 (13,480)	335 (1,509)	6.01 (2.01)	44,984
44,984	43,610	44,879	34,779	44,879	44,984

Table 11.4
Net investment-to-production ratio by type of firm, 1992–1995

Time	Private/ Enterpr.	Private/ Ltd.	Private/ J. Stock	Coop./ General	Coop./ Producer	State/ Ltd.	State/ J. Stock
1992/Q1	0.00	0.27	0.25	0.01	−0.02	−1.81	−0.04
	(0.10)	(4.03)	(1.17)	(0.19)	(0.10)	(5.49)	(0.69)
1992/Q2	0.03	0.01	0.05	0.05	0.01	−0.52	0.00
	(0.25)	(0.30)	(0.24)	(0.36)	(0.11)	(1.68)	(1.13)
1992/Q3	0.02	0.05	−0.01	0.01	0.03	−0.17	−0.67
	(0.15)	(0.86)	(0.27)	(0.25)	(0.38)	(0.60)	(17.01)
1992/Q4	0.09	−0.01	0.41	0.03	−0.01	−0.08	0.06
	(0.46)	(1.57)	(3.31)	(0.63)	(0.11)	(0.17)	(1.19)
1993/Q1	0.04	0.00	0.00	−0.01	0.05	−0.16	−0.09
	(0.18)	(0.30)	(0.15)	(0.12)	(0.70)	(0.48)	(1.45)
1993/Q2	0.04	0.04	0.05	0.01	−0.04	−0.01	−0.08
	(0.15)	(0.35)	(0.43)	(0.15)	(0.20)	(0.56)	(1.32)
1993/Q3	0.03	0.04	0.07	0.03	−0.07	−0.08	−0.06
	(0.21)	(0.47)	(0.36)	(0.24)	(0.31)	(0.49)	(1.13)
1993/Q4	0.03	0.02	0.07	0.02	0.05	0.01	0.06
	(0.16)	(1.39)	(0.63)	(0.26)	(0.30)	(0.66)	(0.42)
1994/Q1	0.01	0.08	0.07	−0.02	−0.09	0.28	−0.14
	(0.23)	(1.97)	(1.08)	(0.16)	(0.01)	(5.13)	(2.86)
1994/Q2	0.15	0.03	0.01	−0.01	−0.05	−0.03	−0.72
	(1.13)	(0.35)	(0.35)	(0.13)	(0.05)	(0.10)	(19.62)
1994/Q3	0.11	0.03	0.10	−0.01	−0.09	0.01	−0.10
	(0.68)	(0.43)	(0.80)	(0.17)	(0.04)	(0.14)	(3.01)
1994/Q4	0.08	0.12	0.15	0.06	−0.05	−0.03	0.04
	(0.49)	(1.73)	(0.98)	(0.60)	(0.04)	(0.26)	(0.39)
1995/Q1	0.04	0.03	−0.20	−0.02	−0.08	0.00	−0.11
	(0.35)	(0.42)	(3.44)	(0.08)	(0.09)	(0.09)	(1.21)
1995/Q2	0.00	0.02	0.06	0.00	−0.10	0.02	−0.07
	(0.06)	(0.39)	(0.36)	(0.14)	(0.18)	(0.09)	(0.98)
1995/Q3	0.00	−0.01	0.08	0.02	−0.08	0.40	−0.08
	(0.06)	(0.51)	(0.41)	(0.19)	(0.16)	(2.03)	(1.64)
1995/Q4	0.01	0.02	0.09	0.05	−0.06	0.19	0.05
	(0.09)	(0.32)	(0.54)	(0.28)	(0.66)	(0.93)	(0.59)

Table 11.4
(continued)

State/ SOE	State/ Subsd.	Foreign/ Ltd.	Foreign/ J. Stock	Mixed/ J. Stock	Mixed/ Ltd.	Other/ Other	All
0.00 (0.34)	−0.33 (0.11)	0.07 (0.34)	0.13 (0.36)	0.20 (1.03)	−0.03 (0.03)	−0.03 (0.11)	0.03 (1.64)
0.02 (0.77)	−0.04 (0.03)	0.11 (0.60)	3.68 (18.94)	0.03 (0.32)	0.00 (0.10)	0.07 (0.66)	0.06 (2.30)
0.03 (0.51)	−0.03 (na)	0.19 (0.70)	0.59 (1.76)	0.14 (0.60)	0.01 (0.73)	−0.03 (0.07)	−0.14 (8.76)
0.05 (0.92)	−0.04 (na)	0.26 (1.10)	0.73 (3.39)	0.80 (4.52)	1.89 (5.86)	0.00 (0.09)	0.08 (1.50)
−0.06 (0.25)	−0.28 (0.02)	0.08 (0.41)	0.04 (0.28)	−0.04 (0.09)	0.18 (0.60)	0.07 (0.27)	−0.03 (0.78)
0.12 (2.79)	−0.11 (0.12)	0.08 (0.25)	0.32 (1.23)	0.03 (0.36)	0.21 (0.60)	−0.09 (0.47)	0.03 (1.55)
0.09 (2.96)	−0.03 (na)	0.14 (0.42)	0.02 (0.22)	−0.02 (0.12)	0.36 (1.45)	0.00 (0.12)	0.03 (1.50)
0.00 (0.65)	−0.22 (na)	0.46 (1.92)	0.19 (0.54)	0.05 (0.23)	0.32 (0.60)	−0.06 (0.43)	0.05 (0.96)
−0.15 (0.47)	na	0.15 (0.82)	0.03 (0.19)	0.06 (0.37)	−0.02 (0.14)	−0.03 (0.21)	0.00 (1.92)
−0.21 (1.31)	na	0.13 (0.54)	0.07 (0.41)	0.00 (0.17)	−0.02 (0.13)	0.03 (0.17)	−0.15 (9.36)
−0.79 (10.95)	na	0.12 (0.44)	0.05 (0.39)	−0.03 (0.17)	−0.02 (0.11)	0.01 (0.22)	−0.05 (3.38)
−0.06 (0.52)	na	0.31 (1.51)	0.08 (0.35)	0.04 (0.17)	0.08 (0.33)	0.11 (0.30)	0.10 (1.25)
−0.09 (0.26)	na	0.10 (0.48)	0.10 (0.49)	−0.04 (0.18)	−0.02 (0.05)	0.09 (0.22)	−0.04 (1.27)
−0.05 (0.18)	na	0.10 (0.66)	0.05 (0.31)	−0.05 (0.86)	0.00 (0.10)	0.19 (0.67)	−0.01 (0.66)
−0.06 (0.20)	na	0.23 (1.44)	0.01 (0.22)	−0.03 (0.16)	0.01 (0.11)	0.11 (0.42)	−0.01 (1.07)
−0.03 (0.37)	na	0.21 (0.70)	0.05 (0.22)	0.01 (0.26)	−0.02 (0.07)	0.45 (0.97)	0.05 (0.49)

Table 11.5
Depreciation-to-production ratio by type of firm, 1992–1995

Time	Private/ Enterpr.	Private/ Ltd.	Private/ J. Stock	Coop./ General	Coop./ Producer	State/ Ltd.	State/ J. Stock
1992/Q1	0.03 (0.03)	0.04 (0.06)	0.07 (0.06)	0.05 (0.06)	0.05 (0.08)	1.84 (5.48)	0.16 (0.77)
1992/Q2	0.04 (0.06)	0.05 (0.17)	0.07 (0.08)	0.05 (0.07)	0.05 (0.04)	0.55 (1.67)	0.16 (0.70)
1992/Q3	0.03 (0.05)	0.06 (0.28)	0.09 (0.19)	0.05 (0.07)	0.07 (0.11)	0.20 (0.60)	0.88 (18.45)
1992/Q4	0.04 (0.07)	0.11 (1.51)	0.12 (0.28)	0.10 (0.39)	0.05 (0.04)	0.11 (0.14)	0.16 (0.99)
1993/Q1	0.03 (0.03)	0.05 (0.23)	0.08 (0.09)	0.05 (0.05)	0.07 (0.11)	0.25 (0.36)	0.19 (1.44)
1993/Q2	0.04 (0.08)	0.05 (0.10)	0.09 (0.16)	0.05 (0.06)	0.08 (0.18)	0.16 (0.33)	0.22 (1.35)
1993/Q3	0.04 (0.07)	0.05 (0.11)	0.10 (0.11)	0.07 (0.10)	0.12 (0.29)	0.18 (0.43)	0.19 (1.10)
1993/Q4	0.04 (0.04)	0.11 (1.30)	0.14 (0.25)	0.09 (0.16)	0.06 (0.05)	0.19 (0.26)	0.12 (0.19)
1994/Q1	0.05 (0.09)	0.06 (0.23)	0.22 (1.63)	0.07 (0.10)	0.09 (0.01)	0.53 (2.59)	0.27 (4.62)
1994/Q2	0.06 (0.13)	0.05 (0.21)	0.10 (0.18)	0.06 (0.07)	0.08 (0.01)	0.07 (0.07)	0.84 (19.62)
1994/Q3	0.05 (0.05)	0.06 (0.27)	0.11 (0.22)	0.07 (0.09)	0.09 (0.04)	0.07 (0.05)	0.23 (3.01)
1994/Q4	0.09 (0.33)	0.07 (0.23)	0.13 (0.33)	0.08 (0.14)	0.07 (0.01)	0.11 (0.27)	0.11 (0.28)
1995/Q1	0.05 (0.07)	0.06 (0.17)	0.35 (3.52)	0.06 (0.04)	0.09 (0.08)	0.07 (0.04)	0.21 (1.55)
1995/Q2	0.04 (0.04)	0.06 (0.21)	0.09 (0.14)	0.06 (0.05)	0.13 (0.16)	0.05 (0.02)	0.25 (2.10)
1995/Q3	0.04 (0.04)	0.08 (0.42)	0.10 (0.13)	0.07 (0.05)	0.14 (0.10)	0.06 (0.06)	0.23 (2.40)
1995/Q4	0.05 (0.06)	0.09 (0.55)	0.13 (0.27)	0.08 (0.15)	0.30 (0.55)	0.05 (0.03)	0.13 (0.48)

Table 11.5
(continued)

State/ SOE	State/ Subsd.	Foreign/ Ltd.	Foreign/ J. Stock	Mixed/ J. Stock	Mixed/ Ltd.	Other/ Other	All
0.12 (0.73)	0.42 (0.12)	0.06 (0.06)	0.07 (0.06)	0.11 (0.27)	0.03 (0.03)	0.07 (0.07)	0.11 (0.73)
0.12 (0.62)	0.18 (0.22)	0.07 (0.17)	0.09 (0.13)	0.10 (0.22)	0.04 (0.05)	0.15 (0.32)	0.11 (0.53)
0.12 (0.36)	0.03 (na)	0.05 (0.07)	0.15 (0.37)	0.08 (0.12)	0.18 (0.44)	0.06 (0.05)	0.29 (9.48)
0.13 (0.84)	0.04 (na)	0.07 (0.12)	0.06 (0.09)	0.05 (0.04)	0.10 (0.18)	0.06 (0.05)	0.12 (1.03)
0.12 (0.29)	0.34 (0.01)	0.05 (0.07)	0.11 (0.14)	0.07 (0.09)	0.06 (0.08)	0.08 (0.10)	0.11 (0.76)
0.14 (0.57)	0.17 (0.21)	0.05 (0.08)	0.11 (0.15)	0.07 (0.07)	0.09 (0.07)	0.18 (0.45)	0.12 (0.73)
0.27 (2.22)	0.03 (na)	0.06 (0.11)	0.13 (0.17)	0.07 (0.07)	0.07 (0.07)	0.06 (0.05)	0.14 (1.15)
0.23 (1.90)	0.22 (na)	0.14 (0.48)	0.13 (0.19)	0.05 (0.04)	0.06 (0.05)	0.15 (0.37)	0.13 (1.11)
0.20 (0.52)	na	0.10 (0.49)	0.11 (0.12)	0.07 (0.07)	0.13 (0.19)	0.10 (0.20)	0.14 (2.26)
0.25 (1.31)	na	0.11 (0.72)	0.11 (0.15)	0.08 (0.09)	0.07 (0.10)	0.07 (0.10)	0.26 (9.36)
0.83 (10.94)	na	0.06 (0.11)	0.11 (0.12)	0.11 (0.20)	0.06 (0.05)	0.07 (0.12)	0.16 (3.36)
0.15 (0.46)	na	0.10 (0.30)	0.12 (0.18)	0.09 (0.13)	0.06 (0.05)	0.08 (0.10)	0.09 (0.27)
0.14 (0.28)	na	0.06 (0.06)	0.12 (0.19)	0.11 (0.18)	0.06 (0.07)	0.07 (0.08)	0.14 (1.39)
0.12 (0.22)	na	0.08 (0.25)	0.11 (0.10)	0.18 (0.83)	0.05 (0.06)	0.08 (0.11)	0.14 (1.24)
0.13 (0.18)	na	0.10 (0.26)	0.12 (0.15)	0.11 (0.21)	0.05 (0.05)	0.07 (0.09)	0.13 (1.40)
0.14 (0.22)	na	0.08 (0.12)	0.11 (0.14)	0.09 (0.13)	0.06 (0.06)	0.09 (0.11)	0.11 (0.43)

Table 11.6
Investment-to-depreciation rates by type of firm, 1992–1995

Time	Private/ Enterpr.	Private/ Ltd.	Private/ J. Stock	Coop./ General	Coop./ Producer	State/ Ltd.	State/ J. Stock
1992/Q1	3.04 (10.59)	21.66 (288.18)	12.42 (43.71)	1.33 (2.87)	0.98 (2.05)	0.30 (0.88)	1.87 (6.47)
1992/Q2	6.60 (30.54)	115.81 (2565.19)	4.07 (14.16)	2.97 (12.21)	1.93 (6.77)	0.49 (1.03)	4.05 (49.23)
1992/Q3	3.92 (12.75)	6.96 (40.14)	3.27 (13.72)	1.98 (11.03)	3.86 (17.75)	0.38 (1.02)	2.03 (5.37)
1992/Q4	7.58 (30.44)	6.44 (28.71)	4.87 (14.92)	4.68 (21.06)	1.04 (2.10)	0.47 (1.16)	3.74 (13.91)
1993/Q1	6.60 (26.30)	3.87 (17.58)	2.51 (8.78)	2.45 (15.10)	2.12 (8.43)	1.09 (4.88)	1.78 (7.48)
1993/Q2	5.53 (21.76)	6.64 (34.34)	3.63 (7.79)	1.70 (3.58)	1.28 (2.96)	2.46 (9.89)	2.76 (12.74)
1993/Q3	5.71 (26.36)	5.37 (23.65)	13.31 (105.60)	2.75 (7.61)	0.94 (1.90)	1.29 (2.87)	1.98 (7.29)
1993/Q4	12.07 (96.52)	4.32 (19.50)	3.66 (7.65)	2.09 (3.93)	1.98 (3.60)	1.59 (3.08)	4.51 (33.05)
1994/Q1	3.27 (10.88)	6.74 (46.72)	2.31 (10.71)	1.46 (6.36)	0.00 (0.00)	7.50 (27.19)	1.55 (17.71)
1994/Q2	4.66 (15.88)	8.39 (115.53)	2.55 (7.94)	1.63 (4.87)	0.40 (0.57)	1.63 (3.44)	2.60 (19.17)
1994/Q3	6.22 (24.19)	7.11 (46.00)	5.38 (45.97)	1.42 (4.64)	0.02 (0.02)	1.81 (3.49)	1.94 (10.10)
1994/Q4	3.14 (10.19)	5.91 (50.01)	2.86 (6.01)	2.75 (15.81)	0.38 (0.53)	1.21 (1.96)	2.34 (6.28)
1995/Q1	3.01 (10.67)	5.79 (77.99)	2.24 (7.01)	0.95 (1.90)	0.86 (1.86)	0.97 (1.29)	1.22 (6.70)
1995/Q2	2.34 (4.38)	4.81 (42.75)	2.61 (6.58)	1.26 (2.06)	2.45 (6.37)	1.39 (1.65)	1.34 (2.89)
1995/Q3	1.62 (3.05)	3.95 (27.81)	3.42 (20.30)	1.51 (3.11)	0.28 (0.69)	2.30 (6.78)	1.50 (5.55)
1995/Q4	1.95 (2.75)	2.84 (9.05)	4.09 (21.36)	2.08 (4.00)	2.26 (3.45)	4.38 (10.52)	2.04 (3.59)

Table 11.6
(continued)

State/ SOE	State/ Subsd.	Foreign/ Ltd.	Foreign/ J. Stock	Mixed/ J. Stock	Mixed/ Ltd.	Other/ Other	All
1.30	0.21	4.73	2.59	2.03	0.08	0.62	4.99
(4.30)	(0.32)	(11.12)	(3.78)	(5.43)	(0.17)	(1.16)	(112.14)
1.58	0.40	7.13	10.71	1.70	1.68	3.37	27.20
(3.78)	(0.57)	(25.20)	(36.32)	(2.97)	(3.45)	(7.70)	(1183.5)
1.40	0.00	30.69	11.59	43.13	4.71	3.66	4.85
(3.96)	(na)	(127.65)	(36.92)	(226.18)	(14.46)	(8.75)	(40.77)
1.98	0.00	15.00	10.11	11.69	35.36	8.81	5.05
(4.26)	(na)	(50.12)	(27.51)	(54.70)	(81.87)	(29.64)	(23.25)
0.95	0.29	5.24	4.62	0.53	1.69	2.13	2.46
(3.61)	(0.27)	(16.44)	(12.69)	(0.88)	(3.50)	(2.89)	(12.40)
1.08	0.20	5.94	5.09	2.00	4.05	1.93	3.60
(2.51)	(0.29)	(14.08)	(11.05)	(5.13)	(5.94)	(3.51)	(20.08)
6.37	0.00	25.06	2.37	1.33	3.78	0.88	5.38
(128.11)	(na)	(107.16)	(5.32)	(3.36)	(7.21)	(1.61)	(66.63)
1.55	0.00	9.05	5.39	10.48	7.08	1.53	4.28
(5.63)	(na)	(32.42)	(14.89)	(50.49)	(11.40)	(2.52)	(30.69)
2.31	na	10.18	2.44	5.47	1.30	1.62	4.32
(31.47)		(64.30)	(5.77)	(22.24)	(1.44)	(3.57)	(35.52)
0.66	na	16.91	3.23	1.64	1.27	5.01	5.57
(1.90)		(171.82)	(6.79)	(3.10)	(1.73)	(15.12)	(83.95)
1.54	na	15.55	2.47	1.07	1.46	1.89	5.14
(16.60)		(106.42)	(3.68)	(1.56)	(3.29)	(2.76)	(41.69)
1.48	na	25.44	3.46	1.89	4.27	6.49	5.43
(3.62)		(255.50)	(4.98)	(3.84)	(8.68)	(23.91)	(72.92)
0.66	na	7.51	2.45	0.73	4.49	3.04	3.00
(2.15)		(28.02)	(7.68)	(1.33)	(12.77)	(3.64)	(42.74)
0.65	na	5.91	1.92	1.98	3.35	5.28	2.79
(1.07)		(16.65)	(3.45)	(7.56)	(7.49)	(9.30)	(23.78)
1.15	na	7.28	1.56	1.08	2.31	2.38	2.72
(3.60)		(25.47)	(1.82)	(1.62)	(6.03)	(3.02)	(17.91)
0.81	na	7.77	2.58	1.55	1.43	6.08	2.79
(1.15)		(24.25)	(5.41)	(2.36)	(2.04)	(9.23)	(10.63)

seen from the table, the most substantial investors by this criterion were foreign-owned and privately owned limited liability companies, followed by privately owned individual businesses, privately owned and foreign-owned joint stock companies and mixed-ownership companies. State-owned firms and cooperatives invested relatively little over the period, with state-owned/limited liability companies investing less than depreciation in 1992. Finally, it is worth noting that privately owned individual and limited liability firms showed a declining tendency to invest between 1992 and 1995, reflecting the fact that these firms started growing from a low capital base and possibly also the fact that, after the massive bank lending to new private firms in the early phase of the transition (see Dyba and Svejnar 1995), these firms gradually had less access to bank capital.

11.3   Econometric Models and Evidence

In our empirical analysis, we estimate separate equations for depreciation and net investment to establish the behavioral patterns of each of these two components of gross investment. All equations are estimated by ordinary least squares. In future research it will be useful to explore the availability of instrumental variables to correct for possible endogeneity of regressors.

11.3.1   Depreciation

Czech laws and regulations permit firms to carry out straight-line depreciation of book value capital up to limits defined for various categories of capital goods. From the profit tax standpoint, depreciation is treated as cost of production. In our analysis we estimate the share of book value capital that depreciation accounts for in different types of firms. In particular, since depreciation does not display strong seasonal patterns (table 11.3), we start by estimating the following linear depreciation equation:

$$D_{i,t} = \alpha + \delta K_{i,t} + \varepsilon_{i,t}, \tag{11.1}$$

where D denotes the quarterly value of depreciation, K the book value of capital, and δ the depreciation rate. We have included a constant term, which allows more flexibility, since we may always view this specification as a first approximation of a depreciation process (see Lízal 1999a).

Table 11.7 presents the coefficient estimates of equation (11.1), covering the 1993–1995 period for which capital data are available, for the sample as a whole, and table 11.8 does the same for each category of firms. Coefficient of interest δ is reported as a quarterly percentage rate. As the F-test statistics presented below each of

Table 11.7
Estimated depreciation rate δ in percentage of capital stock

$D_{i,t} = \alpha + \delta K_{i,t} + \varepsilon_{i,t}.$

Coefficient	Ordinary least squares	Between	Within	Random effect
α	34,400***	29,300**	na	52,600***
	(7,500)	(13,700)		(16,900)
δ	1.306***	1.261***	0.944***	1.184***
	(.004)	(.011)	(.022)	(.011)
Rsq.	.675	.737	.890	.878
NOB/NI	34,779/4,935	34,779/4,935	34,779/4,935	34,779/4,935

Notes: Tests *p*-values
1. AB = AiBi: 0.00
2. AiB = AiBi: 1.00
3. AB = AiB: 0.00
4. FE vs. RE: 0.00
*,**,***: Significant at 10%, 5%, 1%, respectively.
Obs. = N. of Obs. = Number of observations = NOB = N.
Ad. Rsq. = Adjusted $R^2 = \bar{R}^2$.
Rsq. = R^2.
Ni = Number of individuals = NI.

the two tables indicate, the specification with a single intercept and a single slope coefficient is preferable to specifications in which these vary by industry. Moreover, Hausman test statistics presented below each of the two tables indicate that the fixed-effects specification is superior to the corresponding random-effects model at the 1 percent significance test level. We hence use the results from the parsimonious specification and fixed-effects (within) method of estimation. (The ordinary least squares (OLS), between, and random-effects estimates are reported for comparison.)

The overall rate of depreciation is estimated to be about 1 percent of the capital stock per quarter or 4 percent at the annual rate (table 11.7). Since the legally permissible depreciation rate in the Czech Republic varies from 2 to 20 percent per year, depending on the type of capital, our results indicate that the firms' capital stock tends to be dominated by low-depreciation capital such as buildings.

In table 11.8, we present estimates of the depreciation rate by firm type. The 1.74 percent coefficient of quarterly depreciation for the state-owned/state-registered firms represents the base to which the coefficients for other types of firms are related, and the coefficients for other types of firms thus indicate the deviation from the 1.74 coefficient of the state-owned/state-registered firms. As may be seen from the table, one cannot reject the hypothesis that the 1.74 percent quarterly depreciation rate found for state-owned/state-registered firms also reflects the depreciation rate of

Table 11.8
Estimated depreciation rate δ in percentage of capital stock

$$D_{i,t} = \alpha + \delta K_{i,t} + \sum_G \delta_{G,i} G_{i,t} K_{i,t} + \varepsilon_{i,t}.$$

Coefficient	OLS	Between	Within	Random effect
α	25,300*** (5,500)	16,300** (6,600)	na	33,200*** (8,800)
δ (State/SOE)	1.633*** (.025)	2.294*** (.094)	1.738*** (.076)	1.581*** (.037)
δ_G Private/Entrepreneur	−.118 (.327)	−.272 (.496)	−1.019 (.808)	−.391 (.502)
δ_G Private/Ltd.	.181** (.079)	−.257** (.107)	−.510** (.259)	.052 (.121)
δ_G Private/J. Stock	.117*** (.020)	−.469*** (.044)	−.552*** (.112)	.107*** (.029)
δ_G Cooperative/Other Coop.	.099 (.204)	−.223 (.328)	−.082 (.466)	.019 (.296)
δ_G Cooperative/Producer Coop.	−.354 (.788)	−.877 (1.774)	−.120 (1.051)	−.180 (.882)
δ_G State/Ltd.	.098 (.057)	−.173* (.092)	−1.434*** (.182)	−.214** (.092)
δ_G State/J. Stock	−.086*** (.016)	−.483*** (.031)	−.524*** (.070)	−.091*** (.021)
δ_G State/Subsidized	−.192*** (.061)	.059 (.053)	−.954 (20.4)	−.173*** (.067)
δ_G Foreign/Ltd.	1.390*** (.066)	.904*** (.106)	1.234*** (.159)	1.430*** (.098)
δ_G Foreign/J. Stock	2.226*** (.025)	1.912*** (.046)	.120 (.092)	1.709*** (.040)
δ_G Mixed/J. Stock	.159*** (.030)	−.003 (.055)	−.291*** (.078)	.154*** (.037)
δ_G Mixed/Ltd.	.445*** (.130)	.079 (.317)	.567 (.364)	.570*** (.205)
δ_G Other	−.191 (.201)	.179 (.324)	−.930*** (.295)	−.252 (.223)
Industry dummies	Yes	Yes	Yes	Yes
Quarter dummies	Yes	Yes	Yes	Yes
Rsq.	.864	.953	.899	.877
NOB/NI	34,779/4,935	34,779/4,935	34,779/4,935	34,779/4,935

Notes: Tests *p*-values   *,**,***: Significant at 10%, 5%, 1%, respectively.
1. AB = AiBi: na   Obs. = N. of Obs. = Number of observations = NOB = N.
2. AiB = AiBi: na   Ad. Rsq. = Adjusted R^2 = $\bar{R}^2$.
3. AB = AiB: 0.00   Rsq. = R^2.
4. FE vs. RE: 0.00   Ni = Number of individuals = NI.
                        G_is are dummy variables taking on value of 1 if the firm is a member of a given
                        group and 0 otherwise.

privately owned individual businesses, cooperatives, foreign-owned/joint stock companies, and mixed-ownership/limited liability companies. The estimate of the quarterly depreciation rate for foreign-owned/limited liability companies is almost twice as high, whereas estimates for privately and state-owned/joint stock companies is about one third less than the base rate of 1.74. The state owned/limited liability companies generate a -1.43 fixed-effects estimate, which implies a very low rate of depreciation for these firms. This estimated coefficient is also out of line with the OLS, between, and random-effects estimates reported in table 11.8. Given the implausibly low value and the difference in comparison with the other estimates, the state-owned/limited liability estimate needs to be treated with caution.

The difference in the estimated depreciation rates across categories of firms raises the question of whether they are brought about by the particular type of investment carried out recently by the different types of firms or whether they are due to a systematic change of ownership and legal form in firms with certain capital stock during the transition. To check which of these hypotheses receives more support, we have estimated equation (11.1) on data for 1993 and 1995, respectively. The 1993 capital data by and large reflect the capital stock inherited from the period of central planning, whereas the 1995 capital data are already much more influenced by the investment activity undertaken by firms since their commercialization and ownership changes in the early 1990s. The results of these estimations (not reported here in a tabular form) indicate that the depreciation rate of companies with foreign ownership grows more than that of other types of firms over time, suggesting that depreciation is generally rising because of new investment but that (foreign) ownership plays a part as well.

11.3.2 Net Investment

In the Czech Republic, net investment is legally not a cost of production. Net investment hence reflects firms' desire to invest out of taxable retained earnings or funds obtained from government subsidies, bank loans, company bond issues, or equity issues. As we mentioned earlier, transition has brought about a significant reduction of government subsidies to firms, but capital markets have been developing only very gradually. Hence the availability of internal funds has likely had a significant impact on the investment behavior of some types of firms. In particular, we hypothesize that the individually owned or limited liability companies, which tend to be small, will be more rationed in the capital market than the joint stock companies, which tend to be large, or the foreign firms, which can supply themselves with investment finance from other countries.[8] We therefore estimate models that link net investment to factors such as the availability to a firm of internal finance and permit us to test this hypothesis (see, e.g., Fazzari, Hubbard, and Petersen 1988; Oliner and Rudebusch 1992; and van Ees and Garretsen 1994).[9]

11.3.2.1 Investment and Profit

Since our data set contains information on profit for most firms for most of the time periods, we first examine the link between investment and this variable. This corresponds to the use of the cash flow variable (profit plus depreciation) in the Western studies, except that we are able to analyze depreciation separately and hence use net rather than gross investment as the dependent variable and profit rather than profit plus depreciation as the explanatory variable. We estimate two models that link, for each type of firm, its quarterly net investment to the present and past values of its profit.

In the first model we take into account explicitly the strong seasonal component found in the quarterly data and estimate the equation in the four-quarter difference form, thus controlling for the seasonality as well as other firm-specific fixed effects. During some of the quarters we are missing either profit or net investment data for some of the firms, and the data set on which we run the net investment equation is hence smaller (by almost half) than the original data set. To control for possible selection bias in this process, we first run a Heckman-type probit equation, predicting the probability of the firm's being included in the sample on the basis of data on investment, profit, industry, and firm type. The resulting inverse Mills ratio is included as an explanatory variable in the four-quarter difference investment equation. The estimating equation is hence of the form

$$\Delta_4 I_{i,t}^{net} = \beta_1 \Delta_4 \Pi_{i,t} + \beta_2 \Delta_4 \Pi_{i,t-1} + \gamma M_{i,t} + \varepsilon_{i,t}, \tag{11.2}$$

where I^{net} denotes net investment, Π gross profit and M the inverse Mills ratio from the probit estimation. To assess the seasonal and industry effects, we use the Anderson-Hsiao decomposition of the residuals generated by a level version of equation (11.2), using the estimated (within) coefficients from (11.2). These level residuals are regressed on quarterly and industry dummy variables.

Table 11.9 presents the estimates of equation (11.2), together with the analysis of implied residuals. The reported specification is based on current and one-quarter lagged profit, since longer lags proved to be mostly insignificant and their inclusion did not materially alter the results. As may be seen from the table's first column, the overall regression that constrains the coefficients to be identical for all types of firms indicates that there is a statistically very strong positive relationship between profit and investment, with a one-crown increase in profit resulting in a 0.1 crown instantaneous and 0.12 crown long-term increase in investment.

Estimates by type of firm are presented in columns 2–13 of table 11.9. As may be seen from these columns, enterprise profitability has a strong positive effect on investment in all types of firms except for privately owned/limited liability companies and foreign-owned and mixed-ownership firms. The result for foreign-owned and mixed-ownership firms is consistent with the financing hierarchy and credit rationing hypotheses. In the case of privately owned/limited liability companies the finding is a bit counterintuitive. It must be noted, however, that these three types of firms displayed a major decrease in profits in 1993 and to some extent also in 1995 (see tables 11.A.4–11.A.7). It is therefore possible that the lack of a positive relationship between their profit and investment reflects this fluctuation in profit, a conjecture that we explore below.

The second-stage analysis of the residuals of equation (11.2), presented in the lower panel of table 11.9, indicates that there is a strong seasonal pattern in the overall regression. In particular, the coefficients on quarterly dummies imply a rising investment pattern over the four quarters, with a strong increase in the fourth quarter. From the regressions run by firm type we see that this overall pattern is driven by investment behavior of state-owned companies that are state-registered or joint stock, as well as by foreign owned/limited liability companies, cooperatives, and to a lesser extent private joint-stock companies. These findings are consistent with the summary statistics examined earlier.

The second model that we estimate uses current and lagged quarterly values of variables in levels rather than four-quarter differences:

$$I_{i,t}^{net} = \alpha + \beta_1 \Pi_{i,t} + \beta_2 \Pi_{i,t-1} + \varepsilon_{i,t}. \tag{11.3}$$

Because it does not require a four-quarter lag, this model allows us to use all the data more effectively. Most importantly, it allows us to estimate a richer specification for the four quarters of 1994, a period for which we have data on more variables. The estimates of equation (11.3) are reported in table 11.10. The results are based on a random-effects specification, which was found to be better supported by the data than a quarter-to-quarter fixed-effects model.

As can be seen from table 11.10, the overall specification that constrains the coefficients to be the same for all types of firms during the entire 1992–1995 period yields a 0.094 coefficient on current-quarter profit and a 0.034 coefficient on lagged profit. These coefficients are similar to those observed in table 11.9, suggesting that the less data-intensive second model is able to capture the systematic features of investment behavior. As in table 11.9, the estimates for the 13 specific types of firms reported in table 11.10 indicate that the firms that do not reflect the overall pattern

Table 11.9
Net investment and profit: Heckman's two-step estimation based on four-quarter difference and analysis
of residuals

$$\Delta_4 I_{i,t}^{net} = \beta_1 \Delta_4 \Pi_{i,t} + \beta_2 \Delta_4 \Pi_{i,t-1} + \gamma M_{i,t} + \varepsilon_{i,t}$$

	All	State/SOE	Private/ Enterpr.	Private/ Ltd.	Private/ J. Stock	Coop.
Pred. Succ %	60.0	55.8	61.0	63.3	56.9	60.6
N. of Obs.	20,491	2,962	722	5,073	1,101	2,120
Ad. Rsq.	0.012	0.022	0.017	0.004	0.021	0.013
β_1	0.095***	0.114***	0.057***	−0.023**	0.128***	0.189***
	(0.006)	(0.014)	(0.018)	(0.009)	(0.027)	(0.036)
β_2	0.019***	−0.032**	0.035*	−0.034***	0.037	−0.124***
	(0.007)	(0.014)	(0.020)	(0.011)	(0.030)	(0.039)
γ	−768**	−717	−20	−46	−894	176
	(321)	(447)	(122)	(101)	(978)	(300)
Ad. Rsq.	0.017	0.039	0.000	0.004	0.052	0.027
Dummy Q1	−6,353***	−3,436***	46	−385	−4,286**	−891***
	(612)	(857)	(311)	(251)	(2,170)	(180)
Dummy Q2	−3,617***	−2,336***	−333	−230	−1,774	−479***
	(520)	(682)	(253)	(216)	(1,881)	(156)
Dummy Q3	−3,125***	−1,556**	−312	−422**	−1,224	−423***
	(508)	(692)	(239)	(201)	(1,836)	(156)
Constant	4,977***	1,709***	498***	897***	3,796**	197
	(463)	(613)	(223)	(183)	(1,613)	(257)
Industry Dummies	Yes	Yes	Yes	Yes	Yes	Yes

Notes: The top part of the table presents estimates of the four-quarter difference equation; the bottom
part presents estimates from the analysis of residuals.
*,**,***: Significant at 10%, 5%, 1%, respectively.
Obs. = N. of Obs. = Number of observations = NOB = N.
Ad. Rsq. = Adjusted R^2 = $\bar{R}^2$.
Rsq. = R^2.
Ni = Number of individuals = NI.

are privately owned/limited liability companies and mixed-ownership companies.
Unlike in table 11.9, privately owned/limited liability companies as well as foreign-
owned companies display an insignificant effect of profit on net investment. Finally,
other firms are also found to have a negative relationship between investment and
profit. The two specifications hence produce identical overall estimates but somewhat different estimates across the 13 types of firms.

As mentioned earlier, profitability of firms varied over the 1992–1995 period, and
the composition of the sample changed from 1994 to 1995. It is hence worth explor-
ing whether the estimates vary over time. In the lower parts of table 11.10, we present

Table 11.9
(continued)

State/ Ltd.	State/ J. Stock	Foreign/ Ltd.	Foreign/ J. Stock	Mixed/ J. Stock	Mixed/ Ltd.	Other
60.3	59.4	63.6	60.0	65.3	70.8	63.9
246	6,481	743	353	432	96	159
−0.004	0.022	0.101	0.075	0.069	0.236	0.102
0.102*	0.117***	0.131***	−0.229***	−0.050*	−0.189***	0.123***
(0.062)	(0.012)	(0.021)	(0.088)	(0.026)	(0.061)	(0.040)
−0.016	0.063***	−0.200***	−0.347***	−0.091***	−0.595***	0.196**
(0.066)	(0.013)	(0.023)	(0.090)	(0.031)	(0.118)	(0.083)
980	−2,374**	−1,092	−6,318	−2,253*	−1,506	716
(2,938)	(1,134)	(1,215)	(5,381)	(1,367)	(2,660)	(1,101)
0.121	0.034	0.045	0.023	0.048	0.738	0.233
−3,764	−14,283***	−12,155***	−17,251	−4,568	−8,198	−2,666
(5,642)	(1,636)	(3,813)	(11,762)	(2,879)	(6,891)	(2,433)
−3,889	−8,936***	−9,260***	9,906	739	−1,892	−2,659
(4,979)	(1,399)	(3,350)	(10,393)	(2,627)	(5,506)	(2,122)
−4,780	−8,024***	−5,697*	−1,175	2,319	−1,227	−3,594*
(4,844)	(1,384)	(3,178)	(10,277)	(2,586)	(4,941)	(2,045)
6,619	10,376***	24,649***	35,424***	5,318**	3,807	453
(4,445)	(1,204)	(3,323)	(8,952)	(2,196)	(4,398)	(1,769)
Yes	Yes	Yes	Yes	Yes	Yes	Yes

separate estimates of equation (11.3) for each year, 1992–1995. As the overall estimates in the first column indicate, there is indeed a sizable variation in the estimated effect of profit on net investment over the four years. Although the overall long-term effect is positive in all years, it is strongly so in 1992 and 1994, when reported enterprise profits were high, and much weaker in 1993 and 1995, when profits were on average lower. In particular, the short- (long-)term effect is estimated to be 0.25 (0.13) in 1992, −0.01 (0.07) in 1993, 0.36 (0.36) in 1994, and −0.01 (0.07) in 1995. The estimates for individual types of firms vary, but for a number of them the results are consistent with this overall pattern. Thus, state-owned/state-registered firms show a strong positive effect in 1992 when their average profits were high, zero effect in 1993 when their average profits declined, and small positive effects in 1994 and 1995 when their profit was low. Private joint stock companies register a strong positive effect in 1992 and 1994, when their profits were high, and smaller effects in the low-profit years of 1993 and 1995. Foreign owned/limited liability companies show a positive effect in 1992 when their average profit was moderately positive, a strongly negative effect in 1993 when the average profit became negative, a very strong positive

Table 11.10
Net investment and profit: Random-effects estimates based on current and one-quarter lagged profit, in levels

$$I_{i,t}^{net} = \alpha + \beta_1 \Pi_{i,t} + \beta_2 \Pi_{i,t-1} + \varepsilon_{i,t}.$$

Coeff.	All	State/SOE	Private/ Enterpr.	Private/ Ltd.	Private/ J. Stock	Coop.
All years						
Obs.	36,814	5,123	1,502	11,169	2,052	3,189
Rsq.	0.036	0.040	0.044	0.000	0.010	0.007
β_1	0.094***	0.108***	0.012**	−0.016***	0.093***	−0.107***
	(0.005)	(0.010)	(2.243)	(0.006)	(0.017)	(0.036)
β_2	0.034***	−0.024***	0.013***	−0.005	0.064***	0.175***
	(0.005)	(0.008)	(6.048)	(0.007)	(0.016)	(0.035)
α	1,775***	435	65***	578***	3,950***	−4
	(199)	(347)	(4)	(81)	(1,149)	(177)
FE vs. RE	0.250	0.406	0.000	0.510	0.919	0.210
1992						
Obs.	6,618	1,593	290	1,471	225	703
Rsq.	0.027	0.105	0.012	0.004	0.053	0.037
β_1	0.249***	0.302***	−0.097**	0.030	0.383**	−0.989***
	(0.016)	(0.024)	(0.042)	(0.034)	(0.155)	(0.220)
β_2	−0.128***	−0.105***	0.002	0.068	0.142	0.997***
	(0.016)	(0.020)	(0.043)	(0.042)	(0.182)	(0.238)
α	2,539***	1,153*	706***	426**	2,040	−276
	(469)	(612)	(207)	(207)	(1,826)	(686)
FE vs. RE	0.741	0.611	0.346	0.236	0.466	0.274
1993						
Obs.	9,744	2,068	490	2,646	328	954
Rsq.	0.040	0.004	0.095	0.010	0.012	0.084
β_1	−0.014*	0.027**	0.013	−0.001	−0.069	−0.150***
	(0.008)	(0.012)	(0.014)	(0.008)	(0.081)	(0.020)
β_2	0.082***	−0.025***	0.107***	0.055***	0.129*	0.167***
	(0.010)	(0.010)	(0.020)	(0.013)	(0.075)	(0.023)
α	1,889***	225	184*	263***	3,577***	111
	(392)	(506)	(103)	(80)	(1,253)	(129)
FE vs. RE	0.012	0.175	0.002	0.025	0.973	0.224

Table 11.10
(continued)

State/Ltd.	State/ J. Stock	Foreign/ Ltd.	Foreign/ J. Stock	Mixed/ J. Stock	Mixed/ Ltd.	Other
390	9,975	1,610	568	672	233	325
0.022	0.043	0.041	0.051	0.010	0.029	0.015
0.048	0.118***	0.026***	−0.212***	−0.057***	−0.063	−0.034
(0.047)	(0.009)	(0.013)	(0.069)	(0.022)	(0.067)	(0.044)
0.010	0.049***	0.001	0.252***	−0.023	−0.062	−0.039***
(0.048)	(0.010)	(0.014)	(0.067)	(0.030)	(0.051)	(0.011)
833	3,633***	4,717***	11,184***	1,993	3,797	4,429***
(2,469)	(653)	(935)	(3,620)	(1,233)	(2,825)	(1,652)
0.664	0.452	0.403	0.259	1.000	0.694	0.563
68	1,860	178	80	86	23	38
0.033	0.016	0.141	0.370	0.150	0.037	0.047
0.028	0.242***	−0.074	0.397***	0.169***	0.251	−0.051
(0.047)	(0.031)	(0.103)	(0.122)	(0.057)	(0.440)	(0.098)
−0.016	−0.177***	0.418***	0.510***	0.104	−0.230	−0.134
(0.061)	(0.035)	(0.102)	(0.129)	(0.090)	(0.878)	(0.106)
−7,476***	7,331***	1,725**	6,016	−526	9,143	395
(2,965)	(1,587)	(837)	(4,004)	(1,026)	(8,343)	(635)
0.574	0.952	0.212	0.912	0.258	0.000	0.337
104	2,476	332	115	120	49	59
0.016	0.082	0.062	0.070	0.012	0.014	0.008
0.036	−0.016	−0.274***	−0.543*	0.106	−0.146	0.006
(0.104)	(0.015)	(0.082)	(0.309)	(0.078)	(0.216)	(0.071)
0.002	0.152***	−0.570***	1.379***	−0.102	0.306	0.096
(0.149)	(0.021)	(0.090)	(0.422)	(0.067)	(0.257)	(0.059)
1,376	4,349***	5,992***	18,135	2,079	6,522	759
(5,645)	(1,317)	(2,054)	(11,062)	(1,581)	(6,519)	(864)
0.775	0.013	0.748	0.377	0.945	0.960	0.962

Table 11.10
(continued)

Coeff.	All	State/SOE	Private/ Enterpr.	Private/ Ltd.	Private/ J. Stock	Coop.
1994						
Obs.	12,299	1,019	595	4,653	716	956
Rsq.	0.139	0.026	0.082	0.000	0.061	0.000
β_1	0.356***	0.032**	0.032	0.012	0.201***	−0.006
	(0.008)	(0.016)	(0.021)	(0.012)	(0.027)	(0.013)
β_2	0.000	0.018	0.044***	−0.013	0.195***	−0.001
	(0.007)	(0.013)	(0.015)	(0.012)	(0.019)	(0.014)
α	625**	−760**	300***	573***	2,195	136*
	(260)	(321)	(108)	(123)	(1,467)	(73)
FE vs. RE	0.975	0.285	0.018	0.680	0.224	0.021
1995						
Obs.	8,153	443	137	2,399	783	576
Rsq.	0.025	0.066	0.063	0.003	0.010	0.020
β_1	−0.011	0.008	0.069	−0.029***	0.078***	0.034
	(0.007)	(0.020)	(0.036)	(0.010)	(0.024)	(0.025)
β_2	0.082***	0.045*	0.063*	0.005	−0.031	0.031*
	(0.007)	(0.024)	(0.048)	(0.010)	(0.025)	(0.018)
α	2,321***	−997**	261	726***	4,690***	217*
	(360)	(493)	(353)	(170)	(1,692)	(129)
FE vs. RE	0.194	0.007	0.000	0.944	0.905	0.000

Notes:
*,**,***: Significant at 10%, 5%, 1%, respectively.
Obs. = N. of Obs. = Number of observations = NOB = N.
Ad. Rsq. = Adjusted R^2 = $\bar{R}^2$.
Rsq. = R^2.
Ni = Number of individuals = NI.

effect in 1994 when average profit increased, and a positive (though less pronounced) effect in 1995 when their average profit (as well as its standard deviation) soared. The other types of firms display more diverse or less systematic patterns.[10]

11.3.2.2 Stock and Flow Measures of Internal Finance

For 1994 (a relatively high-profit year for most types of firms) we have data on a number of additional variables that capture potential sources of funds for firms in the transition setting. In particular, we have data on receivables, receivables overdue, payables, payables overdue, and cash balances. These variables correspond to the stock measures of internal finance used in some of the Western studies (e.g., Fazzari, Hubbard, and Petersen 1988; Galeotti, Schiantarelli, and Jaramillo 1994; Hubbard,

Table 11.10
(continued)

State/Ltd.	State/ J. Stock	Foreign/ Ltd.	Foreign/ J. Stock	Mixed/ J. Stock	Mixed/ Ltd.	Other
119	2,882	702	199	241	78	149
0.109	0.175	0.326	0.200	0.112	0.074	0.051
0.111	0.413***	0.237***	0.039	−0.213***	0.248*	0.049
(0.083)	(0.017)	(0.036)	(0.086)	(0.046)	(0.129)	(0.062)
0.135**	−0.034**	0.455***	0.209***	0.203***	0.041	−0.034***
(0.067)	(0.015)	(0.042)	(0.078)	(0.035)	(0.069)	(0.012)
811	421	3,309***	10,124**	1,476	3,620	1,609
(2,436)	(933)	(1,004)	(4,222)	(1,717)	(4,124)	(1,067)
0.711	0.976	0.721	0.350	0.230	0.648	0.454
99	2,757	398	174	225	83	79
0.009	0.052	0.060	0.175	0.013	0.287	0.053
−0.019	−0.109***	0.039**	0.031	0.043	0.204***	−0.175*
(0.092)	(0.014)	(0.017)	(0.064)	(0.037)	(0.063)	(0.092)
−0.082	0.179***	0.036**	0.193***	−0.164**	0.212***	−0.220*
(0.091)	(0.014)	(0.018)	(0.059)	(0.070)	(0.079)	(0.122)
3,471	2,942***	7,593***	5,838**	3,483*	819	13,473***
(3,901)	(834)	(1,781)	(3,032)	(1,975)	(1,702)	(5,014)
0.872	0.287	0.710	0.166	0.954	0.398	0.000

Kashyap, and Whited 1995; Whited 1992). The overall results presented in the first column of table 11.11 indicate that when these variables are included in the regression, profit continues to have a strong positive effect, with an estimated coefficient of 0.34. Cash has an identical positive coefficient of 0.34, suggesting that it is an important determinant of investment behavior. The coefficients on the other variables are quantitatively smaller and reflect the ambiguous behavior of transition firms with respect to legal obligations. Receivables have a positive coefficient of 0.04, reflecting the fact that they represent a near-term source of cash that may, however, be expected with less than certainty. Receivables overdue in turn have a negative coefficient of −0.08, which is consistent with the idea that these funds are unlikely to be repaid and are thus heavily discounted. Payables have an expected negative (but low) coefficient of −0.01, but payables overdue generate a positive coefficient of 0.03, likely reflecting the fact that some of these may never have to be paid.

At the level of individual categories of firms, profit has a particularly strong effect on net investment among state-owned/joint stock companies, foreign-owned/limited

Table 11.11
Net investment and Firms' financial Conditions: Random-effects estimates, in levels, 1994

$$I_{i,t}^{net} = \alpha + \beta_1 \Pi_{i,t} + \beta_2 R_{i,t} + \beta_3 RO_{i,t} + \beta_4 P_{i,t} + \beta_5 PO_{i,t} + \beta_6.$$

Coeff.	All	State/SOE	Private/ Enterpr.	Private/ Ltd.	Private/ J. Stock	Coop.
Obs.	14,170	1,047	695	5,729	851	988
Rsq.	0.143	0.082	0.035	0.006	0.283	0.059
β_1	0.344***	0.021	−0.044	0.003	0.063***	0.010
	(0.008)	(0.016)	(0.047)	(0.011)	(0.019)	(0.011)
β_2	0.038***	−0.007	0.024	−0.001	−0.056***	−0.002
	(0.003)	(0.005)	(0.028)	(0.005)	(0.016)	(0.004)
β_3	−0.076***	0.014*	0.011	0.012	0.301***	0.028***
	(0.005)	(0.008)	(0.057)	(0.010)	(0.031)	(0.010)
β_4	−0.012***	0.014**	0.005	0.008***	−0.007	−0.010***
	(0.002)	(0.006)	(0.009)	(0.003)	(0.008)	(0.003)
β_5	0.028***	−0.066***	−0.093***	−0.020***	−0.056***	−0.010
	(0.004)	(0.011)	(0.033)	(0.005)	(0.021)	(0.008)
β_6	0.339***	0.164	0.256	−0.006	−0.198	0.272**
	(0.050)	(0.148)	(0.198)	(0.067)	(0.345)	(0.133)
α	548**	−218	580**	464***	−817	128
	(256)	(341)	(236)	(109)	(1,284)	(82)
FE vs. RE	0.122	0.477	0.956	0.008	0.979	0.000

Notes: R = receivables, RO = receivables overdue, P = Payables, PO = payables overdue, C = cash.
*,**,***: Significant at 10%, 5%, 1%, respectively.
Obs. = N. of Obs. = Number of observations = NOB = N.
Ad. Rsq. = Adjusted R^2 = $\bar{R}^2$.
Rsq. = R^2.
Ni = Number of individuals = NI.

liability companies, mixed-ownership/limited liability companies, other firms, and to a lesser extent privately owned/joint stock companies. Cash has a strong positive effect in foreign-owned/limited liability companies, mixed-ownership/joint stock companies, and cooperatives. It has a surprisingly negative effect in state- and foreign-owned/joint stock companies. The latter two sets of companies appear to hold cash balances that are negatively related to their investment behavior. The investment behavior of foreign-owned companies, mixed-ownership/joint stock companies, and to a lesser extent state-owned/joint stock companies is strongly influenced by the value of receivables and receivables overdue. Foreign-owned/joint stock companies, state-owned/joint stock companies, and to a lesser extent foreign-owned/limited liability companies and mixed-ownership/joint stock companies also generate significant coefficients on payables and payables overdue.

Table 11.11
(continued)

State/Ltd.	State/ J. Stock	Foreign/ Ltd.	Foreign/ J. Stock	Mixed/ J. Stock	Mixed/ Ltd.	Other
126	3,106	869	218	264	95	182
0.192	0.198	0.276	0.478	0.551	0.601	0.125
0.113	0.457***	0.380***	−0.101	−0.058	0.224**	0.406***
(0.074)	(0.017)	(0.045)	(0.069)	(0.043)	(0.092)	(0.098)
0.029	0.032***	0.145***	0.402***	0.155***	0.017	−0.081*
(0.024)	(0.006)	(0.022)	(0.038)	(0.016)	(0.052)	(0.044)***
−0.078	−0.082***	−0.173***	−0.495***	−0.107***	0.374***	0.198
(0.048)	(0.010)	(0.050)	(0.069)	(0.026)	(0.107)	(0.070)
−0.006	−0.013**	−0.017	−0.109***	−0.073***	0.004	0.022***
(0.008)	(0.005)	(0.016)	(0.012)	(0.007)	(0.020)	(0.016)
−0.004	0.044***	−0.112*	0.173***	−0.020	−0.078	−0.098
(0.031)	(0.009)	(0.062)	(0.049)	(0.022)	(0.048)	(0.018)
0.180	−0.383**	0.508***	−0.758*	0.873***	4.020	−0.420
(0.687)	(0.151)	(0.091)	(0.444)	(0.338)	(3.277)	(0.447)
2,927	1,304	2,649**	1,182	−1,001	−4,689*	938
(2,630)	(1,035)	(1,052)	(3,707)	(1,154)	(2,406)	(1,014)
0.000	0.056	0.958	0.006	0.074	0.240	0.026

11.4 Concluding Remarks

In this study we have used firm-level data from the Czech Republic to estimate several specifications of depreciation and net investment functions, taking into account firm ownership and seasonality of the data. Our analysis of depreciation leads us to the conclusion that replacement investment displays a similar pattern in many ownership/legal form categories of firms. Important exceptions are foreign-owned/ limited liability companies, whose depreciation rate is almost twice as high as the base rate of 1.74, and privately and state-owned/joint stock companies, whose depreciation rate is about one third less than that base rate. These results reflects the findings of Lizal (1999a), who claims the major differences in depreciation rate are associated with the type of industry.

Our analysis of net investment yields two major findings. First, retained profit is found to be a major determinant of new investment, and the estimate is statistically significant even when we use the most robust fixed-effects (within) estimates based on one-year differences. Our results indicate that a 1-crown increase in profit results in a 0.1 crown instantaneous and 0.12 crown long-term increase in investment. In estimating this effect by type of firm we find that enterprise profitability has a strong positive effect on investment in all types of firms except for privately owned/limited liability companies and foreign-owned and mixed-ownership firms. All the results, except for the one related to privately owned/limited liability companies, are consistent with the financing hierarchy and credit rationing hypotheses, indicating that domestic firms cannot easily borrow investment funds externally and that investment varies with (is financed from) retained profits. In the case of privately owned/limited liability companies, the finding is a bit counterintuitive, because one might expect these firms to be particularly rationed in the capital market. A possible explanation of the insignificant effect of profit on net investment in these firms is that many of these firms operate close to the zero-profit level, and a number of them may not be expanding beyond their existing scale.

Our second finding is that firms take into account various stock (as opposed to only flow) measures of internal finance in making investment decisions. In particular, a firm's stock of cash, receivables, receivables overdue, payables, and payables overdue systematically affect its net investment.

Appendix

Table 11.A.1
Frequency distribution of firms by legal form

Legal form	1992	1993	1994	1995	Total
Entrepreneurship	4.23	4.92	4.80	1.59	4.06
Limited liability	26.83	33.06	47.06	35.58	36.67
Joint stock company	31.99	28.95	31.50	46.17	33.88
General cooperative	7.13	6.47	6.95	6.15	6.70
Industry cooperative	2.64	2.36	0.05	0.36	1.28
State-owned enterprise	25.16	22.04	8.18	5.55	15.00
State subsidized	0.12	0.09	0.00	0.00	0.05
Other	1.90	2.11	1.46	4.60	2.36
Number of observations	10,257	11,644	14,706	9,110	45,717

Table 11.A.2
Frequency distribution of firms by ownership

Ownership	1992	1993	1994	1995	Total
Private	31.11	37.40	50.63	40.85	40.93
Cooperative	9.86	8.94	6.99	6.52	8.04
State	52.62	46.53	31.10	41.11	41.85
International/foreign	4.19	4.88	7.91	7.48	6.12
Mixed	1.65	1.74	2.53	3.70	2.36
Other/unknown	0.57	0.51	0.84	0.34	0.70
Number of observations	10,257	11,644	14,706	9,110	45,717

Table 11.A.3
Frequency distribution of firms by Industry

Industry/NACE[1]	Observations	Percentage
Unknown	669	1.46
Mining of coal	220	0.48
Mining of oil and gas	64	0.14
Mining of metal ores	32	0.07
Other mining and quarrying	701	1.53
Food production	7,171	15.96
Textile	2,652	5.80
Apparel manufacturing	1,773	3.88
Leather and footwear	1,128	2.47
Wood production	1,996	4.37
Pulp and paper	815	1.78
Publishing and printing	1,371	3.00
Chemicals	1,124	2.46
Rubber and plastics	1,308	2.86
Nonmetallic minerals	3,017	6.60
Manufacture of basic metals	1,186	2.59
Fabricated metal products except machinery	4,903	10.72
Machinery	6,103	13.35
Office machinery and computers	92	0.20
Electrical apparatus	1,783	3.90
Radio and television	698	1.53
Medical and precision instruments	1,043	2.28
Motor vehicles	805	1.76
Other transport equipment	756	1.65
Furniture	3,213	7.03
Recycling	336	0.73
Water utilities	755	1.65
Other	3	0.00
Total	45,717	100

Note:
1. NACE = International Standard Industrial Classification (ISIC) (Nomenclature des Activités établies dans les Communautés Européennes)

Table 11.A.4
Means (standard deviations) of principal variables by type of firm, 1992

Owner/ Form	Private/ Enterpr.	Private/ Ltd.	Private/ J. Stock	Coop./ General	Coop./ Producer	State/ Ltd.	State/ J. Stock
Investment/ Capital	na	na	na	na	na	na	na
Depreciation/ Capital	na	na	na	na	na	na	na
Investment/ Labor	8.98 (33.27)	9.96 (71.69)	30.31 (123.5)	3.91 (13)	2.59 (7.1)	2.43 (7.01)	18.64 (76.07)
Investment/ Production	0.764 (0.308)	0.124 (1.582)	0.272 (1.934)	0.087 (0.34)	0.061 (0.199)	0.029 (0.072)	0.176 (1)
Profit	1,071 (4,653)	1,354 (5,315)	3,699 (11,734)	700 (2,859)	523 (3,448)	−2,003 (25,276)	10,436 (45,873)
Labor	94.74 (164.81)	153.6 (222.5)	435 (637)	209 (163)	224 (170)	1,152 (1,065)	1,127 (2,866)
Investment	687 (2,808)	1,184 (5,952)	7,438 (27,429)	850 (2,524)	679 (2,163)	2,641 (8,305)	16,197 (62,462)
Production	10,843 (18,731)	19,468 (28,438)	59,391 (116,413)	12,390 (15,009)	12,857 (11,700)	127,080 (149,797)	142,523 (375,498)
Depreciation	318 (867)	743 (1,933)	2,608 (4,564)	1,193 (16,017)	598 (919)	9,733 (14,311)	10,210 (35,600)
Capital	na	na	na	na	na	na	na
Wage	4.4 (1.35)	4.59 (1.31)	4.97 (2.01)	3.78 (0.97)	3.89 (0.92)	4.88 (0.78)	4.66 (1.06)
N(max)	434	2,319	346	731	271	99	2,663

Table 11.A.4
(continued)

Owner/Form	State/ SOE	State/ Subsd.	Foreign/ Ltd.	Foreign/ J. Stock	Mixed/ Ltd.	Mixed/ J. Stock	Other
Investment/ Capital	na	na	na	na	na	na	na
Depreciation/ Capital	na	na	na	na	na	na	na
Investment/ Labor	11.66 (50.18)	5.79 (8.69)	29.18 (110.56)	48.74 (153.51)	13.7 (37.23)	111.5 (581.1)	9.84 (20.92)
Investment/ Production	0.144 (0.743)	0.076 (0.095)	0.239 (0.791)	1.353 (9.584)	0.403 (2.53)	0.651 (3.2)	0.093 (0.332)
Profit	5,013 (35,442)	4,525 (9,598)	866 (7,875)	37,127 (313,608)	3,778 (13,320)	3,287 (25,534)	1,113 (5,305)
Labor	539 (920)	386 (357)	115 (246)	895 (2,960)	400 (740)	306 (732)	204 (216)
Investment	5,918 (21,959)	3,707 (6,221)	3,573 (15,794)	33,300 (122,324)	3,215 (7,158)	10,703 (30,685)	1,387 (2,500)
Production	66,014 (141,968)	41,684 (33,798)	16,335 (40,967)	285,600 (1,173,000)	63,994 (100,773)	42,369 (103,761)	25,627 (32,995)
Depreciation	4,497 (14,250)	10,579 (12,141)	823 (1,920)	13,900 (58,682)	3,290 (6,618)	6,775 (24,813)	1,342 (1,834)
Capital	na	na	na	na	na	na	na
Wage	4.46 (0.96)	4.51 (1.05)	5.08 (1.78)	5.47 (1.71)	4.66 (1.15)	4.69 (0.93)	4.79 (1.51)
N(max)	2,581	12	287	129	127	39	155

Table 11.A.5
Means (standard deviations) of principal variables by type of firm, 1993

Owner/Form	Private/ Enterpr.	Private/ Ltd.	Private/ J. Stock	Coop./ General	Coop./ Producer	State/ Ltd.	State/ J. Stock
Investment/ Capital	0.07 (0.148)	0.066 (0.158)	0.05 (0.108)	0.024 (0.061)	0.017 (0.048)	0.026 (0.078)	0.026 (0.064)
Depreciation/ Capital	0.037 (0.067)	0.043 (0.087)	0.028 (0.056)	0.016 (0.018)	0.014 (0.022)	0.024 (0.023)	0.016 (0.02)
Investment/ Labor	7.54 (17.28)	8.74 (33.48)	31.03 (125.19)	4.32 (10.01)	3.56 (14.06)	15.39 (62.43)	19.34 (57.29)
Investment/ Production	0.074 (0.205)	0.097 (0.439)	0.158 (0.42)	0.079 (0.184)	0.081 (0.385)	0.144 (0.419)	1.033 (44.9)
Profit	1,034 (6,316)	913 (8,307)	207 (13,030)	810 (3,979)	683 (3,239)	−5,790 (31,442)	2,305 (62,298)
Labor	90 (132)	132 (177)	379 (566)	179 (147)	182 (135)	884 (889)	1,008 (2,562)
Investment	646 (1,894)	961 (2,382)	7,206 (23,419)	885 (2,340)	557 (1,350)	9,569 (33,310)	15,644 (61,812)
Production	10,827 (17,029)	17,077 (25,314)	54,103 (98,033)	12,187 (16,387)	11,770 (11,264)	100,830 (117,097)	141,845 (378,194)
Depreciation	359 (1,006)	668 (1,418)	3,112 (5,421)	669 (2,095)	625 (1,109)	9,040 (11,380)	10,379 (32,326)
Capital	23,578 (77,120)	39,767 (75,792)	208,708 (384,474)	44,935 (68,889)	47,097 (41,867)	459,586 (556,065)	777,125 (2,683,192)
Wage	5.09 (1.41)	5.6 (1.6)	6.16 (2.68)	4.59 (1.16)	4.79 (1.11)	6.4 (1.04)	5.81 (1.42)
N(max)	572	3,257	391	754	275	113	2,687

Table 11.A.5
(continued)

Owner/Form	State/ SOE	State/ Subsid.	Foreign/ Ltd.	Foreign/ J. Stock	Mixed/ Ltd.	Mixed/ J. Stock	Other
Investment/ Capital	0.013 (0.033)	0.002 (0.003)	0.115 (0.208)	0.086 (0.181)	0.02 (0.066)	0.122 (0.232)	0.026 (0.049)
Depreciation/ Capital	0.015 (0.02)	0.019 (0.03)	0.05 (0.087)	0.039 (0.068)	0.015 (0.013)	0.079 (0.166)	0.021 (0.019)
Investment/ Labor	10.08 (31.05)	5.53 (5.66)	30.53 (101.74)	51.04 (142.1)	13.28 (39.97)	32.68 (78.36)	11.55 (23.16)
Investment/ Production	0.22 (2.745)	0.042 (0.049)	0.289 (1.346)	0.26 (0.694)	0.075 (0.219)	0.35 (0.908)	0.198 (0.492)
Profit	2,247 (37,776)	4,527 (8,464)	−726 (14,069)	−10,588 (77,925)	2,214 (10,071)	−436 (18,576)	1,303 (6,275)
Labor	488 (850)	407 (355)	169 (458)	802 (2,785)	368 (644)	240 (567)	194 (210)
Investment	5,400 (18,988)	3,686 (4,974)	7,425 (27,399)	54,169 (211,834)	4,310 (11,247)	9,498 (27,430)	7,051 (18,216)
Production	64,615 (141,421)	41,851 (34,478)	26,799 (83,701)	305,212 (1,361,490)	56,282 (81,129)	35,043 (84,967)	23,290 (36,495)
Depreciation	5,187 (14,930)	11,666 (11,239)	2,100 (7,684)	28,431 (154,475)	3,182 (5,418)	3,275 (7,924)	1,387 (1,740)
Capital	421,418 (1,113,766)	3,254,432 (3,694,429)	82,302 (245,969)	752,431 (2,413,205)	253,069 (423,279)	137,377 (332,314)	93,082 (127,073)
Wage	5.42 (1.18)	5.56 (0.7)	6.27 (2.09)	6.85 (1.99)	5.74 (1.2)	5.63 (1.27)	5.82 (1.92)
$N(max)$	2,566	10	406	144	133	66	205

Table 11.A.6
Means (standard deviations) of principal variables by type of firm, 1994

Owner/Form	Private/ Enterpr.	Private/ Ltd.	Private/ J. Stock	Coop./ General	Coop./ Producer	State/ Ltd.	State/ J. Stock
Investment/ Capital	0.054 (0.129)	0.059 (0.137)	0.04 (0.092)	0.019 (0.059)	0.002 (0.003)	0.023 (0.052)	0.017 (0.037)
Depreciation/ Capital	0.036 (0.064)	0.037 (0.068)	0.024 (0.049)	0.014 (0.028)	0.009 (0.002)	0.022 (0.019)	0.014 (0.01)
Investment/ Labor	13.08 (47.46)	12.69 (69.5)	31.08 (190)	4.74 (11.33)	0.71 (1.29)	7.64 (14.8)	17.29 (48.53)
Investment/ Production	0.153 (0.787)	0.127 (1.397)	0.223 (1.466)	0.076 (0.319)	0.013 (0.024)	0.25 (2.16)	0.132 (0.985)
Profit	1,108 (3,619)	1,602 (7,313)	5,936 (42,895)	931 (6,095)	189 (244)	292 (28,059)	8,966 (49,711)
Labor	83 (111)	122 (166)	428 (970)	162 (143)	38 (17)	730 (764)	809 (1,918)
Investment	836 (4,014)	1,227 (5,694)	9,031 (36,900)	810 (2,214)	38 (68)	7,164 (19,368)	13,021 (57,018)
Production	9,923 (13,967)	17,756 (27,419)	69,140 (187,588)	12,889 (24,053)	2,187 (654)	99,866 (116,022)	135,249 (384,889)
Depreciation	400 (976)	703 (1,705)	5,421 (21,348)	678 (1,332)	171 (21)	7,353 (11,612)	9,194 (27,232)
Capital	22,630 (47,006)	39,080 (87,244)	423,510 (1,561,458)	52,673 (80,917)	20,984 (3,125)	451,189 (718,105)	771,171 (2,455,390)
Wage	5.84 (1.7)	6.39 (1.85)	6.95 (2.19)	5.24 (1.3)	6.65 (0.49)	7.37 (1.3)	6.56 (1.58)
N(max)	695	5,758	870	1,018	8	126	3,225

Table 11.A.6
(continued)

Owner/Form	State/ SOE	State/ Subsid.	Foreign/ Ltd.	Foreign/ J. Stock	Mixed/ Ltd.	Mixed/ J. Stock	Other
Investment/ Capital	0.01 (0.034)	na	0.089 (0.159)	0.043 (0.059)	0.024 (0.065)	0.049 (0.128)	0.056 (0.13)
Depreciation/ Capital	0.014 (0.025)	na	0.042 (0.08)	0.022 (0.016)	0.019 (0.031)	0.041 (0.07)	0.03 (0.052)
Investment/ Labor	7.01 (25.78)	na	37.92 (119.8)	38.76 (59.66)	15.55 (34.16)	10.54 (25.4)	18.97 (49.31)
Investment/ Production	0.055 (0.17)	na	0.275 (1.179)	0.171 (0.322)	0.103 (0.245)	0.085 (0.201)	0.15 (0.395)
Profit	436 (14,432)	na	2,909 (20,102)	3,253 (112,464)	5,763 (24,781)	3,098 (20,397)	1,807 (11,437)
Labor	279 (378)	na	150 (358)	742 (2,242)	482 (693)	367 (555)	132 (129)
Investment	2,241 (8,125)	na	7,561 (30,788)	49,257 (269,262)	7,739 (21,954)	6,969 (28,591)	9,348 (43,367)
Production	37,294 (65,591)	na	34,040 (99,953)	239,548 (946,759)	104,716 (235,027)	64,032 (109,975)	32,749 (95,218)
Depreciation	3,053 (6,199)	na	2,170 (7,170)	20,116 (88,377)	6,699 (21,833)	3,012 (5,914)	1,264 (2,213)
Capital	247,935 (559,310)	na	98,893 (264,924)	862,069 (2,893,561)	520,282 (1,544,992)	160,024 (380,825)	98,488 (227,349)
Wage	6.07 (1.39)	na	7.21 (2.26)	8.31 (2.46)	7.24 (2.56)	7.07 (2.48)	7.05 (2.43)
N(max)	1,186	0	881	243	272	99	306

Table 11.A.7
Means (standard deviations) of principal variables by type of firm, 1995

Owner/Form	Private/ Enterpr.	Private/ Ltd.	Private/ J. Stock	Coop./ General	Coop./ Producer	State/ Ltd.	State/ J. Stock
Investment/ Capital	0.044 (0.083)	0.049 (0.122)	0.039 (0.095)	0.018 (0.033)	0.01 (0.037)	0.029 (0.064)	0.019 (0.042)
Depreciation/ Capital	0.025 (0.026)	0.032 (0.072)	0.021 (0.021)	0.015 (0.018)	0.011 (0.008)	0.019 (0.014)	0.015 (0.015)
Investment/ Labor	7.72 (21.15)	9.78 (33.11)	27.47 (92)	5.92 (11.87)	4.05 (13.6)	20.37 (79.27)	18.9 (43.17)
Investment/ Production	0.059 (0.178)	0.086 (0.473)	0.177 (0.524)	0.082 (0.182)	0.085 (0.221)	0.211 (1.142)	0.196 (2.606)
Profit	−256 (10,130)	1,634 (15,237)	1,863 (46,211)	866 (4,082)	−575 (2,703)	4,113 (28,060)	4,960 (43,822)
Labor	198 (166)	242 (249)	486 (912)	210 (106)	183 (104)	845 (689)	823 (1,861)
Investment	1,233 (3,780)	2,217 (6,816)	11,126 (42,637)	1,300 (2,840)	1,101 (4,959)	11,698 (26,618)	14,696 (48,980)
Production	23,349 (18,695)	36,820 (51,071)	80,336 (176,629)	18,157 (24,172)	7,237 (6,521)	175,272 (193,357)	150,705 (403,516)
Depreciation	982 (1,342)	1,535 (2,665)	6,554 (23,430)	1,034 (2,025)	837 (979)	8,896 (9,002)	11,171 (33,449)
Capital	64,694 (88,694)	79,192 (137,220)	468,711 (1,661,331)	70,002 (66,750)	69,941 (33,302)	623,811 (790,346)	868,185 (2,655,066)
Wage	6.96 (2.21)	7.23 (1.85)	7.84 (2.36)	6.16 (1.55)	5.97 (1.23)	9.11 (1.53)	7.68 (1.8)
N(max)	144	2,593	873	560	33	103	2,900

Table 11.A.7
(continued)

Owner/Form	State/ SOE	State/ Subsid.	Foreign/ Ltd.	Foreign/ J. Stock	Mixed/ Ltd.	Mixed/ J. Stock	Other
Investment/ Capital	0.01 (0.047)	na	0.092 (0.15)	0.035 (0.066)	0.021 (0.066)	0.09 (0.204)	0.078 (0.114)
Depreciation/ Capital	0.013 (0.016)	na	0.035 (0.047)	0.024 (0.029)	0.021 (0.026)	0.047 (0.048)	0.027 (0.028)
Investment/ Labor	8.4 (20.88)	na	39.05 (85.64)	44 (77.46)	17.16 (66.15)	7.32 (18.47)	42.4 (81.88)
Investment/ Production	0.072 (0.298)	na	0.242 (0.889)	0.168 (0.333)	0.094 (0.291)	0.048 (0.081)	0.277 (0.64)
Profit	417 (18,895)	na	9,204 (89,970)	0 (98,735)	−1,350 (32,291)	5,460 (19,792)	2,637 (15,642)
Labor	327 (297)	na	358 (650)	912 (2,384)	568 (688)	433 (579)	195 (87)
Investment	3,170 (8,325)	na	14,789 (34,643)	51,272 (223,421)	11,816 (34,962)	6,671 (19,701)	9,492 (25,383)
Production	50,778 (72,823)	na	93,468 (169,777)	392,873 (1,453,467)	126,977 (260,081)	67,426 (100,698)	381,909 (133,915)
Depreciation	4,184 (6,910)	na	6,847 (17,428)	32,934 (131,052)	9,030 (27,184)	3,585 (9,777)	2,339 (2,657)
Capital	361,926 (765,303)	na	252,529 (478,841)	1,270,628 (3,849,551)	652,680 (1,778,220)	175,129 (474,067)	121,550 (131,445)
Wage	7.31 (1.7)	na	8.91 (3.31)	9.6 (3.46)	8.09 (1.85)	8.37 (2.26)	8.36 (2.78)
N(max)	502	0	445	191	234	94	427

Table 11.A.8
Gross investment/production by type of firm, 1992–1995

Time	Private/ Enterpr.	Private/ Ltd.	Private/ J. Stock	Coop./ General	Coop./ Producer	State/ Ltd.	State/ J. Stock
1992/Q1	0.03 (0.09)	0.31 (4.04)	0.31 (1.16)	0.06 (0.19)	0.04 (0.07)	0.03 (0.09)	0.11 (0.40)
1992/Q2	0.07 (0.25)	0.06 (0.26)	0.12 (0.30)	0.10 (0.35)	0.06 (0.12)	0.03 (0.06)	0.16 (0.98)
1992/Q3	0.05 (0.18)	0.11 (0.82)	0.09 (0.20)	0.06 (0.24)	0.10 (0.35)	0.03 (0.08)	0.21 (1.52)
1992/Q4	0.13 (0.47)	0.10 (0.43)	0.52 (3.35)	0.13 (0.49)	0.05 (0.11)	0.03 (0.07)	0.22 (0.75)
1993/Q1	0.08 (0.18)	0.05 (0.19)	0.07 (0.16)	0.04 (0.11)	0.12 (0.70)	0.09 (0.26)	0.10 (0.29)
1993/Q2	0.07 (0.22)	0.08 (0.35)	0.14 (0.40)	0.07 (0.14)	0.05 (0.09)	0.15 (0.43)	0.14 (0.53)
1993/Q3	0.07 (0.25)	0.10 (0.48)	0.17 (0.34)	0.10 (0.22)	0.05 (0.12)	0.10 (0.20)	0.13 (0.30)
1993/Q4	0.07 (0.16)	0.13 (0.54)	0.22 (0.58)	0.11 (0.23)	0.11 (0.33)	0.21 (0.60)	0.18 (0.43)
1994/Q1	0.07 (0.24)	0.14 (1.96)	0.29 (2.63)	0.05 (0.13)	0.00 (0.00)	0.81 (4.36)	0.13 (1.77)
1994/Q2	0.21 (1.17)	0.08 (0.29)	0.12 (0.33)	0.05 (0.11)	0.03 (0.04)	0.04 (0.05)	0.12 (0.60)
1994/Q3	0.16 (0.68)	0.09 (0.35)	0.21 (0.86)	0.06 (0.15)	0.00 (0.00)	0.08 (0.14)	0.13 (0.58)
1994/Q4	0.17 (0.75)	0.19 (1.92)	0.28 (1.16)	0.14 (0.59)	0.02 (0.03)	0.08 (0.14)	0.15 (0.32)
1995/Q1	0.09 (0.34)	0.09 (0.54)	0.15 (0.66)	0.04 (0.07)	0.02 (0.02)	0.07 (0.10)	0.10 (0.53)
1995/Q2	0.04 (0.05)	0.07 (0.34)	0.16 (0.42)	0.07 (0.14)	0.03 (0.04)	0.06 (0.10)	0.18 (1.40)
1995/Q3	0.04 (0.05)	0.07 (0.32)	0.18 (0.48)	0.09 (0.19)	0.06 (0.15)	0.46 (2.08)	0.14 (0.83)
1995/Q4	0.06 (0.06)	0.11 (0.63)	0.21 (0.52)	0.13 (0.27)	0.24 (0.39)	0.24 (0.94)	0.17 (0.40)

Table 11.A.8
(continued)

Time	State/ SOE	State/ Subsd.	Foreign/ Ltd.	Foreign/ J. Stock	Mixed/ J. Stock	Mixed/ Ltd.	Other/ Other	All
1992/Q1	0.12 (1.01)	0.09 (0.01)	0.13 (0.34)	0.19 (0.38)	0.31 (1.29)	0.00 (0.00)	0.04 (0.09)	0.14 (1.66)
1992/Q2	0.14 (0.60)	0.13 (0.19)	0.18 (0.59)	3.76 (19.03)	0.13 (0.47)	0.04 (0.09)	0.22 (0.59)	0.17 (2.26)
1992/Q3	0.14 (0.58)	0.00 (na)	0.24 (0.71)	0.74 (1.82)	0.22 (0.66)	0.18 (0.52)	0.03 (0.06)	0.15 (0.97)
1992/Q4	0.18 (0.66)	0.00 (na)	0.33 (1.09)	0.80 (3.46)	0.86 (4.52)	1.99 (5.87)	0.05 (0.07)	0.20 (1.14)
1993/Q1	0.07 (0.22)	0.06 (0.02)	0.13 (0.44)	0.14 (0.23)	0.03 (0.06)	0.23 (0.66)	0.45 (0.87)	0.08 (0.27)
1993/Q2	0.26 (3.23)	0.07 (0.09)	0.13 (0.27)	0.43 (1.24)	0.10 (0.36)	0.30 (0.60)	0.09 (0.15)	0.15 (1.64)
1993/Q3	0.36 (3.80)	0.00 (na)	0.20 (0.42)	0.15 (0.21)	0.06 (0.10)	0.43 (1.49)	0.05 (0.12)	0.16 (1.78)
1993/Q4	0.22 (2.44)	0.00 (na)	0.60 (2.36)	0.32 (0.59)	0.11 (0.23)	0.38 (0.60)	0.22 (0.45)	0.18 (1.22)
1994/Q1	0.05 (0.19)	na	0.25 (1.26)	0.14 (0.19)	0.13 (0.37)	0.11 (0.14)	0.10 (0.27)	0.14 (1.67)
1994/Q2	0.04 (0.08)	na	0.23 (1.09)	0.18 (0.39)	0.08 (0.16)	0.05 (0.08)	0.12 (0.20)	0.10 (0.51)
1994/Q3	0.04 (0.12)	na	0.18 (0.43)	0.16 (0.38)	0.08 (0.17)	0.04 (0.10)	0.10 (0.25)	0.11 (0.46)
1994/Q4	0.09 (0.24)	na	0.42 (1.57)	0.20 (0.29)	0.13 (0.24)	0.14 (0.33)	0.28 (0.67)	0.19 (1.37)
1995/Q1	0.05 (0.18)	na	0.16 (0.48)	0.22 (0.51)	0.07 (0.14)	0.03 (0.05)	0.16 (0.23)	0.10 (0.49)
1995/Q2	0.07 (0.31)	na	0.19 (0.61)	0.15 (0.30)	0.13 (0.49)	0.06 (0.10)	0.27 (0.68)	0.13 (0.87)
1995/Q3	0.06 (0.12)	na	0.33 (1.42)	0.14 (0.23)	0.07 (0.11)	0.06 (0.11)	0.19 (0.44)	0.13 (0.67)
1995/Q4	0.10 (0.47)	na	0.29 (0.70)	0.16 (0.21)	0.11 (0.27)	0.04 (0.04)	0.54 (1.00)	0.16 (0.51)

Notes

Lízal's research on this chapter was in part supported by OSI/HESP grant RSS 899/1996. Svejnar's research was in part supported by Phare ACE grant no. P96-6095-R. The authors would like to thank Jan Hanousek for useful comments and suggestions and the Czech Statistical Office for supplying the data. All remaining errors are ours.

1. See, e.g., Jorgenson 1971; Nickell 1977; Abel 1980; Abel and Blanchard 1986; Shapiro 1986; Fazzari, Hubbard, and Petersen 1988; Hayashi and Inoue 1991; Blanchard, Rhee, and Summers 1990; and Bond and Meghir 1994.

2. See, e.g., Thornton 1970; Desai 1976; Gomulka 1978, 1986; Greene and Levine 1976; Weitzman 1979; Brada and Hoffman 1985; and Terrell 1992, 1993.

3. See, e.g., Belka et al. 1994; EBRD 1995; and Eickelplasch 1995.

4. See Fazzari, Hubbard, and Petersen 1988 and Gertler 1988 for overviews of this literature.

5. As Lizal and Svejnar (1998) show, the behavior of gross investment offers some support for the neoclassical models. In future research it will also be useful to examine in more detail the possibility of estimating dynamic structural models of investment. As Lizal (1999b) shows, however, in the Czech case the parameters of these models imply unrealistic beliefs about the long-term sustainability of soft budget macroeconomic policies.

6. These checks are similar to those in Lizal, Singer, and Svejnar 1995. Namely, the firm's capital at the start and end of each quarter should be positive; the average labor force in a given quarter should be more than 20 employees; investment should be nonnegative; production should be positive; depreciation should be positive and less than the total capital value; investment should be smaller than end-of-period capital stock; average wage should be higher than 2,000 Czech crowns per month (minimum wage); sales should be nonnegative; one-year lagged production, sales and labor should be nonnegative or missing.

7. One large firm that met the nine criteria reported a 90 percent drop in output during the third quarter of 1993. This deviation affected the summary statistics (see, e.g., the large standard deviation in the third-quarter 1993 investment-to-production ratio in table 11.3) and some regression estimates. We have therefore eliminated this observation from the data set. Finally, data on capital stock are unavailable for 1992, and we hence use 1992 data for analyses that do not involve the capital stock variable.

8. In the first phase of the transition, Western banks opened branches and subsidiaries in the transition economies primarily to serve these foreign firms, many of which had been their established clients.

9. We have also tested the validity of the neoclassical/accelerator models of investment by including an output sales variable as a regressor. The estimated coefficient on this variable was usually insignificant and occasionally had a negative rather than positive sign.

10. The privately owned/individual businesses have a pattern that is unrelated to the behavior of average profit over time. They register a negative effect in 1992 (a profitable year) and a positive effect in 1993–1995, despite the fact that their average profit in 1993–1994 was similar to that in 1992 but became negative in 1995. The privately owned/limited liability firms show no effect in 1992 and 1994, when their average profit was relatively high, but they register a small positive effect in 1993 (a low-profit year) and a small negative effect in 1995 (a high-profit year). The foreign-owned/joint stock firms show a positive effect in each year despite major fluctuations (including negative values) in average profit; mixed-ownership/joint stock companies have a positive effect in 1992, zero effect in 1993–1994 and a negative effect in 1995; and mixed ownership/limited liability companies have a zero effect in 1992–1993 and a positive effect in 1994–1995.

References

Abel, Andrew B. 1980. Empirical investment equations: An integrative framework. In *Carnegie-Rochester Conference Series on Public Policy* 12:39–93.

Abel, Andrew B., and Olivier J. Blanchard. 1986. The present value of profits and cyclical movements in investments. *Econometrica* 54:249–273.

Belka, M., M. Schaffer, S. Estrin, and J. Singh. 1994. Evidence from a survey of state-owned, privatised and emerging private firms. Paper presented at workshop, "Enterprise Adjustment in Eastern Europe," World Bank, Washington, D.C., 22–23 September.

Blanchard, Olivier J., C. Rhee, and L. Summers. 1990. The stock markets, profits and investment. Working paper no. 3370, National Bureau of Economic Research, Cambridge, Mass.

Bond, Stephen, and Costas Meghir. 1994. Dynamic investment models and the firms's financial policy. *Review of Economic Studies* 61:197–222.

Brada, Josef, and Dennis L. Hoffman. 1985. The productivity differntial between Soviet and Western capital and the benefits of technology imports to the Soviet economy. *Quarterly Review of Economics and Business* 25:7–18.

Desai, Padma. 1976. The production function and technical change in postwar Soviet industry: A re-examination. *American Economic Review* 66:372–381.

Dyba, Karel, and Jan Svejnar. 1995. A comparative view of economic developments in the Czech Republic. In *The Czech Republic and economic transition in Eastern Europe*, ed. Jan Svejnar, 21–45. San Diego, Calif.: Academic.

European Bank for Reconstruction and Development (EBRD). 1995. *Transition report*. London: Author.

Eickelplasch, A. 1995. Aspekte der Wettbewerbsfahigkeit der ostdeutschen Industrie. Vierteljahreshefte des DIW, no. 2195.

Fazzari, Steven M., Glenn R. Hubbard, and Bruce C. Petersen. 1988. Financing constraints and corporate investment. *Brookings Papers on Economic Activity* 1:141–206.

Galeotti, Marzio, Fabio Schiantarelli, and Fidel Jaramillo. 1994. Investment decisions and the role of debt, liquid assets and cash flow: Evidence from Italian panel data. *Applied Financial Economics* 4, no. 2:121–132.

Gertler, Mark. 1998. Financial structure and economic activity. *Journal of Money, Credit and Banking* 20:559–588.

Gomulka, Stanislaw. 1978. Import technology and growth: Poland 1971–1980. *Cambridge Journal of Economics* 2:1–16.

Gomulka, Stanislaw. 1986. *Growth, innovation and reform in Eastern Europe*. Madison: University of Wisconsin Press.

Gomulka, Stanislaw, and P. Jasinski. 1994. Privatisation in Poland: Principles, methods and results. In *Privatisation in Central and Eastern Europe*, ed. S. Estrin. New York: Longman Press.

Greene, Donald W., and Herbert S. Levine. 1976. Implications of technology transfers for the USSR. *East-West Technological Co-operation*.

Hayashi, F., and T. Inoue. 1991. The relation between firm growth and q with multiple capital goods: Theory and evidence from Japanese panel data. *Econometrica* 59:731–754.

Hubbard, Glenn R., Anil K. Kashyap, and Toni M. Whited. 1995. Internal finance and firm investment. *Money, Credit, and Banking* 27:681–701.

Jorgenson, Dale W. 1971. Econometric studies of investment behavior: A survey. *Journal of Economic Literature* 9:1111–1147.

Lízal, L. 1999a. Depreciation rates in a transition economy: Evidence from Czech panel data. *Prague Economic Papers* 3:261–277.

Lízal, L. 1999b. Does a soft macroeconomic environment induce restructuring on the microeconomic level during the transition period? Evidence from investment behaviour of Czech enterprises. Working paper no. 147, *CERGE-EI*, Prague.

Lízal, L., and Jan Svejnar. 1998. Enterprise investment during the transition: Evidence from Czech panel data. Working paper no. 1835, *CEPR*, London.

Lízal L., M. Singer, and J. Svejnar. 1995. Manager interests, enterprise breakups and performance of state enterprises in transition. In *The Czech Republic and Economic Transition in Eastern Europe*, ed. Jan Svejnar, 211–232. San Diego, Calif.: Academic.

Nickell, S. 1977. *Uncertainty and lags in the investment decisions of firms.* Cambridge: Cambridge University Press.

Oliner, Stephen D., and Glenn D. Rudebusch. 1992. Sources of the financing hierarchy for business investment. *Review of Economics and Statistics* 74:643–654.

Shapiro, Matthew D. 1986. The dynamic demand for capital and labor. *Quarterly Journal of Economics* 101:513–542.

Terrell, Katherine. 1992. Productivity of Western and domestic capital in Polish industry. *Journal of Comparative Economics* 16:494–514.

Terrell, Katherine. 1993. Technical change and factor bias in Polish industry. *Review of Economics and Statistics* 75:741–747.

Thornton, Judith. 1970. Value added and factor productivity in Soviet industry. *American Economic Review* 60:863–871.

van Ees, Hans, and Harry Garretsen. 1994. Liquidity and business investment: Evidence from Dutch panel data. *Journal of Macroeconomics* 16:613–627.

Weitzman, Martin L. 1979. Technology transfer to the USSR: An economic analysis. *Journal of Comparative Economics* 3:167–177.

Whited, Toni M. 1992. Debt, liquidity constraints, and corporate investment: Evidence from panel data. *Journal of Finance* 47:1425–1460.

12 Conglomeration in Banking: Incentives and Market Discipline

Arnoud W. A. Boot and Anjolein Schmeits

12.1 Introduction

In recent years we have witnessed numerous consolidation and restructuring trans-actions in banking sectors around the world. Banks are becoming increasingly larger and more diversified. Noteworthy examples of consolidation for the U.S. banking industry are the mergers between Chase Manhattan and Chemical Bank, Bank One and First Chicago/NBD, and NationsBank and BankAmerica and the cross-industry merger between Citicorp and Travelers. In Japan, a spectacular merger has produced the Tokyo-Mitsubishi Bank, with more than $700 billion in assets. Examples for Western Europe are the mergers between Union Bank of Switzerland and Swiss Bank Corporation, the acquisition of the Belgian Bank (BBL) by the Dutch financial conglomerate (ING), and the merger between the Swedish bank Nordbanken and the Finnish bank Merita.

In many of the recent restructuring transactions, a broadening of the scope of the banks' activities has accompanied scale expansion. Banks that have traditionally focused on relationship-based activities now increasingly combine transaction- and relationship-based activities. Modern universal banks, for example, engage in lend-ing (often relationship-based) but also in proprietary trading (purely transaction-oriented). These mixtures of activities have become more and more common; conglomeration seems to be the current trend. Although few would readily deny that some diversification is valuable, banks seem to engage in an ever broadening variety of activities. As a consequence, banks have increasingly become somewhat opaque institutions. This distinguishes banks from many of their competitors, such as non-banking financial institutions like mutual funds and finance companies (see Merton 1993), which often choose to specialize and therefore are much more transparent. The question that arises, then, is: what is the optimal conglomeration of bank activ-ities? This question is of particular relevance, since self-inflicted opaqueness may come to haunt banks in a more competitive environment.

In this chapter we address this issue and examine the optimal organizational structure of bank activities. We focus on market discipline and internal incentives as key factors in determining the overall risk and decisions of financial institutions. We concentrate on internal incentives that arise from interactions between different divi-sions (or activities) in a conglomerate bank in the absence of synergies. In particular, we argue that internal incentives and also the effectiveness of market discipline are different depending on whether bank divisions operate as stand-alone entities or as part of a conglomerate. The argument that we develop is as follows. A drawback of combining different activities in one financial institution is reduced transparency and therefore a reduction in the effectiveness of market discipline. That is, outsiders, including the bank's financiers, may not be able to assess the performance of a conglomerate bank sufficiently, and—more importantly—have little control over the bank, whereas bank managers may have excessive discretion. The absence of market discipline may result in free-rider problems between divisions, since each division may not fully internalize the consequences of its own actions.

The primary mechanism that we see for market discipline is its effect on the bank's cost of capital. Banks should face a cost of capital reflecting the riskiness of their activities. Conglomeration, however, may obscure this process and invite cross-subsidization and free riding among divisions. As a consequence, market discipline might become ineffective.

We see as a noteworthy recent example of free riding and cross-subsidization the bankruptcy of Barings, a British bank with a long and exemplary tradition as a merchant bank. In this case, the cost of not inducing market discipline on proprietary trading activities turned out to be almost prohibitive. A conflict between the "old" relationship tradition and the new transaction-oriented activities was at the root of Barings' problems. As we discuss later in the chapter, this (emerging) conflict helps us substantiate the growing importance of internal cost-of-capital allocation mechanisms, like risk-adjusted return on capital (RAROC) and value at risk (VAR) in multidivisional banks.

Our analysis also points at some distinct *benefits* of conglomeration. As is well known, limited liability of shareholders may invite risk-taking behavior (Jensen and Meckling 1976). Diversification through implicit coinsurance reduces these incentives. As we show in this chapter, the limited-liability effect and its interaction with risk-taking incentives are important considerations for the optimality of conglomeration.

Building on related work (Boot and Schmeits 1999), we emphasize here that explicitly considering internal incentive problems and the potential mitigating effects of diversification has implications for the optimal organizational structure and scope of a bank's activities. In particular, we identify two determinants of the optimal organizational structure of banks: the degree of market discipline (or transparency) to which a division is subject if it operates as a stand-alone division, and the degree of competition in the market in which the division operates. Our main insights are as follows. Effective market discipline for stand-alone activities reduces the potential benefits of conglomeration. With ineffective market discipline, conglomeration further undermines market discipline but may nevertheless be beneficial. This is the case, for example, if competitive rents are low. A more competitive environment therefore may induce conglomeration. We also argue that internal cost-of-capital allocation schemes may create internal discipline that complements the conglomerate's weak external discipline. Such schemes should respond to a division's actual rather than anticipated risk choices. Finally, we argue that conglomeration may offer benefits that managerial incentive contracts cannot replicate. That is, conglomeration can serve as a commitment device for coinsurance among divisions.

The organization of this chapter is as follows. In section 12.2 we discuss the benefits and drawbacks of conglomeration, with a particular focus on the internal incentives that may arise from interactions among different bank divisions if they are integrated in one financial institution. In section 12.3 we illustrate the potential conflicts between proprietary trading and relationship banking activities in a numerical example that builds on Boot and Schmeits 1999. We also interpret the Barings debacle in this context. Section 12.4 discusses internal cost-of-capital allocation mechanisms ([EVA] and RAROC) and incentive contracting issues. Section 12.5 concludes the chapter.

12.2   General Overview

Consider two bank divisions, A and B, that need external debt financing to invest in a project and may either operate as stand-alone entities or as part of a conglomerate. Each division makes partially obervable risk choices that affect the probability of its project's success. External financing is potentially subject to effective market discipline. The degree of market discipline imposed determines the sensitivity of each division's funding costs with respect to its risk-taking behavior. That is, the funding cost the market sets not only anticipates risk choices after contracting, but also partially responds to risk choices directly. This interpretation captures the notion that the market receives information about the bank division's credit quality (or credit rating) over time, which then becomes reflected in the bank's funding cost. The degree of market discipline generally depends on the type and specificity of a division's assets. High asset specificity may give rise to proprietary information and lack of transparency, and hence little market discipline. The level of market discipline also depends on the maturity of the bank division's assets, since that maturity determines the speed with which information can be used for repricing purposes (see also Flannery 1994). Higher levels of market discipline mitigate a division's incentive problems to take excessive risk, since the division immediately faces the consequences of doing so.

If division A and division B operate as stand-alone firms, they are funded separately and independently in a competitive credit market. If the divisions operate as part of a conglomerate, however, they are funded as a conglomerate. The pooled funding cost of a conglomerate then only partially reflects the risk choices of each division; that is, both divisions share the consequences of their risk choices. As a consequence, divisions can increase risk without being fully charged for the costs, even if market discipline is perfect. Thus even for an arbitrarily high degree of market discipline, divisions may choose to free ride on the bank at large. Conglomeration thus may induce a moral hazard in teams effect (Holmström 1982). Simultaneously, however, the divisions may coinsure each other; that is, the multidivisional bank's returns are more predictable and default is less likely. This reduces default costs (holding incentives fixed) but also has three incentive effects on each division's risk choices. First, coinsurance lowers the pooled funding rate and hence reduces risk-taking incentives induced by limited liability (*diversification effect of coinsurance*). This effect alone will improve each division's risk choices. Second, the default probability of the bank becomes partially immune to each division's risk taking. This reduces a division's expected costs of financial distress, thus inducing extra risk taking (*negative incentive effect of coinsurance*). Third, since the conglomerate bank's pooled funding rate is less sensitive to each division's risk choices than the division's funding rate as a stand-alone entity (the other division "smoothes"), each division now only partially internalizes the higher funding costs associated with risk taking. Thus market discipline becomes less effective, inducing inefficiencies—free riding—in each division's decisions (*negative incentive effect of reduced market discipline*).

These considerations highlight the costs and benefits of conglomeration. The degree of market discipline is a crucial parameter. In the case of perfect market discipline of stand-alone activities, conglomeration could not improve incentives. Risk choices in the stand-alone divisions would then be optimal, and the negative incentive effects of conglomeration would dominate. Even then, however, conglomeration might still be value-maximizing, if the "exogenous" reduction in default risk (due to diversification) offered substantial benefits (i.e., better preservation of future rents).

In general, we could say that more market discipline favors a stand-alone organizational structure and reduces the benefits of conglomeration. Imperfect market discipline could boost the case for conglomeration, notwithstanding that conglomeration always further reduces market discipline. Conglomeration might have benefits that substitute for ineffective market discipline. The expected benefits, however, need to be strong enough to make conglomeration dominate the stand-alone option. An important determinant here is the competitive environment. Conglomeration is most valuable when rents are relatively low. The intuition is that high competitive rents would mitigate excessive risk taking in the stand-alone case, and conglomeration therefore is more likely to worsen matters. Thus, ceteris paribus, in a competitive environment, conglomeration is optimal.

12.3 The Potential Conflict between Proprietary Trading and Relationship Banking

12.3.1 A Numerical Example

In this section, we illustrate the potential adverse incentive and spillover effects of interactions among different divisions in a conglomerate bank in the context of a bank that engages in both relationship banking and proprietary trading, a combination that is increasingly characteristic of modern banking. We now give a numerical example involving these interactions that considers the risk choices of two divisions—as stand-alones or in a conglomerate—simultaneously.[1] Suppose that the divisions, A and B, each need \$1 of external debt financing to invest in their project. Division A can be interpreted as a relationship lending division, division B as a proprietary trading division. At the time of investment, the manager of division A chooses a level of monitoring effort m, which affects the risk of division A's project. We can think of division A's manager monitoring the activities of a borrower to which the division has lent, thereby increasing the probability of repayment of the loan. A higher level of monitoring corresponds to lower risk. Let the private costs of monitoring equal $4m^2$. A monitoring level $m \in [0,1]$ results in a success probability $\frac{1}{2}(1+m)$. In the case of project success, division A's partially contractible project return X equals 2.75. Otherwise, division A's payoff equals 0. Upon success division A generates future (relationship-based) rents with a capitalized value $F(m) = 0.5m^{1/2}$. In the case of division A's default, these rents will be lost. The future rents $F(m)$ reflect the longer-term scope of relationship banking activities. That is, a bank may need to invest heavily in relationships at the outset to benefit in the longer term. We assume that division A's rents are division-specific and cannot be expropriated without a complete loss in value. Division A, if financed as a stand-alone entity, is subject to external market discipline $\alpha_A \in [0,1]$. The parameter α_A represents the probability with which the monitoring (or risk) choice of division A can be observed by the market and thus can directly be contracted on. With a probability $(1 - \alpha_A)$ the division's risk choice can only be anticipated by the market. Thus, division A's funding cost can with a probability α_A fully reflect its actual risk; with a probability $(1 - \alpha_A)$ a moral hazard problem exists, where the market can only anticipate, rather than actually observe, the risk level.

Division B is (short-term) transaction-oriented. The manager of division B chooses a risk level $p \in [0, 1]$, which results in a success probability p and a return of $Y(p) = 3(p - 2)^2$ in the case of success. In the case of failure, division B's payoff equals 0. This payoff structure reflects that trading activities are more short-term oriented and do not depend on relationship-specific effort. The degree of external market discipline that division B is subject to equals $\alpha_B \in [0, 1]$. We assume a zero risk-free interest rate and universal risk neutrality.

Each divisional manager maximizes her division's expected surplus net of the funding cost. Two different organizational structures can be distinguished: stand-alone or conglomerate. In the stand-alone option, each division operates separately and is funded independently in a competitive market. Given the success probabilities $\frac{1}{2}(1 + m)$ and p, the funding cost for division A then equals $2(1 + m)^{-1}$ and that for division B equals p^{-1}. If division A and B are integrated in one firm, they are funded as a conglomerate. In that case both divisions coinsure each other. We assume that the two-divisional bank will default only if the projects of both divisions fail.[2] The competitive funding rate that applies to the conglomerate bank then equals $\{1 - [1 - \frac{1}{2}(1 + m)](1 - p)\}^{-1} = 2[2 - (1 - m)(1 - p)]^{-1}$ per dollar invested and depends on the risk choices in both divisions, m and respectively p. In a multidivisional bank these risk choices need to be determined simultaneously. The risk choice of trading division B therefore may have an impact on the risk choice in the relationship banking division A and vice versa. Our focus is on how the choices of trading division B may undermine, or negatively affect, the choices relationship banking division A makes.

Let m_A and p_B be the respective divisions' privately optimal risk choices if they operate as stand-alone entities, and define m_C and p_C as division A and division B's risk choices, respectively, in the case of conglomeration. Table 12.1 and table 12.2 then represent the difference in incentives in a conglomerate and the stand-alone option as a function of the market discipline parameters α_A and α_B, respectively. Table 12.3 represents the difference in the total expected net surplus between conglomeration and the stand-alone option.

From tables 12.1 and 12.2 we see that conglomeration improves incentives in both bank divisions if the degree of market discipline to which each division is subject if it operates as a stand-alone is small (i.e., if $\alpha_A < 0.49$ and $\alpha_B < 0.37$). In this case conglomeration is always optimal, since it maximizes the total net surplus created by the respective divisions. For $\alpha_B > 0.37$, however, the proprietary trading division chooses more risk in a conglomerate, which negatively affects the incentives in the relationship lending division A. For $\alpha_A > 0.49$, the incentives in both divisions worsen if they are integrated. The negative incentive effects in a conglomerate then

Table 12.1
Differences in incentives $m_C - m_A$ in division A as a function of market discipline parameters α_A and α_B

α_A \ α_B	0.0	0.1	0.2	0.3	0.4	0.5	0.6	0.7	0.8	0.9	1.0
0.0	0.0429	0.0430	0.0432	0.0433	0.0434	0.0436	0.0437	0.0438	0.0440	0.0441	0.0443
0.1	0.0340	0.0341	0.0343	0.0344	0.0345	0.0346	0.0347	0.0349	0.0350	0.0351	0.0353
0.2	0.0251	0.0252	0.0253	0.0254	0.0255	0.0256	0.0257	0.0258	0.0260	0.0261	0.0262
0.3	0.0163	0.0164	0.0165	0.0165	0.0166	0.0167	0.0168	0.0169	0.0170	0.0171	0.0171
0.4	0.0076	0.0077	0.0077	0.0078	0.0078	0.0079	0.0080	0.0080	0.0081	0.0082	0.0082
0.5	-0.0010	-0.0009	-0.0009	-0.0008	-0.0008	-0.0007	-0.0007	-0.0006	-0.0006	-0.0006	-0.0006
0.6	-0.0094	-0.0094	-0.0093	-0.0093	-0.0093	-0.0093	-0.0092	-0.0092	-0.0092	-0.0092	-0.0092
0.7	-0.0177	-0.0177	-0.0177	-0.0177	-0.0177	-0.0177	-0.0177	-0.0176	-0.0176	-0.0176	-0.0178
0.8	-0.0259	-0.0259	-0.0259	-0.0259	-0.0259	-0.0260	-0.0260	-0.0260	-0.0260	-0.0260	-0.0260
0.9	-0.0340	-0.0340	-0.0340	-0.0341	-0.0341	-0.0342	-0.0342	-0.0342	-0.0343	-0.0343	-0.0343
1.0	-0.0418	-0.0419	-0.0419	-0.0420	-0.0421	-0.0421	-0.0422	-0.0422	-0.0423	-0.0423	-0.0424

Table 12.2
Differences in incentives $p_C - p_B$ in division B as a function of market discipline parameters α_A and α_B

α_A	α_B 0.0	0.1	0.2	0.3	0.4	0.5	0.6	0.7	0.8	0.9	1.0
0.0	0.0488	0.0348	0.0215	0.0088	-0.0033	-0.0149	-0.0260	-0.0367	-0.0470	-0.0570	-0.0668
0.1	0.0489	0.0348	0.0215	0.0088	-0.0033	-0.0149	-0.0260	-0.0367	-0.0471	-0.0571	-0.0668
0.2	0.0489	0.0349	0.0215	0.0088	-0.0033	-0.0149	-0.0260	-0.0367	-0.0471	-0.0571	-0.0668
0.3	0.0490	0.0349	0.0216	0.0089	-0.0033	-0.0149	-0.0260	-0.0367	-0.0471	-0.0571	-0.0669
0.4	0.0490	0.0350	0.0216	0.0089	-0.0033	-0.0149	-0.0260	-0.0368	-0.0471	-0.0572	-0.0669
0.5	0.0491	0.0350	0.0216	0.0089	-0.0033	-0.0149	-0.0261	-0.0368	-0.0472	-0.0572	-0.0670
0.6	0.0491	0.0350	0.0216	0.0089	-0.0033	-0.0149	-0.0261	-0.0368	-0.0472	-0.0573	-0.0670
0.7	0.0492	0.0351	0.0217	0.0089	-0.0032	-0.0149	-0.0261	-0.0368	-0.0472	-0.0573	-0.0671
0.8	0.0492	0.0351	0.0217	0.0089	-0.0032	-0.0149	-0.0261	-0.0368	-0.0473	-0.0573	-0.0671
0.9	0.0493	0.0352	0.0217	0.0090	-0.0032	-0.0149	-0.0261	-0.0369	-0.0473	-0.0574	-0.0672
1.0	0.0493	0.0352	0.0218	0.0090	-0.0032	-0.0149	-0.0261	-0.0369	-0.0473	-0.0574	-0.0672

Table 12.3
Differences in total expected net surplus between the conglomerate and the stand-alone option

α_A	α_B 0.0	0.1	0.2	0.3	0.4	0.5	0.6	0.7	0.8	0.9	1.0
0.0	0.2038	0.1777	0.1564	0.1394	0.1262	0.1163	0.1094	0.1050	0.1030	0.1032	0.1052
0.1	0.1875	0.1614	0.1400	0.1230	0.1098	0.0998	0.0928	0.0884	0.0864	0.0865	0.0885
0.2	0.1713	0.1451	0.1237	0.1066	0.0933	0.0834	0.0763	0.0719	0.0698	0.0698	0.0718
0.3	0.1552	0.1289	0.1075	0.0904	0.0771	0.0670	0.0599	0.0555	0.0533	0.0533	0.0553
0.4	0.1394	0.1131	0.0916	0.0745	0.0611	0.0510	0.0394	0.0394	0.0372	0.0371	0.0390
0.5	0.1240	0.0976	0.0761	0.0589	0.0454	0.0353	0.0236	0.0236	0.0213	0.0212	0.0231
0.6	0.1088	0.0824	0.0608	0.0436	0.0301	0.0199	0.0081	0.0081	0.0058	0.0056	0.0075
0.7	0.0939	0.0674	0.0458	0.0285	0.0150	0.0047	-0.0072	-0.0072	-0.0095	-0.0097	-0.0079
0.8	0.0792	0.0527	0.0310	0.0137	0.0001	-0.0102	-0.0223	-0.0223	-0.0246	-0.0248	-0.0231
0.9	0.0648	0.0382	0.0164	-0.0010	-0.0146	-0.0249	-0.0371	-0.0371	-0.0398	-0.0398	-0.0381
1.0	0.0507	0.0241	0.0023	-0.0152	-0.0289	-0.0392	-0.0515	-0.0515	-0.0543	-0.0543	-0.0526

Table 12.4
Optimal organizational structure as a function of competitive environment $(F(m))$ and market discipline/transparency (α_A)

α_A	$F(m)$		
	Low	Medium	High
Low	Conglomerate	Conglomerate	Stand-alone
High	Conglomerate or stand-alone	Conglomerate or stand-alone	Stand-alone
Limit $\alpha_A \to 1$	Stand-alone	Conglomerate or stand-alone	Stand-alone

undermine the benefits of relationship banking. If the expected benefits from diversification are sufficiently high, however, conglomeration could still be optimal. For $\alpha_A > 0.70$ (see table 12.3), this will never be the case.

From our example it is clear that effective market discipline of stand-alone activities (i.e., high levels of α_A and α_B) makes conglomeration less attractive. With ineffective market discipline (low levels of α_A and α_B), conglomeration may worsen incentives but may nevertheless be beneficial. Whether this is the case will also depend on the level of the future rents $F(m)$. This is where the competitive environment comes in. If the capitalized future rents to be generated by division A are not too high, the benefits of conglomeration may dominate the negative incentive effects. If the future rents are high, division A's risk choices in the stand-alone option approach first best, and the negative incentive effects associated with conglomeration generally dominate the potential benefits. If we change the future rents from the relatively modest level $F(m) = 0.5m^{1/2}$, as we have assumed so far, to $6m^{1/2}$, conglomeration always worsens incentives in division A (and often in division B) and is never optimal. Conglomeration therefore is more beneficial in a competitive environment with low future rents $F(m)$.

We have summarized these implications in table 12.4. As we highlight in Boot and Schmeits 1999, the optimality of combining different activities will also depend on the degree of heterogeneity among those activities. For very heterogeneous activities, conglomeration is most detrimental.

12.3.2   Implications for the Interpretation of the Barings Case

The numerical example in section 12.3.1 has shown that proprietary trading within a conglomerate bank may suffer from a lack of effective market discipline, and as a result, excessive risk taking may occur that undermines the bank's relationship-specific activities. A noteworthy example of a banking institution in which proprietary trading gained importance rapidly was the Barings Bank, a British bank with a long tradition in corporate banking that went into bankruptcy following extraordinary trading losses in its Singapore operations (recall the noteworthy trader Nick Leeson). Some interpret the Barings debacle as a meltdown caused by a clash of cultures: agressive and ambitious traders versus traditional and conservative bankers. For them, better internal controls and external supervision aimed at aligning incentives seem obvious remedies. We believe that the economics of banking dictate a much more fundamental analysis, one that transcends the specifics of Barings and calls into question the banks' strategic choices in general. We argue that although internal controls and supervision may indeed *control* incentives, they do not, however, *align* incentives but merely bring about desired behavior through "brute force". In the Barings case, trading units, although undoubtedly ill supervised, faced little market discipline. Barings' (relationship-oriented) corporate banking activities in the United Kingdom were effectively underwriting the risky proprietary trading activities in Singapore. Barings Singapore therefore faced an artificially low cost of capital and could free ride on Barings UK. This interpretation highlights the potentially divergent incentives of different organizational units when combined in one institution.

Our line of argument suggests that the market discipline on the trading activities was obscured within the conglomerate. In the absence of market discipline banks may allocate capital only arbitrarily to their different activities and charge a cost per unit of capital that is potentially even more arbitrary. The demise of Barings suggests that this was indeed the case. The implication is that the proprietary trading activity is free riding on the bank at large. This may have three consequences: (1) proprietary trading appears more profitable than it really is, (2) a proprietary trading unit does not sufficiently internalize risks, and (3) banks' other—mainly relationship-oriented—activities face an unfairly high cost of funds. The implications of this are twofold. First, proprietary traders may operate with little market discipline. Consequently, the only corrective mechanisms on their operations are internal controls and external supervision. Second, banks may become less competitive in their relationship-oriented activities, since these are effectively subsidizing the trading activities. Thus, proprietary trading undermines the banks' real competitive edge. We now turn to a more detailed analysis of the trading activity.[3]

Banks' trading activities have been a considerable source of earnings in the last few years. But have they been as profitable as some believe? Trading activity involves substantial risks, thus establishing the fair risk-adjusted cost of funds is important. Banks try to resolve this by allocating costly capital to the trading unit. Thus, the trading unit's funding cost is artificially grossed up by adding the cost of its "capital at risk." This internal capital allocation process not only is arbitrary but may also be flawed.

The presumption in these internal capital allocations is generally that capital has one price. A bank's cost of capital might be set, for example, at 15 percent. Some believe that capital is twice as expensive as (risk-free) financial market debt financing. Whatever the presumption, capital does *not* have one price. Standard capital structure theory tells us that the per unit cost of capital depends on the risks to which this capital is exposed. More risk generally implies a higher cost of capital. Two important implications now follow. First, the per unit cost of capital will not be the same for all of the bank's activities. The level of risk and the risk characteristics will determine the unit cost of capital for each of the activities. Applying a bank's cost of capital to its proprietary trading unit is therefore wrong. Given the generally well-diversified (and thus low) risks found in the bank at large, the (nondiversifiable) risks taken in the trading unit dictate a much higher cost of capital.

The second implication is more general: banks should not choose to engage in certain activities solely because they have the capital to do so. The critical observation here is that "putting capital to use" elevates its per unit cost. Therefore, engaging in proprietary trading to exploit the bank's capital will elevate the cost of this capital and as a consequence increase the cost of funds for the bank at large. Banks that consider themselves "overcapitalized" and decide to put this capital to use may thus not create value at all. This argument may also explain why banks consider capital (prohibitively?) expensive. If potential investors anticipate that banks will put their capital to use at all costs, they will gross up their required return accordingly. Banks then can issue equity only at discount prices.[4] These beliefs and anticipations create a perverse equilibrium. Given the bankers' state of mind—fixed-priced, expensive capital that needs to be put to use as quickly as possible—the market responds rationally by charging a high price for capital. And given these anticipations by the market, the bankers' beliefs are justified and confirmed in equilibrium.[5]

The arguments above could help explain why banks have granted proprietary trading an artificially low cost of capital at the expense of a (potentially) prohibitively high cost of capital for the bank as a whole (see also Rajan 1996). This is the free riding we alluded to earlier. As a consequence, other—mainly relationship-oriented—activities are implicitly taxed. Banks then may mistakenly conclude that relationship banking activities are not profitable. In terms of our divisions A (relationship banking) and B (proprietary trading), these effects would lead to lower monitoring m in division A and higher risk (lower p) in division B. For our insights on the optimality of conglomeration, these arguments show that for heterogeneous activities it is difficult to overcome the potentially adverse incentive effects. Designing an optimal capital (cost) allocation mechanism is crucial.

12.4   Internal Cost-of-Capital Allocation Mechanisms and Incentive Contracting Issues

In this section we analyze the impact of an internal cost-of-capital allocation mechanism on division A's risk choice in a conglomerate and on the optimal organizational structure. We subsequently address how the use of incentive contracts, that is, managerial compensation mechanisms, would affect our analysis. In particular, we discuss whether stand-alone divisions could replicate the incentives in a conglomerate without a change in organizational structure, and vice versa.

12.4.1   Internal Allocation of Cost of Capital

From section 12.3.1 it is clear that integrating separate divisions in a conglomerate firm is desirable if it results in better monitoring (or risk) choices in the divisions. If it does not, free riding (implying high risk) may dominate, and division A and division B may prefer to operate as stand-alone entities. Potentially valuable diversification benefits may then remain unexploited. This inefficiency results from the reduction in market discipline following conglomeration, which outweighs the potential diversification benefits. An increase in the impact of market discipline in a conglomerate firm therefore could reduce free riding and facilitate socially desirable integration.

An internal cost-of-capital allocation mechanism could create internal discipline that complements external market discipline. Such an internal cost-of-capital allocation mechanism could align incentives and allow division A to benefit optimally from the diversification benefit of integration.[6] The impact of a given level α_A of market discipline on division A's choice of monitoring intensity can be increased by an internal allocation of the cost of capital to the respective divisions by a CEO. (Let's assume that the CEO acts in the interest of the conglomerate firm's shareholders.)

Internal allocation of cost of capital could be introduced in the following way. The CEO first allocates a *differential charge* to the respective divisions to reflect *intrinsic* differences in riskiness. Thus, the CEO does not charge a pooled rate to both divisions but instead differentiates between division A and division B in the cost of capital charged. This is analogous to charging the cost of capital that the market would charge if division A and division B were operated and funded as separate entities. Simultaneously, the CEO could restore market discipline by increasing the *sensitivity parameter* in the cost of capital charged to division A with respect to m.[7] That is, he internally leverages the now diluted external market discipline parameter α_A. The CEO need not be better informed with respect to the incentive problems in division A than outsiders. If he is equally informed, he can still undo the diluted

market discipline in the conglomerate. If the CEO has better information than outsiders, the total—internal *and* external—market discipline can become even larger.
This is implicitly the case in, for example, Stein 1997, where the CEO engages in
"winner-picking" and can reallocate scarce resources among competing projects in a
conglomerate.

Observe that both a differential charge to reflect intrinsic differences in riskiness
and a more active risk choice–dependent charge (via the sensitivity parameter) are
necessary. The latter truly combats moral hazard incentives by imposing "internal"
market discipline.[8] These observations provide a foundation for the recent attention
to RAROC and other capital allocation systems.

Since the late 1980s, a number of large banks have invested heavily in systems
designed to measure the risks associated with their different lines of business (see
James and Houston 1996). These efforts have been undertaken partly in response to
regulations with respect to capital adequacy rules (e.g., the Basle risk-based capital
requirements of 1988 and the Federal Deposit Insurance Corp. Improvement Act
[FDICIA] of 1991). In addition to monitoring risks to comply with regulation, many
banks and financial institutions have also adopted internal capital allocation and
performance measurement systems as part of their strategic response to increased
competition and the resulting growth of fee-based services. These mechanisms generally have a twofold purpose. First, they provide a basis for the allocation of risk
capital (equity) to different bank activities (divisions) for risk management purposes.
Second, they serve as a basis for performance evaluation and incentive compensation within multidivisional banks. Risk-based capital allocation systems are often
lumped together under the name "Risk-adjusted return on capital." RAROC systems replace traditional measures of performance like return on assets (ROA) and
return on equity (ROE) with a measure that takes into account the riskiness of individual bank divisions. RAROC systems assign capital to business units as part of a
process of determining the risk-adjusted rate of return and ultimately the "economic
profit" (or EVA) of each division. Their objective is to measure a business unit's
contribution to shareholder value and thus to provide a basis for effective capital
budgeting and incentive compensation at the business unit level (Zaik et al. 1996).
Capital is allocated to individual business units on the basis of each division's contribution to the overall volatility of the bank's market value. This measure of the
business unit's contribution to shareholder value therefore also takes into account
potential internal diversification benefits. The equity capital (i.e., the economic or
risk capital) allocated to each division is then multiplied by the cost of equity to determine the appropriate capital charge for the division. The economic profit or EVA

for the division subsequently is determined by subtracting this capital charge from each division's earnings (net of taxes, interest payments, and expected credit losses).

James and Houston (1996) and Zaik et al. (1996) analyze the capital budgeting process at Bank of America, where equity capital is defined as a value-at-risk (VAR) measure. VAR is defined as the amount of capital that a bank at large can lose (at a certain confidence level) as a consequence of unexpected losses without becoming insolvent or suffering deterioration of its credit rating. The capital charge for each business within the bank is obtained by multiplying economic capital or VAR by the corporate-wide cost of equity capital. RAROC is computed by dividing each division's risk-adjusted net income by the amount of economic capital assigned to that division, based on the risk calculation. This RAROC measure can then be compared to the appropriate cost of equity for the division to evaluate the division's performance.

Stoughton and Zechner (1999) analyze financial institutions' decentralized capital allocation decisions in the presence of capital adequacy restrictions when the bank's required equity capital (and thus its cost of capital) depends on the risk of the different activities. Their paper addresses the question of how much equity capital should be charged to each division so as to internalize the effect of individual investment decisions and risk choices on a multidivisional bank's overall level of risk. They also discuss the relevance of strict position limits against discretionary trading through the use of an optimal compensation function. Stoughton and Zechner's paper shows that in a world with asymmetric information, when each division's investment decision cannot be contracted on, the optimal capital allocation mechanism requires the bank to compute economic capital for the use in EVA and RAROC calculations. This concept of economic capital is related to the widespread use of VAR. The method proposed by Stoughton and Zeckner involves the central authority of the financial institution specifying a mechanism under which divisions are allocated a capital charge equal to a division-specific price multiplied by their own VAR. The price is chosen so that the economic capital is equal in realization to the incremental VAR, which takes into account the externality that one division's risk imposes on that of the institution's other divisions. The price must be customized for the division's own investment opportunities.[9]

In view of our analysis, the RAROC, VAR, and EVA concepts clearly seek to mitigate the negative incentives that conglomeration can bring about. A proper application of these concepts would lead each division to fully internalize its risk and would overcome (most of) the disadvantages of conglomeration that we focus on in this chapter.

12.4.2 Incentive Contracting Issues

In our discussion, we have assumed that the manager of a stand-alone division maximizes the firm's expected surplus net of funding costs. The manager thus maximizes
shareholder value. This is basically equivalent to the manager's receiving an equity-
linked compensation contract. One might suggest that matters could be improved if
the manager were motivated to maximize the total value of the stand-alone division
(including the value of debt). Observe that with an equity-linked compensation contract the manager is induced to take more risk, to the detriment of the debtholder.
Shareholders, however, cannot credibly design a compensation structure for the
manager such that his actions are aimed at maximizing firm value, because shareholders have an incentive to renegotiate such a compensation contract ex post (after
debt financing is obtained). The manager in the stand-alone case thus cannot be
motivated to choose an optimal monitoring level. Given the assumption of universal
risk neutrality and the informational structure in our analysis, the use of an equity-
linked compensation contract then can be rationalized, since it maximizes the manager's second-best monitoring intensity.[10]

Time inconsistency problems between managers and shareholders in a stand-alone
firm thus prevent the design of ex ante optimal compensation contracts. The next
question is whether stand-alone firms can mimic the incentives in a conglomerate
and the benefits of conglomeration through incentive contracts.

The answer to this question, in the context of our framework, is negative. In order
to mimic the incentives provided in a conglomerate through the use of incentive
contracts, the shareholders of a stand-alone division would have to offer the divisional
manager a contract in which they agree to cross-subsidize the other stand-alone division in the case it defaults. Observe that it is exactly this cross-subsidization (coinsurance) that induces the benefits of conglomeration. Such a contract, however, is
not robust, since in this case the shareholders also cannot precommit against rene-
gotiating the contract ex post. That is, the ex post unwillingness of the shareholders
of a stand-alone division to cross-subsidize a defaulting division makes incentive
contracts that replicate the coinsurance in a conglomerate infeasible ex ante. This
time inconsistency problem is ruled out in the case of conglomeration. By buying a
share in a conglomerate firm, a shareholder precommits to cross-subsidize a defaulting division in a conglomerate. Conglomeration therefore can serve as a commitment device for coinsurance.

These conclusions are similar to the findings in Aron 1988 and Ramakrishnan and
Thakor 1991. Both of these papers compare the benefits of diversification with those
achieved by incentive contracting mechanisms and also conclude that conglomera-

tion and the use of managerial compensation contracts are imperfect substitutes from an agency perspective. Aron (1988) develops a model in which a risk-neutral principal receives an imperfect signal of a risk-averse manager's effort choice for different activities and compares the benefits of merger (diversification) with the use of compensation contracts based on the manager's performance relative to similar activities. Diversification can be differentiated from relative-performance contracts by the signals that can be used to create incentives for managers. Aron shows that the benefit of diversification vis-à-vis relative-performance contracts depends on the correlation between the different activities involved. Relative-performance contracts are valuable when the observable returns of stand-alone activities are positively correlated, whereas diversification dominates when the activities in a conglomerate are negatively correlated or uncorrelated. Ramakrishnan and Thakor (1991) present a model in which a risk-neutral principal must motivate two risk-averse agents that make unobservable effort choices that stochastically affect their output. The principal can choose between having the agents operate independently (stand-alone) or having them cooperate in a conglomerate (integration). Their paper shows that the degree of correlation between activities dictates the choice between integration or the stand-alone option. The benefits of incentive contracts and diversification in both Aron 1988 and Ramakrishnan and Thakor 1991 crucially depend on risk-sharing considerations. We do not consider risk-sharing benefits here but instead focus on the incentive effects associated with diversification.

We could also ask whether a stand-alone firm can replicate the diversification benefits of conglomeration by hedging its default risk with a third party in the financial market. For example, the manager of division A could enter into a contract in which he receives an amount equal to the cross-subsidy from division B if division A defaults or pays an amount equal to the cross-subsidy to division B if B defaults, or both. Although hedging could be an alternative commitment device for a divisional manager, this option has the potential problem that the division's default risk not only depends on exogenous factors but is also influenced by the divisional manager's monitoring intensity (i.e., depends on m). A division's default risk thus is (partly) endogenous and hence firm-specific. Hedging such controllable risks is problematic, since a market for trading firm-specific default risk is subject to rampant moral hazard problems.

We next turn to the issue of the optimal design of incentive contracts in multidivisional firms. A sizable recent literature extends the traditional principal-agent theory, which focuses on single-agent problems, to the context of multidivisional firms and examines the benefits and drawbacks of forming teams in agency contexts (see, e.g.,

Holmström 1982; Holmström and Milgrom 1990; Varian 1990; Itoh 1991; and Ramakrishnan and Thakor 1991). Contributions to this literature focus on the benefits of team effort and payoff pooling in multidivisional firms. Holmström (1982) addresses the merits of relative-performance evaluation and finds that relative-performance contracts can reduce moral hazard costs by allowing for better risk sharing if the outputs of different activities are correlated. If outputs are independent, and each activity's output can be observed separately, however, the optimal compensation schedule for each agent depends solely on her own output. Holmström and Milgrom (1990) obtain similar results, allowing for cooperation (team effort) and potential information sharing between agents in a multidivisional firm. They find that cooperation among agents can be beneficial if the agents can monitor each other and have better information than the principal (see also Varian 1990).[11] Ramakrishnan and Thakor (1991) and Itoh (1991) discuss the benefits of cooperation in the absence of correlation among the outputs of different activities. In these papers, agents can supply effort to facilitate each other's activities and can thus engage in team production with interdependent incentive schemes. Itoh (1991) shows that when agents are risk neutral and team effort is not desirable, each agent's compensation contract should depend on his own output only. If team effort is optimal, interdependent contracts could be beneficial. Finally, Ramakrishnan and Thakor (1991) show that if risk-averse agents can monitor each other's effort choices, optimal incentive contracts make each agent's wage depend both on her own output and on the output of the other agents, since this improves both team effort and risk sharing (payoff pooling).

These results provide a foundation for what we envision as the divisional objective functions when the divisions are part of a conglomerate (see also Boot and Schmeits 1999). The divisional managers are compensated based on the net payoff of their own division and thus receive an equity type of claim in their division. As indicated above, such a claim would be optimal if the outputs of the activities in division A and division B were uncorrelated and could be observed separately by the principal (e.g., the CEO).

The analysis above also underscores the increasing importance and popularity of internal-equity types of compensation mechanisms in multidivisional firms (e.g., EVA or economic profit). Two drawbacks, however, should be mentioned here. First, although divisional payoff–related compensation mechanisms may improve a division manager's incentives, influence activities may hamper the effectiveness of such incentive contracts (see, e.g., Milgrom and Roberts 1990; Rajan and Zingales 1995; and Wulf 1998). These influence activities may be mitigated if each division optimizes the total surplus of the conglomerate firm. Observe, however, that effort aversion is best served by linking the manager's compensation to the output of his own division (Holmström 1982). Second, compensating the divisional manager based on a divisional equity claim instead of the traded equity of the conglomerate limits the possibility for information feedback and performance monitoring by the market (see Holmström and Tirole 1993 and Milbourn 1999). Both drawbacks point to the existence of limitations in the use of managerial performance contracts in conglomerate firms and imply that a conglomerate firm may be unable to mimic the incentives provided by stand-alone divisions.

12.5 Concluding Remarks

In this chapter we have focused on internal incentives and market discipline as potential determinants for conglomeration in banking. We have argued that conglomeration *can* be beneficial, particularly when rents in banking are relatively low and market discipline is weak. The viability of conglomerate banks may, however, crucially depend on internal capital allocation systems and proper managerial incentive contracts. In this context, we discussed the popular VAR, RAROC, and EVA concepts.

On a more general level, the chapter has highlighted *the* major challenge facing modern banks: how to identify and protect their true comparative advantages when their activities become increasingly heterogeneous. We believe that relationship banking continues to be important for the viability of most financial institutions. Relationship banking has suffered, however, from the proliferation of transaction-oriented banking. Indeed, financial markets have gained market share, potentially at the expense of traditional commercial banking. Also, interbank competition may have increased. Banks now find it more difficult to hold on to their clientele than in the past. Borrowers may be tempted to switch to other financiers, and traditional relationships may suffer. As we have argued, however, the proliferation of transaction-oriented banking next to relationship banking in the same financial institution may pose the biggest threat. Combining these activities may undermine relationship banking activities. In the context of the Barings debacle, we have argued that relationship lending activities may implicitly subsidize transaction-oriented activities. Consequently, relationship banking may suffer.

Future research should be directed at further developing the basic themes of this chapter. Though we may have provided some important insights into the functioning of conglomerate banking institutions, they largely remain a black box.

Notes

We thank participants of the Davidson Institute Conference, May 1998, for valuable comments. In particular, we thank Erik Berglöf, the discussant.

1. This numerical example is chosen in such a way that it captures all the possible equilibria that can occur. It therefore represents the most general case. For a more formal exposition, see Boot and Schmeits 1999.

2. In can be verified that in our example each division realizes cash flows sufficiently high to facilitate full debt repayments for the conglomerate and thus survival of the conglomerate bank.

3. It is important to realize that much of modern investment banking is not solely transaction-oriented, but proprietary trading definitely is. Such trading involves arbitrage between different markets and different financial products. Arbitrage strictly speaking does not involve risk. On an intraday basis, however, traders do not cover all their positions and thus accept considerable risk. This is a type of speculation. Banks also speculate on an interday basis; this is "real" speculation. They may use their "vision" and try to benefit from anticipated developments in interest rates, exchange rates, and so on.

4. One could counter that much of the banking literature has focused on equity holders' incentives to engage in excessively risky activities. Observe that these moral hazard incentives depend on the possibility of shifting risk to debt holders (or the deposit insurer) without compensating them. The debt holders then effectively subsidize risky activities. Although these incentives might be relevant for poorly capitalized institutions (e.g., U.S. savings and loans in the 1980s), they are much less compelling for adequately capitalized institutions.

5. Another compelling argument is that banks' credit ratings have become increasingly important because of the proliferation of off–balance sheet banking. The viability of banks in their off–balance sheet activities (e.g., writing guarantees, as in underwriting and securitization) necessitates sufficient capitalization and high credit ratings (see Boot and Greenbaum 1995).

6. Recall that division A (contrary to B) has future rents $F(m)$ at stake that could benefit from diversification.

7. Similarly, he could do this with respect to the risk choice parameter p of division B. For expositional reasons, however, we will focus the discussion in this section on division A's choice of m.

8. Observe that the differential charge by itself would remove the diversification benefit of coinsurance from the respective bank divisions' nominal funding costs. Passively increasing each division's funding costs (capital charges) therefore would worsen incentives. An internal cost-of-capital allocation can therefore be effective only if sufficient "internal" discipline is imposed as well. This is where the sensitivity parameter comes in.

9. Stoughton and Zeckner furthermore show that asymmetric information makes capital allocation more sensitive to risk taking. That is, in the presence of asymmetric information, a bank allocates more capital for a given increase in volatility than in the presence of symmetric information.

10. Observe that, depending on the informational structure and the risk preferences that we consider, other compensation structures are also possible. For example, the manager of the stand-alone firm could be offered a fixed wage if the project generates a sufficiently high cash flow and face a (non)monetary penalty otherwise. If the penalty imposed in the case of default is severe, a first-best solution would be attainable in this case. Such a compensation structure can be effective if the divisional manager is risk averse and the project's cash flow is observable or verifiable. Some general results regarding managerial compensation mechanisms are derived in Holmström 1979 and Harris and Raviv 1979.

11. In both Holmström 1982 and Holmström and Milgrom 1990 the optimal remuneration schemes are linear in each agent's output.

References

Aron, Debra J. 1988. Ability, moral hazard, firm size and diversification. *Rand Journal of Economics* 19:72–87.

Boot, A., and S. Greenbaum. 1995. The future of banking: What should corporate America expect? *Business Week Executive Briefing* 8.

Boot, A., and A. Schmeits. 1999. Market discipline and incentive problems in conglomerate banks. Working paper, University of Amsterdam.

Flannery, M. 1994. Debt maturity and the deadweight costs of leverage: Optimally financing banking firms. *American Economic Review* 84:320–331.

Harris, M., and A. Raviv. 1979. Optimal incentive contracts with imperfect information. *Journal of Economic Theory* 20:231–259.

Holmström, B. 1979. Moral hazard and observability. *Bell Journal of Economics* 10:74–91.

Holmström, B. 1982. Moral hazard in teams. *Bell Journal of Economics*: 324–340.

Holmström, B., and P. Milgrom. 1990. Regulating trade among agents. *Journal of Institutional and Theoretical Economics* 146:85–105.

Holmström, B., and J. Tirole. 1993. Market liquidity and performance monitoring. *Journal of Political Economy* 101:678–709.

Itoh, H. 1991. Incentives to help in multi-agent situations. *Econometrica* 59:611–636.

James, C., and J. Houston. 1996. Evolution or extinction: Where are banks headed? *Journal of Applied Corporate Finance* 9:8–23.

Jensen, M., and W. Meckling. 1976. Theory of the firm: Managerial behavior, agency costs and ownership structure. *Journal of Financial Economics* 3:305–360.

Merton, R. C. 1993. Operation and regulation in financial intermediation: A functional perspective. In *Operation and Regulation of Financial Markets*, ed. P. Englund. Stockholm: Economic Council.

Milbourn, T. 1999. The executive compensation puzzle: Theory and evidence. Working paper, London Business School.

Milgrom, P., and J. Roberts. 1990. Bargaining costs, influence costs, and the organization of economic activity. In *Perspectives on Positive Political Economy*, ed. J. Alt and K. Shepsle, 57–89. Cambridge: Cambridge University Press.

Rajan, R. 1996. Why banks have a future: Toward a new theory of commercial banking. *Journal of Applied Corporate Finance* 9:114–128.

Rajan, R., and L. Zingales. 1995. The tyranny of the inefficient: An enquiry into the adverse consequences of power struggles. Working paper, University of Chicago and National Bureau of Economic Research, Cambridge, Mass.

Ramakrishnan, R., and A. Thakor. 1991. Cooperation versus competition in agency. *Journal of Law, Economics and Organization* 7:248–283.

Stein, J. 1997. Internal capital markets and the competition for corporate resources. *Journal of Finance* 52 (March): 111–133.

Stoughton, N., and J. Zechner. 1999. Optimal capital allocation using RAROC™ and EVA®. Working paper, University of Vienna.

Varian, H. 1990. Monitoring agents with other agents. *Journal of Institutional and Theoretical Economics* 146:153–174.

Wulf, J. 1998. Influence and inefficiency in the internal capital market: Theory and evidence. Working paper, University of Pennsylvania, Philadelphia.

Zaik, E., J. Walter, G. Kelling, and C. James. 1996. RAROC at Bank of America: From theory to practice. *Journal of Applied Corporate Finance* 9:83–93.

13 Financial Reallocation in Russian Groups

Enrico C. Perotti and Stanislav Gelfer

13.1 Introduction

Developed countries have taken an increasingly skeptical view of the efficiency of diversified conglomerates. Overwhelming evidence suggests that Western diversified groups tend to trade at a discount relative to a portfolio of independent firms in related industries; they have on average a lower Tobin's Q; they tend to be broken up; and their share price significantly increases when that occurs (for a review, see Rajan and Zingales 1997). Scharfstein (1997) studies investment patterns in divisions in conglomerate firms and concludes that such firms appear to practice some form of suboptimal "socialist" reallocation of resources across divisions, moving funds from profitable firms in high-Q industries to support investment in lower-Q sectors.

The leading explanations for the underperformance of these groups have focused on the agency conflict between investors and empire-building managers (Jensen 1986). More recently, some authors have argued that internal power conflicts force inefficient redistribution of resources to more poorly performing divisions.

In sharp contrast, industrial-financial groups persist and often prosper in many developing countries (Khanna and Palepu 1996), where diversified business groups often dominate private-sector activity. Some theoretical rationales for such groups have pointed to the incentive to resolve scarcity in the capital and the intermediate product markets. The emergence of such groups may also be a function of the weak institutional environment in emerging market economies of Asia, Latin America, and Eastern Europe. In countries with weak law enforcement, unstable regulatory systems, and vast corruption, these groups may have extensive governance functions. They may support internal trade, ensure close monitoring of management decisions, and manage a privileged access to political favors, such as subsidized credit, favorable regulation and licensing, and access to strategic resources. In conclusion, groups may emerge to capture scarcity rents or compensate for lack of markets, or both.[1]

In Russia, a historical reliance on implicit contracting, the oligopolistic structure of industry, and underdeveloped capital markets have given the development of business groups additional scope. Following the inception of privatization in 1993, new Russian banks took large equity positions in the Russian industrial sector. Most Russian groups obtained their assets through debt-equity swap programs, government provisions, and privatization sales. Taking advantage of the limited competition offered by capital market investors, they began to consolidate holdings in controlling blocks by 1994 (Johnson 1997)

The emerging corporate structure were termed financial-industrial groups (FIGs). FIGs have sometimes been officially constituted by the Russian government or at other times have been formed spontaneously. Official recognition of FIGs came in December 1993 by presidential decree. Under this decree, FIGs receive a number of benefits, such as the right to receive blocks of shares in privatized enterprises from the Russian State Property Committee, or Goskomimushchestvo (GKI), preferential reserve requirements from the Russian central bank, and preferential access to licenses and permits.[2]

Given Russia's history of development and its current market conditions, such groups may constitute an optimal organizational structure. Weak law enforcement makes arm's-length contingent contracting impossible. Russia never experienced a form of capitalism based on reliable contractual relations of the Anglo-Saxon style. During the Soviet era, directors of enterprises relied on relational contracting to ensure supply delivery and performance. High transactions costs associated with segmented information and poor contractual enforcement in Russia suggest that centralized ownership of assets may lead both to better corporate and better contractual governance. Holding companies such as FIGs may thus be an optimal construction for carrying out the required reallocation of ownership and governance in Russia.

Executives of many bank-centered groups routinely claim that they and other banks play the same role in the Russian economy today as investment bankers did in the U.S. economy at the turn of the 20th century.[3] In this chapter we investigate this argument, with the goal of identifying useful policy recommendations.

We start with an empirical analysis of the relationship between internal finance and investment in independent and group-affiliated Russian enterprises. We compare firms that are members of official FIGs or are owned by a large Russian bank (or both) with a control set of large firms categorized by dispersed ownership or management and employee control (or both). We find that investment is sensitive to internal liquidity for the second set of firms but not for the first.

Such results can be reinterpreted as evidence of extensive financial reallocation across group firms. The interesting question, naturally, is how to interpret this finding. One interpretation is that group firms have an internal capital market that facilitate access to finance for good projects by reallocating resources across firms. An alternative view may be that the desire of the controlling shareholders to shift resources around in order to appropriate them better (for instance, by shifting them to firms in which their equity interest is greater) drives reallocation of resources.

To test these competing views, we assess the quality of the investment process in group and nongroup firms by regressing individual firms' absolute and relative investment on our measure of Tobin's Q. The result supports the notion that group firms allocate capital better than independent firms.

Following Johnson (1997), who argues persuasively that FIGs should be subdivided into bank-led groups and industry groupings, we then distinguish between bank-led groups, which are more hierarchical, and industry-centered groups, which may be more defensive arrangements. Whereas investment is not significantly correlated with cash flow in industry-led group firms (unlike in independent firms), there is a *negative* significant correlation between investment and cash flow for bank-led group firms, suggesting a more extensive financial reallocation and the use of profitable firms as cash cows. Most intriguingly, the greater sensitivity of group firms' investment to Q can be attributed entirely to firms in bank-led groups, in which the controlling bank may have a stronger profit motive and authority to reallocate resources. Finally, independent firms with a high stock market valuation appear also to have fewer liquidity constraints, suggesting that the Russian equity market may already provide a positive informational function.

Overall, we conclude that although the FIGs appear to serve a useful governance function, there are no reasons to encourage or subsidize their formation.

13.2   Sources and Measurement of Capital Constraints

Corporate finance theory aims to understand the process by which capital is allocated to the corporate sector. Under the neoclassical Modigliani-Miller theorem, in a world with efficient capital markets, in the absence of transactions costs or distortionary taxation, the value of a company is independent of its financing structure, provided that the mode of financing does not affect the firm's productive activity. The main implication is that firms are indifferent between financing their investment programs from internal or external sources.

In a world with asymmetric information between insiders and outsiders, however, raising external equity capital may be costly because of adverse selection (Myers and Majluf 1984). Moreover, when managerial self-interest leads to principal-agent problems, investors will be reluctant to fund corporations, and external equity finance may be either unavailable or costlier than internal finance. But although debt may have a disciplinary effect on managers in terms of restraining their own interests (e.g., empire building; see Jensen 1986), high leverage also extracts a cost in the form of potential financial distress, credit rationing, and higher costs associated with monitoring.

Financial distress costs are likely to be greater in a context such as that in Russia, where agency and informational problems are severe. Thus external capital may be not just very costly but simply unavailable, and Russian firms may therefore ultimately be forced to forgo valuable investment or restructuring opportunities. A general conclusion is that funding investment by raising external capital may be more costly than generating funds internally. Thus the availability of internally generated funds may have an effect on investment decisions. Additional financing problems arise in countries such as Russia, where contracts may be hard to verify and enforce. When parties have to rely on incomplete or implicit contracts, the allocation of control rights becomes more important than contractual rights (Modigliani and Perotti 1997); a hierarchical structure may be more effective than arm's-length contractual relationships.

Scharfstein and Stein (1997) show that in a conglomerate with diffuse ownership, a biased incentive structure may lead strong divisions to subsidize investment in weak divisions.[4] The command structure of most FIGs however, includes a holding company (either a bank or a company) with the right to residual cash flow and control over the assets of the FIG. In such a case the corporate headquarters reallocates resources efficiently across the FIG's controlled business units and monitors managerial decisions, even if it may overexpand relative to what external investors would prefer (Stein 1997).

Ultimately, the advantages and disadvantages of groups across countries are an empirical question. Most of the testing has been conducted within the context of the Q model of investment, developed by James Tobin. Q is defined as the ratio of the market value of a firm to the replacement value of its capital assets and is therefore a shadow value of an additional unit of capital. In equilibrium the marginal Q is unity.

An important feature of the Q model of investment is that because the securities market evaluation of a firm summarizes market expectations about its future profitability, with Q as a regression it becomes possible to isolate the effects of internal finance on investment. This in turn makes it possible to test empirically the importance of financial factors. Additionally, the empirical model may be augmented by various variables relating to agency conflicts and financial distress, such as the stock of debt, value of capital stock, cash flow, and stock of liquid assets.[5]

If a firm maximizes the market value of the shares of its existing shareholders, under perfect competition and linear production and cost functions the following equation can be derived:

$$\frac{I}{K} = \beta_0 + \beta_1 Q + \beta_2 \frac{X}{K} + \beta_3 \frac{B}{K} + \beta_4 \frac{L}{K},$$

where L is a stock of liquid assets, B is debt, X is a cash flow Q is Tobin's Q, I is investment, and K is the replacement cost of capital assets.

In general, cash flow is correlated with profitability; thus in an investment equation, cash flow may be correlated with investment, because it is a proxy for valuable investment opportunities. If Q is a good proxy for the profitability of prospective investment, however, the significance of the coefficients on the financial variables other than Q can be interpreted as evidence of financial constraints, since the availability of internal finance does seem to affect the level of investment.

In practice, empirically implementing the Q model presents some problems. Measures of Q are calculated using share prices, which reflect the average Q of the firm, whereas the theoretically relevant variable is marginal Q. Thus measured Q may not be very useful in reducing omitted variable bias on a liquidity coefficient. Moreover, traditional Q theory does not take into account other factors (such as irreversibility) associated with the firm's investment decisions. For these reasons, empirical researchers simply postulate that investment profitability should be an increasing function of the value of investment opportunities as measured by proxies for Q such as the market-to-book ratio.

One solution to this problem is to compare the effects of internal finance across two different sets of firms. If the error in the measurement of Q is the same across both sets of firms, then a significant difference in the effects of liquidity between two samples signals that the null hypothesis of perfect capital markets must be rejected. In Fazzari, Hubbard, and Petersen 1988 the division of the sample was based on the dividend payout policy: firms that retained most of their earnings were thought to be liquidity constrained. The appropriateness of this criterion in their sample was recently challenged by Kaplan and Zingales (1997), who also raise doubts about the legitimacy of interpreting a higher positive coefficient on cash flow in investment equations as evidence of stronger liquidity constraints.[6]

Our approach is related to the empirical work of Hoshi, Kashyap, and Scharfstein (1990) on Japanese firms belonging to *keiretsu* groups. They compare the strength of the relationship between the investment and measures of internal finance, such as cash flow, of firms that have strong relationship with banks against that of firms without such ties. They find that cash flow is a more important determinant of investment for independent firms than for firms that are members of a *keiretsu* group. Their evidence shows that for *keiretsu* firms, sensitivity of investment to cash flow is indeed insignificant, whereas nonaffiliated firms experience more binding cash constraint.[7] Hoshi, Kashyap and Scharfstein interpret this as evidence that main-bank monitoring mitigates information problems in capital markets.[8]

This question as to whether group governance resolves capital constraints is important in the case of Russia, where enterprises are in great need of funds to finance restructuring. Moreover, the fundamental rules for a proper corporate governance system for public companies are either not in place or not effective, particularly in companies in which rapid privatization has led to a strong degree of managerial self-control. This limits the role of capital market in financing.

13.3 Empirical Evidence

We now employ the methodology described in section 13.2 to test the hypothesis that in the environment of poorly developed capital markets, where information and agency problems are severe, Russian FIGs help relax firms' liquidity constraint. As in recent empirical literature on information and agency problems in capital markets, we use accounting data. In the case of Russia, the quality of these data is questionable. The accounting book values of total assets present a particular problem for this study, because in empirical literature total assets are used as a scaling factor when working with panel data. In the case of Russian data, there is little knowledge of how the historical value of assets has been adjusted throughout the transition period and what is included in its definition as accounting standards change. To account for this problem, we use total assets as well as total revenue as a proxy for the size of the firm to scale all variables.

13.3.1 Sample Description

We use individual firm data from companies listed in the publication *200 Largest Russian Enterprises, 1996*, compiled by the Russian weekly economic journal *Expert*. Financial information in this publication was directly collected from either Russian public companies or their financial advisers. Only original financial documents such as annual reports and balance sheets were used.[9] Financial statistics were obtained from Skate Kapital Press.

Since it is necessary for the purpose of estimation to calculate a proxy for Tobin's Q, we had to drop from our sample those firms that do not have an established secondary market for their shares. We constructed a consistent sample with sufficiently complete financial indicators for 76 Russian public companies. For each firm, the sample includes data from balance sheets for January 1, 1995, and January 1, 1996, as well as the income statement for the year of 1995. Price per share is from Skate Stock Data Group as of February 1, 1997. All financial details are in Russian rubles and are not adjusted for inflation. To account for inflation, all figures are converted

Table 13.1
Distribution of group and nongroup firms across sectors

Industry	Group firms	Nongroup firms
Oil and gas	12 31.6%	14 36.8%
Utility	9 23.7%	3 7.9%
Nonferrous metals	3 7.9%	2 5.3%
Steel	4 10.5%	6 15.8%
Machinery	5 13.2%	7 18.4%
Transport	2 5.3%	6 15.8%
Other	3 7.9%	0 0%
Total	38 100%	38 100%

into U.S. dollars at the historical rate. Table 13.1 shows the distribution of group
and nongroup firms in the sample by industry.

We use three criteria to distinguish between group and nongroup firms in the
sample. First, firms listed in the *Industrial-Financial Groups Registry Book* for 1996
are classified as group firms. In our sample, 14 firms were given a "group" catego-
rization based on this criterion. Second, we rely on information about ownership
structure available from Skate Kapital Press and *Expert*. Firms in which major
shareholders are Russian banks and oil companies are classified as group firms. Although the ownership information available to us is incomplete, it enables us to include in "group" status another 15 firms. These are either firms in which Menatep
Bank or ONEXIM Bank and their affiliates are major shareholders or firms in
which YUKOS or Sidanco oil companies are major shareholders. Third, we have
included nine utility firms, which form a group called "Unified Energy Systems of
Russia."

The nongroup sample includes firms in which shareholding either is dispersed
among different owners whose largest stake is less than 20 percent or is concentrated
in the hands of management and employees or an affiliated holding company. This
seems a sound way to divide our sample, because firms with insider control, dispersed ownership, or both may face more severe agency costs than other firms.

Table 13.2
Descriptive statistics

Statistic	Nongroup firms	Group firms
Number of firms	38	38
Average investment–to–total assets ratio	0.514	0.794
Average cash flow–to–total assets ratio	0.024	0.019
Standard deviation of investment–to–total assets ratio	0.591	0.925
Standard deviation of cash flow–to–total assets ratio	0.641	0.516
Average total assets, Jan. 1, 1995	759.625	464.878
Average total assets, Jan. 1, 1996	1133.218	816.973

Source: Authors' calculations based on samples selected from Skate Kapital Press data.
Note: Cash flow is net income minus change in inventories minus change in accounts receivable plus change in accounts payable. Investment is change in fixed assets. All variables are scaled by the beginning of the period total assets. Flow values are calculated for January 1, 1995, and January 1, 1996. Stock variables are for the January 1, 1995.

Table 13.2 shows some relevant statistics for the two sets of firms in 1995–1996. Investment normalized by initial total assets is larger for group firms; they tend to invest more, and their investment is more volatile. The distribution of the two types of firms across different industrial sectors is not too different. The cash flow–to–capital ratio is almost identical for both groups, although it is more volatile among the group firms. Both groups almost doubled the value of their assets during the period.[10]

Table 13.3 shows that nongroup firms tend to hold a larger stock of cash than group firms; the difference is marginally significant. This strategy may be an endogenous response to the existence of credit constraints in nongroup firms. Note that the payables–to–total assets ratio constitutes a much larger portion of liabilities than bank debt for both sets of firms. From table 13.2 one can see that the bank debt–to–total assets ratio is remarkably low for both sets of firms. This is consistent with the fact noted by other researchers that Russian firms obtain little credit from the banking system. Firms in both categories are of roughly similar size (as measured by revenue).

Table 13.4 presents indicators of investment opportunities and profitability for both categories of firms. Income-based profitability measures as well as market-to-book ratios are very similar for both categories, as is the fixed asset–to–total assets ratio. Net income over revenues shows that profit margins are higher for group firms.

If fixed assets–to–total assets ratio is a reliable measure of asset tangibility, it can proxy for the firms' ability to attract credit; bank debt should then be similar for both types of firms. In addition, the two sets of firms are equally profitable, generate

Table 13.3
Additional descriptive statistics

Statistic	Nongroup firms		Group firms	
	Mean	SD	Mean	SD
Employment	20,991.216	17,324.736	42,411.625	66,659.857
Change in bank debt	3.877	10.283	0.769	3.235
Bank debt–to–total assets ratio	0.037	0.099	0.046	0.078
Change in accounts payable	0.636	0.642	0.673	0.861
Accounts payable–to–total assets ratio	0.237	0.147	0.294	0.480
Change in cash	0.924	2.963	1.338	4.547
Cash–to–total assets ratio**	0.033	0.052	0.017	0.022
Total liability–to–total assets ratio	0.281	0.179	0.340	0.482
Logarithm of total revenue	6.115	1.238	6.433	1.735
Revenue–to–total assets ratio	1.346	1.160	1.245	0.863

Note: Changes refer to the period 1995–1996. Income statement statistics are for 1995. Asterisks indicate significance of the nonparametric independent-sample *t*-test on the difference in sample means between the two sets of firms.
** significant at the 10% level.

Table 13.4
Financial ratios for group and nongroup firms

	Nongroup firms		Group firms	
	Mean	SD	Mean	SD
Market capitalization–to–book value of equity ratio	0.492	1.041	0.487	0.848
Net income–to–total revenue ratio	0.096	0.123	0.126	0.136
Net income–to–total assets ratio	0.143	0.189	0.153	0.150
Total bank debt–to–equity ratio	0.114	0.515	0.096	0.263
Income before taxes–to–total assets ratio	0.238	0.273	0.245	0.212
Fixed assets–to–total assets ratio	0.569	0.178	0.539	0.184

Note: Table presents the following financial ratios: our proxy for Q, the market-to-book ratio, calculated as market capitalization as a proportion of book value of equity; net income as a proportion of total revenue; net income as a proportion of total assets; income before taxes as a proportion of total assets; and fixed assets as a proportion of total assets. Leverage is total bank debt over equity book value. Income statement statistics are for 1995 and balance sheet statistics are for January 1, 1995.

a comparable amount of cash flow, and have very large stocks and flows of trade payables. Nevertheless, group firms invest more; investment is also more variable across firms in this category, consistent with the possibility of intragroup financial reallocation.

One final comment on our measure of investment. Since we do not have a direct measure, we obtain a proxy by using the deflated change in a firm's fixed assets. This value may be distorted by accounting adjustments in 1996 relative to 1995 to factor in past inflation; such distortion almost certainly overestimates measured investment. On the other hand, to be able to perform our test, we need such adjustments not to be systematically different between the group firms and the control sample. We cannot come up with any reason why that would be the case.

These statistics are not inconsistent with the notion that the independent firms are cash constrained. Firms in both categories are of roughly the same size and have similar cash flow, but the nongroup firms hold more cash, which can be interpreted as a buffer against sudden liquidity problems. Their lower level of investment is also consistent with this hypothesis, as is the greater variation in the investment-to-capital ratio. The recent higher increase in bank debt is, on the other hand, not consistent with the hypothesis. In any case these comparisons are only suggestive, as none of the differences in the average are statistically significant at the 5 percent level and only a few are significant even at the 10 percent level.

The general regression includes as independent variables a proxy for Tobin's Q, two measures of liquidity, stock of debt, and profitability measure. To eliminate the effects of scale, all variables other than the proxy for Tobin's Q are normalized by the beginning-of-period total assets.

We next estimate the following equation:

$$\frac{I_t}{K_{t-1}} = \beta_1 + \beta_2 M\_B + \beta_3 \frac{CF_t}{K_{t-1}} + \beta_4 D^* \frac{CF_t}{K_{t-1}} + \beta_5 \frac{DEBT_{t-1}}{K_{t-1}} + \beta_6 \frac{IBT_t}{K_{t-1}} + \beta_7 \frac{CASH_{t-1}}{K_{t-1}}.$$

We use both flow and beginning-of-period stock measures of liquidity. Cash flow (CF/K) records the inflow of cash to the firm during the period of investment: it is defined as after-tax income less change in inventories and accounts receivable plus the change in accounts payable. The stock measure of cash $(CASH/K)$ measures the stock of cash at the beginning of the period when a firm decides on its investment. The stock of debt $(DEBT/K)$ is included in the regression with no strong prior: in the literature a high level of debt may affect agency conflict; at the low level typical of the Russian context, we are rather inclined to interpret it as a sign of access to scarce credit. As a proxy for Tobin's Q we use the market value of equity over the book value of equity (M_B). It is here calculated at the beginning of the period; we later also use the end-of-period value. Investment (I/K) is measured as the change in fixed assets over the period. We also include the income before taxes–to–total assets ratio (IBT/K) as a proxy for profitability, because this measure may be related to sales and production.[11] We do not use sales directly in our regression because the correlation coefficient between revenue and cash flow is greater than the regression R^2 and thus may endanger the accuracy of any inference resulting from the regression.

To condition on whether the firm is part of an industrial-financial group or is independent, we use an interactive dummy variable times the cash flow (Group D^*CF/K), where D is a dummy indicating group status. This tests whether the coefficient on a particular cash flow variable is different for the two groups. We will use other interactive dummies in later sections to control for various other qualitative features such as industry effects.

13.3.2   Estimation Results

Table 13.5 presents estimates of the investment models, including financial variables, for group and nongroup firms. Column 1 in table 13.5 shows the estimates of the basic regression, which is the most closely related to the Q model of investment. Our proxy for Tobin's Q is highly significant and has the expected sign. In addition, all financial variables have large significant coefficients, suggesting that internal finance does matter for investment.

One main result of table 13.5 is that the availability of internal funds has a positive effect on investment, presumably because of credit constraints. The other main result is that the investment has a substantially different sensitivity to cash flow for group and independent firms: the estimated difference in the cash flow coefficient between group and nongroup firms (the coefficient on the group dummy times cash flow) is negative and significant. These results are consistent with the hypothesis that nongroup firms are financially constrained, whereas the sensitivity of investment to the cash flow for the group firms is zero (or perhaps even slightly negative). This suggests that cash flow is strongly reallocated within the group, to the point that investment is uncorrelated with individual firms, or in the case of a negative coefficient, that some firms that tend to be cash rich act as cash cows for the group as a whole. This may imply that a close relationship with a bank or a group structure resolves agency or market imperfections and enables some Russian industrial firms to raise investment funding while perhaps constraining cash-rich firms' use of free cash flow.

The estimated effect of bank debt is positive and significant at the 10 percent level. In the case of Russia, bank debt is quite low relative to assets, and because of high past inflation, what debt exists is largely newly accumulated debt. Thus firms with

Table 13.5
Effects of cash flow on investment

	1	2	3	4	5
(Constant)	0.3991*** (0.1039)	0.4051*** (0.1154)	0.3147** (0.1231)	0.2984** (0.1224)	0.4372*** (0.1238)
M_B	0.2071** (0.0813)	0.2079** (0.0821)	0.1595* (0.0846)	0.1697** (0.0843)	0.1886** (0.0836)
CF/K	0.5728** (0.2358)	0.5767** (0.2395)	0.4459* (0.2452)	0.4584* (0.2454)	0.6112** (0.2374)
D^*CF/K	−1.2743*** (0.3255)	−1.2787*** (0.3297)	−1.1535*** (0.3305)	−1.1604*** (0.3311)	−1.3639*** (0.3286)
$DEBT/K$	2.1555* (1.1946)	2.1608* (1.2038)	1.7806 (1.1992)	1.86221 (1.1992)	2.7144** (1.2455)
$CASH/K$	—	−0.2406 (1.9494)	−2.5432 (2.2703)	—	—
IBT/K	—	—	0.7612* (0.4035)	0.5182 (0.3408)	—
$ShLiquid$	—	—	—	—	0.2194 (0.1861)
GOV	—	—	—	—	−0.2184 (0.1547)
$EMPLOY$	1.1E−06 (1.5E−06)	1.1E−06 (1.5E−06)	1.2E−06 (1.5E−06)	1.3E−06 (1.4E−06)	7.4E−06 (1.6E−06)
F-statistic	5.0052***	4.1149***	4.1663***	4.6344***	4.0470***
Adj. R^2	0.211	0.199	0.228	0.225	0.2214
Wald test F-statistic coefficients restrictions					
Null hypothesis: $c(3) + c(4) = 0$	11.730***	11.577***	12.196***	11.966***	12.506***

Note: Dependent variable is investment–to–total assets ratio (I/K), where I is defined as a change in fixed assets and K is beginning-of-period total assets. Independent variables include M_B: market value of equity divided by beginning-of-period book value of equity; CF/K: cash flow during investment period as a proportion of beginning-of-period total assets; D^*CF/K: dummy variable times CF/K, with dummy equal to 1 if a firm is a member of a group and 0 otherwise. $DEBT/K$: beginning-of-period stock of bank debt as a proportion of beginning-of-period total assets; $CASH/K$: stock of cash as a proportion of beginning-of-period total assets; IBT/K: proxy for profitability calculated as income before taxes as a proportion of beginning-of-period total assets; $ShLiquid$: dummy variable that equals 1 if a firm's shares are "moderately" or "actively" traded and 0 otherwise; GOV: dummy variable equal to 1 if State Property Committee owns more than 20 percent of a firm. Employment size $(EMPLOY)$ is included in all regressions. Standard errors appear in parentheses. Statistics for several firms that are outliers in debt and investment have been removed. Number of observations: 76.
*** significant at 1% level; ** significant at 5% level; * significant at 10% level.

higher debt are perhaps those that have been able to secure money through borrowing. If those are generally firms with better investment opportunities, a positive sign is not surprising. Since the significance is only marginal, however, we hesitate to interpret this result further.[12] Other variables we included, such as trading liquidity, profitability, employment and government ownership are not significant determinants of investment.

In our view the regression reported in column 1 of table 13.5 is the most sensible.[13] We did, however, estimate several other specifications without any change in the main conclusions: the pattern of investment sensitivity to cash flow is remarkably robust across different specifications. Table 13.5 presents the estimation results for the regression equations, where a proxy for productivity was added without any substantive difference in the results (columns 3 and 4 of table 13.5). Estimated coefficients and their standard errors also do not vary much. We also add the stock of cash to the model (column 2). This variable has an insignificant effect, and it does not materially affect any of the other coefficients.

Column 5 introduces two dummy variables to the regression. The first is a dummy for firms in which the Russian Federation State Property Committee has a substantial stake (more than 20 percent), to control for the possibility of a different investment pattern under government ownership. Moreover, to test whether firms that are traded actively on the Russian stock market are better appreciated by investors and are therefore able to invest more, we add a dummy for firms with a high trading volume. There is no evidence in support of these effects, as both dummy variables are found to be insignificant.

In these regressions we also tried to include industry dummies, to see if firms in high–cash flow industries drive the results. None of the coefficients on these dummy variables were significant, and however, we do not report them.

At the bottom of table 13.5 we report the result of a Wald test to determine whether the coefficient on cash flow in the investment equation is significantly different from zero. The result of the test suggests that for the group firms total cash flow has a negative sensitivity to investment; this would imply that firms with larger cash flows have less investment.

The interpretation of this result is very important in assessing the impact of group memberships on investment behavior. A benign interpretation is that groups redistribute resources from cash-rich firms to support investment by cash-poor companies. Alternatively, this result is also consistent with the popular belief that FIGs in Russia do not provide capital and proper governance to member firms but rather skim the cash generated by the firms to strengthen their banks or simply channel the money for their private needs. Later in this chapter we test these alternative hypotheses explicitly.

These results are qualitatively very interesting. In particular, we are surprised by the strength and significance of our proxy for Q in the investment patterns of Russian industry. An interpretation is that stock market prices in Russia are starting to be informative about the quality of firms, a hypothesis that we also study further later in the chapter.

We next separate the group sample into a bank-led group category and an industry-led group category to see whether indeed there are structural differences between the two governance structures (table 13.6). This set of regressions confirms our view that there are structural differences between bank-led and industry-led groups. Industry-led group firms show no sensitivity of investment to cash flow, as the Wald test attests. In contrast, the total coefficient on bank-led group firms is negative and significant. This confirms a much stronger degree of redistribution from cash-rich firms to cash-poor firms in bank-led groups. Intuitively, this type of financial reallocation is possible only within groups with a strong governance structure, where a holding company has controlling blocks of equity.

What can we conclude from these results? Are bank groups actively moving funds to better investment opportunities, constraining high–cash flow firms not to overspend? Or are they just skimming cash from profitable firms? We try to answer these questions in the next set of regressions.

Table 13.7 reports results from regressions in which we eliminate all financial variables to measure investment's sensitivity to Q across different types of firms. The Q theory of investment implies that the higher is a firm's Q, the higher should be its level of investment, as the stock market values more highly the present value of new capacity. We also attempted to use other variables of performance variables, which proved not to be significant; we leave these out in the table. In column 1, the general regression reports that investment is positively correlated with our Q proxy for the whole sample, which suggests that the average investment decision in the best Russian industrial companies is correlated with the stock market's view of the company's profitability. The regression in column 2 shows that among group firms, investment is more sensitive to the Q proxy, implying a greater sensitivity to the market assessment of valuable investment opportunities. We interpret this as evidence of a better capital allocation decision within the groups than outside. Perhaps in the insider-controlled independent firms, investment decisions are driven only by availability of internal finance and are less dependent on expected profitability, whereas inside the group the controlling shareholders, who have a sharper interest in future profits vis-à-vis size, are able to control the process better. The regression in column 3 shows

Table 13.6
Effects of cash flow on investment: Differentiating between industry-led groups and bank-led groups

	1	2	3
(Constant)	0.2502 (0.1370)	0.2479 (0.1315)	0.5179 (0.0857)
M_B	0.1611* (0.0837)	0.1740** (0.0829)	0.2328*** (0.0802)
CF/K	0.4914** (0.2374)	0.5334** (0.2344)	0.3134* (0.1685)
IL^*CF/K	−0.5924*** (0.1616)	−0.6078*** (0.1608)	−0.4866*** (0.1349)
BL^*CF/K	−2.6370*** (0.9078)	−2.6293*** (0.9046)	−1.7593*** (0.8520)
$DEBT/K$	1.9899* (1.1588)	2.1970* (1.1438)	
$CASH/K$	−2.4598 (2.2991)		
IBT/K	0.8208* (0.4173)	0.5441 (0.3420)	
$EMPLOY$	1.13E−06 (1.53E−06)		
IL	0.0078 (0.0977)	0.0526 (0.0907)	
BL	0.2185 (0.1966)	0.2510 (0.1937)	
F-statistic	3.5933***	4.3034***	6.1097***
Adjusted R^2	0.2569	0.2606	0.2142
Wald test F-statistic coefficients restrictions			
Null hypothesis: $c(2) + c(3) = 0$	0.4362	0.2429	1.6513
Null hypothesis: $c(2) + c(4) = 0$	6.0563**	5.8267**	2.9879*

Note: All variables are as in table 13.5 except BL^*CF/K: dummy variable BL times CF/K, with dummy BL equal to 1 if a firm is a member of a bank-led group and 0 otherwise; IL^*CF/K: dummy variable times CF/K, with dummy IL equal to 1 if a firm is a member of an industry-led group and 0 otherwise. Standard errors appear in parentheses. Statistics for several outliers in debt and investment have been removed. Number of observations: 76.
*** significant at 1% level; ** significant at 5% level; * significant at 10% level.

Table 13.7
Relationship between investment and Q

Variable	1	2	3
Constant	0.5135***	0.5006	0.4709
	(0.0917)	(0.0902)	(0.0899)
M_B	0.2271**	0.1030	0.1239
	(0.0869)	(0.1059)	(0.1043)
$Group^*M\_B$		0.3026*	
		(0.1530)	
IL^*M_B			0.1039
			(0.0772)
BL^*M_B			1.0186***
			(0.3839)
F-statistic	6.8246**	5.5018***	5.0903***
Adjusted R^2	0.0721	0.1071	0.1406

Note: Dependent variable is investment–to–total assets ratio (I/K), where I is defined as a change in fixed assets and K is beginning-of-period total assets. Independent variables include M_B: Market value of equity divided by the beginning-of-period book value of equity; $Group^*M\_B$: $Group$ dummy times M_B, with dummy equal to 0 if a firm is independent and 1 otherwise. BL^*M_B: dummy variable BL times M_B, with dummy equal to 1 if a firm is a member of a bank-led group and 0 otherwise; IL^*M_B: dummy variable IL times the M_B, with dummy equal to 2 if a firm is a member of an industry-led group and 0 otherwise. Standard errors appear in parentheses. Statistics for several outliers in debt and investment have been removed. Number of observations: 76.
*** significant at 1% level; ** significant at 5% level; * significant at 10% level.

that if we differentiate between industry-led groups and bank-led groups, the bank-led groups' coefficient is clearly larger and significant. In fact, the regressions provide no evidence that in industry-led groups investment has a greater correlation with Q than in independent firms.

In the next section, we investigate the role of government ownership as well as the impact of stock market trading and valuation on the degree of credit constraints.

13.3.3 The Effect of Share Liquidity and Valuation

Thus far we have established that group firms tend to be less cash constrained than independent firms. We interpret this result within a framework of imperfect information and agency problems in capital markets; group membership helps the firms escape their liquidity constraints. Other factors, however, might also play an important role. Some Russian FIGs were formed by the government; others came about through asset consolidation by banks. The same heterogeneity presumably holds for independent firms.

Our sample consists only of firms that are publicly traded, which begs the question of what role the stock market exercises in monitoring the firms and influencing their investment decisions. We thus investigate the volume of trading on the stock market and relative market valuation as measures of attention to the firm's performance. The rationale for this distinction comes from the possibility that more public information is available about firms that are actively traded. In particular, the market's role may be more important for nonaffiliated firms.

A low liquidity of share trading does not directly imply that a firm has poor prospects; its owners may prevent circulation of shares and information for control considerations, however, or be unable to communicate credibly with financial investors. Thus a firm whose shares are actively traded may have a lower investment–to–cash flow sensitivity because of either control or information considerations.

Controlling for these various effects also implicitly tests for the endogeneity of group membership; factors that lead a firm to join or to be captured by a group may be correlated with factors that would make liquidity more informative about the firm's investment opportunities. For example firms that do not join a group may be firms with better investment opportunities that do not need membership to communicate with the market, as they have better access to other sources. In this case investment will be less correlated with cash flow. Alternatively, firms with little visibility or poor access to alternative sources may be more easily captured by (or yield to) a group than firms without these difficulties.

13.3.4   The Impact of a Liquid Secondary Share Market

To explicitly control for both liquidity of shares and group status, we create four dummy variable with values as follows:

1. If a firm is nongroup and its shares have low liquidity, its value is 0.

2. If a firm is group and its shares have low liquidity, its value is 1.

3. If a firm is nongroup and its shares have high liquidity, its value is 2.

4. If a firm is group and its shares have high liquidity, its value is 3.

We allow these dummies to interact with cash flow and run the regression models used in table 13.7. Results are presented in table 13.8.

Structural coefficients in these regressions do not change substantially from those in previous estimates. Cash flow and the stock of debt are still highly significant. The coefficients on interactive dummies are significant only for group firms. Specifically, the interactive dummy for group firms with low liquidity of shares is highly significant, large, and negative.

We can draw a preliminary conclusion from these results. Although being in a group alleviates the credit constraints of member firms, the effect is particularly significant

Table 13.8
Trading volume of shares and state ownership effects

Variable	Coefficient
(Constant)	0.2513*
	(0.1464)
M_B	0.0635
	(0.0909)
CF/K	0.6061**
	(0.2417)
IBT/K	0.4627
	(0.3299)
$DEBT/K$	2.7771**
	(1.2040)
$Group\&LowLiquid*CF/K$	−1.5180***
	(0.3382)
$NoGroup\&HighLiquid*CF/K$	−0.2507
	(0.7020)
$Group\&HighLiquid*CF/K$	0.0326
	(0.2178)
$Group\&LowLiquid$	0.0769
	(0.1734)
$NoGroup\&HighLiquid$	0.0469
	(0.1446)
$Group\&HighLiquid$	0.1394*
	(0.0723)
F-statistic	4.0156***
Adj. R^2	0.287

Note: Dependent variable is investment–to–total assets ratio (I/K); all independent variables are as defined for previous tables.
*** significant at 1% level; ** significant at 5% level; * significant at 10%

for the subset of firms with low liquidity of shares. These firms account for most of the reduced correlation between investment and cash flow in group firms.[14]

If liquidity of shares is an exogenous factor, then group status may help those firms that need it most (as information problems are presumably more severe for firms whose shares are not actively traded). It is also possible that their shares are less liquid because of their membership in a group. For instance, when a bank holds a controlling stake in a firm, the firm may be less transparent. Or the negative correlation may suggest that the banks running the groups use these firms as cash cows.

The significance of trading liquidity for investment sensitivity within the groups may also suggest that the Russian equity market is aware of firms with better investment opportunities and focuses its attention on these firms. Of course, further investigation is necessary to establish the validity of this interpretation. If this is true, then market prices on the Russian stock market have already started to have some significance in guiding investment and relaxing financial constraints. Alternatively, the equity market may be focusing attention on firms that can generate enough internal finance to fund their investment choices. In either case, this has interesting implications for the emergence of a complementary role for the market in information gathering and ultimately financing. However, the fact that liquidity's influence on sensitivity does not extend to nonaffiliated firms suggests that it is premature to talk about a corporate governance role for the equity market in Russia.

13.3.5 Industry Effects

Thus far we can strongly reject the hypothesis that liquidity has the same effect on investment for independent and group firms in Russia. Our comparison between the two samples may be biased, however, by the possibility that independent firms operate in higher-growth industries, where internal cash flow may proxy for the value of investment opportunities, whereas group firms may be operating in low-growth industries. This would induce a positive bias on the coefficient for nongroup firms.

In table 13.9 we control for sectoral effects. We introduce industry dummies and have them interact with cash flow in the basic regression. Our prime suspects are the power, oil, and metal industries: these sectors are the most profitable in Russia and are very cash rich, and they may drive the sensitivity of investment to cash flow. None of the interactive dummy coefficients emerge as significant, however, for either the group or the independent firms. Finally, the difference in cash flow coefficients for group and nongroup firms is similar to previous estimates within each sector. On balance there is no evidence that industry factors drive our results.

13.3.6 Market Valuation Effects

In this section we explore how market perceptions of a firm affect its ability to raise investment finance. We also test how important market valuation of the firm is for group and nongroup firms. Generally, the market perceives firms that have a high market-to-book ratio as having good investment prospects, which should make it easier for them to raise investment capital. This should be especially true for independent firms, whereas for group firms market valuation may not be as important, as they have alternative sources of capital finance.

To explore this idea we again divide the sample of firms. As a proxy for firms' future prospects we use the market-to-book ratio, the indicator usually employed in the empirical literature. Thus we regard firms with a market-to-book ratio above (below) the sample median as having better (worse) investment prospects.

Table 13.9
Effects of cash flow on investment: Industry effects

	1	2	3	4
(Constant)	0.4257***	0.4237***	0.4099***	0.4179***
	(0.1040)	(0.107)	(0.1029)	(0.1037)
M_B	0.2047**	0.2099**	0.2086**	0.2096**
	(0.0808)	(0.0808)	(0.081)	(0.0808)
CF/K	0.6218**	0.6161***	0.5961**	0.6156**
	(0.2335)	(0.2354)	(0.2392)	(0.2347)
D^*CF/K	−1.8013**	−1.3376***	−1.3236***	−1.3428***
	(0.7072)	(0.321)	(0.3246)	(0.3217)
$DEBT/K$	2.4093*	2.2139**	2.194*	2.258*
	(1.2016)	(1.1747)	(1.1971)	(1.1792)
$POWR^*CF/K$	0.2496	—	—	—
	(0.3321)			
OIL^*CF/K	—	−0.3092	—	—
		(0.7146)		
MET^*CF/K	—	—	0.0212	—
			(0.3332)	
$TRANS^*CF/K$	—	—	—	−0.1084
				(0.2314)
F-statistic	4.913***	4.895***	4.858***	4.951***
Adj. R^2	0.225	0.220	0.218	0.221

Note: Dependent variable is investment–to–total assets ratio (I/K), where I is defined as a change in fixed assets and K is beginning-of-period total assets; all independent variables are as before except the industry dummy (D), which is equal to 1 if a firm is a member of a group and 0 otherwise. Interactive dummies: OIL: 1 if a firm is in oil and gas; POWR: 2 if a firm is a utility company; MET: 3 if a firm is in the non-ferrous metals industry; TRANS: 6 if a firm is a transportation industry; all of these dummies are multiplied by CF/K. Standard errors appear in parentheses.
*** significant at 1% level; ** significant at 5% level; * significant at 10% level.

Table 13.10 reports the regression results for the set of group and nongroup firms. In addition to the variables used in the previous regressions, we add here an interaction term that is cash flow times a dummy that equals 1 if a firm's market-to-book ratio is above the sample median.

The results indicate that the coefficients on the interaction term for the independent firms are negative and significant: investment in firms with a high market-to-book ratio is less sensitive to cash flow than for the low-Q firms. This points to an interesting conjecture, namely, that a positive assessment by the equity market reduces liquidity constraints on stand-alone firms. At a minimum, this suggests that the market has some ability to identify independent firms that can successfully fund their best investments.

Table 13.10
Effects of firms' market valuation on financial constraints

Variable	Nongroup firms	Group firms
(Constant)	0.3051**	0.4059**
	(0.1176)	(0.2622)
M_B	0.0213	0.4422***
	(0.1094)	(0.1385)
CF/K	3.0427**	−1.3368
	(1.2330)	(0.9957)
High M_B^*CF/K	−2.2435*	0.6243
	(1.1959)	(1.0254)
$DEBT/K$	3.9556	2.9105*
	(2.4537)	(1.4984)
F-statistic	3.1307**	5.5909***
Adj. R^2	0.1872	0.3378
Wald test F-statistic coefficients restrictions		
Null hypothesis: $c(3) + c(4) = 0$	4.8494**	

Note: Dependent variable is investment–to–total assets ratio (I/K), where I is defined as a change in fixed assets and K is beginning-of-period total assets. Independent variables include M_B: market value of equity divided by beginning-of-period book value of equity; CF/K: cash flow during investment period as a proportion of beginning-of-period total assets. $DEBT/K$: beginning-of-period stock of bank debt as a proportion of total assets. Interaction dummy: *High M_B^*CF/K*: cash flow times dummy variable *High M_B*, which is equal to 1 if M_B is above the sample median. Standard errors are in parentheses. *** significant at 1% level; ** significant at 5% level; * significant at 10% level.

In all likelihood, these coefficients are not precisely estimated given the small sample size; we believe, however, that the results are suggestive. Note also that running two separate regressions as opposed to using dummy variables to separate between group and nongroup firms largely preserves our previous findings.

The cash flow variables are found to be insignificant for the group firms. For the group firms a high valuation does not affect financial constraints, whereas for independent firms a high valuation seems to be very important in reducing financial constraints. This is consistent with the hypothesis that for group-affiliated firms financing is governed within the group, whereas other firms depend more on market valuation.

13.4   Conclusions

The main questions investigated in this chapter have been whether the structure of Russian FIGs offers an efficient form of corporate governance and helps alleviate capital market imperfections for large Russian firms. The evidence presented in the chapter has shown that firms that are members of industrial-financial groups are subject to an intense degree of financial reallocation, which may lead to a reduced dependence on internal funds to finance investment expenditures, unlike in unaffiliated companies, or to a greater degree of opportunistic appropriation of their cash flows. The incompleteness of Russian balance sheets so far does not allow a complete answer as to which interpretation is correct. Additionally, a high market valuation of independent firms' investment opportunities seems to relax their financial constraints.

One element supporting the beneficial role of Russian FIGs is the greater sensitivity of investment to market measure of expected profitability among firms that are members of such groups. Yet we feel that we cannot draw a strong conclusion from one year of data. We intend to assess the significance of these results once more-complete data and data for more years become available.

In any event, we believe that given the scarcity of finance in Russia these days there can be no argument in favor of subsidizing group formation or expansion. As the control sample used here suggests, other firms appear quite credit constrained, and we believe that any transfer of resources to group structure would further deprive ordinary firms of access to credit and finance. The 1998 financial crisis in Russia in itself suggests that an excessive concentration of financial resources and obligations in groups may end up being very costly for the Russian financial markets and investment financing in general.

Notes

We thank Stijn Claessens, Irena Grosfelt, and participants at seminars at the Davidson Institute, Department and Laboratory of Applied Theoretical Economics (DELTA) and Russian-European Centre for Economic Policy (RECEP) for useful comments. We retain responsibility for our errors.

1. A difference in the Western experience with such groups may be that corporate control in developing countries is more concentrated, often in the hands of family holding companies or banks.

2. Although these benefits were confirmed in December 1995 in the Law on Financial-Industrial Groups, this has not led to visible explicit concessions for the FIGs.

3. Ramirez 1995 shows that the involvement of J. P. Morgan bankers on U.S. firms' board of directors around 1900 appears to have improved those firms' access to capital and argues that bank monitoring curtailed the principal-agent conflict and diminished informational asymmetries between investors and managers.

4. Scharfstein (1997) finds that investment by subsidiaries of divisions of conglomerates is higher than for stand-alone competing firms in low-Q industries and lower than for those firms in high-Q industries.

5. Usually agency costs are assumed to be increasing in debt and decreasing in cash flow and liquidity, although the theory is ambiguous on this point; leverage may constrain excess investment by forcing management to pay out cash flow (Jensen 1986).

6. This criticism does not affect our results where one group of firms has a positive correlation of investment to cash flow and the other has a zero or negative correlation.

7. It is not clear, however, that the result can be fully attributed to the role of the banks: Berglöf and Perotti (1994) show that the dominant control configuration in the *keiretsu* group is horizontal, supported by corporate cross-holdings. This is consistent with the finding that non-*keiretsu* firms with a main-bank relation appear to be credit constrained.

8. Hoshi, Kashyap, and Scharfstein (1994) find that *keiretsu* firms that weakened their ties to banks by raising money directly from capital markets became more liquidity constrained than before. A related result on the Chilean *grupos* following financial deregulation is in Hermes and Lensink 1998.

9. One should treat these data with care because of the uncertain quality of reporting by Russian firms. Although some of these accounts are audited, some of the sample companies report their financial information according to Russian accounting standards. We nevertheless believe that these sources are more reliable than the information available from the Russian Federation Statistical Agency.

10. A simple correlation analysis between investment and cash flow suggests that nongroup firms spend about one third of cash flow on investment, whereas for group firms the correlation is negative.

11. In the literature, production is included to the regression for practical reasons. Since liquidity and production are correlated, liquidity might proxy for accelerator effects, which appear to be important in the empirical investment literature. This point is discussed in Fazzari, Hubbard, and Petersen 1988 and Hoshi, Kashyap, and Scharfstein 1994.

12. As many firms in the sample have increased their leverage, we also tried including the change in bank debt; the coefficients were again positive but not significant at the 10 percent level.

13. We have conducted a few diagnostic tests. A Lagrange-Multiplier test for serial correlation was not significant. No evidence of heteroschedasticity was found, using both ARCH and White tests. The RESET test on functional form mis-specification was insignificant.

14. Recall that trading volume was not significant by itself in the basic regression.

References

Berglöf, E., and E. Perotti. 1994. The governance structure of the Japanese financial Keiretsu. *Journal of Financial Economics* 36:259–284.

Fazzari, S., G. Hubbard, and B. Petersen. 1988. Financing constraints and corporate investment. *Brookings Papers on Economic Activity* 1:141–206.

Hermes, Niels, and Lensink, Robert. 1998. Baking reform and the financing of firm investment: An empirical analysis of the Chilean experience, 1983–1992. *Journal of Economic Studies* 34, no. 3:27–43.

Hoshi, T., A. Kashyap, and D. Scharfstein. 1990. *Bank monitoring and investment: Evidence from the changing structure of Japanese corporate banking relationships.* In *Asymmetric information, investment, and capital markets*, ed. R. Glenn Hubbard, 105–126. Chicago: University of Chicago Press.

Hoshi, T., A. Kashyap, and D. Scharfstein. 1994. Corporate structure, liquidity, and investment: Evidence form Japanese industrial groups. *Quarterly Journal of Economics* 6:33–60.

Jensen Michael C. 1986. Agency costs of free cash flow, corporate finance and takeovers. *American Economic Review*. 76:323–329.

Johnson, Juliet. 1997. Understanding Russia's emerging financial-industrial groups. *Post-Soviet Affairs* 13, no. 4:333–365.

Kaplan, Steven N., and Zingales, Luigi. 1997. Do investment-cash flow sensitivities provide useful measures of financing constraints? *Quarterly Journal of Economics* 112, no. 1:169–215.

Khanna, Tarun, and Krishna Palepu. 1996. Corporate scope and (severe) market imperfections: An empirical analysis of diversified business groups in an emerging economy. Unpublished manuscript, Graduate School of Business Administration, Harvard University, Boston.

Myers, Stewart C. and Majluf Nicholas F. 1984. Corporate financing and investment decisions when firms have information that investors do not have. *Journal of Financial Economics* 13, no. 2:187–221.

Rajan, Raghuram G., and Zingales, Luigi. 1997. Power in a theory of the firm. Working paper no. 6274, National Bureau of Economic Research, Cambridge, Mass.

Ramirez, Carlos. 1995. Did J. P. Morgan men add liquidity? Corporate investment, cash flow, and financial structure at the turn of the twentieth century. *Journal of Finance* (June).

Scharfstein, David. 1997. The dark side of internal capital markets II: Evidence from diversified conglomerates. Massachusetts Institute of Technology, Cambridge, Mass. Mimeographed.

Scharfstein, David, and Jeremy Stein. 1997. The dark side of internal capital markets: Divisional rent-seeking and inefficient investment. Working paper no. 5969, National Bureau of Economic Research, Cambridge, Mass.

Stein, Jeremy. 1997. Internal capital markets and the competition for corporate resources. *Journal of Finance* 52:111–134.

Index